Sunday lunch 1920's style in the north of the Yucatán Peninsula, Mexico. Mestizos pose for the photograph with several Maya servants.

Quirigua, in the Motagua Valley
(Guatemala), where archeologists have
uncovered a giant stele ▲ 306.

Library of Congress Cataloging-in-Publication Data

Route of the Mayas. English
Route of the Mayas/ [Gallimard editions].
p. cm.– (Knopf guides)
Includes bibliographical references and index.
ISBN 0-679-75569-1
1. Mayas – Antiquities – Guidebooks. 2. Mexico – Antiquities – Guidebooks.
I. Gallimard (Firm) . II. Title. III. Series.
F1435.R83513   1995
917.2604'53 – dc20
CIP 95-1871

First published June 1995
Second edition September 1996

NUMEROUS SPECIALISTS AND ACADEMICS HAVE
CONTRIBUTED TO THIS GUIDE.
SPECIAL THANKS TO: MICHEL ANTOCHIW,
ANDRÉ AUBRY, CLAUDE-FRANÇOIS BAUDEZ,
JEAN-LUC BRACONNIER, ALAIN BRETON

THE ROUTE OF THE MAYAS:
EDITORS: Pierre-Yves Mercier *assisted by* Isabelle
de Coulibœuf, Marie-Hélène Carpentier, Clarisse
Deniau (architecture), Odile Simon (nature),
Grégory Leroy (practical information)
LAYOUT: Isabelle Roller, Nathalie Victor-Pujebet,
Michèle Bisgambiglia (nature)
PICTURE RESEARCH: Natalie Saint-Martin
GRAPHICS: Élisabeth Cohat
NATURE: Frédéric Bony, Philippe J. Dubois *with*
Michel Antochiw, Michel Boccara, Noëlle Demyk,
Gérard Rocamora
HISTORY: Michel Antochiw, Claude-François
Baudez
THE MAYAS TODAY: Michel Boccara, Alain Breton
MAYAN TEXTILES: Danièlle Cavaleri
ARCHITECTURE: Bruno Lenormand *with*
Michel Antochiw, André Aubry, Alain Breton,
Claude-François Baudez
THE ROUTE OF THE MAYAS AS SEEN BY ARTISTS:
Nicole Dagnino, Luisa Galeotti de González,
Zipacná de León
THE ROUTE OF THE MAYAS AS SEEN BY WRITERS:
Lucinda Gane

ITINERARIES:
EASTERN YUCATAN: Michel Antochiw,
Claude-François Baudez
WESTERN YUCATAN: Michel Antochiw,
Claude-François Baudez
CHIAPAS: André Aubry Claude-François Baudez,
Alain Breton
HIGHLANDS OF GUATEMALA: Claude-François
Baudez, Jean-Luc Braconnier

SOUTHEASTERN MAYA: Claude-François Baudez,
Jean-Luc Braconnier
PETÉN: Claude-François Baudez, Jean-Luc
Braconnier
BELIZE: Michel Antochiw, ClaudeFrançois Baudez

PRACTICAL INFORMATION:
Seymourina Cruse, Grégory Leroy

ILLUSTRATIONS:
NATURE: Anne Bodin, Jean Chevallier, Gismonde
Curiace, François Desbordes, Claire Felloni,
Gilbert Houbre, Bernard Hugueville, François
Place, Pascal Robin, Franck Stefan
ARCHITECTURE: Jean-Marie Guillou, Jean-Benoît
Héron, Pierre Hugo, Claude Quiec, Christian
Rivière, Jean-Sylvain Roveri, Amato Soro, Oliver
Verdy
THE MAYAS TODAY: Anne Bodin, Philippe Munch
LITERATURE: Flo Villacèque
ITINERARIES: Anne Bodin, François Desbordes,
Jean-Marie Guillou, Philippe Munch,
Claude Quiec
PRACTICAL INFORMATION: Maurice Pommier
MAPS: Vincent Brunot *with* Stéphane Girel,
Isabelle-Anne Chatellard (colorist)
COMPUTER GRAPHICS: Kristof Chemineau,
Paul Coulbois, Latitude (maps for practical
information and endpapers), Patrick Mérienne
(nature)

PHOTOGRAPHY:
Éric Guillemot, Patrick Léger *with* Emmanuel
Chaspoul, Jean-Pierre Courau, Seymourina Cruse,
Mireille Vautier

WE WOULD ALSO LIKE TO THANK:
Danièlle Cavaleri (Ethnic Consultants), Françoise
de Tailly (Inguat Paris), Marco Tulio Ordóñez
(Inguat Guatemala-Ciudad)

TRANSLATED BY WENDY ALLATSON.
EDITED AND TYPESET BY BOOK CREATION SERVICES, LONDON.
PRINTED IN ITALY BY EDITORIALE LIBRARIA.

THE ROUTE
OF THE MAYAS

KNOPF GUIDES

CONTENTS

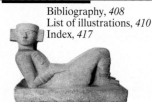

EASTERN YUCATÁN

WESTERN YUCATÁN

CHIAPAS

HIGHLANDS OF GUATEMALA

SOUTHEASTERN MAYA

PETÉN

BELIZE

▲ THE ROUTE OF THE MAYAS

1. CANCÚN
2. TULUM
3. CHICHÉN ITZÁ
4. MÉRIDA
5. UXMAL
6. CAMPECHE
7. BELIZE CITY
8. CORAL REEF
9. BELMOPAN
10. MELCHOR DE MENCOS
11. TIKAL
12. FLORES

TULUM
▲ 177

CHICHÉN ITZÁ
▲ 205

UXMAL
▲ 222

GULF OF MEXICO

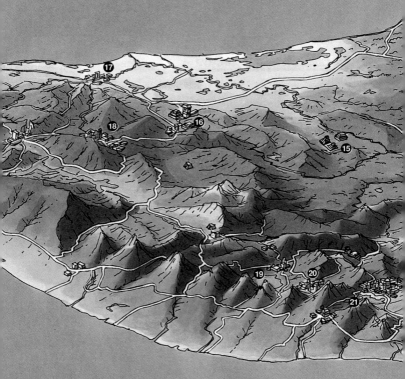

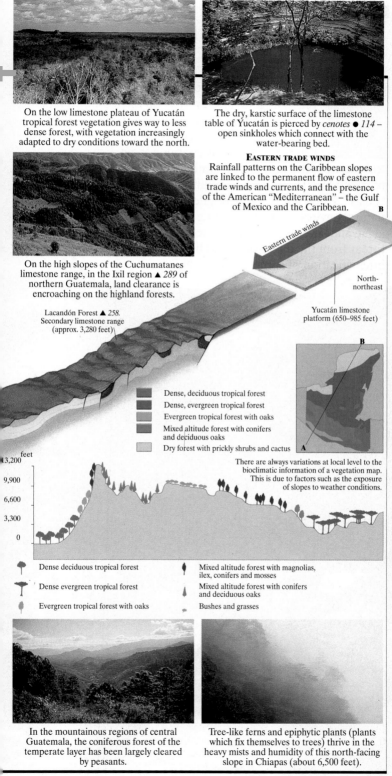

On the low limestone plateau of Yucatán tropical forest vegetation gives way to less dense forest, with vegetation increasingly adapted to dry conditions toward the north.

The dry, karstic surface of the limestone table of Yucatán is pierced by *cenotes* ● *114* – open sinkholes which connect with the water-bearing bed.

EASTERN TRADE WINDS
Rainfall patterns on the Caribbean slopes are linked to the permanent flow of eastern trade winds and currents, and the presence of the American "Mediterranean" – the Gulf of Mexico and the Caribbean.

B

Eastern trade winds

North-northeast

Yucatán limestone platform (650–985 feet)

On the high slopes of the Cuchumatanes limestone range, in the Ixil region ▲ *289* of northern Guatemala, land clearance is encroaching on the highland forests.

Lacandón Forest ▲ *258*.
Secondary limestone range (approx. 3,280 feet)

B

Dense, deciduous tropical forest
Dense, evergreen tropical forest
Evergreen tropical forest with oaks
Mixed altitude forest with conifers and deciduous oaks
Dry forest with prickly shrubs and cactus

A

feet
13,200
9,900
6,600
3,300
0

There are always variations at local level to the bioclimatic information of a vegetation map. This is due to factors such as the exposure of slopes to weather conditions.

Dense deciduous tropical forest

Dense evergreen tropical forest

Evergreen tropical forest with oaks

Mixed altitude forest with magnolias, ilex, conifers and mosses

Mixed altitude forest with conifers and deciduous oaks

Bushes and grasses

In the mountainous regions of central Guatemala, the coniferous forest of the temperate layer has been largely cleared by peasants.

Tree-like ferns and epiphytic plants (plants which fix themselves to trees) thrive in the heavy mists and humidity of this north-facing slope in Chiapas (about 6,500 feet).

17

■ CORAL REEFS

STONE BASS, OR WRECKFISH
If threatened, the wreckfish changes
color: the lower part of its body turns
white and the upper part almost black.

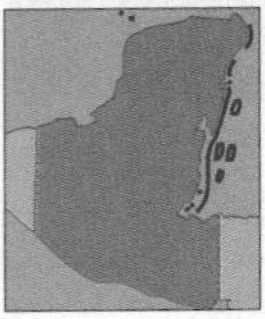

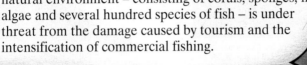

The coral reefs of the Caribbean are barely 20,000
years old and have evolved on the fossilized remains
of older corals destroyed during the last Ice Age.
Since then the sea level has risen, forming numerous
lagoons. The corals continue their slow process of
formation in the warm, clear waters and, in so doing, form a
barrier which shelters an incredibly richly stocked marine
"oasis". However, the very fragile ecological balance of this
natural environment – consisting of corals, sponges, limestone
algae and several hundred species of fish – is under
threat from the damage caused by tourism and the
intensification of commercial fishing.

BLACK-TIPPED SHARK
This coastal shark lives in groups of six to
eight individuals. It is renowned for its
agility and amazing leaps out of the water.

Sand star

Fan coral,
or sea fan

Morbius cat

Moving basin
sponge

Moray

Sea cucumber

Sea melon

Capitaine

ROYAL ANGELFISH
One of the most brightly colored fish on the reef, the royal angelfish has a blue, tiara-like mark on its head.

Bonito

ATLANTIC BIG-EYE
Although it prefers deep water, this striking fish does frequent shallower waters at certain times of year.

Sea cactus, or sea candle, a cylindrical, or "pillar", coral.

Royal gramma
This tiny, timid fish sometimes swims upside down above the many places of refuge provided by the depths of the reef.

Sea urchin

BLACK ANGELFISH
This fish can grow to almost 12 inches and weigh up to 5½ lbs.

SQUIRREL FISH
This tiny, nocturnal predator feeds on crabs and shrimps.

Royal trigger fish
The trigger fish can keep one eye on a predator while looking for somewhere to hide with the other.

WHITE-SPOTTED FILE FISH
The file fish sometimes changes its single-colored livery to one covered with white spots.

BOXFISH
The boxfish feeds on micro-organisms which it dislodges by blowing onto the sand.

MANGROVES

BIRTH OF A MANGROVE
The leaves and flowers of mangroves are at the
end of the branch (**1**). When it reaches maturity,
the fruit germinates on the tree (**2**).

The coastal strips of marshland around the Yucatán
Peninsula and along the Pacific shores of
Guatemala are rich in plant and animal life.
Between the tropical forest and the Caribbean,
impenetrable networks of vegetation – mangroves –
invade the muddy deposits which teem with aquatic life. Their
long, submerged and intertwined roots provide shelter for fish
and shellfish, while their numerous "islets" harbor colonies of
nesting birds.

Magnificent frigate bird

BOA CONSTRICTOR
The boa constrictor is the largest snake in
Central America. Harmless to human beings,
it hunts birds, mammals and reptiles and
crushes them to death.

LOGGERHEAD TURTLE
These turtles live in shallow waters, feeding
on fish, jellyfish, shellfish and algae. Between
May and September they leave the sea to lay
their eggs on the beaches.

The mangrove's stilt roots
enable it to grow on the
loose substratum of the
salt marshes.

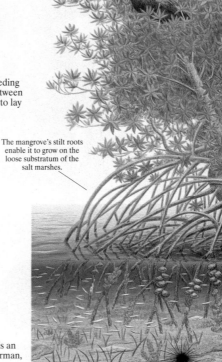

BROWN PELICAN
Extremely awkward on land, this bird is an
extremely strong flier and a skilled fisherman,
using its beak as a fishing net.

Barnacle

Oyster

Algae

The fruit produces a dart-like plantlet about 11 inches long (**3**) which frees itself from the branch, falls into the mud and takes root (**4**).

Mangrove roots form a sort of buttress around the tree and become inextricably entangled. The animals which seek refuge among the roots attract large numbers of predators.

Fanworms

Sponges

MANATEE, OR SEA COW ▲ *312*
The manatee lives in the fresh waters of estuaries and coastal lagoons. It is disturbed by the turbulence caused by motor boats and has disappeared from areas where this kind of traffic is frequent.

SCARLET IBIS
The scarlet ibis nests in the most inaccessible parts of the mangrove. Overhunted for its superb red plumage, today it is on the verge of extinction.

Male performing his courtship display

MAGNIFICENT FRIGATE BIRD
This superbly aerial bird makes headlong chases to catch a fish that has just surfaced or to snatch another bird's prey.

Brown heron

Great white heron, or American egret

BROWN HERON
This wading bird nests on mangrove "islets" along with other species of heron.

NEOTROPIC CORMORANT
This common bird rarely wanders out to sea. It is also often seen on inland lakes.

■ "MILPA"

Agricultural techniques are the same in the highlands and lowlands, but the calendar is different.

Milpa – a Mexican word derived from Nahuatl, meaning "freshly cleared ground" – is an area of cultivated forest. In Maya tradition trees are ancestors and cutting them down would be commiting murder. To ensure that the forest regenerates, land must be cleared according to precise rules and rituals which require an excellent knowledge of the environment and the many species of plant life. Corn is not the only crop grown on the plot. A number of different crops are developed through a remarkable combination of archaic techniques and highly complex systems of irrigation, drainage, terracing and soil classification, all adapted to the particular region.

"Coa" **LAND CLEARANCE** Land is cleared using the axe or *bat* and the machete-like *coa* or *lotche*, and is usually carried out in August when the wood is at its most tender. A hardworking peasant can clear 2–3 *mécates* (960–1,430 square yards) per day.

BURNING. The Maya walk round their plots lighting fires with a torch at regular intervals and whistling to invoke beneficent winds – an act considered vital for a successful harvest.

Peasant (*kolkab*) in a fertile area of the *milpa* (*kolce* in the Yucatecan Maya dialect).

Choul

Layer of topsoil

The average surface area of a field is slightly more than 5 acres.

SOWING. Corn is sown "between the stones" with a sort of dibble called a *choul*, a traditional tool which has undergone only one development since prehistoric times: the point, originally hardened by fire, has been replaced by a steel tip.

Implement for extracting the cob from its sheath

WEEDING. Since the 1970's, weedkillers have gradually replaced the use of the *coa* for weeding. However, peasants are becoming increasingly aware of their disadvantages and are adopting less harsh methods.

HARVEST. The women and children help with the harvest and, sometimes, other peasants who in turn enlist help for their own harvest. The average yield is in the order of 1,320 lbs of corn per 2½ acres.

Corn

The stems of the cobs are "broken" in September–October to prevent the grain being rotted by rain or pecked by birds.

Beans

Marrow

VARIETIES OF CORN

The several varieties of this starch-rich cereal crop are classified according to color and ripening period (2–5 months). It is almost always grown with beans and marrows, whose seeds are sown in the same hole as the corn seeds.

MIXED CROPS

Red and black beans

Marrow

Gourd

Sweet potato

Tomatoes

Bananas

Chili

In the richer areas of soil – usually located in small, damp depressions known as *k'op* – the peasants plant various food crops: pulses, tubers, fruit and vegetables and, of course, chilies ● 86.

Stony ground where corn is grown "between the stones"
Pasel

Forest canopy

Cenote

Palm tree left during clearance

Permeable, karstic layer

MILLING

After the harvest, the corn has to be turned into flour. Today the millstone has been replaced by a hand- or motor-operated mill.

MAKING TORTILLAS

The rhythmic sound of women slapping corn pancakes into shape can be heard late in the morning in any Maya village.

TROPICAL FOREST

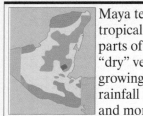

Maya territory has the largest expanse of tropical forest in Central America. In the drier parts of Yucatán, the so-called lowlands, this is "dry" vegetation consisting of relatively low-growing, deciduous trees. Further south the rainfall increases and the forest becomes taller and more luxuriant as, for example, in Petén and Chiapas. This wet jungle, or tropical rainforest, is found up to altitudes of around 6,500 feet where it is replaced by conifers. The uncontrolled development of agriculture and stockbreeding and the exploitation of timber in recent decades have destroyed a large part of this ecosystem, in spite of the creation of nature reserves.

The tropical forest constitutes the richest ecosystem in the world and contains almost half the world's flora and fauna. A wide diversity of species is often accompanied by low numbers of individuals in any given area, with the result that populations are small and vulnerable. This biodiversity also gives rise to complex food chains and an appropriate distribution of species within a particular environment, each fulfilling its own ecological function.

AMAZON PARROT ▶
Amazon parrots fly rapidly through the forest in small, noisy bands.

BLUE COTINGA ▶
The brilliant color of the male can look dull when seen against the light.

▲ GREAT CURASSOW
This flightless bird is under threat today from deforestation and hunting.

KING VULTURE ▶
Its keen sense of smell enables this bird to locate animal carcasses, even when in flight.

▲ NINE-BANDED ARMADILLO
The armadillo is hunted for its flesh and skin.

▲ OCELLATED TURKEY
This bird lives on the edge of the forest. It has been hunted to extinction in many regions of Central America.

▲ BAIRD'S TAPIR
The tapir is the largest land mammal in Central America and can weigh up to 440 lbs.

▲ COLLARED PECCARY, OR MEXICAN HOG
The peccary is widely hunted by the Indians.

▲ AGOUTI
This rodent is commonly found in the undergrowth, near water.

RESPLENDENT QUETZAL ◀
Mainly found in the mountain forests of Chiapas and Verapaz ▲ *293*.

SCARLET MACAW ▼
Its powerful beak enables it to crack open the shells of the hardest fruit.

KEEL-BILLED TOUCAN ▲
This toucan prefers the high tree-tops where it feeds on fruit.

HARPY EAGLE ▼
This rare, forest-dwelling eagle hunts mammals, reptiles and birds.

BLACK HOWLER MONKEY ▲
Once the sacred animal of the Maya, this monkey is now threatened by the disappearance of the tropical forest.

VIRGINIA OPOSSUM ▶
This small, nocturnal omnivore is a marsupial.

BLACK-HANDED SPIDER MONKEY ◀
The spider monkey's prehensile tail and long limbs enable it to move from tree to tree with amazing speed and agility.

OCELOT ▼
Found only in tropical regions of America, this cat is important in Mayan culture.

PUMA ▼
One of the most adaptable of all cats, the puma is found throughout the American continent from humid forests to mountains.

RING-TAILED COATI ▲
Mainly diurnal, the coati uses its tail to improve its balance when climbing trees.

TAYRA ▲
Active at night and in the morning, the tayra feeds mainly on rodents. It has become increasingly rare as a result of deforestation.

JAGUAR ▲
This beautiful big cat is a formidable hunter. For the Maya the jaguar embodied the night sun.

FOREST LAYERS

CACAO
The Maya already knew how to prepare the "nectar of the gods" using the beans from the cacao tree, which can reach heights of 50 feet.

The tropical forest of Central America is so rich that in some places there are more than a hundred species of trees in an area of 2 acres. Its various layers of vegetation harbor a wide variety of flora and fauna and have a particularly complex structure, characterized by the profusion of lianas (woody, free-hanging climbing plants) and epiphytes such as orchids and bromeliads. The trees usually have large, rigid leaves and huge buttressed roots, like those of the silk-cotton tree.

Young trees can reach heights of up to 165 feet.

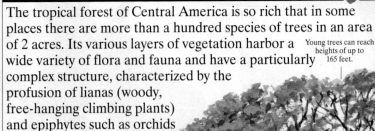

CANOPY

LIFE AT ALL LEVELS
Young trees harbor insects, bats and predatory animals, while the canopy is the domain of monkeys and multicolored butterflies. Snakes and tree frogs live in the intermediate layer and mammals find shelter among the smaller trees and undergrowth.

SAPODILLA
This lactiferous tree produces chicle, a form of latex used to make chewing gum ▲ 330.

Epiphytes

INTERMEDIATE LAYER

"STANTOPEA OCULATA"
This epiphytic orchid with its heady perfume grows "upside down" on the branches of tall trees.

Palm tree forming part of the lower level of smaller trees. Palms do not grow very tall and need a minimum amount of light.

Some lianas strangle and kill their host trees.

SHRUB LAYER

"LYCASTE SKINERI"
This pink orchid, the national emblem of Guatemala, is found mainly in the wet, mountain forests.

The soil on the forest floor is poor and the trees have shallow but extensive root systems.

HISTORY

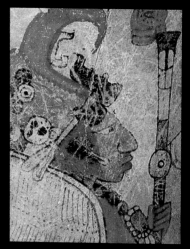

● HISTORY

7000 BC
Cereals begin to be cultivated in the Tehuacan Valley, Mexico.

1700 BC
First ceremonial buildings in farming villages in the Mexican Valley.

12000 BC	8000 BC	4000 BC	2000 BC	1500 BC

13000–9000 BC
Paintings and engravings at Lascaux (France) and Altamira (Spain).

3250–3100 BC
Invention of writing in the Near East (seals and clay tablets bearing pictographic symbols). Cuneiform writing is developed in Mesopotamia.

2600–2100 BC
Egyptian Old Kingdom.

c. 1500 BC
The Aryans conquer India.

ORIGINS

Humankind is thought to have arrived on the American continent at least 20,000 years ago, when a period of glaciation dried up the Bering Strait and made it possible to

have developed in isolation. The reduced or non-existent role of stockbreeding in American societies (apart from the use of llamas and other camelids in the

a slower rate of displacement of populations and individuals, because of the absence of horses and practical limitations such as the lack of the wheel. But although it may

> Until c. 6000 BC the American continent was populated by small bands of hunter-gatherers whose economic activities became increasingly specialized.

the only explanation for the sometimes disconcerting similarities between, for example, Mayan art and the art of the civilizations of Southeast Asia. The alternative would be to attribute these resemblances to analogous environments, parallel histories or simply the artistic limitations of the human mind and intellect.

walk from Siberia to Alaska. Compared with the history of the Old World, American history is relatively recent and its cultures

Andean cultures) helps to explain early forms of nomadism (unrelated to the movement of flocks), reduced mobility and

be true that transatlantic contacts were not a determining factor, cultural diffusion would appear to be

2000 BC

MAYA TERRITORY AND SUBDIVISIONS

GULF OF MEXICO

Yucatán

3

MEXICO

CARIBBEAN SEA

2

Chiapas

BELIZE

1

GUATEMALA

HONDURAS

PACIFIC OCEAN

EL SALVADOR

To understand the cultural variations within Maya territory, it is important to identify at least three main areas, each characterized by their own specific forms and historical development:

1. The Pacific coast and the highlands of Guatemala and El Salvador;
2. The central and southern lowlands;

3. The northern lowlands.
The history of Mayan civilization has been divided into three main periods, referred to as Preclassic, Classic and Postclassic, which are in turn divided into Early, Middle and Late. These are sometimes subdivided once again to give classes such as Protoclassic, Terminal Classic and Protohistoric.

MESOAMERICA

From 2000 BC the population of Mesoamerica was, generally speaking, sedentary. This is a precondition for the creation of societies sufficiently complex to be called civilizations. The term "Mesoamerica" was first used to refer to an area of civilization that included central and southern Mexico, Guatemala, Belize, El Salvador and parts of Honduras, Nicaragua and Costa Rica. Within this vast territory, whose frontiers have altered throughout history, the homogeneity of Mesoamerica has changed. But, in spite of their differences, the Mesoamerican civilizations have certain common characteristics that

give the region its unity, whether looked at from an economic standpoint (the importance of the maize–squash–bean crops, agricultural techniques, trade networks and markets) or from an artistic, religious or intellectual angle. The Late Preclassical Stele 10 from Kaminaljuyú (below).

30

| 1200 BC | 600 BC | 500 BC | 900 AD | | |
| Building of the first Olmec centers in Mexico. | Beginning of the Preclassic Maya civilization. | Start of the Zapotec civilization at Monté Alban. | | | c. 0 Teotihuacán begun. |

| 1000 BC | 800 BC | 400 BC | 200 BC | 100 BC |

| 1200 BC | 800 BC | 753 BC | 336–323 BC | 146 BC |
| Trojan War and collapse of the Hittite empire. | Beginning of the Etruscan civilization. | Foundation of Rome. | Empire of Alexander the Great. | Carthage destroyed by the Romans. |

PRECLASSIC AND PROTOCLASSIC (2000 BC–AD 250)

CALENDAR

The Maya are famed for having possessed the most elaborate form of writing in America ● *42* and for having been the only people to measure time using the Long Count (a system starting from an imaginary point corresponding to 3114 BC) ● *44*. Paradoxically they do not appear to have invented either but inherited the already complex systems developed by the successors of the Olmecs along the coast of the Gulf of Mexico and in Oaxaca, where calendric and other types of glyphs, as well as numbers represented by bars and dots (all dating from 600–450 BC), have been identified. Stele C at Tres Zapotes, on the Gulf coast, bears a date which uses the same type of numbers but without the period glyphs, and corresponds to 31 BC. On the Pacific coast, dates from the 1st and 2nd centuries AD have been found on the sites of El Baúl (detail of stele, below left, dating from the Late Classic period).

THE OLMECS

San Lorenzo and La Venta (sculpture below) were inhabited by the Olmecs in 1250 and c. 1100 BC respectively. Monumental sculpture (above) played an important role in these centers. Olmec society had a clearly defined hierarchy, highly developed traditional crafts, and an extensive trade network, and its works of art were spread widely across the whole of Mesoamerica by the 1st millennium BC.

THE OLMEC HERITAGE

During the Late Preclassic the sites of Izapa on the Pacific coast and Kaminaljuyú in the highlands demonstrated the sophistication of the calendar and writing system by extending and developing the Olmec heritage. If the Izapa and Kaminaljuyú sculptural styles provide the transition between Olmec and Mayan art of the Early Classic period, it would seem reasonable to suppose that direct contacts existed between the Olmecs and the Maya in other areas. For instance, during their early history the Maya, surprisingly, developed a taste for gigantism, as illustrated by the structures of La Danta and El Mirador which reach heights of 230 feet! In spite of conditions unfavorable to agriculture, important centers developed in the northern lowlands during the Middle and Late Preclassic periods, probably as a result of trade developments. Komchén and Cerros (in Belize) seem to have been staging posts for Yucatec maritime trade.

31

● History

c. 250
Beginning of the Maya
Classic period.

250–650
Golden age of
Teotihuacán.

100   200   300   400   500

c. 200
End of the Han
Dynasty (China).

**c. 400–c.
1450**
Byzantine
empire.

476
Fall of the last
Western Roman
emperor.

Classic (250–1000)

A PERIOD OF PROGRESS

In the Classic Maya period, rules of dynastic succession were established and royal power began to manifest itself in art. Both aspects were notably combined in the central lowlands at the end of the 3rd century. The Classic Maya civilization marks the end of a long process of development begun by the latest in the 6th or 5th century BC. The complex societies that built such sites as Nakbé and El Mirador ultimately adopted and then developed the calendar and writing system inherited from the west and south. However, the corbeled vault was a local invention, since it was never used in the highlands. The early steles of Tikal ▲ 324 and Uaxactún ▲ 328 bear an image of the king accompanied by a text which gives, among other things, his name, his date of accession and the name of his city. They provide evidence of the emergence of the state as a system of social and political organization and also of the birth of rival states who would divide up the Maya territory between them. Carved panel (left) at Palenque ▲ 243.

A HIERARCHICAL SOCIETY

Mayan society was divided into classes and professions such as craftsmen and merchants. It was subject to the authority of a centralized government which ruled a territory whose boundaries were clearly defined. The political authority, headed by the king who represented his community, had an army and administration at its disposal. The emblem glyphs appear to designate the state rather than the city, which would explain why several cities used the same emblem. The political map of the Classic Maya territory was a constantly changing mosaic, with the various states acquiring and then losing control of secondary centers which passed into other hands. The Classic Maya civilization was essentially urban. Although they did not look like modern-day towns and cities, Maya centers performed the same function and were responsible for important artistic and intellectual achievements.

DEFINITION
The term "Classic" is used here to define development characterized by the simultaneous appearance of the Mayan corbeled vault in architecture, steles, hieroglyphic writing ● 42 (below) and the calculation of time using the Long Count ● 44.

c. 600 Height of the Zapotec civilization:	c. 800 Beginning of the decline of the Maya civilization.	c. 900 End of the Zapotec civilization at Monte Albán.	c. 950 Arrival of the Toltecs at Tula.
600	**700**	**800**	**900**	**100**

c. 610 Birth of Islam.	685 Buddhism becomes the state religion of Japan	800 Charlemagne crowned emperor in Rome.	900–1000 Viking expeditions to America.

EARLY CLASSIC (250–600)

The only good example of the subdivision of the Classic period is found in the central lowlands. The highlands, to the south, passed under the control of Teotihuacán and

developed along alternative lines characterized by a combination of local Mayan and central Mexican elements. When the great Mexican city fell to the northern barbarians, its trading posts and

colonies experienced a degree of difficulty in re-establishing themselves. For example, Kaminaljuyú and the surrounding region suffered a period of decline in spite of the fact that trading links with the lowlands remained intact. Little is known of the Early Classic period in the northern lowlands. Tikal was one of the most important cities of that period. Stele 29 bears the earliest known date on a Mayan monument (corresponding to AD 292), while evidence of the presence and authority of Teotihuacán is apparent on Stele 4 on the same site. The erection of steles at the end of the period is illustrated for the first time at Tikal (Temple 1, right), with the celebration of the end of the eighteenth *katun* of the eighth *baktun* (July 6, 396) ● 44.

The end of the Early Classic is marked by a period of decline which was represented by a worsening in the quality of funeral paraphernalia and an interruption of the custom of periodically erecting steles. This period, referred to as the "hiatus", lasted from 534 until 593 and, at Tikal, until 692. It is presumed that the collapse of Teotihuacán and its empire provoked a serious crisis for the Mayan dynasties. The return to normal, with the resumption of the erection of steles, marks the beginning of the Late Classic period.

LATE CLASSIC (600–800)

Tikal's ▲ *322* most impressive structures date from this period. It also marked the height of the glory of Palenque ▲ *243*, which did not become important until the 7th century and began to decline from 800 onwards. The golden age of Yaxchilán ▲ *248* began in c. 630 with Bird Jaguar II. Copán ▲ *299*, whose valley was occupied from the Middle Preclassic period became the most important city on the eastern frontier of Maya territory with the foundation of the Yax Kuk Mo dynasty in the 5th century. Quirigua ▲ *306*, founded shortly afterwards, was dominated by its great neighbor and rival until 737, when it captured and put to death Eighteen Rabbit, the powerful king of Copán. During this period cities in

central Yucatán ▲ *190*, such as Becán, Xpuhil (bottom right) and Chicanná, reached their apogee. Figurine from Jaina ▲ *230* (below).

TERMINAL CLASSIC (800–1000)

The end of the eighteenth *katun* of the ninth *baktun* (AD 790) was celebrated by the erection of the greatest number of steles known. At this time population density had reached a maximum in the central lowlands. The northern lowlands would soon become famous. With the exception of cities such as Dzibilchaltún ▲ *216*, northern Yucatán remained sparsely populated with no majorly important cities.

The situation changed during the 9th century, however, with the development of the Puuc ▲ *220* cities of Uxmal, Labná, Sayil and Kabáh (due to the combined action of foreign Putún and Chontal groups from the Tabasco coast) and of the Chenes and Río Bec centers to the south.

c. 1220–1400
Fall of Chichén Itzá and dominance
of Mayapán in Yucatan.

1100	1150	1200	1250	1300

1099
First crusade and
capture of
Jerusalem.

c. 1200
Apogee of the Mongol
empire (conquest of
northern China).

1206
Treaty of Guadalajara
between Castile, Aragon
and Navarre.

c. 1240
Major construction of
cathedrals throughout
Europe

CAUSES OF THE DECLINE

In spite of many hypotheses, it is now known that the decline was not so much a sudden collapse or abrupt disappearance as a process of cultural decay which took place over a period of a century. There were a number of contributory factors. Famine was always a risk after a succession of poor crops from the unstable tropical soil. Also the political fragmentation into city-states caused great rivalry as cities tried to surpass their neighbors in magnificence and incurred expenditure which proved ruinous. The final failure of the Maya civilization highlights the fragility of its foundations and its inability to adapt. The first disasters caused the break-up of trade networks, rebellions, wars and invasions, a chain reaction which accelerated the process of disintegration.

THE BEGINNING OF THE DECLINE

In the 9th century the central lowlands experienced a decline marked by the end of the steles and architectural activity, which represented a breakdown in the organization of traditional political and religious power. Although the population did not disappear, it was significantly reduced during the ensuing period. Centers such as Copán and Palenque ceased to function after 800. By 830 only one tenth of the city of Tikal was occupied. The most recent stele of the central lowlands (AD 909) was found at Toniná ▲ *242*. The only exception to this general collapse was Ceibal ▲ *331*, which experienced its golden age between 830 and 930. The foreign style of its steles is undoubtedly due to Putún influence. This Mexicanized group from the coast of Tabasco or the north of Yucatán is thought to have reached the Río Pasión by following the Usumacinta upstream. In northern Belize ▲ *340*, which escaped the general decline, some major structures were built.

CHICHÉN ITZA ▲ 205
This city experienced its golden age during the Postclassic period. The Caracol (above), detail of fresco and a Chacmool (below), and columns from the Temple of the Warriors (right).

POSTCLASSIC (1000–1500)

EARLY POSTCLASSIC (1000–1250)

From AD 1000 Chichén Itzá ▲ *205* became one of the most important sites in the lowlands. During this period the city was characterized by the development of a series of new features which were urban, architectural and iconographic in character and of Mexican origin. Certain of these elements, such as the *tzompantli* (platform carved with human skulls), had already been introduced to the Puuc ▲ *218* by the Putún–Chontal Maya. Others seem to have come direct from Tula, the Toltec capital of the Mexican basin during the Early Postclassic. During the Postclassic period, Chichén Itzá is therefore described as Maya-Toltec (fresco from the Temple of the Jaguars, left). The connection between Tula and Chichén Itzá has still not been clarified. Indeed, the latter is the only Maya–Toltec site in the lowlands, and there is no known staging post between Chichén Itzá and Tula, which are separated by a distance of some 870 miles.

COASTAL AND MOUNTAIN SITES

Apart from Chichén Itzá, there were very few Early Postclassic sites of any importance in the north. In the central Maya territory some Classic cities were inhabited by groups who lived among the ruins without building anything of significance.

However, this was not the case in northern Belize ▲ 340, where sites such as Lamanai (remains above), Nohmul, Cerros and Altún Ha were the object of much architectural activity. A few coastal sites constituted other exceptions and suggest the existence of maritime trade along the Yucatecan coast. The changes observed in the end of the Classic period were beginning: sites on plains were abandoned in favor of easily defended locations perched on hills or plateaux, a development attributed to new

external influences which, by following the natural routes of the Río Usumacinta and Río Motagua, correspond to Chichén Itzá's dominance of Yucatán.

LATE POSTCLASSIC (1250–1525)

After the fall of Chichén Itzá, Mayapán ▲ 212 became the dominant city in Yucatán. The new capital was, once again, the object of Mexican influence but differed considerably from its predecessor, as it did from all the cities of the Classic Maya. The ten thousand or so inhabitants of this walled city were crowded around a political and ceremonial center. The fine masonry of the Puuc sites and Chichén Itzá was replaced by a crude, dry-stone bonding, and the design of the houses changed. So, too, did the form of worship: domestic oratories and sanctuaries were built and huge incense burners, fashioned in terracotta designed to represent the gods (Postclassic censer, right) ● 48. Mayapán was the center of an alliance that dominated Yucatán until the mid 15th century. There seems to have been more settlement then than during the Early Postclassic period: the eastern coast of the peninsula in particular, with the sites of Xel-Há, Cozumel, Tulum ▲ 177 and Santa Rita, was a maritime trade zone. There were also later sites in the region of Lago Petén Itzá (Topoxté). After the fall of Mayapán, north Yucatán was once again politically

fragmented into a series of small "rival states". The highlands witnessed the development of small centers in powerful (rival) regional capitals. At the time of the Spanish conquest Mixco Viejo ▲ 268 was the capital of the Pokomams, Zaculeu ▲ 284 of the Mams, Iximché of the Cakchiquels and Utatlán of the Quichés. The Quichés extended their territory at the expense of their neighbors until the late 15th century, when their king was defeated by the Cakchiquels.

HISTORY

1560	1562	1564	1566	1568

1562
Diego de Landa has a large number of Mayan manuscripts burned.

1556
Abdication of Charles V and accession of Philip II to the Spanish throne.

1561
Madrid becomes the capital of Spain.

1562. Beginning of the Wars of Religion in France.

1563. Council of Trent ends after establishing principles of the Counter Reformation.

1565
The Spanish conquer the Philippines.

1565
Foundation of the Portuguese colony of Rio de Janeiro.

THE SPANISH CONQUEST (16TH–17TH CENTURIES)

FROM CORDOBA TO CORTÉS

The Spanish conquest of the Americas began with the colonization of Hispaniola (modern Haiti and the Dominican Republic) and Cuba, and continued with forays launched from these islands. In 1517 Hernández de Córdoba (right) led an expedition in search of slaves, gold and new territory. He discovered the Isla Mujeres ▲ 174, near Cozumel, and then sailed along the coast of Yucatán to Champotón ▲ 230, where he suffered heavy losses at the hands of the Maya. The next expedition, led by Juan de Grijalva, took five months to sail round the peninsula as far as the Río Pánuco. Finally

He traveled round the peninsula and across the Gulf of Mexico landing at Veracruz, where he burned his boats (the grounded fleet, center). The Aztecs were

Hernán Cortés (below) set sail on February 18, 1519 with eleven vessels.

conquered in a year, but it took another twenty years to conquer Yucatán.

TOWARDS THE HIGHLANDS

In 1523 Cortés asked his lieutenant, Pedro de Alvarado (above, right), to explore the territory now known as Guatemala. The efficient but bloodthirsty Alvarado occupied the province of Soconusco on the Pacific coast and confronted the

Quichés, putting them to flight when he killed their chief Tecún Umán (far right). At Utatlán ▲ 288, the Quiché capital, he killed the royal family and successfully attacked Iximché ▲ 276, the capital of the Cakchiquels. His brother Gonzalo occupied Zaculeu ▲ 284, the Mam capital. The Tzutuhils were defeated at Atitlán, and the Pipils at Escuintla. The terrified Maya of the

Guatemalan highlands surrendered *en masse*, and Alvarado founded the capital at Santiago de los Caballeros, now Ciudad Vieja ▲ 275. There was continued resistance in Chiapas. Luis Marín attacked but was only partly successful against the Tzotzils and Tzeltals in 1524. Eight years later Mazariegos took them by surprise, but rather than surrender the Indians threw themselves into the Sumidero canyon ▲ 260. In 1528 Mazariegos founded Villa Real, now San Cristóbal da las Casas ▲ 233. Alvarado had founded Comitán, and the two lieutenants, now rivals, divided up the land and the people among their soldiers.

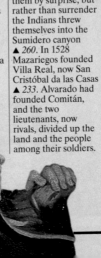

COLONIZATION

The colonial regime was firmly established with Montejo in Yucatán and Alvarado in Guatemala. There were a few short-lived attempts to shake off the Spanish yoke, but a firm hand soon destroyed any hope of autonomy. However, the region inhabited by Chol groups in central Guatemala, to the southwest of modern Belize, remained inaccessible and unconquered. Fray Bartolomé de

1571 A tribunal of the Inquisition is established in Mexico.	1572 The Jesuits arrive in Mexico.

1570 · 1572 · 1574 · 1576 · 1578
1570

1568 The Spanish explore Oceania.	1570 The Council of the Indies promulgates a law prohibiting mestizos from holding office as lawyers or caciques.	1572 In Spain, Sister Theresa of Avila writes *The Book of the Foundations*. She is canonized in 1622.	1576 An epidemic kills 40 percent of the Indians in New Spain

CARTE DES PROVINCES DE TABASCO, CHIAPA, VERAPAZ, GUATIMALA, HONDURAS et YUCATAN.

RESISTANCE

In 1525 Cortés travelled to Honduras to quash a bid by one of his lieutenants for independence. He stopped at Tayasal ▲ *321*, the capital of the Itzás. Almost a century later missionaries from Yucatán paid a second visit to the city without obtaining anything from its king, Canek. A third expedition failed in 1622, and it was not until 1697 that the city fell to the troops of Martín de Ursua, governor of Yucatán. Another expedition left Guatemala for Tayasal, where it was to join up with troops from Yucatán. It occupied Dolores, the center of the unvanquished Lacandons. The Maya territory was finally conquered over two centuries after Columbus had first "discovered" America.

GUATEMALA AND NEW SPAIN

Las Casas and his Dominicans succeeded where all military initiatives had failed. They established their mission there and brought the region, subsequently named Verapaz, peacefully under Spanish rule. However, vast areas of jungle, between the mountains of Guatemala and northern Yucatán, remained unconquered. Maya warrior (right) depicted on a Classic vase.

The function of Captain General of Guatemala was created in 1542 and subsequently incorporated in the *Audiencia de los Confines*, whose jurisdiction covered the whole of Central America down to Costa Rica and included Yucatán. In 1565 the *Audiencia* was moved to Panamá, while Guatemala and Yucatán became part of New Spain

(Mexico). Five years later the *Audiencia de Guatemala* was established to cover Chiapas, Honduras, El Salvador, Costa Rica and Nicaragua. Yucatán remained annexed to Mexico.

AUDIENCIA DE LOS CONFINES
The *Audiencia*, a legislative and legal tribunal established in 1543, counter–balanced the powers of the Captain General in Guatemala.

THE COLONIAL REGIME

THE INDIANS AS ROYAL SUBJECTS

Spanish America formed a vast unit of over six million square miles that was subject to the same legal regime and administered by royal officials. Under Spanish law the Indians were considered subjects of the Spanish crown and slavery was outlawed, which harmed the purses and angered the early conquistadors. They were opposed by jurists, theologians and men of the church including Vitoria, Montesinos and especially Las Casas ▲ 234, who had witnessed the abuse of the Indians during the conquest of Cuba. As Bishop of Chiapas he continued his humanitarian work (Las Casas' book, below). Spanish laws and especially the *Recopilación de las Leyes de Indias*, promulgated in 1681 by Charles II (above), gave the empire a strong legal unity. However, regional variations were taken into account by the Crown and the Council of the Indies. Codicils were added to the general laws to provide solutions to local problems.

> **AUTOS-DA-FÉ**
> Indian beliefs persisted in spite of Christianization. At Maní (Yucatán), Landa ● 42 ordered an *auto-da-fé* during which Indians were tortured and executed, and hundreds of idols and more than twenty Mayan codices burnt. *Auto-da-fé* at Solotepec (right).

THE INDIANS UNDER THREAT

As well as being slaughtered during the Conquest itself, the Indians also fell victim to viral infections transmitted by the Spaniards which

decimated the population. The survivors were concentrated in the villages (*reducciones*) and made subject to the Indian nobility, who collected tributes in the name of the Spanish authorities. Spaniards were forbidden to live in Indian villages, and only monks came into contact with the native population. To aid them in their mission, the monks appointed a *maestro cantor* or *fiscal* in each village who taught the catechism and presided over the recitation of prayers. The increase in the power of the *maestros* and the simultaneous re-emergence of ancient beliefs resulted in *autos-da-fé*. These in turn provoked rebellions, including those of Canek (Yucatán) in 1671, Chiapas in 1692, and the Tzeltal rebellion at Cancuc, which was harshly repressed by Cosio in 1713.

RIVALRY WITH BRITAIN

Guatemala and Chiapas, situated far from the pirate-infested coasts and lacking the mineral resources which altered the established agricultural order, lived peacefully through the colonial period. Yucatán, exposed to the plundering of the pirates and too sparsely populated to offer any form of effective resistance, fell victim to the numerous attacks that caused the depopulation of what is now the coast of Quintana Roo. The British had established themselves near the Laguna de Términos, in southern Campeche, and occupied a vast territory where they exploited the mahogany and logwood (used in dyeing) and threatened navigation in the Gulf of Mexico. Driven out by the Spanish in 1716, they established themselves firmly

1731
Rebellion (begun in 1729) by the
Natchez Indians of Louisiana, against
the French presence, is finally crushed.

1789
Ratification of the American
Constitution. George Washington
becomes first president of the USA.

1713
The Treaty of Utrecht
confirms British
maritime supremacy.

1763
The French cede their
North American
territories to the British.

1776–83
American War of
Independence concluded
by the Treaty of Paris

along the coast of
present-day Belize,
protected by the fleet
anchored off Jamaica.
Naval battle (below)
between the British
and Spanish in 1747.
In 1763 Spain
conceded the
territory of British
Honduras to the
British. The act was
confirmed by the
Treaty of Versailles
in 1783, although
ownership was not
finalized until the
British victory of St
George's Caye in
September 1798. The
poor soil and absence
of natural resources
on the peninsula
meant that the
province of Yucatán
could not become
rich. The Indians,
subject to the
encomienda paid
regular tributes to the
Spanish in cotton,
honey, leather, salt
meat and logwood.

AFTER INDEPENDENCE

MEXICO AND THE UNITED PROVINCES OF CENTRAL AMERICA

The call for
independence issued
at Dolores by the
Mexican priest
Miguel Hidalgo,
together with the
liberal Constitution
of Cadiz proclaimed in
Spain in 1812
(above), reinforced
the Creole spirit of
independence. The
struggle fought in
central Mexico was
echoed in Yucatán.
Mexico declared
independence in
1821, followed
immediately by
Yucatán, Chiapas and
Guatemala. The
representatives of
Chiapas demanded
reannexation to
Mexico, which was
accepted in 1822.
With the fall of the
Mexican emperor
Agustín de
Iturbide in
1823, Central
America
parted
company with
Mexico and
Chiapas declared
independence. Then
in 1824 a plebiscite
decided that
Chiapas should
be part of the
Mexican
Confederation.
The United
Provinces of Central
America, separated
from Mexico, lasted
until 1839 but could
not withstand the
mounting waves of
nationalism, and the
Spanish colonies
became independent
countries.

CONSTITUCION
política de la
MONARQUÍA ESPAÑOLA,
PROMULGADA EN CÁDIZ

39

● HISTORY

1835
Beginning of hostilities
between Texas and
Mexico.

1864–7
Maximilian of Austria
becomes Emperor of
Mexico.

1800	1820	1840	1860	1880	1900

1810
Rebellions as Spanish
colonies fight for
independence.

1819
The USA buys
Florida from
Spain.

1848
Annexation of
Mexican territory by
the USA.

1861–5
American
Civil War.

1898
Spanish–American war in
Cuba and the Philippines.
Annexation of Hawaii.

YUCATÁN

After Mexican independence, in a

long struggle fuelled by the Mexican government under the dictatorship of Santa Anna,

Federalists were set against Centralists. Yucatán held out against the Mexicans and declared independence from Mexico in 1841, as Texas had in 1836. The so-called "Caste War" ▲ 186 posed a threat to the whites of Yucatán, but after the American invasion Mexico supported the local government against the rebels. Yucatán was reunited with Mexico in 1848, followed by Campeche ▲ 228 in 1857.

HONDURAS AND EL SALVADOR

During the 20th century Honduras and El Salvador have both experienced political instability and relations between them have been difficult. For instance, the "Soccer War" in 1969 was only brought to an end by the intervention of the OAS (Organization of American States). Encouraged by the success of the Sandinista revolution in Nicaragua in 1979, guerrilla movements developed in El Salvador ▲ 314.

During the 1980's the US increased its military presence in Honduras to support the anti-Sandinista Contadora group in El Salvador. With the end of the revolution in Nicaragua in 1990, Honduras and El Salvador enjoyed a return to peace.

> **PEACE ACCORDS**
> Costa Rica, Guatemala, Nicaragua, El Salvador and Honduras signed a series of accords between 1987 and 1989. The civil war in El Salvador ended.

DIFFICULTIES IN CHIAPAS

Chiapas lived through the first years of independence torn between two options for their country: rule by the conservatives (the big landowners, army and high-ranking clergy), who wanted to unite it around a strong, centralized power; or by the reformists (supported by the liberals and republicans), who preferred a federation of free and independent sovereign states. The conflicts were not

resolved until after the reformist triumph of 1864. However, new conflicts immediately broke out in an attempt to prevent their re-election. The victor, Miguel Utrilla, established peace in 1879. The liberals took the precaution of transferring the capital from San Cristóbal to Tuxtla Gutiérrez in 1892. The revolution (above) rekindled the old conflict between the conservatives and liberals, who formed

an alliance to protect their own land interests at the expense of social achievements. The oil industry currently represents a large proportion of Mexican national production. Disputes between farmers and Indians over land-ownership, the complicity between the oligarchy and the local authorities which was at the root of an absence of laws for the protection of individuals and society as a whole, the

terror instilled by the white guard, the lack of accountability, the general corruption and poverty, all culminated in the 1994 rebellion.

1910
In Mexico the revolutionaries Francisco Madero and Pancho Villa seize power.

1969
War between El Salvador and Honduras.

1987–9
Peace accords in Central America (Costa Rica, Guatemala, Nicaragua, El Salvador and Honduras).

1915	1930	1945	1960	1975	1990

1914–18
World War One.

1917
Russian Revolution.

1939–45
World War Two.

1957
Creation of the EEC.

1993
Signing of ALENA (free trade agreement between the USA, Canada and Mexico).

MEXICO

Mexico adopted an imperial system in 1863 and was governed by Maximilian of Habsburg (receiving the crown of Mexico, above). The liberals subsequently expelled the new emperor, who for a time had the support of French troops sent by Napoleon III. Juárez restored the republic in 1867. A vast plan for reform adopted throughout the country included the construction of railway lines and industrialization projects, while the dictatorship of Díaz (inset, far left) encouraged the creation of vast estates and the modernization of the country. However, the state of serfdom to which the peasants were reduced and the absence of democracy led to the 1910 revolution (left), dominated by the figures of Pancho Villa and Emiliano Zapata. The ensuing period of unrest lasted until the political stability established in the 1930's by the PRI, who are still in power today.

GUERRILLA RESISTANCE
On January 1, 1994, there was a rebellion by Indians in Chiapas (below). The government negotiated.

GUATEMALA

Guatemala came into being as a nation in 1839 and adopted a liberal government, which was overthrown by the conservative Rafael Carrera. Carrera governed from 1844 to 1856 and was succeeded by Justo Rufino Barrios, who came to power following a liberal revolution and implemented many reforms. By the early 20th century, American capital controlled virtually the entire Guatemalan economy. Political unrest brought General Ubico to power, where he remained until 1944. After Arévalo, the land reforms decreed in 1954 by Colonel Jacobo Arbenz Guzman provoked the *coup d'état* led by Colonel Castillo Armas (anti-Arbenz rebel, below), who restored land to the companies. The repressive measures of successive military governments gave rise to the creation of guerrilla resistance from 1963, consolidated by the FAR (Fuerzas Armadas Revolucionarias). The country was caught up in a wave of violence, assassinations and terrorism, followed by repressive measures imposed by the army and paramilitary groups. Thousands of Indians fled to Mexico during the 1980's. The return of constitutional government in 1985 began to change things. Despite pressure from the army, negotiations continued with the guerrillas.

BELIZE

Britain's annexation in 1859 of part of Verapaz (Guatemala) put the two nations on a potential war footing. Maps of Guatemala still included Belize as part of the country. New agreements adopted a *status quo* which was, sooner or later, accepted by both countries. After World War Two the colony of British Honduras suffered a very violent economic crisis which favored the establishment of unions and political parties. Belize finally declared independence on September 21, 1981, and George Price was elected Prime Minister. Generally speaking, Belize is a poor country which lives mainly by agriculture and increasingly tourism, based on its tropical beaches and archeological sites. However, its current poor road network is an obstacle to its development ▲ 335.

41

● WRITING

About eight hundred different symbols have been recorded in Mayan texts. The number is too great for an alphabetic or syllabic form of writing but too small for a purely logographic form. The somewhat whimsical records (opposite) of Waldeck ● 56.

The Maya are the only civilization on the American continent to have developed a form of writing capable of expressing all types of thought and language through a combination of signs and symbols. As early as the Classic period the Maya had books in the form of long strips of bast paper folded in a "concertina" and covered with a fine layer of lime on which the scribe painted texts and images. There were also carved and painted inscriptions. In recent years considerable progress has been made in deciphering these texts, due to a better understanding of the true nature of the writing, in which certain symbols express concepts while others are a transcription of syllables.

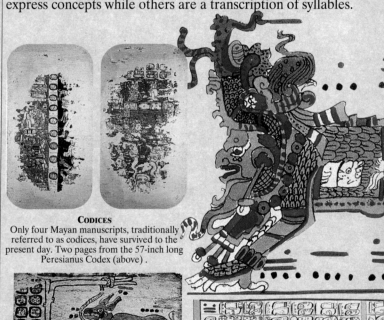

CODICES

Only four Mayan manuscripts, traditionally referred to as codices, have survived to the present day. Two pages from the 57-inch long Peresianus Codex (above).

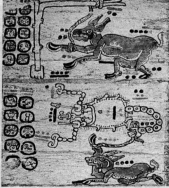

The Dresden Codex (center) is a treatise on divination and astronomy, while the Madrid Codex (above) consists of horoscopes and almanacs to assist priests in their predictions and ceremonies.

READING ORDER

Mayan writing is presented in the form of blocks of glyphs which are arranged either in rows or columns. These glyphic blocks are usually intended to be read from left to right and from top to bottom in pairs of columns. They are made up of various symbols or glyphs: a principal symbol with affixes.

VERB-OBJECT-SUBJET
In this example taken from the Dresden Codex, each figure is accompanied by a text of four glyphic blocks. The first block, the verb, designates the action: presenting an offering. The second, the object, is the offering itself (the same glyph appears in the hand of each figure). The third names the figure, and the fourth is the omen for this period: good or bad depending on the divinity.

The third block (above) represents the turkey-cock (*cutz*) by using the symbol *cu* and the symbol read as *tzu*.

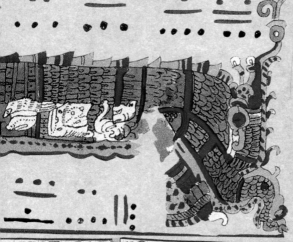

The dog (*tzul*) is represented in the third block (above) which consists of the glyphs *tzu* and *lu*.

LANDA ALPHABET
In the 16th century the Bishop of Yucatán tried to transcribe the European alphabet into Mayan symbols – an impossible task as Mayan writing is syllabic.

43

LONG COUNT
Years were calculated from an initial date corresponding to 3114 BC in the western calendar. The units used were the day (*kin*), the 20-day month (*uinal*), the 360-day year (*tun*), the period of 20 *tuns* (*katun*) and the period of 20 *katuns* (*baktun*).

The Maya perfected the discoveries of their post-Olmec predecessors in the fields of positional arithmetic and the calendar, which used independent cycles. The principal cycles were the divinatory cycle or *tzolkin* (260 days), the solar year or *haab* (365 days), and the Great Cycle of 5,200 *tun* (5,200 x 360 days) or Long Count. Their mastery of the calculation of time enabled them to write their history and, above all, to predict the future by means of a cyclical conception of chronological units, as illustrated by their inscriptions.

"KATUN" CALENDAR ROUND
Landa ● 55 reproduced the *katun* cycle on this wheel. The Short Count dates an event in relation to the end of a *katun* (period of 20 *tuns*), while 260 *tuns* (260 x 360 days) elapsed between two *katuns*. Hence the thirteen segments in Landa's wheel.

STELE E AT QUIRIGUA
1. Initial Series
2. 9 *baktuns* and 17 *katuns*
3. 0 *tun* and 0 *uinal*
4. 0 *kin* and 13 *ahau* (260-day calendar)
5. Ninth Lord of the Underworld and Glyph F (undeciphered)
6–8. Supplementary Series

52-YEAR CYCLE. The Long Count can be shortened by indicating the date on the *tzolkin* (260-day) cycle and on the *haab* (365-day) cycle. A combination of two positions from these cycles can only be repeated every 52 years. A cycle of this length is, therefore, exact.

1	2	5	6	9	12

For numerical notations the Maya used a system of bars and dots.
A bar represented 5 and a dot 1.

CALCULATION

To write 1995 (right):
3 bars represent the
number of units
(15 x 1 = 15), 3 bars
(below) and 4 dots
represent the number
of twenties
(19 x 20 = 380), and
4 dots represent the
number of four
hundreds (4 x 400 =
1,600). Thus
1,600 + 380 + 15 =
1995.

HISTORY AND ASTRONOMY

Although many historical facts specific to
each city are recorded in the inscriptions of
the Classic period, astronomical observations
– such as the solar eclipses described in the
13th-century Dresden Codex ● 42 (fragment
above) – are not always represented.

NUMBERS

Unlike the western
decimal system which
increases in value
from right to left, the
vigesimal Maya
system used two
symbols (the dot and
the bar) which
increased in vertical
columns from bottom
to top. The lowest
value was that of the
units (0 to 19), the
next was the 20s, then
the 400s, the 160,000s
and so on.

CALLIGRAPHY AND THE INITIAL SERIES

Another system of
calculation used
glyphs ● 42, in the
form of a complete
figure, which mainly
symbolized the
numbers and periods
in certain Initial
Series. These appear
at the beginning of
many inscriptions and
indicate the time that
has elapsed since the
initial date of the
Mayan calendar.
On Stele E at
Quirigua ▲ 306
(detail and general
view, left) the
numbers are
represented by bars
and dots and the
periods by a head in
profile. On the panel
from the "Palacio" at
Palenque (right),
numbers and periods
are represented by a
complete figure,
while on the panel
from Yaxchilán (far
left), the numbers are
represented by heads
and the periods by
entire figures.

● HUMAN SACRIFICE AND SELF-SACRIFICE

A jaguar (below left) devours a human heart after tearing it out. Bas-relief from Chichén Itzá ▲ 205. Wars between city-states (right) brought prisoners and sometimes sacrificial victims.

For a long time the Maya have been contrasted with the bloodthirsty Aztecs. They have been presented as a non-violent, intellectual people who were not given to bloody sacrifices. The most recent discoveries, however, have shown that, although the numbers of victims were much lower than those of their neighbors, human sacrifice played a major role in Mayan religion from the very beginning. Iconography and texts from the Classic period also reveal that the sacrifice of a victim and self-sacrifice had the same value. Sacrifice was a payment that had to be made to natural and supernatural powers to obtain such favors as rain, a good harvest, victory and universal harmony.

SELF-SACRIFICE

Self-sacrifice, a characteristic rite of Mesoamerica, was as important to the Maya as the sacrifice of a victim. The supplicant would offer their own blood, which had been obtained through one of various methods, some more painful than others, using instruments such as needles, sting-ray spines and knives. A rope of thorns passed through the tongue of the victim (below, detail from a bas-relief at Yaxchilán ▲ 248).

"TZOMPANTLI"
From the year AD 1000, victims' skulls were skewered on rods and arranged in rows in the manner of the Aztec *tzompantli*. A sculpted version of the "skull rack" exists at Chichén Itzá ▲ 205 (above).

TEARING OUT THE HEART
The many scenes depicting human sacrifice by tearing out the heart date mainly from the 11th century AD. Notable examples exist at Chichén Itzá ▲ 205 where they appear on repoussé gold pectoral disks (right) or painted on buildings.

> "A VEIL OF AGONY SPREADS ACROSS THE VIRGIN LIDS, AND THE BLOOD THAT SPATTERS THE SACRIFICIAL KNIFE ... HALOES THE HEADS OF THE GODS, SACRED AND INDIFFERENT."
>
> MIGUEL ANGEL ASTURIAS

SUN AND EARTH

Sacrificial scenes were seldom represented on monuments, but the instruments associated with the night sun and the jaguar (its symbolic representation) were quite common. This seems to confirm that the recipients of the sacrifice were the sun, which was thereby invested with the power to be reborn the next morning, and the earth, which was made fertile. As well as tearing out the heart, decapitation and sacrifice by arrows were also practiced. The method of selection between the various forms of sacrifice is unknown. The Maya also performed a double sacrifice which involved tearing out the heart for the sun and decapitation to release a flow of blood which would slake the earth's thirst.

IN BLOOD AND PAIN

It is quite probable that everyone had to shed their blood during certain festivals. The religious and political authorities, and therefore the king, were obliged to do so most frequently. The sacrifice was all the more valuable if the bleeding was accompanied by pain. Some of the practises appear unbearable from a modern standpoint.

This two-part censer (left) represents an "old god" offering a severed head. It was found at Tikal and dates from the Early Classic period (c. AD 450).

During the Middle Preclassic period the Maya made fairly crude, ceramic figurines. These were mostly solid, with the exception of whistles and hollow rattles, and represented animals and people. After disappearing for almost six centuries, the figurines once again featured on the archeological inventory of the Early Classic period. The new characters and forms were used as intermediaries during communication rituals with the other world. They disappeared during the Postclassic period and were replaced by over-simplified statuettes of the human body.

FIGURINE-WHISTLES
During the Classic period hollow figurines were often used as whistles. This "woman with rabbit" from Campeche (Mexico) is a rare image of a woman.

MOVEMENT
The more elaborate figurines represent moving figures – such as dancers, warriors or ball players.

CENSERS AND ELABORATE DECORATION
It seems that in Mesoamerica censers appeared at the same time as the first ceramics. Copal was burnt in these containers, whose form varied depending on the period and subject. This censer from Teapa (above) has elaborately decorated wings surrounding the central figure (Late Classic).

The smoke from the incense made it possible to address the great ancestors, the nocturnal sun, the earth and other natural forces.

This late 7th-century AD cylindrical winged censer from Palenque (below) stands 3½ feet high.

COSMIC CONTAINER
A two-part censer found at Tikal, dating from AD 800. A man wearing a bird-helmet is seated on the container-body of a terrestrial monster.

TYPES OF CENSER
The simplest form of censer was a bowl decorated with dots on the sides. Cylindrical winged censers were usually decorated with an image of the sun.

TWO-PART FIGURES
The incised decoration of this censer found at Uaxactún (Early Classic) represents clothing and body paint.

NEW CENSERS
New censers appeared at Mayapán around AD 1250. These were in the form of a cylindrical vase, which acted as the container and was mounted on a truncated base. Leaning against the base a full-length figure painted in several colors often represented a god. During this time censers became a significant part of ceramic production.

49

CLASSICAL COSMOGONY AND THE POSTCLASSICAL PANTHEON

The Mayan religion was developed over the centuries from a fundamental belief in returning power to the world. During the Preclassic and Classic periods natural forces (earth, sky, death, corn, lightning) were represented in the form of hybrid creatures or symbols whose images changed according to what they were actually required to embody. During the Postclassic period these images became fixed; the creatures acquired a personality and became immutable divinities who formed part of a hierarchical pantheon.

ARCHITECTURE
The architecture of the city-states of the Classic period was a joyous representation of all or part of the universe. It created an ideal setting for rituals associated with power and its legitimacy (rites of accession, funeral ceremonies and the worship of dynastic ancestors) and rituals designed to achieve universal order and harmony (the regulation of calendars by means of deambulation, rites performed to feed the earth and the sun, and to make the rain fall).

GOD K
The creature of the Late Classic period traditionally known as God K (Kauil), is represented with a smoking axe embedded in his forehead and symbolized by lightning. He is shown here (above) in both figurative and glyphic form.

Heroes of myths, demons of the underworld, numerous spirits and possibly some gods abound in the scenes painted and engraved on the (mainly funerary) ceramic vases, which tended to be less subject to the official art form. Cosmogonic representation (above) on a vase from Uaxactún, dating from the Late Classic period.

COSMIC MONSTER. This creature from the Classic period is both celestial and subterranean. The world of the natural and supernatural powers is centered around the basic life-death opposition represented by the two heads of the terrestrial monster: the living earth and the skeletal nocturnal sun.

A MULTIPLICITY OF CREATURES
An entire population of creatures associated with humidity, fertility and the fecund earth, with features suggesting reptilian or froglike origins, developed alongside the cosmic monsters. Other types of grotesque figures, with feline features, are represented as solar creatures, the spirits of sacrifice, war and death. They pass from one extreme to the other, just as life ends in death, and death in rebirth.

THE KING RULES
In the monumental art of the city-states the figure of the king represents the center of the universe. Around him are organized the cosmic powers depicted as monsters and grotesque figures who are more spirit-like than god-like. The monstrous appearance of Stele D and its altar at Copán has been accentuated by Frederick Catherwood (lithograph, 1844).

SCULPTURE
The monumental sculpture of the Classic period, usually associated with architecture or in the form of steles, often shows the king in a cosmic setting, with images of the earth and the underworld beneath his feet and the sky above his head. Details (left and right) from the back of an 8th-century AD royal throne.

CLASSICAL COSMOGONY AND THE POSTCLASSICAL PANTHEON

CHANGING BELIEFS

The changes in beliefs and rituals that occurred during the Postclassic period were the result of Mexican influences and the weakening of political structures. By the beginning of the Early Postclassic period, monumental art no longer celebrated royal power but two orders of rival warriors. The steles disappeared and worship focused on war and human sacrifice. Gods, especially those of Mexican origin, began to appear. The names of divinities that were not established until the Late Postclassic period were all too readily attributed to images from the Classic, which were probably representations of natural forces. For example, because of their long noses, the masks on the façades of Yucatec sites have been designated as those of the rain god Chac, whereas they are probably masks of the cosmic – and more usually terrestrial – monster.

Carved stone, found at Jonuta (Mexico), showing a kneeling priest making an offering.

THE PANTHEON

With the founding of Mayapán in c. 1250 (the combined result of a wave of Mexican influence and a weakening of royal power) there developed a veritable pantheon of gods, all endowed with a physical personality. Places of worship became much more numerous, with oratories and sanctuaries as well as temples. Stele (left) at Yaxchilán showing a high priest holding a scepter which is half-man, half-serpent.

DISCOVERING THE
WORLD OF THE MAYAS

After the Spanish Conquest of Central America the already declining Maya civilization became the subject of many investigations, particularly with the rediscovery during the 18th and 19th centuries of cities buried deep in the forest. With a few notable exceptions, such as Diego de Landa, the Spanish conquerors had shown little interest in the region's history. The study of Mayan civilization (or "Mayanism") developed initially as a result of the efforts of European and American travelers and adventurers, and subsequently as professional archeologists gradually began to solve the mysteries of the world of the Mayas.

THE EARLY CONQUERORS

The first contact between Europeans and the Maya was an exchange of gifts which took place in 1502 on the Isla Guanaja during one of Columbus' voyages. In 1517 Hernandez de Córdoba found the Maya on the Isla Mujeres ▲ 174 and continued his voyage as far as Champotón ▲ 230. On February 18, 1519 Cortés set sail with eleven ships and, after stopping at the Isla de Cozumel, landed at Veracruz. It took him less than two years to conquer Mexico but another twenty to bring Yucatán under Spanish control.

FORGOTTEN RUINS

The ruins of ancient cities, which had lain silent and forgotten for centuries, were discovered by missionaries and officials from the colonial administration. However, their reports, both official and private, were rarely acted upon.

PALENQUE ▲ 243.
In 1476 the priest from a nearby village was surprised to find "stone houses" in the forest. It took forty-two years for the governor of the province to send an official who requested further investigations. In 1785 Bernasconi drew a plan of the site. In 1786, after visiting Palenque, Captain Antonio del Río concluded that these ruins, like those of Yucatán, pre-dated the Spanish Conquest and were the work of a single "nation".

DIEGO DE LANDA ● 43
The Spanish Conquest was legitimized by the christianization of the Indians, with the first Franciscans landing in 1535. While persecuting the Maya in the name of the "true faith", Diego de Landa – the future Bishop of Yucatán – was also interested in their history and customs. In his *Relación de las cosas de Yucatán* (above), found in 1864 he describes ruined cities.

JUAN GALINDO
The son of actors, Juan Galindo (above) left his native Ireland for America at the age of sixteen. By 1827 he was in Guatemala. He was appointed military governor of Petén and went on many voyages of discovery.

It was during one such voyage in 1834 that he discovered Copán ▲ 299. He remained there for a month, describing and sketching its monuments, drawing plans of the site and region and carrying out excavations.

THE "WINDOWS" OF COPÁN
After the site was abandoned in the 9th century AD, the river flooded the center of the city, leaving only a 100-foot section on which walls, stuccoed floors and tunnels were clearly visible. Galindo mistakenly called the site *Las Ventanas* because he thought it was a wall pierced by windows.

JEAN-FRÉDÉRIC WALDECK (1766–1857). In 1832 the 66-year-old artist and adventurer Waldeck arrived at Palenque to draw and give a description of the ruins for a work on the civilizations of Mexico ● *130*. He stayed thirteen months before going on to Yucatán. His drawings were used to illustrate the work of Brasseur de Boubourg ▲ *292*.

TWO DIFFERENT APPROACHES

Waldeck was a man of the Enlightenment who shared the liberalism and thirst for knowledge of the French Encyclopedists and believed that civilization was superior to the "primitive" state. He therefore believed in the intervention of Europe in the development of the cultures of the New World. The cautious interpretations of the liberal and democratic Stephens heralded the scientific discourse.

JOHN LLOYD STEPHENS (1805–53)

Although he was far from being the first to visit the Maya sites, Stephens was the first to make them accessible to the general public through his publications. Breaking with the strong "diffusionist" tradition, he declared his support for the independent development of Amerindian civilizations, and the Maya in particular. Born into a wealthy New England family, Stephens studied law before undertaking a series of voyages, accounts of which he later published. In 1836 he met the young English architect Frederick Catherwood who showed him a report by the mineralogist Del Río, illustrated by Waldeck. Captivated by the beauty of its ruins, the two men decided to visit Central America but were initially prevented by a war there. They finally managed to enter the region in 1839 and visited Copán, Quirigua, Toniná and Palenque over the next three years.

TEOBERT MALER
The German archeologist Teobert Maler (right) completed the work of Maudslay by taking some admirable photographs, which are still referred to today.

DÉSIRÉ CHARNAY
Charnay was the first to photograph the Maya sites (right) in 1859. His pictures were used to illustrate *Les Anciennes Villes du Nouveau Monde* (published in 1863).

ALFRED MAUDSLAY
The quality of Maudslay's photographs was not only due to improved techniques such as the dry-gelatin negative (invented in 1882), but also to his systematic approach, which was based on the collection of interpretative documents. The four volumes devoted to the archeology of the Maya sites in the collection *Biologia Centrali-Americana* (1889–1902) are a fine example of the genre.

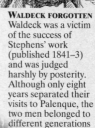

WALDECK FORGOTTEN
Waldeck was a victim of the success of Stephens' work (published 1841–3) and was judged harshly by posterity. Although only eight years separated their visits to Palenque, the two men belonged to different generations of culture and thought.

Drawing made by Waldeck in 1832 of a temple at Palenque (above). Photograph taken by Maler at Uxmal (below).

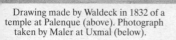

FREDERICK CATHERWOOD ● *130*
The development of new reproduction and photographic techniques made it possible to produce drawings that were much more objective. After the failure of the daguerreotype process, Frederick Catherwood decided to use a *camera lucida*, which enabled him to produce these extremely accurate drawings. View of Sayil (1843) ▲ *221* (right), and views (below left and bottom right) of the ruins of Palenque (1841).

FIRST PROFESSIONAL EXCAVATIONS

The first professional excavations in Maya territory were at Copán ▲ *299* from 1891 to 1895 by Harvard's Peabody Museum. From 1914 to 1958 the Washington Carnegie Institution was in the forefront of Maya archeology with its excavation of the major sites of Chichén Itzá, Copán, Kaminaljuyú and Uaxactún. This last site made it possible to establish the main lines of Maya history and divide them into three periods: Preclassic (2000 BC–AD 250), Classic (250–1000) and Postclassic (1000–1500). The University of Pennsylvania's Tikal Project (1956–70) was one of the most ambitious in terms of the number of people involved, the length of the project and the diversity of aspects studied.

A series of discoveries in the early 1960's gave Mayan studies a new lease of life. The paintings of Bonampak ▲ *249* and a number of sculptures from other sites demonstrated the importance of war, torture and human and self-sacrifice in the Mayan culture ● *46*.

In 1958 Heinrich Berlin noted the presence in the inscriptions of several major sites of a type of glyph whose main symbol was virtually exclusive to each of these sites. These "glyph-emblems" suggested that Mayan texts might have a historic and local – rather than a calendric – content ● *42*.

THE LATEST DISCOVERIES

It is likely that current research will lead to a better understanding of the origins of the Maya civilization. Evidence suggests that great cities such as El Mirador and Nakbé, with their grand pyramid complexes, were built by the immediate forebears of the Classic Maya, who were most probably direct descendants of the Olmecs ● *31*.

THE LIFE OF KINGS
In the 1960's Tatiana Proskouriakoff noticed that the period covered by each group of steles at Piedras Negras ▲ *332* never exceeded sixty years. This led her to consider the possibility that each group related to the life of a particular king and that the initial date of the group referred to the birth of the king and the second to his accession to the throne. She tested her hypothesis at Piedras Negras and Yaxchilán ▲ *248* by demonstrating that the glyphs associated with the various dates represented the birth, accession and death of the king whose name and titles followed. The inscriptions did not therefore relate solely to religion and the measurement of time.

PROGRESS IN THE STUDY OF MAYAN WRITING ● *42*
At the end of the 19th century documents were collected which enabled progress to be made in the study of the Mayan writing system. Its decipherment had been made possible in 1864 when the Abbé Brasseur ▲ *292* discovered Landa's 16th-century text, *Relación de las cosas de Yucatán*, in which Landa describes the calendar and gives the names of the days and months with their respective glyphs, producing what he

believed to be an alphabet but which was in fact a syllabary. In 1866 Brasseur noticed that the same symbols appeared in the Madrid Codex and on the sculpted monuments of Yucatán, Petén and Chiapas. In spite of

local variations it was the same system but it was different from the symbols observed in the manuscripts of Central Mexico, especially those of the Aztecs. The concept of an independent Mayan civilization was thus born.

In 1950 the Maya were still perceived, through their inscriptions, as a peaceable and religious people, concerned with the passage of time,

astrology and prophecies. It was thought that their writing was logographic, in other words that the textual units represented entire words.

THE MAYA TODAY

Maya territory covers the eastern part of Mesoamerica: southeast Mexico (Yucatán Peninsula and the State of Chiapas), Belize, Guatemala and the west of El Salvador and Honduras. It covers an area of around 125,000 square miles divided into highlands and lowlands – the same area inhabited by the Maya at the time of the Spanish Conquest. Today more than three million people (predominantly Quichés and Yucatecans) speak one of the twenty-eight Mayan dialects, which subdivide into nine large groups.

Most of the Maya are peasants living in villages and tiny rural communities, although they are swelling the urban and suburban populations in increasing numbers. Lacandón Indians from Chiapas ▲ 258 (above) at the turn of the century.

The Indians left their villages in search of work or to escape oppression. Tens of thousands of Guatemalan refugees settled in California, thus contributing to the spread of their languages beyond their traditional borders.

Since the Spanish Conquest and colonization, the Maya have been forced to live alongside mestizos and other ethnic groups.

After a severe decline during the 16th and 17th centuries, the Maya population is slowly increasing.

TENSION AND CONFLICT

The recent increase in the Maya population has led to discrepancies in the growth of the various ethnic groups (there are 400 Lacandóns and 800,000 Yucatecan Maya, while the Quiché-Cakchiquel-Tzutuhil population exceeds one million) and their occupation of land. This has given rise to conflict when local governments have refused to take it into account. Lacandón Indians (right). Distribution of Maya groups (below).

In the face of the exploitation, segregation and violence of colonial policies, the Maya developed strategies of passive resistance on a daily basis. When this was not enough they resorted to open rebellion.

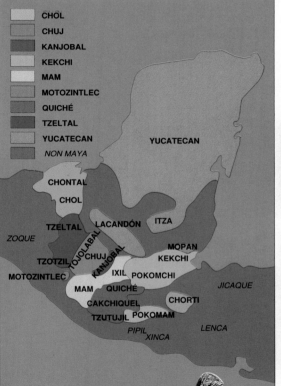

CHOL
CHUJ
KANJOBAL
KEKCHI
MAM
MOTOZINTLEC
QUICHÉ
TZELTAL
YUCATECAN
NON MAYA

YUCATECAN

CHONTAL
CHOL
ZOQUE
TZELTAL LACANDÓN ITZA
TZOTZIL TOJOLABAL CHUJ KANJOBAL MOPAN
MOTOZINTLEC IXIL POKOMCHI KEKCHI
MAM QUICHÉ JICAQUE
CAKCHIQUEL CHORTI
TZUTUJIL POKOMAM
PIPIL LENCA
XINCA

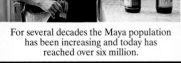

For several decades the Maya population has been increasing and today has reached over six million.

63

The organization of Indian communities around a village center dates back to the post-Conquest period. It is the result of the *reducciónes* policy conducted by the civil and, more especially, the religious authorities who imposed their own *imago mundi* (influenced, in particular, by the organization of the sacred area of the cloister) on these new settlements. Today these villages still retain the broad outlines of their original appearance and are a focal point for markets, small traders and religious festivals.

COSMIC TREE
The "center of the world and center of the sky" (often a silk-cotton tree) spreads its branches above the village square (**1**).
✝ Palín ▲ *269* (above).

COMPOSITION

Village and town squares feature votive chapels (**2**), associated with various districts and used as stopping-off points during processions. Each village has its own patron and other tutelary saints. There is often a fountain (**3**), a public wash-house (**4**) (painting by Samuel Sotz, right), and an ancestral altar (**5**).

FROM THE SPANISH CONQUEST TO THE PRESENT DAY

After the Conquest, villages where the indigenous population gathered were used as a means of colonial control (through preaching, the collection of tributes, recruitment of labor). Their architecture was based on the neoclassical designs of the Renaissance: perpendicular streets radiating outwards around which the church (**6**), the priest's residence (**7**) and the town hall (**8**) represented the centers of power ● *122*.

● RURAL COMMUNITIES

The Indians live in rural communities, whose size has depended on location and historical period, which are centered around an *ejido* (a square area given over to village buildings) and communal lands. The efforts of the colonial administrators to reduce communities to the smallest possible area were generally unsuccessful. Very early on the Indians abandoned their villages and dispersed to escape the abuses of administrative authority and reoccupied, as far as they could, their former dwellings and places of worship. The Catholic Church responded by building rural chapels and erecting crosses at key points in the landscape: by the roadside, on mountain tops and passes and near springs.

A WORLD IN MINIATURE

Each community is a "world" in miniature, a microcosm of the universe in which the Earth is a flat quadrilateral surrounded by four seas and orientated in relation to the sun's course (the sun's feet or lower parts lie to the East, his head or upper part to the West, while the North and South represent his left and right hands). The mountains (**1**), the ancient pyramids (**2**) and the church (**3**) are steps leading to the heavens, while the grottos, gulfs and sepulchers lead to the underworld.

ARCHEOLOGICAL SITES

Maya territory abounds with archeological sites which bear testament to the distant past. These survivors existed long before the villages which housed the kings and warriors of yesteryear (described in the *Rabinal Achi* ● *148*), figures of authority who were replaced by saints with the arrival of Christianity in the 16th century. Although chapels (**4**) were built on the pyramids (**2**), the sites have always been respected and feared and are often visited by groups offering up prayers to ask for rain or making conciliatory offerings before certain festivals or dance performances.

PATHS, TRACKS AND PASSES. The land is criss-crossed by a vast network of paths, tracks and the more important *caminos reales* (**5**).

MOUNTAIN TOPS

The mountain tops (**6**) mark the limit of the world as well as the frontier with neighboring communities. According to local mythology they often indicate successive stages in the journey of a founding hero, who set up boundary stones to mark the limits of his territory and thus legitimize his claim.

THE FOUR "CORNERS OF THE EARTH"

Around the villages where ancient calendric practices ● *70* are still observed, particularly those in Guatemala, four special sites symbolize the four "corners of the earth". From year to year the *alcaldes del mundo* – the so-called "year bearers" appointed by the communities ● *68* – move between these "corners".

"ALTAR DE COSTUMBRE" OR LOCAL ALTAR
An arrangement of flat stones, blackened with soot and spotted with wax, in an area scattered with shards, withered petals, pine needles and a few feathers, indicates a place of prayer, offering and sacrifice ● *46*. Some of these altars (**7**) have stone crosses or even idols in human form. Many show the position of pre-Hispanic places of worship.

SACRED SITES
In the Indian representation of the world all the sacred sites in the community are revered. Their local names reflect their natural characteristics.

"CALVARIO"

The *calvario* or "house of the ancestors" is the counterpart of the church or "house of the saints". It is situated to the west of the village, often on the outskirts, overlooking the cemetery.

CEMETERY
Tombs, consisting of a simple mound marked by a cross or plant, alternate with the cement tombs of the mestizos. Tombs are repainted on All Souls' Day ● *74*.

RIVERS
Rivers are used for washing and fishing. Fish are caught with nets, poison or dynamite (**8**).

RURAL CHAPEL

Rural chapels (**9**) provide a place of worship for the inhabitants of small villages (*rancherías, aldeas, caseríos*). They are also the venue for the ceremonies held for Santa Cruz (May 3), and the festival of springs, which marks the long-awaited start of the rainy season and the agricultural cycle ■ *22*.

The family is the basic unit of social organization. It is within the family that most of the productive and domestic tasks are performed. In certain regions the family forms part of a larger group, or lineage, made up of people living in the same village, or immediate vicinity, who often share the same name. One such grouping is the *calpul* (also known as the *chinamit* or *molab*), the remnant of the former *parcialidades*, which consisted of indigenous groups forcibly regrouped into new communities. Another is the *barrio* or district, a grouping created by the colonial administration.

THE MUNICIPALITY

Generally speaking, each community has the status of a municipality (*municipio*) and has a body of officials under the authority of the mayor (*alcalde*). Municipal officials are not elected by the community as a whole, but are appointed by nomination or co-option.

INDIANS, MESTIZOS AND WHITES

The different interests and traditions of the Indians, mestizos and whites in the countries of the Mayan world are often in conflict. In Guatemala, for example, the professionalization of municipal posts since the 19th century has marginalized the indigenous authorities.

COLLECTIVE WORK

Community officials have the right to mobilize an unpaid workforce to carry out work deemed to be in the local interest: for example, repairing a public building or constructing a bridge. This recruiting system is sometimes abused to serve private or external interests (such as the construction of roads and railway lines, or the levying of gangs of seasonal workers for the plantations), a reminder of the times when civic duties were an essential part of the colonial system and were used as a means of controlling and exploiting local populations.

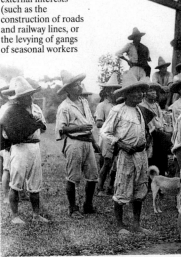

INSIGNIA
The most commonly found symbol of local power is undoubtedly the *vara* (wand of office) carried by holders of high civil office. This is often a silver-knobbed cane decorated with ribbons.

MUNICIPAL COUNCIL
The municipal council is responsible for the day-to-day maintenance, policing, and administrative and financial management of the community. During festivals and on market days a full council sits beneath the gallery of the town hall holding public audiences, recording and judging complaints and requests, and maintaining public order.

DIVISION OF POWER
As in any peasant community where politics and religion are intimately linked and where the destiny of its members is ruled by supernatural forces which control every undertaking, the municipality does not have a monopoly on local power. Religious offices controlled by the priesthood and brotherhood also hold important prerogatives, especially in ritual matters.

● FORTUNE-TELLERS AND HEALERS

Fortune-telling and healing play an important part in the complex ceremonies that are central to the religious life of the Maya. They are practiced by traditional priests whose often ambivalent and ambiguous powers are primarily a product of their own personal talents, revealed in dreams and developed during many years' apprenticeship to their elders. Sometimes these priests are believed to be "sorcerers" (*aj itz*), able to transform themselves into powerful, flesh-eating animals (*nahual*). As "calendar priests" they oversee the use of the 260-day (divinatory) and 365-day (solar) Counts ● *44*.

RITUAL ORATIONS
Mastery of the ritual orations is one of the skills of the healer. These orations are central to the therapeutic process and draw part of their effectiveness from the healer's ability to invoke the aid of supernatural powers in healing the patient.

TOOLS OF THE TRADE AND ROLE OF THE FORTUNE-TELLER
Fortune-tellers use a wide range of objects and accessories to enable them to "see" into the future: translucent stones, quartz crystals and *tz'ite* seeds are always found in the pouches worn over their shoulder or on their belt.

POR ROSA ELENA CURRUCHICH

HABLA NALOS IMARENE

Censers from Amatenango and Chamula (Chiapas).

CONTROLLING TIME

Fortune-tellers present the passage of time in spatial terms. Each day of the 260-day divinatory calendar has its own number and symbol.

SMALL PLATE FROM CHAMULA ▲ 238

In 1969 a small wooden plate was discovered, still in use, on which a series of vertical lines marked in charcoal represented the eighteen 20-day months and the five unlucky days.

During seances fortune-tellers answer the questions of those seeking advice by throwing crystals and seeds onto a towel spread on the ground and observing the patterns formed as they fall. Each pattern corresponds to a day on the divinatory calendar and to a specific number–symbol combination whose lucky or unlucky associations predict the success of a particular undertaking, such as marriage, seed sowing or building a house.

A UNIVERSAL APPROACH

Healers master therapeutic techniques such as the use of medicinal herbs, the splinting of fractures and the extraction of venom, all of which are linked to an understanding of the natural world. With their profound knowledge of the balances required by their system of beliefs healers can repair the loss of part of the soul, reestablish the circulation of the vital fluids within the body, identify, locate and expel pathogenic agents sent by a sorcerer, invoke supernatural powers and master the ritual orations. Since all ailments and illnesses are considered to be the result of a disfunction of the component parts of the individual, healing is a matter of performing rituals to reestablish the basic unity between the individual and society, the body and the cosmos, time and space.

● FESTIVALS OF THE BROTHERHOODS

MAXIMÓN BROTHERHOOD
The Santa Cruz brotherhood of Santiago
Atitlán worships the unorthodox Saint
Maximón, a master of the magic arts and
the patron saint of sorcerers ▲ 281.

One of the main concerns of Spanish evangelists
was to impose the worship of saints upon the
Maya and to establish brotherhoods within the
communities to serve and preserve this practise.
These brotherhoods (*cofradías*) played an
important role in religious and social life. They
were given land and livestock, and provided part
of the tribute demanded by the Spanish. In the 19th century the
missionary orders were stripped of their wealth and privileges
and expelled by the liberal regimes. The brotherhoods
remained, acting as a melting pot for a syncretic religion, born
of the union of Catholic doctrines and traditional beliefs and
reintroduced a number of practises which, until then, had
remained semi-clandestine.

Each saint has a
votive brotherhood
and an altar-
sanctuary, which
contains their
effigy and
possessions and is
watched over by
brotherhood
officials. The
altar-sanctuary is
for private rituals
and preparations
for ceremonies.
The Tenejapa
brotherhood,
(right), in
ceremonial costume
▲ 238.

> "WHILE THE CHILDREN ON THEIR BACKS WERE AMAZED BY THE CHANTING AND THE LIGHTS, THE WOMEN SMILINGLY WATCHED NOT ONLY THE IMAGES OF THE SAINTS, BUT ALSO THEIR MEN CARRYING THEM ... INTOXICATED BY THEIR EFFORTS AND THEIR OFFERING."
>
> MICHEL BUTOR

FESTIVAL OF THE PATRON SAINT

Brotherhood officials gather on their saint's festival to perform rituals which mark the reunion of the living and the dead and commemorate the mythical passage from primordial darkness into the light of day. Participants include members of other brotherhoods, musicians, dancers and firework-makers, as well as parents and friends. Next, the saint is worshipped in public beneath a canopy of leaves in the court of the sanctuary, then in the church, and finally in the festal procession (the "high day"). Eight days later the saint is taken to another sanctuary prepared by the new brotherhood officials.

Transfer of the Saint by the Brotherhood (left) by the artist Chavajay.

PROCESSION

The end of the festival, when the saint is borne aloft, is reminiscent of the ancestral inauguration of the sun's course. The ceremonial bearing of these heavy saints' catafalques (the festivals of Cubulco and San Andres Sajcabajá, left) symbolizes the permanent sacrifice of mankind to the service of the universal powers and the binding contract to ensure universal harmony.

The all-pervasive scent of incense and the many flowers distributed on the altars and during the performance of rituals show a desire to please the ancestral spirits, who are believed to like them. The fragrances are supposed to unite the souls of the living and the dead in a single aromatic cloud, as stated in the ritual orations. The explosions of fire-crackers and *bombas* let off by the firework-makers, mark the various stages of the rituals. (Smoke from fire-crackers on the steps of the church of "Chichi", above.) It is the plumassiers' task to decorate the church doors and the niches containing images of the saints with a profusion of feathers, pieces of cloth and garlands.

Procession at Santiago Atitlán ▲ *281*: painting by Martín Ratzan (1982).

The major Christian festivals, whose prominence depends on the local influence of the Catholic Church, form the third aspect of religious festivals. The cult of the Virgin and the festivals marking the main stages in the life of Christ are often the affair of the official clergy and the Ladinos. Apart from pilgrimages to particular statues of the Virgin or Christ, the religious year is divided into three: the Christmas cycle (Nativity, Epiphany, Candlemas), the Easter cycle (Carnival, Holy Week, Ascension, Whitsun, Corpus Christi), and All Souls' or All Saints' Day.

HOLY WEEK

Although the brotherhoods take part in the celebration of Holy Week, the festival is organized by a committee under the control of the Catholic priest. Each day commemorates an episode in the Passion with a procession. On Easter Day in Antigua the streets are carpeted with flower petals and colored wood-shavings.

ALL SOULS' DAY

All Souls' Day, which is celebrated in the smallest hamlets by Indians and Ladinos alike, is primarily a family festival. Houses are decorated with altars piled high with food and gifts to welcome the returning souls of the dead. During the night of November 1 to November 2 the living go to the cemetery to honor their dead with food, alcohol, various offerings, music and dancing.

FLAGS

Tzeltal Indians during the carnival of Tenejapa (Chiapas).

> "EVERYTHING WAS AS ARRANGED: COSTUMES, CLOUDS OF INCENSE. THE PROCESSIONS WERE ALREADY UNDER WAY; THE TOWN WAS VIBRANT WITH ANTICIPATION ... IMAGES OF CHRIST, OF THE VIRGIN AND CHILD ON MAKESHIFT WOODEN CARTS." DEBORAH EISENBERG

CARNIVAL

Little is known of the historical process by which Carnival was introduced into Indian culture, but it is a festival that symbolizes the dual heritage of the Mayan religious tradition. It combines certain characteristics of European carnivals (inversion of hierarchies, lack of distinction between the sexes, ritualized rebellion) and elements from local mythology and history.

Carnivals are at their most spectacular and interesting in Chiapas where "monkeys" and "savages" surround the two villages of Chamula ▲ *238* and Bachajón respectively, transporting them back in time to a previous creation and reinstating the original primordial chaos. It is then up to the civil and religious authorities to ritually re-establish social and cultural order. The Carnival is the modern equivalent of the so-called *uayeb* rites of the ancient Maya and of the ceremonies that accompanied the five-day transition (*ch'ay k'in*) between two solar years. It marks the arrival of the New Year.

THE CHRISTMAS CYCLE

The Nativity, which is rarely celebrated in the villages, is primarily an urban, mestizo festival. The evening of December 16 marks the start of the Christmas novena, punctuated by *posadas* (halts of the Virgin). Mary and Joseph are carried through the streets in search of a house (chosen in advance) that will offer them shelter. Receiving the couple is a great honor. The scene is re-enacted each evening until December 24 when the Holy Family reaches Bethlehem (in this case the church) and joins the nativity scene set up for the occasion.

During the pre-Hispanic period dance, including *palo volador*, war dances and dynastic dramas, was a highly codified form of expression. The Spanish quickly understood that they could capitalize on this form of ritual performance to "colonize" the Indian imagination and spread their ideological message of military and religious conquest among the vanquished nations. Contemporary Spanish dances represented recent Christian victories over the Arabs, a subject which was readily adapted to the new situation and resulted in the *bailes de la Conquista*.

"BAILES DE LA CONQUISTA"
There were different versions of these dances, depending on whether they were presenting Spanish themes (*baile de Moros y Cristianos, Rey Moro, Tamorlan*) or local motifs. In the *baile de Cortés*, the conqueror of Mexico (often on horseback) confronts the Aztec king Moctezuma.

PATZKA
The dancers (below) are dressed in rags, armed with sticks carved with animal motifs (serpents, deer), and wearing goitrous masks. They represent the ancestors of the community of Rabinal ▲ 292 who, in the original dance, carried the patron saint to the high altar, thus triggering the sun's rotation and the first rainfall.

MASKS ● 85
Masks are carved from lightweight wood and painted in bright colors. They represent characters from local myths (jaguars, monkeys, deer, devils and ancestors) and key historical figures (the Spanish, Indian chiefs and kings, princes and princesses of bygone days). Like all effigies, masks are thought of as living beings and, as such, are watched over and fed. In vocal dances the sacred words are spoken by the voices of the masks.

DANCE OF SAN JORGE
This dance, inspired by the biblical episode of Saint George and the Dragon, illustrates the fight between the forces of Good and Evil. The dragon is made of cloth and cardboard.

"PALO VOLADOR"

The *palo volador* originated in central Mexico and was being performed in Guatemala before the Conquest. Two groups of dancers ("monkeys" and "angels") climb, two by two, to the top of a mast fixed firmly in the ground. They then throw themselves from the top, with one foot attached to a rope. As the rope unfurls it causes the *canasta* – a pyramidal structure fixed over a mobile fork set into the point of the mast – to rotate. Another dancer stands on the *canasta*, 50–65 feet above the ground.

COSTUMES AND ACCESSORIES

Spectacular historical dances provide an opportunity to display lavish and brightly colored costumes: velvet jackets and trousers, silk scarves and fringed hats. These *bailes de seda* contrast sharply with the so-called ancestral dances (*Patzkas, Pascares, Viejitos*) performed by dancers dressed in rags with various accessories according to the theme.

"RABINAL ACHI"

Although not particularly spectacular, a performance of the *Rabinal Achi* is still an exceptional event. The text of this pre-Hispanic dance (written in ancient Quiché) has been preserved in its entirety ● *148*. It re-enacts the trial of a Quiché warrior, accused of an incursion into Rabinal territory ▲ *292*, and describes the judicial ritual leading to his sacrifice.

INDIAN DANCES

Some Indian dances are silent, some are vocal and have been passed down by word of mouth, while others have long, recitative dialogues recorded in the *Rabinal Achi* or the *Balam Kej*.

77

Music and song play an important part in Mayan rituals and celebrations. The aerophones of the ancient Maya have been replaced by various kinds of flutes, while percussion instruments, and especially xylophones and drums, have enjoyed greater continuity. As in popular music, where ancient forms co-exist with old Spanish folk tunes, Christian hymns and songs of praise have not completely suppressed Indian recitatives. For example, the *bolonchon* of the Tzotzils, the funerary songs of the Chols and the shamanist incantations of the *h'men* (sorcerers from Yucatán) remain an integral part of traditional rituals and ceremonies.

"MARIMBA"
The national instrument of Guatemala, the *marimba* (right), is extremely popular throughout the region. It is a type of xylophone derived from the African *balafon*, which was introduced to the American continent by black slaves during the 16th century. It consists of strips of rosewood of various lengths, connected to a group of resonators enclosed by a piece of gold-beater's skin or pig-gut membrane. Sound is produced when the wooden strips are struck.

FLUTES AND DRUMS
A flute and large skin-covered drum form the most popular combination of instruments in Indian music. They accompany the central figures in processions and

rituals and punctuate the orations delivered at the entrance to brotherhood sanctuaries. During mass the players stand beneath the porch.

VIOLIN AND "ADUFE"
The Quichés play this pair of instruments (below right) to honor the dead. They are an example of the intermingling and inventiveness of Indian traditions: the rustic violin is made of cypress wood; the sound-post is made from the tail of a rattlesnake and the bow (carved in one piece) is strung with greased horsehair. The square drum consists of two skins stretched over a wooden frame. Its local name, *tupe*, comes from the Spanish *adufe* – in turn derived from the Arabic *duff*, a similar instrument which is its distant ancestor.

"MATRACA"
The *matraca* is a small wooden board to which pieces of metal are loosely attached. These are shaken by rapidly rotating the wrist to produce a rattling noise. It is played only at Easter, to replace the church bells which remain silent for this period of mourning.

The *marimba* is played by at least three people at once who strike it using wooden sticks with hard rubber ends.

VIOLIN, HARP AND GUITAR
Although these are derived from instruments introduced by the Spanish, their rusticity distinguishes them from their ancestors. While the violin and guitar are widespread, the harp is played only by the Tzotzils and Kekchis.

CONCHES AND TURTLE SHELLS
Conches were once used as trumpets to issue rallying or alarm calls. During the Bachajón carnival they are played together with turtle shells struck with corn cobs.

WOODEN DRUMS
The *tun*, the descendant of the drum that the Aztecs called the *teponaztli*, is still heard in the Guatemalan highlands. Its barrel, which varies in size, has two incised tongues of wood.

● FURNITURE AND ACCESSORIES

Yucatecan house ● 126.

Furniture in Indian houses usually consists of a few basic items: one or more beds, depending on the size of the family, consisting of a wooden frame covered with boards or slats – the sleepers lie on a rush mat and wrap themselves in blankets; chests, a few shelves and hanging cords providing storage space; and a ladder, carved out of a tree trunk, giving access to the rafters where tools, baskets and other materials such as ropes and boards, are stored. Tables, chairs, cupboards and even bolsters and mattresses are relatively recent additions. The most frequently used room is still the kitchen, the hub of domestic activity centered around the women and the hearth.

HEARTH
Three hearth stones, placed on the ground or raised, support the various cooking pots: the pot for cooking corn in limewater (the *nixtamal*); the earthenware disk for grilling tortillas (the *comal*); and the earthenware or iron pots for simmering black beans. A mill stone (*metate*), enamel plates and dishes, and earthenware jars are also used.

Gourd spoons ● 85.

DOMESTIC ALTAR

Every house has a corner containing a small domestic altar (below) or *mesa* (table) arranged with religious pictures, candles, incense and tobacco. It is decorated with flowers, fruit and special little loaves for the prayer vigils held on occasions such as All Souls' Day (the Day of the Dead) or to commemorate a death (on the seventh and fortieth days, one year and every seventh year after the death). Every day short prayers are said for the souls of the dead, recently lost loved ones and ancestors.

HAMMOCKS

The hammock, which these days is most probably imported from the Caribbean (the close links between Yucatán and the Caribbean are all too often forgotten), is a basic "bedroom" item in Yucatán and the lowlands. It was traditionally made from loosely woven agave fibers (there was once a thriving hammock industry in Yucatán), but today the use of cotton or nylon thread, bought in the nearest town, is on the increase. The weaver incorporates various motifs (*jaspeado, franjas, perritos*) into the warp.

81

● MARKETS AND SMALL TRADERS

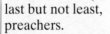

In Yucatán and Chiapas markets are essentially an urban phenomenon with a few cities holding the monopoly on this type of trade. In Guatemala, however, the institution is widespread and has given rise to vast trade networks. Markets are held frequently – one or twice a week at each location – throughout Guatemala and attract wholesalers, professional retailers, occasional traders (who come to sell either a small surplus or traditionally made articles), all kinds of street vendors (hawkers, shoe-shiners, ice cream sellers) and, last but not least, preachers.

ASSOCIATED ACTIVITIES
The most important of these activities is the porterage of merchandise. The market also offers people an opportunity to find employment. Some wholesalers act as moneylenders as well as recruiting and transporting labor on behalf of the *fincas*. Indian borrowers can only repay their debt through a work contract with a plantation of the Pacific coast ▲ 290.

SOUVENIR PHOTOS
Street photographers sometimes provide their customers with an unsophisticated backdrop against which to pose.

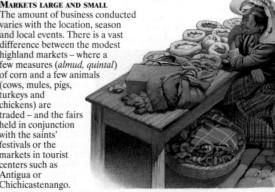

MARKETS LARGE AND SMALL
The amount of business conducted varies with the location, season and local events. There is a vast difference between the modest highland markets – where a few measures (*almud, quintal*) of corn and a few animals (cows, mules, pigs, turkeys and chickens) are traded – and the fairs held in conjunction with the saints' festivals or the markets in tourist centers such as Antigua or Chichicastenango.

"MINIFUNDIO"
Divided into tiny, intensively cultivated plots, land is a precious commodity.

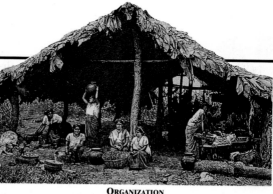

ORGANIZATION
The market is divided into specific sections: bread with lime, salt or sugar (*panela*); flowers, incense and spices, including cinnamon, annatto, and fresh and dried chilies; fruit (anona, melons, marmalade plums, papaws, bananas, mangos, oranges); and vegetables (corn, cabbages, beans, carrots, garlic, onions, tomatoes) ◆ *374.*

In another section displays of home-made breads and confectionery (*dulces*) alternate with displays of tortillas and *atole* (corn pancakes and gruel). Some stalls sell cloth, clothes, traditionally made goods (hats, pottery, furniture, mats, saddlery, wool) and manufactured goods (cigarettes, transistor radios, machetes). The cattle market is set apart.

A VARIETY OF TRADES
Vendors of fruit and vegetables, hats and other goods sell their wares alongside knife grinders and shoe-shiners.

One of the most striking features of Indian markets is their calm atmosphere. Most market business is carried out in a low voice and is devoid of any form of aggression or street-crying (unlike the sales techniques used by the street vendors who abound in other quarters). Most transactions involve quite small sums of money.

The traditional Indian economy is, first and foremost, agricultural. Maya (meaning "man of corn") peasants are linked by a quasi-genetic and sacred bond to the land, which is the object of all their attentions. The *milpa* and garden are used to cultivate food crops (corn, beans, marrows and other vegetables) while different plots produce crops for processing (sugar cane and reeds) and sale (onions, garlic and coffee). These crops suffer greatly from the limitations inherent in the *minifundio* system ● 83 – even if the harvest does not fail, it only produces a small surplus and part-time work on coastal or forest plantations is often necessary. For some households the sale of traditional crafts provides only a small income to cover part of the household needs, in others it represents a significant source of supplementary income.

Terracotta bus, wooden horse and pottery from Rabinal.

POTTERY

Mayan potters produce a wide range of items in varying shapes and sizes, from all kinds of functional crockery – baked naturally in the sun or glazed in a kiln – to tiles, animals, human figures and nativity scenes.

WORKING WITH PALMS

Different types of wild palm are plaited to make matting and hats. Hats are manufactured from handmade strips which are sewn together before being pressed into their final shape.

MASKS

Usually made of wood but sometimes of leather, masks are one of the most important elements in the Mayan dances of the highlands ● 76. Tourism has led to an increase in their production and they are now a common sight on market stalls.

LEATHERWORK

The origins of leatherwork lie with the stock-breeders, and it is a craft which tends to be practiced by the Ladinos rather than the Indians. Bags and saddlebags, belts, machete cases, saddlery and harnesses are sold at village markets or in the retail workshops of large towns and cities.

In the 19th century the cultivation of sisal brought prosperity to Yucatán ▲ 196.

ENGRAVED AND PAINTED GOURDS

Decorated gourds are a specialty of one of the districts of Rabinal ▲ 292. They are cut, scooped out and dried before being engraved or painted. The dye for the yellow background used to be obtained by a complicated process which involved extracting the color from a worm (*nij*), while the red and black pigments used for the animal and

flower motifs came from annatto (*achiote*) and charcoal respectively.

PREPARING TORTILLAS
These corn pancakes
are always served
with Mayan food.

Black chili sauce is a traditional Yucatecan recipe cooked in the open air. The Indians grill the long, red chilies on a *comal* (usually the top of an oil drum). They have to be cooked for quite a long time so that they turn from red to black without burning. If they are overcooked they lose their taste, but if they are undercooked they will be too hot and spicy. Tradition has it that if a woman coughs while they are cooking it is a sure sign that she is jealous.

THE SAUCE
INGREDIENTS: 60 red chilies,
6 tomatoes, 4 onions, a pinch of annatto
(red food coloring),

2 lbs cornflour with added lime,
1 cockerel or turkey (6 lbs), salt and pepper.

1. Cook the chilies on a wire tray in a partly open oven at gas mark 2, 300°F for about 3½ hours (in a well-ventilated room).

2. Crush the blackened chilies, using your hand to obtain a fine powder. Finely chop the tomatoes and onions.

3. Blend the crushed chilies with a paste of cornflour mixed with water until you obtain a *kol* (thick paste).

4. Add the tomatoes, onions, annatto, pepper and salt. The Yucatecans prefer this sauce to be very thin.

86

5. Add water until the sauce is thin and will cover the meat during cooking. It can be bought ready made (in Spanish: *recado de chilmole*).

6. Put a quarter of the sauce aside for the stuffing. Place the cockerel in a cooking pot, cover with sauce and cook for about 3 hours.

THE STUFFING
INGREDIENTS: The whites of 15 hard-boiled eggs, 6 to 8 tomatoes, apazote (*chenopodium ambrosiodes*) leaves or, alternatively, oregano or marjoram, 1 lb ground pork, lard.

7. Make a stuffing with the tomatoes, apazote leaves, egg whites cut into fine strips, and pork mince.

8. Mix the stuffing with the remaining sauce (which may need to be thickened slightly). Fry the mixture gently in a little lard.

9. The Indians usually eat the stuffing separately from the meat and cook it wrapped in a banana leaf. Thicken the stuffing and roll it into a sausage shape. Wrap in foil, making sure it is well sealed, and boil in salted water for about 1 hour.

10. Finally, pour the black chili sauce over the cockerel and serve it either stuffed or with a stuffing sausage.

Young Garinagus.

Ladino child in San Salvador.

Mayan history has been deeply affected on many occasions by the arrival of immigrants who have altered the cultural landscape to a greater or lesser extent. The most significant changes took place with European colonization in the 16th century. Cross-breeding between Spanish settlers and Indians gave rise to the group known as the mestizos, and today they and other groups with some European origins, known collectively as Ladinos, make up the majority of the population. Other non-Indians live alongside the Maya, in particular Garinagus in Belize and Germans in Guatemala.

Deutsche Schule in Quezaltenango

LADINOS
Ladinos are either white or mixed-race (Indian–European, such as the mestizos) people in Central America. Today they form the majority of the population in each country in the region (with the notable exception of Guatemala) and dominate political and social life. They have adopted a westernized lifestyle both in towns and rural areas. Children from the Ladino bourgeoisie of Mérida (center) in the late 19th century.

GERMANS. The Germans settled in Guatemala, and particularly in Verapaz ▲ *294* during the 19th century and became integrated into the population while maintaining their own identity. Other ethnic groups in the region include Mennonites in Belize and Hindus.

GARINAGUS ▲ *343*. These distant descendants of African slaves have been deeply affected by their extended contact with the Arawakan cultures of the island of St Vincent (Antilles). The Garinagus (below right) have developed their own extremely rich and complex culture, which combines African and Caribbean traditions.

Mestizo woman from Yucatán, early 20th century.

Ladino from Chiapas (right).

Mayan Textiles

● TECHNIQUES AND MATERIALS

In the following pages the letters M and G stand for Mexico and Guatemala.

Mayan costume is part of a tradition dating back more than a thousand years and illustrates the fierce attachment of the Maya to their culture. Textiles provide a link between the pre-Colombian past and the present day, acting as a vehicle for history, legend and myth. For two thousand years production methods have hardly changed and the quality of the weaving has depended on the final use of the clothing and the complexity of the techniques used. Techniques introduced by the Spanish in the 16th century, such as knitting, crochet and the use of the vertical treadle-operated loom, became a male preserve, while weaving with the traditional belt loom remained a female activity.

THE "TELAR DE CINTURA"

The *telar de cintura*, or belt loom, consists of seven wooden rods. The vertical threads of the warp are held taut between two end-rods. The top rod, fastened at each end by a cord in the form of an inverted Y, is fastened to a tree. The bottom rod is attached to a belt passed behind the back of the kneeling woman to control the tension. Spacer rods separate the two layers of threads: the heddle, or warp rod, which is for controlling the even- and odd-numbered threads; the saber for compressing the weft; the shuttle for passing the threads between the layers; and the "pin spreader", a slender reed rod, for ensuring that the width of the cloth is consistent.

THE "TELAR DE PIE"

This vertical, treadle-operated loom is used to weave skirts, long lengths of cloth, and woollen and cotton blankets. This type of weaving is done by a predominately male workforce, which is organized in co-operatives in some villages.

WEAVING TECHNIQUES

The most commonly used of the eleven official weaving techniques are plain weave, twill weave, open weave, mottled *ikat* weave and the "additional weft", which creates a single- or double-sided brocade effect (the latter can be used on reversible materials).

LOOMS

Two types of pre-Colombian loom are used: the *telar de cintura* (or *de palitos*) and, less commonly, the *telar de estacas*. Because they are so much a part of her life, a woman's loom and her finest *huipiles* are buried with her.

"IKAT"

This process consists of arranging threads in bundles and knotting them at various points before plunging them into a dye bath so that only the exposed sections are colored. The operation is repeated for each color. The different areas of color are then arranged on the warp to create the design. Preparing *ikat* threads at Sololá, Guatemala (above).

WOOL

Since the introduction of sheep in the 16th century, the inhabitants of the colder regions have used wool to make clothing. The fibers obtained after shearing are washed and dried in the sun before being carded. This is done using two rectangular wooden combs with handles (above) whose inner surface is covered with tiny metal "teeth". The process involves placing the wool in the center of the combs and drawing it from one comb to the other, teasing out the fibers in the same direction. The wool is then spun in the same way as cotton.

SPINNING

The *malacatl* (or *petet* in the Mayan Tzotzil and Tzeltal dialects) is used for spinning cotton and wool. It consists of a slender wooden rod (between 4 and 15 inches long), filed to a point at both ends, with a clay or stone spindle-whorl inserted into the lower end. The process involves holding the cotton fibers in one hand while using the other to turn the spindle whose point is placed into a small gourd to keep it stable. With each phase of twisting, the thread is gradually wound onto the spindle (above).

MODERN DEVELOPMENTS

The traditionally dyed and woven materials produced by complex techniques have become an established part of modern textile design. Since the 19th century, however, they have tended to be replaced by less expensive, man-made fibers. Today there are an increasing number of projects aimed at reviving ancestral skills.

MOMOSTENANGO

> "WHAT WE INDIANS FIND MOST HURTFUL IS THAT, WHILE THEY
> FIND OUR COSTUMES ATTRACTIVE, IT IS AS IF THE PEOPLE WEARING
> THEM DO NOT EXIST."
>
> RIGOBERTA MENCHÚ

THE WHEEL
This more rapid method of spinning involves the use of two wooden wheels, nowadays often replaced by bicycle wheels.

WARPING
This is done prior to weaving. It involves preparing a skein of the same length as the cloth to be woven with the right number of threads for the required width. In order to do this the thread is wound around stakes set in the ground or driven into a plank.

"IXTLE"
Ixtle comes from the agave plant and was utilized to make clothes during the pre-Colombian period. Today it is used for sacking and rope. Preparation and spinning techniques vary according to the region and type of agave (sisal or pita). In Yucatán the leaves are hung over a fire to draw out the sap. When they are soft, they are scraped to remove any excess pulp. The fibers thus obtained are washed, dried and tied in skeins before being spun by the menfolk (tools for spinning *ixtle* are shown above). Near Lake Atitlán, the pulp is crushed with a pestle and the fiber combed, washed and dried in the sun.

COTTON
The more expensive natural white cotton and coffee-colored cotton are used mainly for ceremonial costumes. Once the seeds, leaves and dust have been removed, the cotton is beaten on a leather cushion using two forked sticks to obtain strips for spinning.

93

WOMEN'S COSTUMES

Statuette from the
site of Lagartero
(Chiapas, Mexico)

The most beautiful examples of weaving are found in the highlands of Chiapas (Mexico) and Guatemala. In other regions, such as the Lacandón Forest, Yucatán, Quintana Roo (Mexico), Belize, Honduras and the lowlands of Guatemala, clothes are more simple. For economic, political and social reasons some ethnic groups have abandoned their traditional costume (to which the women have remained more attached) in favor of a western style of dress. Before the Spanish Conquest this costume consisted of a long *huipil* (a sort of over-blouse) and a skirt. The sophistication of the materials and richness of the jewelry were an indication of the wearer's social status. Traditional costume fulfils the same function today. It consists of a *huipil*, a skirt, a belt, a ribbon for tying the hair, a *tzute* and a *rebozo* (shawl).

BELTS
Belts of cotton, wool or, more rarely, silk, are decorated with embroidered or brocaded motifs. The colors and the way in which they are worn vary. They are wound round the waist to hold the skirt in place and the ends are only noticeable if they are decorated. The broad belts of Nahuala, Sacatepéquez, Nebaj, Chajul and San Juan (G) are tied at the front or back. In Chichicastenango the threads of the warp are concealed by floral motifs.

The headdresses of the women of Nebaj are of woven cloth, brocaded with colored threads and with large pompons.

In Santiago Atitlán the women wind long red ribbons, brocaded with geometric motifs, around their head.

Women in Palín use long ribbons to make elaborate headdresses, which are twisted, snake-like, above their foreheads.

94

"TZUTE". The *tzute* consists of one or two rectangular widths of cloth woven on a belt loom then joined together to form a square. Extremely versatile, it can be folded and placed on the head as a protection against the sun, thrown decoratively across the shoulder or opened up and fastened around the neck. It is worn as a cape during festivals.

Belt from Totonicapán (above). Cakchiquel woman (left) from Patzicía (G) wearing a ceremonial *huipil*.

"HUIPIL".
The *huipil* is either square or rectangular in shape. It consists of two or three widths of cloth joined by a seam of vertical stitching which is often embroidered (*randa*), the brocaded section usually forming a cross. The garment is then folded in half and an opening is made in the center for the neck. The stitching at the sides breaks to allow for armholes.

● WOMEN'S COSTUMES

There are two types of *huipil*: those worn every day (*huipiles de cocina*) and ceremonial *huipiles*.

QUICHÉ "HUIPIL" FROM CHICHICASTENANGO (G)
The two-headed eagle, the emblem of Chichicastenango, appears on this *huipil* in stylized, geometric form. When unfolded, the design of the Maya cross is visible.

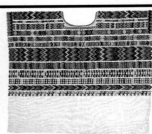

"HUIPIL" FROM RABINAL (G)
The bands of zigzag embroidery on the shoulders represent lightning. Below these are dog's paw (possibly symbolizing the messenger of the Death God), leaf, jar and flag motifs.

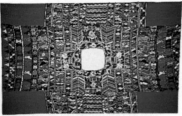

"HUIPIL" FROM SAN JUAN COTZAL (G)
Decorated with alternate bands of animal and plant motifs.

TZOTZIL "HUIPIL" FROM SAN ANDRÉS LARRÁINZAR (M)
Brocaded with lozenge motifs in predominantly red wool on a white cotton background.

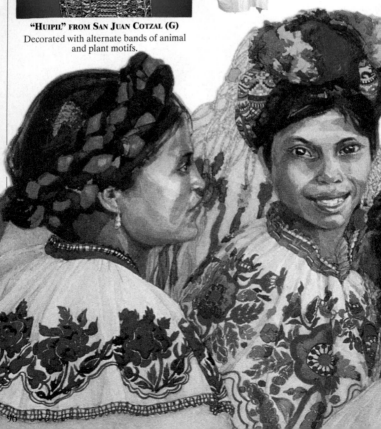

QUICHÉ "HUIPIL" DE NAHUALÁ (G)
Brocaded with predominantly red animal motifs on a white cotton background.

"HUIPIL" FROM SAN MARTIN JILOTEPEQUE
Characterized by its subtle geometric designs, this *huipil* is decorated with velvet inlays around the neck and armholes.

SKIRT OR "CORTE"
The *corte* is made on a vertical loom and is between 3 and 5 yards long. The ends are sewn together to form a tube. It is worn straight (pulled in at the waist by a belt with the excess material pleated at the front or the back) or gathered at the waist. Costume (left) from San Marcos (G) with a silk *ikat* skirt.

"HUIPIL" FROM SAN MATEO IXTATÁN (G)
Embroidered with concentric motifs.

SPANISH COLLARS
In the Totonicapán region (G), Mayan women wear brightly colored embroidered collars, a legacy from the Spanish. Women from San Cristóbal (left).

97

Man from Almolonga (G) wearing traditional costume and holding an *escudo*, the emblem of his brotherhood.

Before the Spanish Conquest basic clothing consisted of a cape (*pati* or *capixay*), a G-string (*maxtatl*) and a long tunic (*xicolli*). On ceremonial occasions the nobility adorned themselves with quetzal-feather headdresses and jewelry. The belt (a remnant of the *maxtatl*) and sandals (*huaraches*) appear on the steles of the Classic period.

The black and white checked woollen aprons (*ponchitos* or *delantales*), the *tzute* ● 99 and the capes worn by the pre-Colombian Maya are still part of the traditional costume.

ALMOLONGA
C.A. PETTERSEN.

The men are gradually abandoning traditional costume, now reserving it for ceremonial occasions. This is due to their greater contact with the outside world, usually for economic reasons (such as seasonal employment – harvesting coffee, picking cotton, cutting sugarcane – or the need to find work, especially in the United States) or for political reasons, for example the persecutions of the 1980's.

ZINACANTÁN (M)
The bachelors of this village in Chiapas wear more brightly colored clothes than the married men, and their characteristic pink over-shirts are decorated with larger pompons.

"TZUTE". The square *tzute* is folded in half diagonally, placed on the head and tied at the nape of the neck. On ceremonial occasions it is draped over the shoulder or worn as a bandeau during certain rituals. *Tzute* (above) from Chichicastenango (G).

TODOS SANTOS (G)
Young Mam men wearing shirts with brocaded collars and handwoven trousers. The black garment worn over the trousers is a remnant of the pre-Hispanic *maxtatl*.

TENEJAPA (CHIAPAS)
A member of the town council in ceremonial dress (below). The straw hat, decorated with multicolored ribbons, is still a common sight in Chiapas (M), especially on ceremonial occasions. Its shape varies, depending on the region.

BELTS
A belt puts the final touch to a costume. Belts are woven on a blue or red ground, sometimes decorated with fine blue stripes. It is brocaded at each end with multicolored motifs and edged with twisted fringes, pompons or macramé work. *Ixil* belt (above) from Chichicastenango.

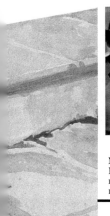

NAHUALÁ (G)
Man wearing a *tzute*, brocaded with multicolored geometric and zoomorphic motifs, over his shoulder.

THE SYMBOLISM OF CLOTHING

Spinning and weaving are closely associated with the symbolism of childbirth and are placed under the patronage of the Moon goddess. As such they are essential to the reproduction of the mythical universe of the Maya. Each weaver acts as a demiurge and each piece of weaving is a microcosm, a projection of the *imago mundi* and, to some extent, a cosmography whose elements are borrowed from mythology and local history. Thus the composition of the designs of a *huipil* can be read like a text which varies in form and content according to ethnic group, community and lineage. The weaver signs her work with her own particular mark.

(1) LOZENGES. The rows of brocaded lozenges, or diamonds, on the central motif evoke the cosmos conceived as a cube with three planes: the sky, the earth and the underworld. In the center of each lozenge is the sun (Our Lord Jesus Christ), embodied by Yaxché, the sacred tree of the Maya.

(2) VULTURE AND BEES. The motif below the rows of diamonds represents the vulture and refers to an episode in local mythology. The next row represents bees, the weaver's family motif. The weaver herself signs her work with star motifs.

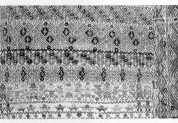

(3) GERMINATION. The design on the sleeves of this *huipil* describes the complete plant germination cycle. It is also decorated with an inscription of the Mayan calendar (18 months of 20 days, plus 5 unlucky days). Taken as a whole it can be interpreted as a prayer by the weaver to invoke the benevolence of the gods.

ANTHROPOMORPHIC AND ANIMAL SYMBOLS

Just as weaving techniques involve counting the number of threads in the warp and the number of rods, so brocaded designs relate to the measurement of the world. The arrangement of motifs and colors is governed by precise rules. The anthropomorphic and zoomorphic figures symbolize the forces of nature according to local mythology.

Wild animals belong to the dark domain of the natural world as opposed to the bright, civilized world of Man. The central motif of this *huipil* from San Juan Cotzal (above) consists of bands of geometric motifs and birds.
Flower and deer motifs (left) embroidered on the collar of a Mam *huipil* from San Marcos (G).

"Huipil" of the Virgin from Magdalenas (M). This shows a detailed chart of the Maya cosmogony (**1**, **2** and **3**, left). Many of the pre-Hispanic motifs and symbols which appear on steles, statuettes, codices, frescos and ceramics are reproduced on modern textiles.

Lintel 24 from Yaxchilán (M), dating from AD 719, depicts Queen Xoc wearing a *huipil* decorated with the same diamond motifs that appear on the modern *huipiles* of Magdalenas (M).

TWO-HEADED ANIMALS. These animals represent the dualistic vision of the world shared by all Mesoamerican cultures. The symbol of the two-headed eagle of Quiché Maya mythology is widely used today on the ceremonial *huipiles* and *tzutes* of Chichicastenango (G).

"HUIPILES" AND "TZUTES" FROM PALÍN (G)
These *huipiles* and *tzutes* are decorated with two-headed eagles surrounded by zigzag, fly and diamond motifs. The Spanish identified the eagle with the Habsburg eagle but, according to the *Popol Vuh* manuscript, the bird is an ancestor of the Quichés.

"HUIPIL" FROM CHAJUL (G). This *Ixil huipil* is often decorated with a front view of two-headed animals, their heads in profile. These motifs were widely used in pre-Hispanic Mayan iconography. Bird motif (above).

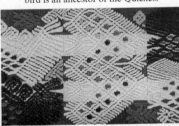

REPTILES. Reptiles wind their way through the designs like a serpent between the earth and sky. The finest examples are found on the *huipiles* of San Juan Sacatepéquez (above), where zoomorphic motifs alternate with a band representing the Feathered Serpent.

PLANTS AND BIRDS. The *huipiles* of Cobán (G) and Venustiano Carranza (M) are characterized by plant and bird motifs. On this *huipil* from Tactic (G) a hummingbird is perched on a clump of tobacco.

TURKEYS. The birds and animals most widely represented are the turkey (above, on a *huipil* from San Pedro Sacatepéquez), peacock, cockerel, deer, squirrel, jaguar, opossum and hummingbird.

FERTILITY
The scorpion, usually associated with flower motifs, is believed to bring rain by causing lightning. These motifs, like the cactus motif (left), decorate the embroidered skirts of the Tzotzils of Venustiano Carranza (M).

BATS
The bat, a common motif on the jackets of Sololá (G), is the symbol of the royal house of Xahilá, whose prince led the Cakchiquels on their legendary journey in search of a permanent home (right).

ZIGZAGS. Zigzags are the symbol of the Lightning god, the dispenser of rain, and are a popular motif on the textiles of many villages. The women of Pantelhó (M) decorate the sleeves of their garments (above) with zigzags and motifs of toads (harbingers of rain).

MONKEYS. Monkeys are associated with disaster and evoke a previous creation. On the *huipiles* of Chenalhó (M) the body of the monkey, represented by three vertical lines, is surrounded by curves representing the arms and legs (above). The motif reminds the Maya of their obligation to worship the gods.

"HUIPIL" FROM SAN JUAN COTZAL. The neck of this *huilpil* (below) is decorated with leaf motifs. The woman who wears it is placed symbolically at the center of the universe, surrounded by four leaves which represent the four points of the compass and correspond to the solstices and equinoxes.

THE COSMIC TREE

The cosmic tree ● 64 also known as *Yaxché* or the Tree of Life, is central to the cosmology of the Maya, who believed that their ancestors came from its roots. It occupies pride of place on the ceremonial *huipiles* of San Pedro Sacatepéquez (left), San Pedro Ayampuc and Chuarrancho (G).

CIRCLES

The tooth-shaped material inlays around the neck of the *huipiles* from Chichicastenango, and the four small circles decorating the front, back and shoulders, are associated with solar worship. Other concentric motifs are embroidered on the "fins" of the trousers of brotherhood members (below).

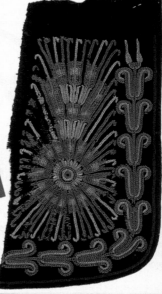

● ACCESSORIES

Pre-Hispanic and contemporary sandals.

Pre-Hispanic iconography attests to a profusion of quetzal-feather headdresses, intricately carved jade jewelry and other finery worn by Mayan dignitaries. Modern accessories have lost this former magnificence and have become much more simple. The women enjoy wearing jewelry, however, and take pride in complementing their clothes with necklaces, rings and earrings. The men make do with sandals and straw hats.

NECKLACE OR "CHACHAL"
The necklace is an important accessory for Mayan women and fine coral necklaces, decorated with silver coins from the colonial period, are a common sight in many villages. Often the women also wear several rows of large glass beads (gold, red or blue, depending on the area) and chains decorated with a heavy cross or, for marriage ceremonies, a huge silver coin.

HEADBAND OR "MECAPAL"
The *mecapal* is indispensable for carrying heavy loads in areas where there are no pack animals. It consists of a flat, leather strip whose ends are joined by a cord. The leather strip is placed on the forehead and the cord used to secure the load.

SANDALS OR "HUARACHES"
In both Mexico and Guatemala *huaraches* are an exclusively male accessory. They have either a leather sole or a rubber one, cut from an old tire, with a single thong which passes between the toes and fastens around the ankle. Some sandals have a heel piece.

BLANKETS
Blankets are an extremely important accessory. As well as providing protection against the cold, they can also be spread on the ground to display produce at market. The smaller, black and white checked *ponchitos* are worn around the waist by the men.

RINGS AND EARRINGS
Mayan women are very fond of rings and earrings. Rings are made of silver or nickel and decorated with a heart, an animal or glass beads. There are long, lightweight, filigree earrings or a heavier variety, made from small coins set off by a stone.

BAG OR "MORRAL"
Although the men do not wear jewelry, they never go anywhere without their *morral* containing seeds, fruit or other items.

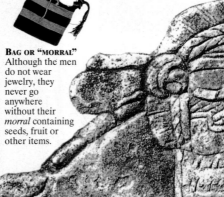

ARCHITECTURE

In spite of very serious practical constraints, such as the absence of metals, pack animals and the wheel, the Maya were the first builders in Mesoamerica. From the outset their architecture aimed to impress by its vast size. The effort initially reserved for pyramidal bases, was soon applied to the actual buildings, particularly with the introduction of the arch, which opened the way for the upward development of architecture, a symbol of prestige.

WALL BONDING
Originally walls were made of rough-hewn blocks of stone, held together by mortar. However, a new concrete casing technique replaced this type of large-stone construction to some extent. The inner surface of the carefully squared stones, often sculpted on the outside, was left irregular so that it would bond with the concrete.

SCULPTED DECORATION
The solidly cemented stones were often decorated with one or several repeating motifs.

DEVELOPMENT OF THE ARCH
1. Archaic (3rd–8th century), rough-hewn bonding. **2.** Classic (9th–16th century), decorative casing.

DIFFERENT TYPES OF CLASSIC ARCH
1. Concave arch.
2. Convex arch.
3. Step arch.
4. Trefoil arch.

BASES
The bases consisted of one or several rock-hewn platforms, decreasing in size as they progressed vertically, forming the trunk of a step pyramid. Each step consisted of a rubble and earth bank, retained by a stone wall.

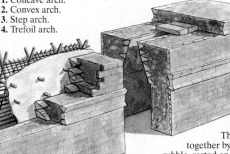

ARCHES
The arch, held together by mortar and rubble, rested on two walls of gradually increasing thickness. The gap was closed by a stone slab. To complete the arch, a wooden framework held each course of stone blocks in place while the concrete was poured on. Apart from its esthetic value, the concrete "veneer" also acted as a casing.

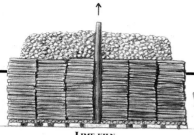

LIME KILN
Crushed carbonate (limestone) was tipped onto a large pile of logs which served as fuel. A vertical piece of wood was placed in the center during construction. When removed, the chimney thus created was filled with hot coals to set fire to the logs.

CARVED RELIEFS
Each element of a figure in relief was individually carved and painted before being put into place. Gradually building up a relief in this way gave a more natural appearance. Relief (right) on Pillar E of House C at Palenque ▲ 243.

PREPARING A STUCCOED WALL
When a wall had to support a relatively heavy stuccoed relief, a preparation made of small stones and mortar was applied. This acted as a reinforcement or tenon for the relief. Stuccoed mask (left) at the Temple of Kohunlich ▲ 189.

POLYCHROME
The Maya used a fairly wide range of colors to paint walls, pillars and stuccoed reliefs. They were probably obtained locally and included blue, vermilion, yellow and white.

FRESCOS
The walls and arches of many buildings (such as Bonampak ▲ 249) were decorated with frescos, often of complex composition. Most surviving frescos are found on internal structures, where they have been protected from the effects of the sun and bad weather.

● TEMPLES AND PALACES

Mayan architecture of all types was traditionally set on stone bases. Prestigious architecture picks up and accentuates this characteristic feature borrowed from archaic dwellings. The various types of imposing structures (the functions of which are often difficult to determine) all attest to a desire for height: from the temple-pyramids, which symbolize the link between heaven and earth, to the structures defined as "palaces" by the early Spanish conquerors, as well as other buildings of intermediate stature.

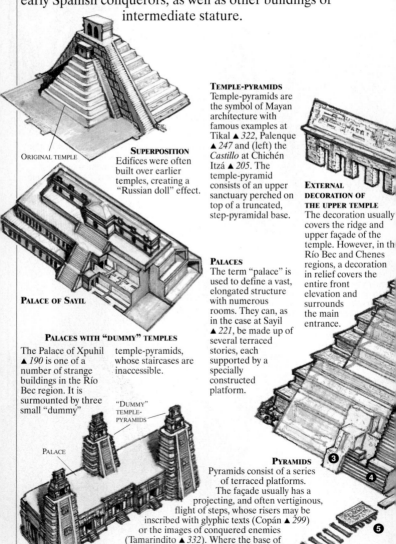

ORIGINAL TEMPLE

SUPERPOSITION
Edifices were often built over earlier temples, creating a "Russian doll" effect.

PALACE OF SAYIL

PALACES WITH "DUMMY" TEMPLES
The Palace of Xpuhil ▲ 190 is one of a number of strange buildings in the Río Bec region. It is surmounted by three small "dummy"

temple-pyramids, whose staircases are inaccessible.

"DUMMY" TEMPLE-PYRAMIDS

PALACE

TEMPLE-PYRAMIDS
Temple-pyramids are the symbol of Mayan architecture with famous examples at Tikal ▲ 322, Palenque ▲ 247 and (left) the *Castillo* at Chichén Itzá ▲ 205. The temple-pyramid consists of an upper sanctuary perched on top of a truncated, step-pyramidal base.

PALACES
The term "palace" is used to define a vast, elongated structure with numerous rooms. They can, as in the case at Sayil ▲ 221, be made up of several terraced stories, each supported by a specially constructed platform.

EXTERNAL DECORATION OF THE UPPER TEMPLE
The decoration usually covers the ridge and upper façade of the temple. However, in th Río Bec and Chenes regions, a decoration in relief covers the entire front elevation and surrounds the main entrance.

PYRAMIDS
Pyramids consist of a series of terraced platforms. The façade usually has a projecting, and often vertiginous, flight of steps, whose risers may be inscribed with glyphic texts (Copán ▲ 299) or the images of conquered enemies (Tamarindito ▲ 332). Where the base of the pyramid is a monumental plinth, it has often been used as a tomb.

3
4
5

PYRAMID INSCRIPT

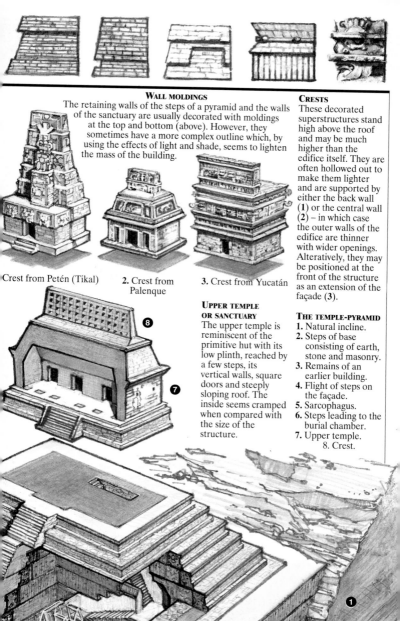

WALL MOLDINGS

The retaining walls of the steps of a pyramid and the walls of the sanctuary are usually decorated with moldings at the top and bottom (above). However, they sometimes have a more complex outline which, by using the effects of light and shade, seems to lighten the mass of the building.

1. Crest from Petén (Tikal)

2. Crest from Palenque

3. Crest from Yucatán

CRESTS

These decorated superstructures stand high above the roof and may be much higher than the edifice itself. They are often hollowed out to make them lighter and are supported by either the back wall (**1**) or the central wall (**2**) – in which case the outer walls of the edifice are thinner with wider openings. Alteratively, they may be positioned at the front of the structure as an extension of the façade (**3**).

UPPER TEMPLE OR SANCTUARY

The upper temple is reminiscent of the primitive hut with its low plinth, reached by a few steps, its vertical walls, square doors and steeply sloping roof. The inside seems cramped when compared with the size of the structure.

THE TEMPLE-PYRAMID

1. Natural incline.
2. Steps of base consisting of earth, stone and masonry.
3. Remains of an earlier building.
4. Flight of steps on the façade.
5. Sarcophagus.
6. Steps leading to the burial chamber.
7. Upper temple.
8. Crest.

CHOOSING A SITE

The best site was a natural incline because it enabled the pyramidal base to be built against the slope. This natural foundation limited the size of the structure to be built.

LENQUE

STELES AND ALTARS

Part of the altar associated
with Stele 22 at Tikal.

In Mayan culture steles fulfilled a political and sacred role
rather than a funerary one. Their dated texts and decorations
commemorated historic events relating to a particular
sovereign, as well as episodes from mythology. They were
usually accompanied by a huge, geometrically carved stone used
as an altar for the sacrifices and offerings associated with
dynastic rituals. The stele-altar combination is found at the foot
of pyramids and in certain holy places.

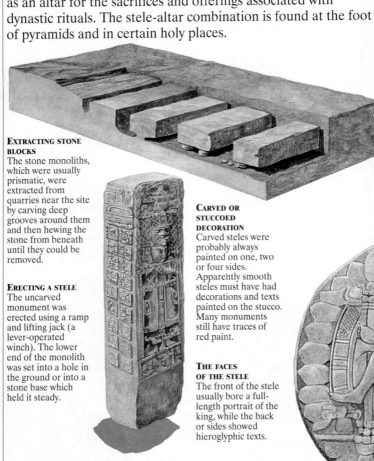

EXTRACTING STONE BLOCKS
The stone monoliths, which were usually prismatic, were extracted from quarries near the site by carving deep grooves around them and then hewing the stone from beneath until they could be removed.

ERECTING A STELE
The uncarved monument was erected using a ramp and lifting jack (a lever-operated winch). The lower end of the monolith was set into a hole in the ground or into a stone base which held it steady.

CARVED OR STUCCOED DECORATION
Carved steles were probably always painted on one, two or four sides. Apparently smooth steles must have had decorations and texts painted on the stucco. Many monuments still have traces of red paint.

THE FACES OF THE STELE
The front of the stele usually bore a full-length portrait of the king, while the back or sides showed hieroglyphic texts.

RAMP Earth ramps, built in stages, were also used to erect steles.

TRANSPORTING STONE BLOCKS
The monoliths were pulled to their future site by dozens of men using ropes and wooden rollers.

"ZOOMORPHIC" ROCK

A variation to the usual stele-altar combination can be found at Quirigua ▲ 306, where a "zoomorphic" rock is paired with a flat, irregularly shaped stone, used as an altar.

ICONOGRAPHY OF A STELE

Stele 22 at Tikal ▲ 324 is a fine example of the political and religious symbolism of this type of monument. It commemorates the performance by King C of one of the rites celebrating the end of the *katun* ● 44. The date is scrupulously recorded and corresponds to AD 771.

SCALE

A stele usually stands between 6½ and 13 feet high, but much larger examples have been found. Stele E at Quirigua is over 38 feet high.

FORM AND ICONOGRAPHY OF AN ALTAR

This altar, associated with Stele 22 at Tikal, is in the fairly common form of a low cylinder. The carved surface (above) shows a captive about to be sacrificed. Around the edge a plaited motif (a royal attribute) is repeated at intervals and there is another image of a bound prisoner.

The ball game was particularly popular among the Maya who built an impressive number of ball courts. Most sites had at least one and the larger cities had several.

The game was not so much a sport or spectacle as a ritual, symbolizing the struggle between the forces of life and death. It was sometimes associated with a divine judgement and may have been used to settle a conflict. After the game, victims (most probably the losers or their representatives) were decapitated.

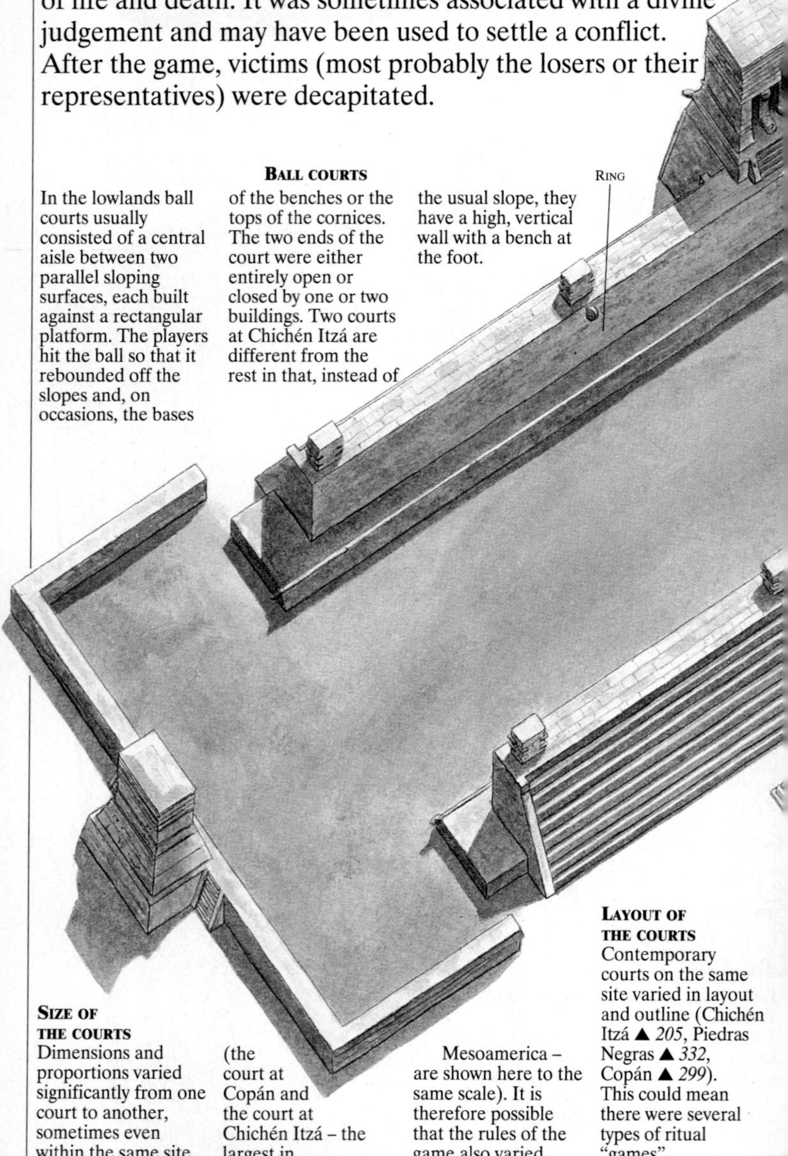

BALL COURTS

In the lowlands ball courts usually consisted of a central aisle between two parallel sloping surfaces, each built against a rectangular platform. The players hit the ball so that it rebounded off the slopes and, on occasions, the bases

of the benches or the tops of the cornices. The two ends of the court were either entirely open or closed by one or two buildings. Two courts at Chichén Itzá are different from the rest in that, instead of

the usual slope, they have a high, vertical wall with a bench at the foot.

RING

SIZE OF THE COURTS

Dimensions and proportions varied significantly from one court to another, sometimes even within the same site

(the court at Copán and the court at Chichén Itzá – the largest in

Mesoamerica – are shown here to the same scale). It is therefore possible that the rules of the game also varied.

LAYOUT OF THE COURTS

Contemporary courts on the same site varied in layout and outline (Chichén Itzá ▲ 205, Piedras Negras ▲ 332, Copán ▲ 299). This could mean there were several types of ritual "games".

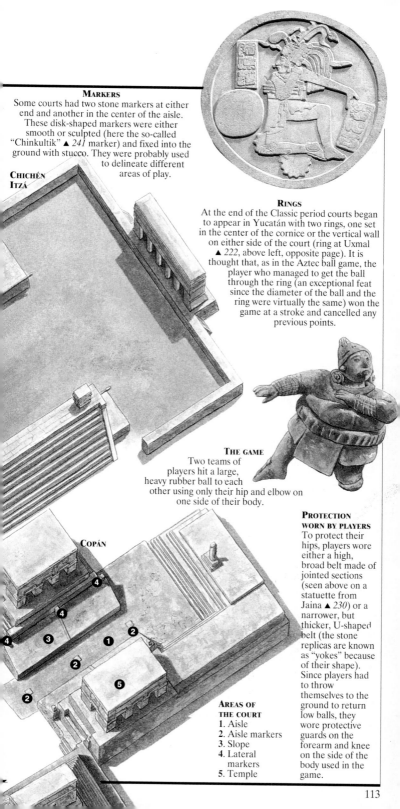

MARKERS

Some courts had two stone markers at either end and another in the center of the aisle. These disk-shaped markers were either smooth or sculpted (here the so-called "Chinkultik" ▲ *241* marker) and fixed into the ground with stucco. They were probably used to delineate different areas of play.

CHICHÉN ITZÁ

RINGS

At the end of the Classic period courts began to appear in Yucatán with two rings, one set in the center of the cornice or the vertical wall on either side of the court (ring at Uxmal ▲ *222*, above left, opposite page). It is thought that, as in the Aztec ball game, the player who managed to get the ball through the ring (an exceptional feat since the diameter of the ball and the ring were virtually the same) won the game at a stroke and cancelled any previous points.

THE GAME

Two teams of players hit a large, heavy rubber ball to each other using only their hip and elbow on one side of their body.

COPÁN

PROTECTION
WORN BY PLAYERS

To protect their hips, players wore either a high, broad belt made of jointed sections (seen above on a statuette from Jaina ▲ *230*) or a narrower, but thicker, U-shaped belt (the stone replicas are known as "yokes" because of their shape). Since players had to throw themselves to the ground to return low balls, they wore protective guards on the forearm and knee on the side of the body used in the game.

AREAS OF THE COURT

1. Aisle
2. Aisle markers
3. Slope
4. Lateral markers
5. Temple

The major Mayan sites were true cities and not just temporarily inhabited ceremonial centers. In spite of their fairly loose-knit network of dwellings, apparently scattered groups of structures and an urban environment consisting of a series of superpositions, the cities in fact fulfilled definite economic, political, administrative and religious functions. Edifices and architectural complexes often represented microcosms and served as a setting for rituals that may have involved movement from one area to another. These various areas had to observe relations of proximity or distance which gave the city its characteristic, open appearance.

BALL COURT

SITE OF BECÁN

PALACE

THE ROUTE OF THE MAYAS
AS SEEN BY ARTISTS

The spectacular development of Mayan pictorial art during the Late Classic period (AD 600–800) both illustrated and accompanied a religious and esthetic ideology which liberated the various forms of Mayan representations from the power of authority and death. The mediums used were various: codices (manuscripts written in hieroglyphics and illustrated with drawings), wall paintings and polychrome vases. The codex was a manuscript co..sisting of a strip of bast paper several yards long, covered with a fine layer of lime and folded in a "concertina". On this page of the Madrid Codex (1) ● 42 the Death God strikes the celestial serpent with his axe to make rain fall. Glyphs representing days on the divinatory calendar are arranged in four rows across the center of the image. Reproductions, made in 1947 by the artist Antonio Tejeda Fonseca, of the frescos of Bonampak ▲ 249 are on display at the Mexican National Museum of Anthropology. In this scene (2) showing Chan Muan surrounded by his generals, the captive at the king's feet symbolizes Death and thus confirms the ruler's omnipotence. The drama of the scene is heightened by the brilliantly colored figures. The subject of this polychrome vase (3) reiterates the theme of human sacrifice ● 46 with its depiction of a captive being led away. It is one of several Late Classic vases, discovered at Altamira, in the State of Campeche (Mexico). One of the vases found at Altar de los Sacrificios ▲ 333 dates from AD 754 and shows a dancer representing the Bird Jaguar (previous page).

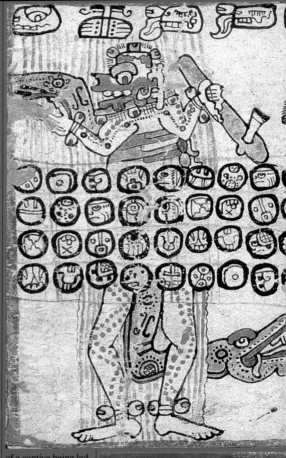

1	2
	3

Even before Independence Guatemala had already produced some extremely talented artists One notable example was José Casildo España, who depicted the descendants of the Maya in a pure neoclassical style. His *Guatemala-Kiché* (1818, below) represents, for the first time in the colonial history of Guatemala, the very real presence of the Maya population. In 1832 the artist and adventurer, Jean-Frédéric Waldeck (1766–1857) ● 56, discovered the world of the Maya and embarked upon an exploration of the temple of Palenque in Chiapas ▲ 244. He produced over one hundred drawings and watercolors of a clearly academic nature. In *Façade orientale du palais de Palenque* (**1**) he drew on the Western Classical repertoire (the nude in the foreground and the posing figures) to present Europe with an idealized perception of the world of the Maya. *Incidents of Travel in Central America, Chiapas and Yucatán* (1841), a work by two cultured and resolutely "modern" travelers, combined the talented writings of John Stephens (1805–52) ● 56, 153, with the remarkable engravings of Frederick Catherwood ● 58. It was an immediate bestseller and exercised a decisive influence over generations of Mayanist scholars. Catherwood's quasi-photographic reproductions give a much more realistic impression of Mayan architecture as, for example, in his *View of a temple to the south of the Castillo of Tulum* ▲ 177 which shows *macheteros* clearing land for cultivation (**2**).

1

2

> "THE BEAUTY OF THE SCULPTURE . . . , THE DESOLATION OF THE CITY AND THE AIR OF MYSTERY THAT ENVELOPED IT INSPIRED IN ME A STATE OF EXCITEMENT MORE ACUTE THAN ANY I HAD EXPERIENCED AMONG THE RUINS OF THE OLD WORLD." JOHN LLOYD STEPHENS

Roban a una muchacha.
Comalapa.
Filiberto Chali.

Andrés Curruchich (1891–1969), a member of the Cakchiquel community in Comalapa ▲ 276, was one of the founders of 20th-century Guatemalan Indian painting. This self-taught artist drew his inspiration from everyday life and traditions. With paintings like *Transfer of the Saint by the Brotherhood* (2) he produced a visual record of the work and daily life of a peasant community where the spiritual and supernatural were all-important. These themes were reiterated and developed by his descendants and by the many popular artists, from Comalapa to Santiago Atitlán ▲ 281, who celebrated the peaceful world to which they aspired. None of these more recent works, although painted at a time of extreme violence, depicts the contemporary massacres or the burning of houses and cornfields. Rather they focus on everyday life (cooking and harvest), festivals (processions, libations and dances) and rituals (healing, marriage and funeral services) revealing an overwhelming interest in the cycle of life and its continuity. José Eladio Mux Curruchich (1955–91) established himself as the champion of this domain, so vital for the development of community values. *Panorama of my Village* (3) consists of a series of

"snapshots" (detail below) of an active society where everyone has their place and function, but not always enough money for a proper marriage ceremony, with the result that young men are sometimes forced into *Kidnapping a Fiancée* (1), under the conspiratorial eye of the young artist Filiberto Chali (b. 1967). Whether in the dark of night or the light of day, the main theme is to survive and celebrate every aspect of life, from the mundane to the supernatural; to reinvest the most basic gestures with their original meaning and provide a reminder of the collective responsibility to re-assert and perpetuate myths and traditions.

1

2	3

Rodolfo Galeotti Torres (1912–88), a mestizo of Italian origin, drew his inspiration from the oral traditions and history of the still unfamiliar world of the Maya, enobling these elements in his sculptures and paintings. His series of portraits of the *Mayan Priest* (**4**) combines artistic quality with ethnographic detail. At the same time, a certain paternalism makes the Indian simply a visual object as in *The Wedding* (**3**) by Alfredo Gálvez Suárez (1946–88), the most outstanding member of the neo-Impressionist school. Some contemporary Guatemalan artists have opened up rich new horizons where ancient symbols are invested with new meaning. The *Gucumatz* (**1**) – the chimeric part-serpent part-quetzal, represented as a transpierced victim – resists aggression with an unbelievable strength forged by centuries of passion and courage. It appears in the work of Rolando Aguilar (b. 1957), an active member of the Indian community, as the root and ideological foundation of the Maya. In the work of Zipacná de León (b. 1948), the *Tree of Ixquic* (**2**), mother of the divine twins

Hunahpu and Xbalanque (mythical figures from the *Popol Vuh* manuscript), conveys a new message – that of a generation of highly creative artists fiercely proud of their cultural heritage.

1	
2	4
3	

"TO CAPTURE A MEMORY AT THE
HEIGHT OF ITS INTENSITY."

WALTER BENJAMIN

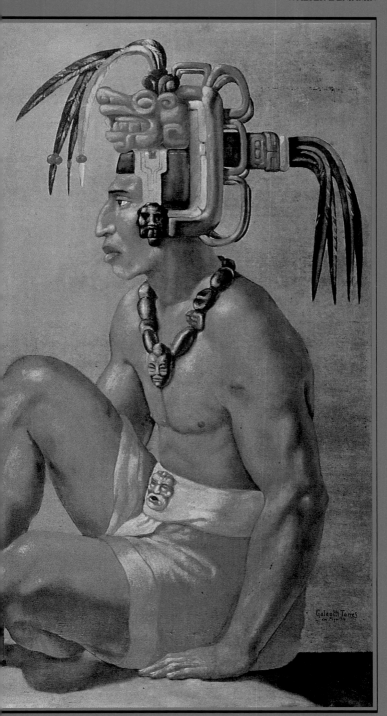

The work of Carlos Mérida (1891–1984) celebrates traditional craft techniques. *The Mestizo Race*, a mosaic installed in the town hall of Guatemala City in 1957, shows the dual influences of Cubism and traditional weaving.

THE ROUTE OF THE MAYAS
AS SEEN BY WRITERS

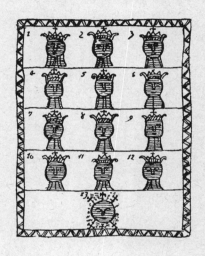

ANCIENT WISDOM

CURATIVES

Francisco Cervantes de Salazar (c. 1500–75) prepared a book of dialogues about life in ancient Mexico which he used in his teaching of Latin.

AL. Those Indian men and women sitting there – what wares are they selling? Most of them seem cheap and of very little worth.

ZUAZO. What the earth brings forth: ají [chili], beans, Persian pears, guavas, mameyes, zapotes, camotes, gícamas, cacomites, mesquites, tunas, gilotes, xocotes, and other fruits of this nature.

AL. I have never heard of such names or seen such fruits! What drinks are those in the large earthenware jars?

ZUAZO. Atole, chía, zotol, made of certain ground seeds.

AL. Outlandish names!

ZA. As ours to them.

AL. What is that dark liquid with which their limbs are smeared, as with pitch, so that they are made blacker than the Ethiopians? And also that filthy, clay-like stuff with which their heads are daubed and incrusted? Explain why they do this.

ZUAZO. The Indians call the liquid *ogitl*, and they use it as a protection against cold and the itch. In their tongue, the clay is called either *zoquitl* or *quahtepuztli*. It is useful for dyeing hair very black, as well as for killing lice.

AL. Medicaments indeed unknown to Hippocrates, Avicena, Dioscorides, and Galen. I notice, too, quite a large supply of worms for sale. For what purpose? I am moved to laughter.

ZA. They are aquatic and are brought from the marsh. The Indians call them *oquilín*, and they themselves eat them and feed them to their little sparrows.

AL. Strange things you tell. Who would ever believe that worms are food for men, since men, when dead, are food for worms?**

FRANCISCO CERVANTES DE SALAZAR,
LIFE IN THE IMPERIAL AND LOYAL CITY OF MEXICO IN NEW SPAIN,
TRANS. MINNIE LEE BARRETT SHEPARD,
PUB. UNIV. OF TEXAS PRESS,
AUSTIN, 1953

TARAHUMARA HERBS

Mexican poet Alfonso Reyes (1889–1959) wrote of the Indians who live in the Chihuahua region and adjacent parts of northern Mexico.

"The Tarahumara Indians have come down,
sign of a bad year
and a poor harvest in the mountains.

Naked and tanned,
hard in their daubed lustrous skins,
blackened with wind and sun, they enliven
the streets of Chihuahua,
slow and suspicious,
all the springs of fear coiled,
like meek panthers.

Naked and tanned,
wild denizens of the snow,
they – for they thee and thou –
always answer thus the inevitable question:
"And is thy face not cold?"

A bad year in the mountains
when the heavy thaw of the peaks
drains down to the villages the drove
of human beasts, their bundles on their backs.

The people, seeing them, experience
that so magnanimous antipathy
for beauty unlike that to which they are used.

Into Catholics
by the New Spain missionaries they were turned
– these lion-hearted lambs.
And, without bread or wine,
they celebrate the Christian ceremony
with their chicha beer and their pinole
which is a powder of universal flavour.

They drink spirits of maize and peyotl,
herb of portents,
symphony of positive esthetics
whereby into colours forms are changed;
and ample metaphysical ebriety
consoles them for their having to tread the earth,
which is, all said and done,
the common affliction of all humankind.
The finest Marathon runners in the world,
nourished on the bitter flesh of deer,
they will be first with the triumphant news
the day we leap the wall
of the five senses."

ALFONSO REYES,
ANTHOLOGY OF MEXICAN POETRY,
SELECTED BY OCTAVIO PAZ,
TRANS. SAMUEL BECKETT
PUB. CALDER & BOYARS,
LONDON 1970

SPIDER SPELLS

Is there a logical explanation for the effects of spider spells? Miguel Angel Asturias (1899–1974) ponders the question.

❝He stopped in front of a desk once varnished black, now ashen like his hair, to take out from a locked drawer his nursery of notes, as he called a diary he kept in folio form...

Earlier he had written, and now reread, 'Little is known of "spider-spell" bites – bites being the popular term – but they cause great suffering in my parish, such is the way of things here, and the same may be said with respect to fabrications about "naguals", or animal protectors, who, through the lies and fictions of the devil, these ignorant people believe to be not only their protectors but their other selves, so much so that it is thought they can change their human form for that of the animal which is their 'nagual', a tale as old as it is foolish. Little is known about, but much suffering is caused by, the stings of these "spider-spells", as was noted above, for there are frequent cases of women who are taken with ambulatory madness and escape from their houses, never to be heard of again, thereby swelling the number of "tecunas", as they are called, a name which derives from the legend of an unfortunate woman named María Tecún who, it is said, took a pinole powder which had been crawled through by spiders as a result of some mischief done to her, some evil of witchcraft, and set out to wander the roads like a madwoman, followed by her husband, who is depicted as being blind like Cupid. He follows her everywhere and finds her nowhere. Finally, after searching heaven and earth, after a thousand trials, he hears her speak in the most inhospitable place in all Creation. And such is the commotion undergone by his mental faculties that he regains his vision, only to see – unhappy creature – the object of his wanderings turn to stone in the place that henceforth is known as María Tecún Ridge.'

'Personally,' Father Valentín read swiftly over his burgeoning crop of notes with two small buzzard's eyes, common to all the Urdáñez family, 'personally, on first

Es ten yan in vol yn vilae, velijun
Dab teeh. lic vaya bal tin tane, lic va

taking charge of the parish of San Miguel Acatán, I visited María Tecún Ridge, and I can testify to what is suffered for various reasons by those who venture there. The altitude fatigues the heart and the eternal cold which reigns at midday and at all hours makes one's flesh and bones ache. Morally, the spirit of the most valiant wilts in the silence, two syllables of a word which here, as at the Pole, takes on all its grandeur: silence due to the altitude, "far from the madding crowd", and above all to the fact that in the constant, swirling mist, no bird ventures, and so saturated is the vegetation that it seems mute, ghostly, swathed always in a cloak of frost or migrating rains. Yet this impression of a dead world due to the silence is accompanied by another no less dismaying. The low clouds and thick mist blot out the surrounding landscape and then it is that a man feels he is going blind himself, so much so that when he moves his arms he can scarcely see his hands, and there are moments when, looking for his feet, he cannot see them, as though he were already in a cloud, changed to a winged being. The close proximity of the abyss completes the picture. If, elsewhere, a man who penetrates deep into the forest goes in fear of wild beasts and senses their presence even before they become flesh before his terrified gaze, here it is the fangs of the earth which assail him, the earth transformed into a wild beast, like a female jaguar whose cubs have been taken from her. The precipices cannot be seen, for they are covered over with fluffy quilts of white cloud, but so evident is their threat that the hours seem like years on a visit to the famous María Tecún Ridge. Inspired by the Holy Virgin, Our Lady, though without formal authorization from my hierarchical superiors, I carried there with me what was necessary to bless the rock, and I must here record under oath that as I completed the blessing, and for no apparent reason, our horses kicked out at one another and whinnied, with their eyes staring from their sockets, as though they had seen the devil himself. **99**

MIGUEL ANGEL ASTURIAS,
MEN OF MAIZE,
TRANS. GERALD MARTIN,
PUB. VERSO, LONDON, 1988

HUNTING MONKEYS

Alexander O. Exquemelin (c. 1645–1705) describes the sights he encountered while sailing along the coast of Costa Rica.

❝We came to a large bay known as Bleeckveldt Bay, after a buccaneer who used to put in there very often, to repair his ship. This was an excellent place for careening, and we set to work as quickly as possible. While some of our men were busy on the ship, the others went hunting in the forest. In these woods are wild pigs which have their navels on their backs, and are called navel pigs on this account; there are also badgers, but not many. We met with few wild boar or badgers, so most of our hunting consisted of shooting monkeys and pheasants for our daily food – mostly monkeys, which are found in great numbers.

Although we were in a wretched state for want of fresh food, we did not take much pleasure in shooting the monkeys, for out of every fifteen or sixteen that we hit, we scarcely got three or four. Unless they were shot stone dead it was impossible to get hold of them, for they would cling by the tail to the tips of thin branches until they died, and even then, hang there until they rotted. The females carry their young on their back like the Negro women carry their babies. If the mother was shot dead and the young monkey remained alive, it would not leave its mother, whether she fell or not, but stay clinging tight to her back.

When anyone passes under a tree full of monkeys, they will spatter him with excrement and break off branches and throw them at his head. When a troop of monkeys has been fired on and one of them is hit, the others immediately gather round and sniff the wound. If there is much blood spurting out, some of them squeeze the wound to check the blood, others get moss from the trees and stick it in the place, while still others fetch certain herbs, which they chew and then press in the wound. I have often observed with great wonder the way these animals stand by each other in time of need and endeavour to help their fellows, though in peril of their lives.

These monkeys are tasty and very nourishing; every day we boiled and roasted so much monkey-flesh we became used to it, and to us it tasted better than pheasant.❞

ALEXANDER O. EXQUEMELIN, *THE BUCCANEERS OF AMERICA*, TRANS. ALEXIS BROWN, PUB. PENGUIN BOOKS, 1969

BEING A HUNTER

In "Journey to Ixtlan", Carlos Castaneda (b. 1931) explains the teachings of don Juan Matus, a Yaqui Indian sorcerer to whom he was apprenticed.

❝'Your hunter's spirit has returned to you,' don Juan said suddenly and with a serious face. 'Now you're hooked.'
'I beg your pardon?'
I wanted him to elaborate on his statement that I was hooked, but he only laughed and repeated it.
'How am I hooked?' I insisted.
'Hunters will always hunt,' he said.
'I am a hunter myself.'
'Do you mean you hunt for a living?'
'I hunt in order to live. I can live off the land, anywhere.'
He indicated the total surroundings with his hand.
'To be a hunter means that one knows a great deal,' he

went on. 'It means that one can see the world in different ways. In order to be a hunter one must be in perfect balance with everything else, otherwise hunting would become a meaningless chore. For instance, today we took a little snake. I had to apologize to her for cutting her life off so suddenly and so definitely; I did what I did knowing that my own life will also be cut off someday in very much the same fashion, suddenly and definitely. So, all in all, we and the snakes are on a par. One of them fed us today.'

'I had never conceived a balance of that kind when I used to hunt,' I said.

'That's not true. You didn't just kill animals. You and your family all ate the game.'

His statements carried the conviction of someone who had been there. He was, of course, right. There had been times when I had provided the incidental wild meat for my family.

After a moment's hesitation I asked, 'How did you know that?'

'There are certain things that I just know,' he said. 'I can't tell you how though.' **

CARLOS CASTANEDA, *JOURNEY TO IXTLAN –*
THE LESSONS OF DON JUAN,
PUB. SIMON & SCHUSTER, NEW YORK, 1973

THE TWO VOLCANOS
English traveler Thomas Gage (1600–56) undertook a survey of the West Indies in 1648, in which he describes Guatemala City.

The chiefest mountains which straighten in this city and valley are two, called volcanoes, the one being a volcano of water, and the other a volcano or mountain of fire, termed so by the Spaniards, though very improperly a volcano may be said to contain water, it taking its name from the heathenish God Vulcan, whose profession and employment chiefly was in fire. These two famous mountains stand almost the one over against the other, on each side of the valley; that of water hanging on the south side almost perpendicularly over the city, the other of fire standing lower from it, more opposite to the old city. That of water is higher than the other, and yields a goodly prospect to the sight, being almost all the year green, and full of Indian *milpas*, which are plantations of Indian wheat; and in the small and petty towns which lie some half way up it, some at the foot of it, there are roses, lilies, and other flowers all the year long in the gardens, besides plantains, apricots and many sorts of sweet and delicate fruits. It is called by the Spaniards, *el* *volcán del agua*, or the volcano of water, because on the other side of it from Guatemala it springs with many brooks towards a town called Saint Christopher, and especially is thought to preserve and nourish on that side also a great lake of fresh water, by the towns called Amatitlan and Petapa. But on the side of it towards Guatemala and the valley it yields also so many springs of sweet and fresh water as have caused and made a river which runneth along the valley close by the city, and is that which drives the water-mills spoken of before in Xocotenango. This river was not known when first the Spaniards conquered that country; but since (according to their constant tradition) the city of Guatemala standing higher and nearer to the volcano in that place and town which to this day is called *la Ciudad Vieja*, or the Old City, there lived in it then about the year 1534 a gentlewoman called Donna Maria de Castilla, who having lost her husband in the wars, and that same year buried also all her children, grew so impatient under these her crosses and afflictions, that impiously she defied God, saying: 'What can God do more unto me now than he hath done? He hath done his worst without it be to take away my life also, which I now regard not.' Upon these words there gushed out of this volcano such a flood of water as carried away this woman with the stream, ruined many of the houses, and caused the inhabitants to remove to the place where now standeth Guatemala. **99

THOMAS GAGE, *THOMAS GAGE'S TRAVELS IN THE NEW WORLD*, ED. A.P. NEWTON, PUB. GEORGE ROUTLEDGE & SONS, LONDON, 1928

MONTEZUMA

THE LEGENDARY RULER

William Carlos Williams (1883–1963) describes the importance of Montezuma to his people.

66Surely no other prince has lived, or will ever live, in such state as did this American cacique. The whole waking aspirations of his people, opposed to and completing their religious sense, seemed to come off in him and in him alone: the drive upward, toward the sun and the stars. He was the very person of their ornate dreams, so delicate, so prismatically colorful, so full of tinkling sounds and rhythms, so tireless of invention. Never was such a surface lifted above the isolate blackness of such profound savagery. It is delightful to know that Montezuma changed his clothes four times a day, donning four different suits, entirely new, which he never wore again; that at meals he was served in a great clean-swept chamber on mats upon the floor, his food being kept warm in chafing dishes containing live coals; that at meals he sat upon a small cushion 'curiously wrought of leather'. But nowhere in his state was the stark power of beauty, the refined and the barbaric, so exquisitely expressed as in his smaller palaces and places of amusement. 'What can be more wonderful than that a barbarous monarch, as he is, should have every object in his domain imitated in gold, silver, precious stones and feathers; the gold and silver being wrought so naturally as not to be surpassed by any smith in the world; the stonework executed with such perfection that it is difficult to conceive what instruments could have been used, and the feather work superior to the finest production in wax and embroidery.' 'There is one palace inferior to the rest, attached to which is a beautiful garden with balconies extending over it supported by marble columns and having a floor formed of jasper elegantly inlaid. Belonging to it are ten pools, in which are kept the different species of water birds found in the country, all domesticated: for the sea birds there are pools of salt water and for

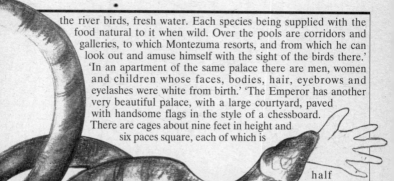

the river birds, fresh water. Each species being supplied with the food natural to it when wild. Over the pools are corridors and galleries, to which Montezuma resorts, and from which he can look out and amuse himself with the sight of the birds there.' 'In an apartment of the same palace there are men, women and children whose faces, bodies, hair, eyebrows and eyelashes were white from birth.' 'The Emperor has another very beautiful palace, with a large courtyard, paved with handsome flags in the style of a chessboard. There are cages about nine feet in height and six paces square, each of which is half covered with a roof of tiles, and the other half has over it a wooden grate, skilfully made. Every cage contains a bird of prey, of all species.' 'In the same palace there are several large halls on the ground floor, filled with immense cages built of heavy pieces of timber, well put together, in which are kept lions, wolves, foxes and a great variety of other animals of the cat kind.' 'The care of these animals and birds is assigned to three hundred men.' Daily the Emperor's wine cellar and larder are open to all who wished to eat and drink. His meals were served by three or four hundred youths who brought on an infinite variety of dishes; indeed, whenever he dined or supped, the table was loaded with every kind of fish, flesh, fruits and vegetables which the country afforded. Both at the beginning and end of every meal they furnished water for the hands, and the napkins used on these occasions were never employed a second time.**

WILLIAM CARLOS WILLIAMS, *IN THE AMERICAN GRAIN*,
PUB. NEW DIRECTIONS, 1956

A ROYAL WELCOME
Spanish Conquistador Bernal Diaz de Castillo (c. 1492–1581) joined Cortés on his 1519 expedition to Mexico and was invited to dinner by Montezuma.

**His cooks had upwards of thirty different ways of dressing meats and they had earthen vessels so contrived as to keep them always hot. For the table of Montezuma himself, above three hundred dishes were dressed, and for his guards, above a thousand. Before dinner, Montezuma would sometimes go out and inspect the preparations, and his officers would point out to him which were the best and explained of what birds and flesh they were composed; and of those he would eat. But this was more for amusement than anything else. It is said that at times the flesh of young children was dressed for him; but the ordinary meats were, domestic fowls, pheasants, geese, partridges, quails, venison, Indian hogs, pigeons, hares and rabbits, with many other animals and birds peculiar to the country. This is certain; that after Cortes had spoken to him relative to the dressing human flesh, it was not practised in his palace. At his meals, in the cold weather, a number of torches of the bark of a wood which makes no smoke and has an aromatic smell, were lighted, and, that they should not throw too much heat, screens, ornamented with gold, and painted with figures of idols, were placed before them. Montezuma was seated on a low throne, or chair, at a table proportioned to the height of his seat. The table was covered with white cloths and napkins, and four beautiful women presented him with water for his hands, in vessels which they call Xicales, with other vessels under them like plates, to catch the water; they also presented him with towels. . . . Fruit of all the kinds that the country produced was laid before him; he ate very little, but from time to time, a liquor prepared from cocoa, and of a stimulative, or

corroborative quality, as we were told, was prepared to him in golden cups.
could not at that time see if he drank it or not, but I observed a number of j
above fifty, brought in, filled with foaming chocolate, of which he took some, w
the women presented to him. At different intervals during the time of dinner, th
entered certain Indians, humpbacked, very deformed, and ugly, who played tr
of buffoonery, and others who they said were jesters. There was also a company
singers and dancers, who afforded Montezuma much entertainment. To these
ordered the vases of chocolate to be distributed. The four female attendants th
took away the cloths, and again with much respect presented him with water
wash his hands, during which time Montezuma conversed with the four o
noblemen formerly mentioned, after which they took their leave with ma
ceremonies. One thing I forgot, and no wonder, to mention in its place, and that
that during the time Montezuma was at dinner, two very beautiful women wer
busily employed making small cakes with eggs and other things mixed therein
These were delicately white, and when made they presented them to him on plate
covered with napkins. Also another kind of bread was brought to him in long
loaves, and plates of cakes resembling wafers. After he had dined, they presented
to him three little canes highly ornamented, containing liquid amber, mixed with an
herb they call tobacco; and when he had sufficiently viewed and heard the singers,
dancers, and buffoons, he took a little of the smoke of one of these canes, and then
laid himself down to sleep; and thus his principal meal concluded. **99**

BERNAL DIAZ DEL CASTILLO,
THE TRUE HISTORY OF THE CONQUEST OF NEW SPAIN,
TRANS. M. KEATINGE, PUB. LONDON, 1927

A BLOODY HISTORY

FIRST IMPRESSIONS

*Hernán Cortés (1485–1554) wrote to the king and queen of Spain in 1519, describing
the land and the people he encountered.*

66The people who inhabit this land, from the island of Cozumel and the cape of
Yucatán to the place where we are now, are of medium height and well-
proportioned bodies and features, save that in each province their customs are
different; some pierce their ears and put very large and ugly objects into them;
others pierce their nostrils down to the lip and put in them large round stones
which look like mirrors; and others still split their lower lips as far as the gums and
hang there some large stones or gold ornaments so heavy that they drag the lips
down, giving a most deformed appearance. The clothes they wear are like large,
highly colored yashmaks; the men cover their shameful parts, and on the top half of
their bodies wear thin mantles which are decorated in a Moorish fashion. The
common women wear highly colored mantles from the waist to the feet, and others
which cover their breasts, leaving the rest uncovered. The women of rank wear
skirts of very thin cotton, which are very loose-fitting and decorated and cut in the
manner of a rochet.
The food they eat is maize and some chili peppers, as on the other islands, and
patata yuca, just the same as is eaten in Cuba, and they eat it roast, for they do not
make bread of it; and they both hunt and fish and breed many chickens such as
those found on *Tierra Firme,* which are as big as peacocks. . . .
They have their shrines and temples with raised walks which run all around the
outside and are very wide: there they keep the idols which they worship, some of
stone, some of clay and some of wood, which they honor and serve with such
customs and so many ceremonies that many sheets of paper would not suffice to
give Your Royal Highnesses a true and detailed account of them all. And the
temples where they are kept are the largest and the best and the finest built of all
the buildings found in the towns; and they are much adorned with rich hanging
cloths and featherwork and other fineries.
Each day before beginning any sort of work they burn incense in these temples and

sometimes sacrifice their own persons, some cutting their tongues, others their ears, while there are some who stab their bodies with knives. All the blood which flows from them they offer to those idols, sprinkling it in all parts of the temple, or sometimes throwing it into the air or performing many other ceremonies, so that nothing is begun without sacrifice having first been made. They have a most horrid and abominable custom which truly ought to be punished and which until now we have seen in no other part, and this is that, whenever they wish to ask something of the idols, in order that their plea may find more acceptance, they take many girls and boys and even adults, and in the presence of the idols they open their chests while they are still alive and take out their hearts and entrails and burn them before the idols, offering the smoke as sacrifice. Some of us have seen this, and they say it is the most terrible and frightful thing they have ever witnessed. 99

HERNÁN CORTÉS, *LETTERS FROM MEXICO*,
TRANS. AND ED. A.R. PAGDEN, PUB. OXFORD UNIVERSITY PRESS, LONDON, 1972

THE INQUISITION
Sailor Miles Philips was abandoned in the West Indies, attacked by Indians and then captured by the Spanish. Here Richard Hakluyt (1551/2–1616) describes his ordeal.

66We were all soon apprehended in all places, and all our goods seized and taken for the Inquisitors' use, and so from all parts of the country we were conveyed and sent as prisoners to the city of Mexico, and there committed to prison in sundry dark dungeons, where we could not see but by candle light, and were never past two together in one place, so that we saw not one another, neither could one of us tell what was become of another. Thus we remained close imprisoned for the space of a year and a half. We were often called before the Inquisitors alone, and there severely examined our faith, and commanded to say the Paternoster, the Ave Maria, and the Creed in Latin, which God knoweth a great number of us could not say, otherwise than in the English tongue. . . . Yet all this would not serve; for still from time to time we were called upon to confess, and about the space of three months before they proceeded to their severe judgement, we were all racked, and some enforced to utter that against themselves, which afterwards cost them their lives. And thus having gotten from our own mouths matter sufficient for them to proceed in judgement against us, they caused a large scaffold to be made in the midst of the market place in Mexico right over against the head church, and 14 or 15 days before the day of judgement, with the sound of a trumpet, they did assemble the people in all parts of the city: before whom it was then solemnly proclaimed, that whosoever would upon such a day repair to the market place, they should hear the sentence of the Holy Inquisition against the English heretics. The

night before they came to the prison where we were, bringing with them certain fool's coats which they had prepared for us, being called in their language *sanbenitos*, which coats were made of yellow cotton and red crosses upon them: they were so busied in putting on their coats about us, and bringing us out into a large yard, and placing and pointing us in what order we should go to the scaffold or place of judgement upon the morrow, that they did not once suffer us to sleep all that night long. The next morning being come, there was given to every one of us for our breakfast a cup of wine, and a slice of bread fried in honey, and so about eight of the clock in the morning, we set forth of the prison, every man alone in his yellow coat, and a rope about his neck, and a great green wax candle in his hand unlighted, having a Spaniard appointed to go upon either side of every one of us: and so marching in this order and manner toward the scaffold in the market place, which was a bowshoot distant or thereabouts, we found a great assembly of people all the ways and so coming to the scaffold we went up by a pair of stairs and found seats ready prepared for us to sit down on, every man in order as he should be called to receive his judgement. Presently the Inquisitors came up another pair of stairs, and the Viceroy and all the chief justices with them. When they were set down, then came up also a great number of friars, white, black and grey, about the number of three hundred persons. Then was silence commanded, and then presently began their severe and cruel judgement. **99**

RICHARD HAKLUYT, *VOYAGES AND DISCOVERIES*,
EDITED, ABRIDGED AND INTRODUCED BY JACK BEECHING,
PUB. PENGUIN BOOKS, 1972

CANNIBALS

Suspicion was rife on both sides. English sailor John Chilton (fl. 1561–85) describes how he was nearly eaten by cannibals in New Spain (Mexico) in 1569.

66The next day in the morning we passed over the river in a canoa; and being on the other side, I went my selfe before alone: and by reason there met many wayes traled by the wilde beasts, I lost my way, and so travelled thorow a great wood about two leagues: and at length fell into the hands of certaine wilde Indians, which were there in certaine cottages made of straw; who seeing me, came out to the number of twenty of them, with their bowes and arrowes, and spake to mee in their language, which I understood not: and so I made signs unto them to helpe mee from my horse; which they did by commandement of their lord, which was there with them. They caried me under one of their cottages, and layed me upon a mat on the ground: and perceiving that I could not understand them, they brought unto mee a little Indian wench of Mexico, of fifteene or sixteene yeeres of age, whom they commanded to ask me in her language from whence I came, and for what I was come among them: for (sayth she) doest thou not know Christian, how that these people will kill and eat thee? To whom I answered, let them doe with me what they will; heere now I am. She replied, saying thou mayest thanke God thou art leane; for they feare thou hast the pocks; otherwise they would eate thee. So I presented to the king a little wine which I had with me in a bottle; which he esteemed above any treasure: for for wine they will sell their wives and children. Afterwards the wench asked me what I would have, and whether I would eat any thing. I answered that I desired a little water

to drinke, for that the countrey is very hote. . . . Having now bene conversant with them about three or foure houres, they bid her ask me if I would goe my way. I answered that I desired nothing els.**

JOHN CHILTON, FROM HAKLUYT'S *PRINCIPAL VOYAGES*,
EXTRACT FROM ERIC NEWBY'S *TRAVELLERS' TALES*, PUB. COLLINS, LONDON, 1985

MEXICO

The dust of history rests in the present land. Robert Lowell (1917–77) questions the nature of history in his poem entitled 'Mexico'.

**The lizard rusty as a leaf rubbed rough
does nothing for days but puff his throat
for oxygen, and tongue up passing flies,
sees only similar rusty lizards pant:
harems worthy this lord of the universe –
each thing he does generic, and not the best.
How fragrantly our cold hands warm to the live coal!
We sit on the cliff like curs, chins pressed to thumbs,
the Toltec temples changing to dust in the dusk –
hair of the vulture, white brow of the moon: this too dust...
dust out of time, two clocks set back to the Toltec Eden,
as if we still wished to pull teeth with firetongs –
when they took a city, they too murdered everything:
man, woman and child, down to the pigs and dogs.**

ROBERT LOWELL, FROM *NOTEBOOK*,
PUB. FABER & FABER, LONDON 1970

SALVADOR

When mass murder becomes commonplace, after a while the evidence is taken for granted. Joan Didion (b. 1934) describes a body dump in El Salvador.

**I drove up to Puerta del Diablo one morning in June of 1982, past the Casa Presidencial and the camouflaged watch towers and heavy concentrations of troops and arms south of town, on up a narrow road narrowed further by landslides and deep crevices in the roadbed, a drive so insistently premonitory that after a while I began to hope that I would pass Puerta del Diablo without knowing it, just miss it, write it off, turn around and go back. There was however no way of missing it. Puerta del Diablo is a 'view site' in an older and distinctly literary tradition, nature as lesson, an immense cleft rock through which half of El Salvador seems framed, a

149

site so romantic and 'mystical', so theatrically sacrificial in aspect, that it might be a cosmic parody of nineteenth-century landscape painting. The place presents itself as pathetic fallacy: the sky 'broods', the stones 'weep', a constant seepage of water weighting the ferns and moss. The foliage is thick and slick with moisture. The only sound is a steady buzz, I believe of cicadas.

Body dumps are seen in El Salvador as a kind of visitors' must-do, difficult but worth the detour. 'Of course you have seen El Playón,' an aide to President Alvaro Magaña said to me one day, and proceeded to discuss the site geologically, as evidence of the country's geothermal resources. He made no mention of the bodies. I was unsure if he was sounding me out or simply found the geothermal aspect of overriding interest. . . .

'Nothing fresh today, I hear,' an embassy officer said when I mentioned that I had visited Puerta del Diablo. 'Were there any on top?' someone else asked. 'There were supposed to have been three on top yesterday.' The point about whether or not there had been any on top was that usually it was necessary to go down to see bodies. The way down is hard. Slabs of stone, slippery with moss, are set into the vertiginous cliff, and it is down this cliff that one begins the descent to the bodies, or what is left of the bodies, pecked and maggoty masses of flesh, bone, hair. On some days there have been helicopters circling, tracking those making the descent. Other days there have been militia at the top, in the clearing where the road seems to run out, but on the morning I was there the only people on top were a man and a woman and three small children, who played in the wet grass while the woman started and stopped a Toyota pickup. She appeared to be learning how to drive. She drove forward and then back toward the edge, apparently following the man's signals, over and over again.

We did not speak, and it was only later, down the mountain and back in the land of the provisionally living, that it occurred to me that there was a definite question about why a man and a woman might choose a well-known body dump for a driving lesson. This was one of a number of occasions, during the two weeks my husband and I spent in El Salvador, on which I came to understand, in a way I had not understood before, the exact mechanism of terror.**

JOAN DIDION, *SALVADOR*,
PUB. CHATTO & WINDUS, LONDON, 1983

ARTS AND CRAFTS

GUADALUPAN

The development of a new Mexican culture incorporating elements of Indian and Spanish styles is described here by Octavio Paz (b. 1914).

❝The curiosity which the Indian past excites should not always be regarded as a mere thirst for the exotic. During the seventeenth century many minds were occupied with the problem of how a colonial order could assimilate the native world. The ancient history of the Indians, their myths, their dances, and their crafts, even their religion, formed a secret and inaccessible universe. At the same time, the old beliefs were mingling with the new, and the remnants of the native culture posed questions to which there was no answer. The Virgin of Guadalupe was also Tonantzin, the coming of the Spaniards was confused with the return of Quetzalcoatl, and the ancient native rituals revealed disturbing analogies with those of the Catholic Church. If certain presages of the coming of Christ were to be found in the pagan faith of the Mediterranean, why should they not be encountered also in the history of ancient Mexico? The Conquest was no longer regarded as an event brought about by the will of Spain alone, but as an occurrence for which the Indians had been waiting, and which had been prophesied by their kings and priests. By dint of such interpretations a supernatural link was established between the ancient religions and Catholicism. The Virgin of Guadalupe, ancient goddess of fertility, on whom so many ideas and psychic forces were focused, became the meeting place of the two worlds and the center of Mexican religious life. Her image embodied the reconciliation of the two conflicting worlds, and at the same time expressed the originality of the nation that was coming to birth. Through the Virgin of Guadalupe, Mexico claims to be heir to two traditions. Baroque colonial art exploited this situation, mixed the Indian with the Spanish tradition, and produced a new form of exoticism. A peculiar form of baroque, which might be labeled 'guadalupan,' was to become the pre-eminent style of New Spain.❞

FROM *ANTHOLOGY OF MEXICAN POETRY*,
COMPILED BY OCTAVIO PAZ, TRANS. SAMUEL BECKETT,
PUB. CALDER & BOYARS, LONDON, 1970

GOLDSMITHS

Thomas Gage was fascinated by the intricate craftsmanship.

66The art, or science, of goldsmiths among them was the most curious, and very good workmanship engraven with tools made of flint or in mould. They will cast a platter in mould with eight corners, and every corner of several metal, the one of gold, and the other of silver, without any kind of solder. They will also found or cast a little cauldron with loose handles hanging thereat, as we use to cast a bell; they will also cast in mould a fish of metal, with one scale of silver on his back, and another of gold; they will make a parrot or popinjay of metal that his tongue shall shake and his head move and his wings flutter; they will cast an ape in mould, that both hands and feet shall stir, and hold a spindle in his hand seeming to spin, yea and an apple in his hand as though he would eat it.99

THOMAS GAGE, *THOMAS GAGE'S TRAVELS IN THE NEW WORLD*, ED. A.P. NEWTON, PUB. GEORGE ROUTLEDGE & SONS, LONDON, 1928

ANCIENT ARTS

In his history of the Conquest, William Prescott (1796–1859) admired the rich colors and ornate designs of ceramics and fabrics.

66The ancient Mexicans made utensils of earthenware for the ordinary purposes of domestic life, numerous specimens of which still exist. They made cups and vases of a lackered or painted wood, impervious to wet, and gaudily coloured. Their dyes were obtained from both mineral and vegetable substances. Among them was the rich crimson of the cochineal, the modern rival of the famed Tyrian purple. It was introduced into Europe from Mexico, where the curious little insect was nourished with great care on plantations of cactus, since fallen into neglect. The natives were thus enabled to give a brilliant colouring to the webs which were manufactured, of every degree of fineness, from the cotton raised in abundance throughout the warmer regions of the country. They had the art, also, of interweaving with these the delicate hair of rabbits and other animals, which made a cloth of great warmth as well as beauty, of a kind altogether original; and on this they often laid a rich embroidery, of birds, flowers, or some other fanciful device. But the art in which they most delighted was their *plumaje*, or featherwork. With this they could produce all the effect of a beautiful mosaic. The gorgeous plumage of the tropical birds, especially of the parrot tribe, afforded every variety of colour; and the fine down of the hummingbird, which revelled in swarms among the honeysuckle bowers of Mexico, supplied them with soft aerial tints that gave an exquisite finish to the picture. The feathers, pasted on a fine cotton web, were wrought into dresses for the wealthy, hangings for apartments, and ornaments for the temples. No one of the American fabrics excited such admiration in Europe, whither numerous specimens were sent by the Conquerors. It is to be regretted that so graceful an art should have been suffered to fall into decay.99

WILLIAM HICKLING PRESCOTT, *HISTORY OF THE CONQUEST OF MEXICO*, PUB. GEORGE ALLEN & UNWIN LTD., LONDON 1913

SCULPTURE
British sculptor Henry Moore (1898–?) was much influenced by Mexican art.

❝Mexican sculpture, as soon as I found it seemed to me true and right, perhaps because I at once hit on similarities in it with some eleventh-century carvings I had seen as a boy on Yorkshire churches. Its 'stoniness', by which I mean its truth to material, its tremendous power without loss of sensitiveness, its astonishing variety and fertility of form-invention, and its approach to a full three-dimensional conception of form, make it unsurpassed in my opinion by any other period of stone sculpture.❞

JOHN RUSSEL, *HENRY MOORE,*
PUB. PENGUIN BOOKS, LONDON, 1973

THE NATURAL WORLD

A MUDDY ASCENT
John Lloyd Stephens (1805–1852) climbed the Volcan de Agua near the city of Copán in Honduras.

❝At half past ten we were above the region of forest and came out upon the open side of the volcano. There was still a scattering of trees, long grass, and a great variety of curious plants and flowers, furnishing rich materials for the botanist. Among them was a plant with a red flower, called the *mano del mico*, or hand-plant, but more like a monkey's paw, growing to a height of thirty or forty feet, the inside a light vermilion color, and the outside vermilion with stripes of yellow. My companion, tired with the toil of ascending even with the aid of the rope, at length mounted an Indian's shoulders. I was obliged to stop every two or three minutes, and my rests were about equal to the actual time of walking. The great difficulty was on account of the wet and mud, which, in ascending, made us lose part of every step. It was so slippery that, even with the staff and the assistance of branches of trees and bushes, it was difficult to keep from falling. About half an hour before

reaching the top, and perhaps one thousand or fifteen hundred feet from it, the trees became scarce and seemed blazed by lightning or withered by cold. The clouds gathered thicker than before, and I lost all hope of a clear day.

At half an hour before twelve we reached the top and descended into the crater. A whirlwind of cloud and vapor was sweeping around it. We were in a perspiration, our clothes were saturated with rain and mud, and in a few moments the cold penetrated our very bones. We attempted to build a fire, but the sticks and leaves were wet and would not burn. For a few moments we raised a feeble flame and all crouched around it, but a sprinkling of rain came down, just enough to put it out. We could see nothing, and the shivering Indians begged me to return. On rocks near us were inscriptions, one of which bore the date of 1548, and on a cut stone were the words:

> ALEXANDRO LDVERT
> DE SAN PETERSBURGO;
> EDVARDO LEGH PAGE,
> DE INGLATERRA;
> *JOSE CROSKEY,*
> *DE FYLADELFYE,*
> BIBYMOS AQUI UNAS BOTEAS
> DE CHAMPANA, EL DIA 26
> DE AGOSTO DE 1834.

It seemed strange that three men from such distant and different parts of the world – St. Petersburg, England, and *Philadelphia* – had met to drink champagne on the top of this volcano. **99**

JOHN LLOYD STEPHENS, *INCIDENTS OF TRAVEL IN CENTRAL AMERICA, CHIAPAS, AND YUCATAN*, ED. RICHARD L. PREDMORE, PUB. RUTGERS UNIVERSITY PRESS, NEW BRUNSWICK, 1949

THE MOUNTAINS

D.H. Lawrence (1885–1930) traveled throughout Mexico between 1922 and 1928. Here he describes a walk to Huayapa.

66The morning is perfect; in a moment we are clear out of the town. Most towns in Mexico, saving the capital, end in themselves, at once. As if they had been lowered from heaven in a napkin, and deposited, rather foreign, upon the wild plain. So we walk round the wall of the church and the huge old monastery enclosure that is now barracks for the scrap-heap soldiery, and at once there are the hills.

154

'I will lift up my eyes until the hills, whence cometh my strength.' At least one can always do *that*, in Mexico. In a stride, the town passes away. Before us lies the gleaming, pinkish-ochre of the valley flat, wild and exalted with sunshine. On the left, quite near, bank the stiffly pleated mountains, all the foot-hills, that press savannah-coloured into the savannah of the valley. The mountains are clothed smokily with pine, *ocote*, and, like a woman in a gauze *rebozo*, they rear in a rich blue fume that is almost cornflower-blue in the clefts. It is their characteristic, that they are darkest-blue at the top. Like some splendid lizard with a wavering, royal blue crest down the ridge of his back, and pale belly, and soft, pinky-fawn claws, on the plain.

Between the pallor of the claws, a dark spot of trees, and white dots of a church with twin towers. Further away, along the foot-hills, a few scattered trees, white dot and stroke of a *hacienda*, and a green, green square of sugar-cane. Further off still, at the mouth of a cleft of a canyon, a dense little green patch of trees, and two spots of proud church.**99**

D.H. LAWRENCE, MORNINGS IN MEXICO,
PUB. MARTIN SECKER, LONDON, 1930

NIGHT

In "Under the Volcano", Malcolm Lowry (1909–57) uses the Mexican landscape to reinforce his theme of self-destructiveness.

66The jungle closed over them and the volcanoes were blotted out. Yet it was still not dark. From the stream racing along beside them a radiance was cast. Big yellow flowers, resembling chrysanthemums, shining like stars through the gloom, grew on either side of the water. Wild bougainvillea, brick-red in the half-light, occasionally a bush with white handbells, tongue downwards, started out at them, every little while a notice nailed to a tree, a whittled, weather-beaten arrow pointing, with the words hardly visible: *a la Cascada* –

Farther on worn-out ploughshares and the rusted and twisted chassis of abandoned American cars bridged the stream which they kept always to their left.

The sound of the falls behind was now lost in that of the cascade ahead. The air was full of spray and moisture. But for the tumult one might almost have heard things growing as the torrent rushed through the wet heavy foliage that sprang up everywhere around them from the alluvial soil.

All at once, above them, they saw the sky again. The clouds, no longer red, had become a peculiar luminous blue-white, drifts and depths of them, as though illumined by moon rather than sunlight, between which roared still the deep fathomless cobalt of afternoon.

Birds were sailing up there, ascending higher and higher. Infernal bird of Prometheus!

They were vultures, that on earth so jealously contend with one another, defiling themselves with blood and filth, but who were yet capable of rising, like this, above the storms, to heights shared only by the condor, above the summit of the Andes –

Down the south-west stood the moon itself, preparing to follow the sun below the horizon. On their left, through the trees beyond the stream appeared low hills, like those at the foot of the Calle Nicaragua; they were purple and sad. At their foot, so near Yvonne made out a faint rustling, cattle moved on the sloping fields among gold cornstalks and striped mysterious tents.

Before them, Popacatepetl and Ixtaccihuatl

continued to dominate the north-east, the Sleeping Woman now perhaps the more beautiful of the two, with jagged angles of blood-red snow on its summit, fading as they watched, whipped with darker rock shadows, the summit itself seeming suspended in mid-air, floating among the curdling ever mounting black clouds. **"**

MALCOLM LOWRY, *UNDER THE VOLCANO*,
PUB. JONATHAN CAPE,
LONDON, 1947

BIRDS
The cacophony of the thousands of birds is one of the lasting memories of Tzinzuntzan for writer Lesley Blanch.

"No one told me about the birds. Every province has its own special birds, like its fruit or flowers, a thousand different fluttering, shimmering creatures, fluting, cawing, shrieking. At Purapechas, by the end of the lake, there is a whole world, or concentration of humming-birds, where these beetle-sized little beauties zoom and dart about the honied trails of vine, 'cup-of-gold', or a plant called *izgujochitl* – 'the flower of the raven'. Pelicans and cormorants in Yucatan. Gaudy macaws and parakeets flashing through the tropic groves round Orizaba. Under the towering ash trees at Tzinzuntzan I heard the nightingale at noon; but it turned out to be a yellow-feathered bird, and I recalled that the Emperor Maximilian imported two thousand nightingales from Germany: where they, perhaps, then crossed with canaries? Everywhere, in the mountains, in the valleys, I see those long-tailed black magpie-like birds, so impudently friendly, which seem to address one personally, as they flutter close to perch on the spear-tip of a cactus or on a window-sill. The Mexicans call them 'ouraki'; in Mayan, they are 'toh'. Their song has the heart-piercing sweetness of a blackbird's trill, with something melancholy added, something which epitomises all Mexico at dusk. **"**

LESLEY BLANCH, *UNDER A LILAC-BLEEDING STAR*,
PUB. JOHN MURRAY,
LONDON, 1963

A JOURNEY BY COACH

Scottish-born traveler Madame Calderon de la Barca (1804–82) spent two years in Mexico and described her experiences in vivid letters which were later published as a book.

❝We climbed into the coach, which was so crowded that we could but just turn our heads to groan an adieu to our friends. The coach rattled off through the streets, dashed through the Alameda, and gradually we began to shake down, and, by a little arrangement of cloaks and serapes, to be less crowded. A *padre* with a very Indian complexion sat between K– and me, and a horrible, long, lean bird-like female, with immense red goggle-eyes, coal-black teeth, fingers like claws, a great goitre, and drinking brandy at intervals, sat opposite to us. There were also various men buried in their serapes. Satisfied with a cursory inspection of our companions, I addressed myself to *Blackwood's Magazine*, but the road which leads towards the Desierto, and which we before passed on horseback, is dreadful, and the mules could scarcely drag the loaded coach up the steep hills. We were thrown into ruts, horribly jolted, and sometimes obliged to get out, which would not have been disagreeable but for the necessity of getting in again. The day and the country were beautiful, but impossible to enjoy either in a shut coach. We were rather thankful when the wheels, sticking in a deep rut, we were forced to descend, and walk forwards for some time. We had before seen the view from these heights, but the effect never was more striking than at this moment. The old city with her towers, lakes, and volcanoes, lay bathed in the bright sunshine. Not a cloud was in the sky – not an exhalation rose from the lake – not a shadow was on the mountains. All was bright and glittering, and flooded in the morning light; while in contrast rose to the left the dark, pine-covered crags, behind which the Desierto lies. At Santa Fé we changed horses, and found there an escort which had been ordered for us by General Tornel; a necessary precaution in these robber-haunted roads. We stopped to breakfast at *Quamalpa*, where the inn is kept by a Frenchman, who is said to be making a large fortune, which he deserves for the good breakfast he had prepared for us. . . . After leaving this inn, situated in a country formed of heaps of lava and volcanic rocks, the landscape becomes more beautiful and wooded. It is, however,

dangerous, on account of the shelter which the wooded mountains afford to the knights of the road, and to whose predilection for these wild solitudes, the number of crosses bore witness. In a wooded defile there is a small clear space called '*Las Cruces*', where several wooden crosses point out the site of the famous battle between the curate Hidalgo and the Spanish General Truxillo. An object really in keeping with the wild scenery, was the head of the celebrated robber *Maldonado*, nailed to the pine-tree beneath which he committed his last murder. It is now quite black, and grins there, a warning to his comrades and an encouragement to travellers. From the age of ten to that of fifty, he followed the honourable profession of free-trader, when he expiated his crimes. The padre who was in the coach with us, told us that he heard his last confession. That grinning skull was once the head of a man, and an ugly one too, they say; but stranger still it is to think, that that man was once a baby, and sat on his mother's knee, and that his mother may have been pleased to see him cut his *first tooth*. If she could but see his teeth now!**99**

MADAME CALDERON DE LAS BARCAS, *LIFE IN MEXICO*,
PUB. CHAPMAN & HALL, LONDON, 1843

SANITATION

Aldous Huxley (1894–63) observed the basics of human life in his journey around the Bay of Mexico. The first extract describes a hotel in Belize; the second a market in Guatemala city.

66Walking through the streets, one saw but little traces of the great calamity of 1930, when a hurricane blew the sea in a huge wall of water right across the town. A heap of bricks, it is true, was all that was left of the principal house of God; but Mammon, Caesar and the Penates had risen fresh and shining from the ruins. Almost all the private residences and all the government offices, all the shops and warehouses, had been rebuilt or repaired. The town as a whole looked remarkably neat and tidy. Even a tidal wave may have something to be said for it. It does at least clear away the slums. Our governments and municipalities are less brutal; but they are also, alas, a good deal less effective.

The sanitary arrangements at the new hotel were all that could be desired; but the proprietor, who was a Spanish-American, was evidently unacquainted, not only with

English spelling, but also (which was worse) with our English euphemisms. At the top of the stairs I found myself confronted by a door, on which were written, in very large black letters, the words: FOR URIN.
Why not, after all? Nevertheless, I was a little startled. We are all like Pavlov's dogs – so conditioned that, when the scatological bell rings, we automatically begin to frown or blush. It is absurd, it is even, if you like to think of yourself as a rational being, rather humiliating. But there it is; that is how the machine happens to work. **99**

66Outside in an overflow market we saw an old Indian woman selling iguanas. They were cheap; you could buy a miniature dragon with three feet of ship-lash tail, all alive, for twenty or thirty cents. Flayed and gutted, the dried carcasses of several more lay in a neat row on the pavement, a pale meat crusty with flies. Near them stood an enormous bowl, full of iguana eggs. Curiosity wrestled with prejudice and was at last defeated; we moved away, leaving the eggs untasted. That evening we happened to pass again along the same street. Business in lizards had evidently been slack; the old woman's pitch was still crawling with monsters. While we were looking, she began to pack up her wares for the night. One by one, she took up the animals and dumped them into a circular basket. The tails projected, writhing. Angrily she shoved them back into place; but while one was being folded away, another would spring out, and then another. It was like a battle with the hydra. The abhorred tails were finally confined under a net. Then, hoisting the lizards on to her head, and with the bowl of their eggs under her arm, the old woman marched away, muttering as she went heaven knows what imprecations against all reptiles, and probably, since she shot a furious look in our direction, all foreigners as well.**99**

ALDOUS HUXLEY, *BEYOND THE MEXIQUE WAY,*
PUB. CHATTO & WINDUS, LONDON 1934

BY TRAIN
American poet Elizabeth Bishop (1911–79) described a train journey in a letter to Marianne Moore.

66Oaxaca is very nice – I like it next best to Mérida, I think. We came from Puebla by *narrow-gauge Pullman*, the tiniest train I have ever seen. It ran all day through a narrow mountain gorge filled with cactus, beside a raging torrent of mud, and it kept coming off the tracks and bumping along on the ties. Then the engineer and the conductor would hop off and somehow boost it back on again – and set up a miniature broadcasting station beside the track to let the day train behind us know where we were so they wouldn't bump into us. We were ten hours late, but apparently that wasn't bad – sometimes it gets stuck for days, and the company seriously suggests that you bring some groceries along.**99**
ELIZABETH BISHOP, *LETTERS*, SELECTED AND EDITED BY ROBERT GIROUX,
PUB. CHATTO & WINDUS, LONDON 1994

MEXICANS
The travel writing of Graham Greene (1904–9) reflects his preoccupations with religion and moral dilemmas. The first of these extracts describes Huichapan station; the second, the nightlife of El Retiro.

66The whole long platform was given up to beggars – not the friendly Indian women bearing tortillas and legs of chicken, preserved fruits dried in the dusty sun, and strange pieces of meat, who pass at every station down the train, not even the kind of resigned beggars who usually sit in church porches waiting dumbly and patiently for alms – but get-rich-quick beggars, scrambling and whining and

159

snarling with impatience, children and old men and women, fighting their wa
along the train, pushing each other to one side, lifting the stump of a hand,
crutch, a rotting nose, or in the children's case a mere bony undernourished hand
A middle-aged paralytic worked himself down the platform on his hands – three
feet high, with bearded bandit face and little pink baby feet twisted the wrong way
Someone threw him a coin and a child of six or seven leapt on his back and after an
obscene and horrifying struggle got it from him. The man made no complaint
shovelling himself further along: human beings here obeyed the jungle law, each
for himself with tooth and nail. They came up around the train on both sides of the
track like mangy animals in a neglected zoo. **99**

66El Retiro is the swagger cabaret of Socialist Mexico, all red and gold and little
balloons filled with gas, and Chicken à la King. A film star at one table and a
famous singer, and rich men everywhere. American couples moved sedately acros
the tiny dance floor while the music wailed, the women with exquisite hair and
gentle indifference, and the middle-aged American business men like overgrown
schoolboys a hundred years younger than their young women. Then the cabaret
began – a Mexican dancer with great bold thighs, and the American women lost a
little of their remote superiority. They were being beaten at the sexual game
somebody who wasn't beautiful and remote was drawing the attention of their men
They got vivacious and talked a little shrilly and powdered their faces, and suddenly
appeared very young and inexperienced and unconfident, as the great thigh
moved. But their turn came when the famous tenor sang. The American men li
their pipes and talked all through the song and then clapped heartily to show that
they didn't care, and the women closed their compacts and listened – avidly. I
wasn't poetry they were listening to or music (the honeyed words about roses and
love, the sweet dim nostalgic melody), but the great emotional orgasm in the
throat. They called out for a favourite song and the rich plump potent voice wailed
on – interminably, a whole night of love. This was not popular art, nor intellectua
art – it was, I suppose, capitalist art. And this, too, was Socialist Mexico. **99**

GRAHAM GREENE, *THE LAWLESS ROADS – A MEXICAN JOURNEY*
PUB. LONGMANS, GREEN & CO
LONDON, 193

TRAVELING
AROUND THE
ROUTE OF THE
MAYAS

▲ "Castillo" at Tulum (Mexico)

▼ Temples at Palenque (Mexico)

▼ Mayan edifices and causeway at Labná (Mexico)

▲ "Caracol" at Chichén Itzá (Mexico)   ▼ Temple 1 at Tikal (Guatemala)

▼ Nunnery quadrangle at Uxmal (Mexico)

▲ Lake Atitlán (Guatemala)   ▼ Field at Quetzaltenango (Guatemala)

▼ Pool in the Lacandón Forest (Mexico)

▲ Livingston Beach (Guatemala)   ▼ Agua Azul Falls (Mexico)

▼ Panamerican road in the highlands (Guatemala)

▲ Tzotzil Indians at Zinacantán (Mexico)

▲ San Antonio Palopó (Guatemala)   ▼ Market at Almolonga (Guatemala)

▲ Dzibalchen (Mexico)   ▼ "Garifunas" in Belize City (Belize)

▼ Santa Lucía Cotzumalguapa (Guatemala)

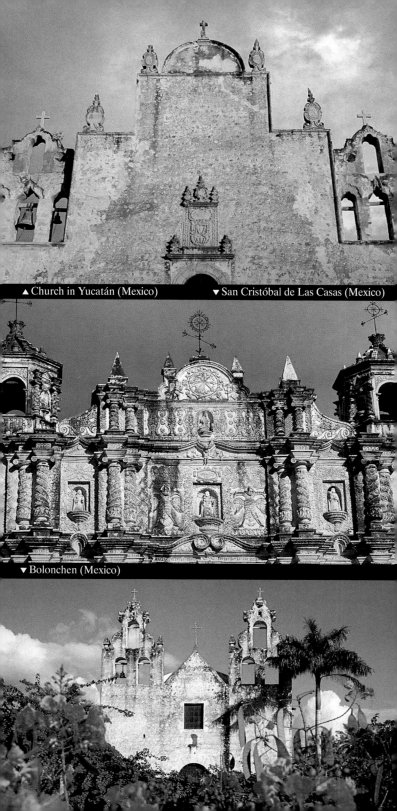

▲ Church in Yucatán (Mexico)   ▼ San Cristóbal de Las Casas (Mexico)

▼ Bolonchen (Mexico)

EASTERN YUCATÁN

QUINTANA ROO
The state of Quintana Roo occupies the eastern half of the Yucatán Peninsula. It covers an area of 19,387 square miles and has a population of 500,000. From 1902 it was governed as federal territory by the military and it only became a state in 1974.

This long, rocky, forested coastal strip is bordered to the north and east by the Caribbean. The coast is protected by the coral reef (yellow coral, above) ■ *18* and has some of the finest beaches in America. In recent years, with the development of Cancún, the tourist trade has become increasingly important.

Detail from wall painting, Cancún, showing the 1910 Mexican revolution.

Before the Spanish Conquest the coastal region of Eastern Yucatán, bordered by the Caribbean, underwent an extraordinary period of development equalled only by the modern tourist boom. The so-called "East" or "East Coast" lay on the long-distance trade routes between Central America, Honduras and Guatemala, on the one hand, and the northern Maya region of Yucatán and the Gulf of Mexico, on the other.

AN UNSETTLED PERIOD. During the Classic period (3rd–9th centuries AD) the major urban centers were concentrated in the forests of Petén ▲ *317*, in Guatemala, and along the Motágua ▲ *296* and Usumacinta ▲ *248* rivers. Northern Yucatán was less developed at this time and did not flourish until the Terminal Classic and, more especially, the Postclassic periods, following the collapse of the great cities. In the eastern region, Cobá ▲ *182* was the only important trading center,

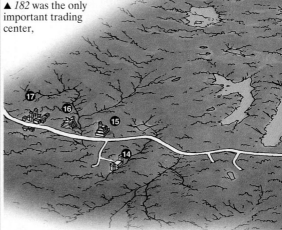

sending salt, shells, honey, wax and cotton to the coasts of Belize and Honduras.

TERRITORIAL AND ECONOMIC RE-ORGANIZATION. When these consumer centers disappeared, large-scale population migration altered the cultural, economic and demographic balance of the entire region. Other major centers developed in the highlands of Guatemala ▲ *261*, northern Yucatán and along the coast of Tabasco. It was from here that navigators organized new (maritime and river) trade routes and controlled the cocoa-producing regions of Guatemala, Honduras and the coast of Belize, establishing trading posts along the Caribbean coast. Many new towns (such as Tulum ▲ *177* and Cozumel ▲ *174*) developed, along with small sanctuaries (providing shelter for some and acting as trading posts for others) where goods could be exchanged or sent inland.

1. CANCÚN   2. ISLA MUJERES   3. PUERTO MORELOS   4. PLAYA DEL CARMEN   5. COZUMEL   6. TULUM   7. COBÁ   8. VALLADOLID   9. FELIPE CARRILLO PUERTO   10. POLYUC   11. PETO   12. CHETUMAL   13. KOHUNLICH   14. RÍO BEC   15. XPUHIL   16. BECAN   17. CONHUAS

CARIBBEAN SEA

🕐 Four days

THE EUROPEAN CONQUEST. Having dispossessed the Indians of their commercial activities, the Spanish proceeded to decimate the population with imported epidemics. Although the villages of Polé (Xcaret), Cozumel and Zama (Tulum) survived for a some time, they were abandoned after being plundered by pirates, and the east coast remained virtually deserted for almost two centuries. Only the English went there to cut wood and replenish their freshwater supplies.
THE CASTE WAR ▲ 186. When the Maya rebelled in 1847, the few inhabitants of the coastal region sought refuge on the Isla Mujeres and the Isla de Cozumel. The Maya, driven back from the regions of central Yucatán, built their sacred capital, Chan Santa Cruz ▲ 184 in the eastern forests. The capital was finally seized by the Mexicans in 1901.

FISHING FOR PLEASURE
The Caribbean coast is an ideal place to fish for *sábalo* (shad), *corvina*, *macabi* or *robalo* (sea bass), barracuda, sailfish, marlin and groupers (below).

171

Cancún's beaches are remarkable both for the color of the sea, which is transparent to a depth of up to 130 feet and ranges from emerald green to sapphire blue, and for their fine, white sand. The sand contains

microscopic fossilized plankton, known as "discoaster", which ensure it always remains cool, even under the blazing sun. Currents and sudden changes in the wind can make these beaches dangerous for bathing. Summer temperatures remain around 104°F with humidity levels of between 70 and 80 percent. The best time to visit Cancún, and indeed the rest of Maya territory, is in the winter, between December and March.

CANCÚN

Since the 19th century the Yucatán Peninsula has been a popular destination for travelers with an interest in archeology. The absence of roads and any kind of tourist infrastructure put the dedication of these intrepid early travelers to the test. The final port of call on these archeological journeys was invariably Chichén Itzá ▲ 205. The Caribbean coast, so naturally beautiful and so rich in beaches and archeological remains, was inaccessible until the early 20th century because of the insurgent Indians of Chan Santa Cruz ▲ 184.

A MODERN RESORT. During the 1970's a vast project was conceived to use this deserted coastline, trapped between the jungle and the sea, to create a series of tourist centers which could compete with the internationally renowned resort of Acapulco, which was already at saturation point. So the tiny island of Cancún, south of the Isla Mujeres ▲ 174, was joined up with the mainland and a vast tourist complex was created. Today, with 300,000 inhabitants, Cancún is one of the most visited tourist resorts in the world.

TWO MAIN AVENUES. The city is crossed by two main avenues. One, the Avenida Tulum, joins the Mérida–Chichén Itzá road at Puerto Juárez to the north, and crosses the city from north to south in the direction of the airport and Tulum ▲ 177. The other, the Avenida Kukulcán, opens onto the Avenida Tulum in the city center, continues east for 5 miles towards the hotel zone and then south along the seafront where it services a further 8 miles of hotels. Finally it turns west towards the airport and Tulum.

THE LAGOON. The vast lagoon between the island and the mainland has been divided into sections: Laguna de Nichputé, Bojórquez, Laguna del Amor and Río Inglés. It is bordered by mangroves ■ 20 and linked to the sea by the Nizuc canal to the south and the Nichputé canal to the north. The lagoon (6 miles long by 3 miles wide) is an ideal place to go fishing, water skiing and diving. There are also boat trips round the lagoon, to the mangroves and archeological sites.

MAYAN REMAINS. The island of Cancún was inhabited by the Maya before the Spanish Conquest. In the center of the island lie the remains of two Mayan sites: SAN MIGUELITO (Xlab-Multun) which overlooks the sea and EL REY (Kin ich Ahau Bonil) which overlooks the lagoon. The site of El Rey consists of a central plaza surrounded by three platforms, a pyramid, two small temples and a vaulted structure. A second plaza has two platforms and a vaulted building with a small oratory in the center. Near the Sheraton Hotel a small structure and a statue of the *Chacmool* are all that remains of the site of YAMIL LU'UM, while the remains of POK-TA-POK can be seen 4 miles away near a golf course of the same name. These Postclassic structures are in the same style as those found along the coast of Quintana Roo.

The beaches of Quintana Roo extend
for over 100 miles along the shores of
the Caribbean.

HACIENDA MUNDACA
A 19th-century smuggler, Fermin Mundaca, made his base on the Isla Mujeres. He was in love with a beautiful Spanish woman and built her a palace and a fort to protect it. But the object of his affections married another man and the pirate died of a

broken heart. The ruined fort and gardens are due to be restored.

The ranch of Miguel Molas at Cozumel (drawing by Frederick Catherwood).

ISLA MUJERES

The Isla Mujeres (Island of Women), situated a few miles north of Cancún, was probably discovered in 1517 by Francisco Hernández de Córdoba ● *36* who was visiting one of the temples when he noticed several female idols. The island is 4 miles long, between 330 and 875 yards wide and lies just over 4 miles from the quay at Puerto Juárez. The tiny fishing village (1,400 inhabitants) at the northern end of the island has retained its traditional appearance. At the southern end is a small Mayan temple (left), damaged by Hurricane Gilbert in 1988. Four openings facing the four points of the compass are an indication that it was used as an observatory. The beaches, washed by a calm, transparent blue sea, are on the southwestern side of the island and include Playa Garrafón, Indios, Lancheros and Pescador. Garrafón is the most interesting as it teems with tropical fish and is an ideal spot for divers, although care should be taken near the coral reef. To the north of Garrafón, the Playa Cocoteros or Los Cocos (also known as North Beach), with its fine sand and transparent waters, is popular among the local population.

A PIRATES' HAVEN. For centuries the Isla Mujeres was used as a base by pirates and smugglers. In 1821 Jean Lafitte was mortally wounded here by the Spanish. Although he died at sea and was buried at Dzilam ▲ *216* in north Yucatán, Lafitte has become a legendary figure in the region.

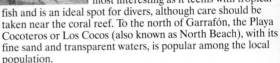

COZUMEL ★

The Isla de Cozumel is the largest of the Mexican islands. It is 33 miles long, 8 miles wide and has a population of fifty

THE "CASTILLO"

The largest edifice on the site overlooks the
Caribbean to the east and, on the landward
side, looks onto a courtyard surrounded by
small buildings. The *Castillo* today (above)
and in 1841 (below, by Catherwood).

CORNER MASK

Stucco mask (above) decorating one of the
corners of the Temple of the Frescos.
Stephens and Catherwood (who made the
drawing) measuring the façade of a temple to
the south of the *Castillo* (top).

BUILDINGS IN MINIATURE
The architects of Tulum used poor quality masonry and concealed any faults with a thick layer of stucco. They tended to favor miniature structures which were sometimes so small that they made any form of human activity difficult (one of the buildings on the site, above). A small sanctuary in the center of an only slightly larger temple (Temple of the Frescos, right), is one of the most typical forms. There are also miniature structures on the shores of the Caribbean which are thought to have been used as landmarks by seafarers.

TEMPLE OF THE FRESCOS
This temple is in fact two superposed Late Postclassic temples, one on top of the other (right). The first sanctuary was covered by a second whose wide entrance is divided by four columns. The interior walls of both structures are completely covered with well-preserved frescos.

FRESCOS
The "cosmic" construction of the decoration is a constant element in the wall paintings of Tulum. The figures are represented with the sky above their heads and the underworld beneath their feet, while the scenes are divided into panels by coiled serpents.

In the inner sanctuary of the Temple of the Frescos, the central iconographic theme is corn. The divinities represented are all connected with this cereal crop. The so-called "Diving God" has two plants in his headdress; in the upper register a kneeling goddess is grinding corn, while above her and to the right, the seated God K (Kauil) ● 50 is presenting a small Maize God to a standing goddess.

THE "DIVING GOD"
Although he is usually interpreted as the image of a specific divinity (the planet Venus or the Bee God), the variations noted in the representations tend to suggest that there are several "Diving Gods". His posture most probably illustrates the theme of the god descending from the heavens to receive the offerings of men.

The Temple of the Frescos, by Frederick Catherwood.

On the back wall of the Temple of the "Diving God", the celestial frieze includes one of the sun's rays and (possibly) a symbol for Venus. It is surmounted by a band terminated at either end by the top half of a creature, probably an image of the sky in the form of a two-headed serpent. The earth is also represented as a two-headed serpent, the counterpart of the celestial monster. Below the earth a central panel depicts the aquatic underworld. The terrestrial scene includes two groups of figures in which a woman is presenting an object to a man, probably a divinity.

181

HOLBOX
Holbox is reached via
the road from Cobá
to Nuevo Xcan which
crosses the Cancún-
Mérida road. At El
Ideal, a road runs
north to Kantunil Kin
and Chiquila. The
village of Holbox, an
ancient port used by
shark fishermen, is
reached by boat.
After sharks (tiger
shark, opposite),
lobsters are the most
highly prized catch.

PUNTA ALLEN
This tiny fishing
village is at the end
of a sandbar looking
across the Bahía de
la Ascensión. The
fishermen of the
village catch lobsters
in the bay with their
bare hands.

COBÁ

This virtually unexplored archeological region, about 30 miles
from Tulum, covers an area of 20 square miles. Cobá was
founded at the beginning of the 7th century and was occupied,
with a few interruptions, until the 15th century. Its
architecture is reminiscent of that of Tikal ▲ *322*. In fact the
two cities flourished at the same time – between the 7th and
10th centuries – when Cobá was the most important city in
northeast Yucatán. This is evidenced by the many steles and
the impressive network of raised causeways (*sacbeob*) leading
to the city. An alliance between Cobá and Tikal made the two
cities important trading centers with products, especially salt,
being delivered there from the coast before being sent on to
Petén.

RECENT EXCAVATIONS. The site (above), initially explored by
Washington's Carnegie Institution, has recently been
excavated and restored by the Mexico National Institute of
Anthropology and History. To the northeast of the main
group, Structure 1 (also known as the "Tallest Pyramid" or
Nohoc Mul) reflects the city's long occupation. A Late
Postclassic structure, similar to those at Tulum, was built on
top of the 78-foot high Late Classic pyramid. At its foot Stele
20 was discovered, one of the best preserved on the site,
dating from AD 684. From the top of the pyramid of the
Castillo, there is a magnificent view across the forest and the
five lakes (including Lake Macanxoc, opposite page)
surrounding the site.

RAISED CAUSEWAYS. *Sacbeob*
leading in five directions link the
central group to the other
architectural groups on the site. These
roads (sixteen have been recorded) are
between 1 and 8 feet above the ground and
about 14 feet wide. Their sides are rough stone
walls, filled with rubble and covered with *sascab*, a
natural limestone cement which sets when wet and

Black-headed gulls and turnstones are a common sight on the coasts of Yucatán.

under pressure. *Sacbeob* also linked Cobá to other sites: Ixil, about 12 miles to the southwest, and Yaxuná, 62 miles to the west. The Cobá–Yaxuná causeway, most probably constructed during the Late Classic period, is perfectly straight, except for the first 20 miles when it must have had to skirt around small communities. It is the longest Maya road discovered to date. A 13-foot limestone cylinder was found on the causeway, weighing around 5 tonnes. It was probably used as a roller for compressing the surface.

TOWARD PUNTA ALLEN

A sandy track runs from Tulum to Punta Allen, a distance of some 35 miles. At Boca Paila there are chalets for visitors from Cozumel and Cancún who come for the deep-sea fishing. The road runs between the sea and the Laguna de Chunyaxché, winding between palm trees and tropical plants, and crosses a wooden bridge with a nearby camping facility. The lagoon is situated in a nature reserve and is a sanctuary for migratory birds such as flamingos, herons and egrets. There are over three hundred species of birds in the reserve, while two species of tropical crocodile (*Crocodylus moreletti* and *Crocodyluus acatus*) inhabit the lagoon.

SIAN KA'AN RESERVE

The Sian Ka'an reserve ("gift from heaven" or "horizon" in Maya) was created in 1986 and incorporated into UNESCO's World Network of Biosphere Reserves. It covers a surface area of 1,737 square miles and is not open to the public. The only accessible area is the coastal strip inhabited by a few fishermen. The former port of Vigia Chico is no longer in use and researchers find accommodation at Punta Allen. Many species which have disappeared elsewhere in the world have survived in this environment where humans have not been allowed to encroach.

WHALES. Several species can be seen around the Yucatán Peninsula. Cuvier's whale or *picuda* (*Ziphius cavirostris*) tends to live only in warm waters. In the past, the most widely hunted species was the sperm whale (*Physeter macrocephalus*), prized for its meat and blubber, but also for its spermaceti, a white waxy substance obtained from oil in the whale's head and used to make cosmetics and candles. Ambergris, an

AN EXTINCT SPECIES
The Caribbean monk seal, the only seal found in tropical Atlantic waters, was a common sight in the early 20th century. The last sighting was in Honduras in 1952.

SEA BIRDS
Birds such as sandpipers and curlews live on the beaches and in the mangroves where they find their food. Wilson's snipes, sandpipers and turnstones frequent the damp areas of the peninsula. The more commonly found seabirds in the Caribbean are the black-headed gull, with its dark head and orange-red beak; the herring gull, white with a yellow beak; the brown (*pontoh*) and white (*sac pontoh*) pelican; the frigate bird (*chimay* in Maya); the brown booby (*alcatraz*), with its white underbelly; and the blue-footed booby; the scissor-bill (*rayador*) which skims along the surface of the water with its beak open; the cormorant (*mach* in Maya); the *anhinga*, a strange animal known as the serpent-bird because of its long neck and beak; and, finally, Cabot's tern, and the royal and common terns.

On the road from Chetumal to Xpuhil.

DOLPHINS
There are five species of dolphin in the Caribbean: the *bufeo* or *tonina* that can be seen in aquariums (at Xcaret, for example); the *manchado* (*Stenella frontalis*) which travels the open sea in bands of up to a thousand individuals; *Stenella attenuata* and the *giradora* dolphin (*Stenella longirostris*), well-known to fishermen; and, living alongside the above species, the smaller and much rarer *Steno bredanensis*.

Fruit sellers in Yucatán at the end of the 19th century.

intestinal secretion used as a fixative for scents in perfumes is also in demand. The rorqual or fin-back whale (*Balaenoptera physalus*) is the largest species (80 feet long) found in the Caribbean, while the orca or killer whale (*Orcinus orca*) is the most common. The best known species in Yucatán is the *ah k'anxoc* or pilot whale (*Globicephala macrochynchus*), so called because it is thought that bands of fifty or sixty individuals often follow one male, who acts as their guide. This is the species that is most frequently found beached and in 1985 there was a mass "suicide" at Xpet Há in northern Yucatán. The fishermen of Holbox were experts at hunting this whale.

MUYIL

From Tulum a road heads south towards Chan Santa Cruz, modern Felipe Carrillo Puerto, the former capital of the insurgent Indians of the Caste War ▲ 186. For over 60 miles, the road runs through what was, up to twenty years ago, thick jungle. Today it is an uninteresting expanse of vast, deforested areas and *ranchos*. About 15 miles south of Tulum, on the road to Chetumal, the ruins of Muyil (also known as Chunyaxché) appear on a rocky promontory on the Laguna de Chunyaxché. The first surveys indicated that the site had been occupied continuously from the 1st century AD to the time of the Spanish Conquest. A *sacbé* (raised causeway) linked the ceremonial center with the lagoon 3 miles away. Six edifices are still standing along the *sacbé*, at intervals of 130 yards. With the exception of the edifice furthest from the lagoon, they all face west. The *Castillo*, situated mid-way along the causeway, and almost 70 feet above the level of the lagoon, supports a circular tower which is the only one of its kind in Mayan archeology.

FELIPE CARRILLO PUERTO

During the Caste War the insurgent Maya (*cruzob*), driven back by the federal troops of Yucatán in 1849, regrouped around a *cenote* in the jungle. And then a miracle occurred: a "Talking Cross" appeared at Kampocolché and promised the Maya a decisive victory. The "little sacred cross" became "Chan Santa Cruz" and its sanctuary the center of a new power. A huge church, the Balam Na, was built in its honor and surrounded by a vast complex of residences, barracks and training grounds. It was here that the *Tatich* or patron of the Cross – the supreme chief – resided, as did his aide-de-camp, the *Tata*

Nohuch Zul or chief of spies (who infiltrated the enemy camp to prepare the attacks), and the *Tata Polin*, the interpreter of the Cross. The rest of the town's population was made up of Servants of the Cross, garrison soldiers who came regularly from the surrounding villages to do their turn on guard duty, and European and Indian slaves used for the building work.

PLACES OF WORSHIP. The *cenote* (left) where the cross appeared and the tiny sanctuary built to commemorate the event can still be seen at the intersection of streets 69 and 58. Several sanctuaries were built, including the sanctuary of Tumul where a woman called Maria Huicab officiated. The great Balam Na became a Catholic church and the barracks behind it were converted into schools. The tiny chapel at the side of the church was built by the Mayan general Francisco May. In 1901 when the town was occupied by federal troops, several villages vied for the honor of hiding the Talking Cross, and the modest churches of the Indian villages continued to preach the cult. Today on May 3 (Santa Cruz) the Maya still visit the small *cenote* of Carrillo Puerto where the Cross first spoke to them, and they still believe that the tower of the Balam Na will not be finished until they once more have control over their own destiny.

BACALAR LAGOON

The lagoon (right), known as the Laguna de Siete Colores, is linked to the Bahia de Chetumal (Chetumal Bay). About 20 miles before Chetumal, a turning leads to the *Cenote Azul* which, with a depth of 295 feet, is one of the most impressive sinkholes after Chichén Itzá ▲ *205*. The road continues along the lake to the village of Bacalar. This once densely populated region declined rapidly after the Spanish Conquest. The village of Salamanca de Bacalar, founded in 1544 by Gaspar Pacheco, was abandoned after an Indian uprising. The village was rebuilt during the 17th century, but remained under constant threat from marauding pirates who plundered it several times, and was eventually abandoned once again. During the first quarter of the 18th century the governor, Antonio Figueroa, built a fort (now a museum) there to

Fresco from Chichén Itzá ▲ *205* representing life in a Yucatecan village during the pre-Hispanic era.

XCALAK
Mid-way between Carrillo Puerto and Chetumal, a road leads to the peninsula of Xcalak. After Majahual a track follows the coast north to Punta Herrero and south to Xcalak. This region has a number of unexplored archeological sites. Although the existence of the coastal sites has been recorded, nothing is known of the interior. During the colonial era the region served as a refuge for the Maya fleeing Spanish

domination. In 1900 the army built a lighthouse and station at Xcalak and a lighthouse at Punta Herrero.

185

During the second half of the 19th century the Yucatán Peninsula was shaken by a violent conflict between the Maya and Europeans. The Indians, heavily taxed by the government, saw their ancestral lands being taken from them. Their chiefs, whose privileges were threatened by liberal laws and the European abuses of power, launched a violent campaign which intensified from 1847 onward. The insurgents held a large territory until the end of the 19th century, but were eventually defeated.

BEGINNING OF THE INSURRECTION

In July 1847 the public execution of one of the Indian rebels and the burning of the Maya village of Tepich and its inhabitants provoked a full-scale insurrection by the Maya in eastern Yucatán. The Indians gave free rein to their hatred of the Europeans, attacking villages, burning, massacring and destroying anything that reminded them of their oppressors.

RECONQUERING THE MAYA

The Maya, armed by English settlers in Belize, regained 90 percent of their ancestral lands and established outposts 5 miles from Campeche and 15 miles from Mérida. But when panic was at its height the Maya inexplicably withdrew to their villages. The Europeans regrouped and, with the end of the war between the United States and Mexico in 1848, were able to procure arms and reinforcements. The Maya were driven back and regrouped around Chan Santa Cruz where they founded the cult of the Talking Cross. Inspired by the oracle that promised them victory, they resisted vigorously for several years.

At the end of the 19th century the Indians, weakened by disease and deprived of weapons, fell easy prey to federal troops who, in 1901, occupied Chan Santa Cruz, (right) following a Mayan withdrawal. Thus, after fifty years of independence, their ancestral lands became federal territory under military control.

Stucco mask from Kohunlich.

observe the English who were in the process of moving into Belize ▲ *335*. In 1859, during the Caste War, the village was captured by the Maya who massacred the population. It was not recaptured until 1901.

CHETUMAL

Chetumal was founded in 1898 following the signing of the Spencer-Mariscal treaty, in accordance with which Mexico recognized the borders of British Honduras (now Belize). A pontoon built in New Orleans was anchored in the bay opposite the village of Payo Obispo from where a watch could be kept on the illegal trade in arms and tropical hardwoods which were being brought down the Río Hondo. Soon the refugees from the Caste War returned from Belize and the village of Payo Obispo began to develop. The name Chetumal probably means "place of red wood" (*chacté*). In 1915 the regional government was transferred from Chan Santa Cruz to Chetumal which became the capital. Situated in a hurricane zone, it was destroyed several times – first in 1916, then in 1942 and, most violently, in 1945 by Hurricane Janet. With a population of 120,000, Chetumal (left) is a modern city and an important trading center for the neighboring villages of Quintana Roo and Belize. As yet Chetumal does not have a well-developed tourist industry.

RÍO HONDO. The Río Hondo forms the natural border between Mexico and Belize. From Chetumal you can travel up the river by boat as far as the village of Subteniente López. Alternatively you can take a boat along the coast to the Laguna Milagros and the town of Calderitas where you can sample the local seafood by the water's edge. The few archeological sites in this region are either unexplored or, like Ichpaatún, have been destroyed.

AROUND CHETUMAL. A road runs west from Chetumal to Ucum, 15 miles away, where it forks south to Belize, crossing the border at La Unión 53 miles away. The other fork leads west to Francisco Escárcega 180 miles away, passing through Kohunlich and the various sites of central Yucatán (Río Bec) ▲ *190*. Beyond Francisco Escárcega, it is possible to continue all the way to Palenque ▲ *243* and Campeche ▲ *228*.

Kohunlich

About 43 miles west of Chetumal, on the main Escárcega road, a track leads south for about 5 miles to the ruins of Kohunlich, a site occupied from the Preclassic to the Postclassic periods. Excavations and restoration work begun in the late 1970's were resumed on a more extensive scale in 1992.

Cattle breeding is one of the traditional economic resources of the Yucatán Peninsula.

Plaza Mayor. Three smooth steles stand on the entrance steps to this great Late Classic plaza. Below them lies a stone altar. At right angles to the entrance is a long platform, lined by various buildings whose doors are flanked by twin columns.

Temple of the Masks. The Temple of the Masks stands at the far end of Kohunlich, beyond numerous structures, including a large ball court ● *112*. Painted stucco masks (opposite page) decorate the four steps of this Early Classic pyramid, on either side of the staircase. They have been protected from the elements and vandals by the construction of a later pyramid over the first. This second pyramid still covers the base of the first. The masks on Steps 2 and 3 have human faces, the symbol *kin* (sun) in their eyes and incisors carved in the form of a T. They are seen inside the jaws of a serpent, most probably representing the sky, formed by two vertical jaws joined by a celestial band (the symbol *lamat*, star, can be seen below the left-hand mask of the third step). Each face is framed by two masks, one on its head and the other under its chin. The ear ornaments are surmounted by a fish mask and extended below by a serpent's mask. On the fourth step the human face is replaced by that of a jaguar beneath a large *kin* symbol. The masks of this pyramid represent the ceremonial aspects of the sun – the star itself and the king with whom it was associated.

Dzibanché. The ruins of Dzibanché lie about 18 miles north of Kohunlich, in a region which was clearly well-populated during the pre-Colombian era and where a great deal of archeological work is being carried out. The ruins have been intensively excavated since 1992. Some remarkable tombs have been discovered in the large pyramids forming part of the main group. Further results of the excavations are awaited with great anticipation.

The silk cotton tree ■ *28*
The silk cotton tree, the Cosmic Tree of the Maya, towers above the villages of Yucatán and is sometimes seen by the roadside (drawing by P. Langlois, late 19th century).

XPUHIL ★

The town of Xpuhil is situated on the road from Chetumal to Francisco Escárcega, just inside the state of Campeche. The ancient ruins of Xpuhil lie just beyond the town. Most of the excavated and restored structures date from the Postclassic period. However, the largest edifice (No. 1) is typical of the earlier Río Bec style which developed between AD 600 and 830 in the northern central lowlands.

TERRESTRIAL MONSTERS. The region designated by archeologists as Río Bec (named after one of its sites), and the more northerly and lesser-known region of Chenes (incorporating the sites of Hochob, Dzibilnocac and Xtampak), are characterized by temples whose doors represent the jaws of the terrestrial monster. These purely decorative temples, which stand on pyramidal towers, are found only in Río Bec architecture.

THREE "DUMMY" PYRAMIDS ● 108. The body of the main edifice (No. 1) at Xpuhil has three additional elements. Each of the outer entrances is surmounted by a frontal mask of the terrestrial monster, with the opening corresponding to its jaws. Stylized masks of this same creature, mainly portrayed in profile and bas-relief, are superposed on either side of the entrance, emphasizing that the edifice represents the earth. The staircases of the structure's three pyramidal towers slope at an angle of 70° and serve no functional purpose. In the center of the staircase huge frontal masks, also of the terrestrial monster, break the monotony of the vast expanse of stonework. The three dummy pyramids are surmounted

TROMPE-L'OEIL
The pyramids of Becán (Structures 1 and 4, above) and Xpuhil (opposite and below, in a reconstruction by Tatiana Proskouriakoff ● 60) are sometimes surmounted by dummy temples with trompe-l'oeil staircases.

Western Yucatán

CRUCERO GANADO

1. MÉRIDA 2. IZAMAL 3. PISTÉ 4. CHICHÉN ITZÁ 5. VALLADOLID 6. MAYAPÁN 7. TEABO 8. MANÍ

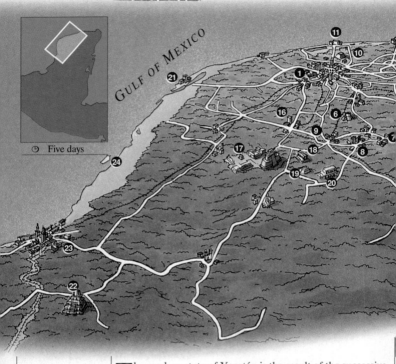

GULF OF MEXICO

🕐 Five days

The characteristically high windows, protected by wrought-iron grilles, of the houses of the aristocracy in the center of Mérida.

The modern state of Yucatán is the result of the successive divisions, begun in the 19th century, of a territory which once covered the entire Yucatán Peninsula. Today it covers a triangular area of 15,425 square miles bordered by the Gulf of Mexico to the north, the state of Campeche to the south, and Quintana Roo to the east. Most of the state's 1,365,000 inhabitants are of Maya origin. The climate is warm and wet virtually all year. From November to March, breezes from the north bring cooler evening temperatures, while from April to September, the streets of the capital, Mérida, are flooded by tropical rains. The rainwater is absorbed by the chalky soil and collects beneath the layer of surface rock and in the *cenotes* (*dzonot* in Maya) ■ *16*. Yucatán is the home of sisal (*Agave sisalana*), grown during the pre-Hispanic period for its fiber. During the 19th century it brought prosperity to the region, but the dispersion of the crop (now grown in Brazil and Tanzania) and competition from artificial fibers, soon put an end to the sisal "boom". The only evidence of this short-lived period of prosperity are the palatial French-style residences in the center of Mérida and the former haciendas – now mostly abandoned – whose distinctive, tall, brick chimneys can be seen from the roads.

CARIBBEAN SEA

ECONOMY.
Today Yucatán produces honey, salt and building materials. In the foothills of the mountains that run east-west across the peninsula, vegetables and citrus fruit are grown in the pockets of alluvial soil between Ticul and Oxkutzcab. Throughout the region, peasants use traditional methods of cultivation to grow vegetables for their own consumption. In the east, cattle are bred on the coastal pastures of the Tizimín region, while along the coast boats from Progreso and the neighboring ports catch local varieties of fish and octopus. Over recent years, the *maquiladoras* (assembly industries), which require a large workforce, have created new jobs in the region. In the clothing industry, for example, ready-cut material is imported from the United States, sewn together in Yucatán, and re-exported to the North.

TOURISM. Archeological sites such as Chichén Itzá ▲ 205 and Uxmal ▲ 218 attract large numbers of visitors. Other tourist attractions in the region include Río Lagartos and Celestún, the largest flamingo sanctuaries in America. Hammocks, embroidered *huipiles* and local shirts (*guayaberas*) are the goods most sought-after by tourists.

TRADITIONAL DRESS
Yucatecan women often wear, white dresses with brightly colored embroidery around the hem and neck. Unlike in the highlands ● 94 this is the only form of traditional dress worn on the peninsula today.

Horse-drawn vehicle in Mérida at the turn of the century.

197

A ncient Tiho, or Ichcanziho, was one of the principal towns in the Maya province of Chacán. On January 6, 1542

Francisco de Montejo, known as El Mozo, confirmed the Spanish occupation of the region by founding the town of Mérida on the ancient site (the Mayan ruins reminded the conquistadors of the Roman ruins of Mérida in Spain). The town's layout is the same as that used for all colonial towns in America: a central square with parallel streets intersecting at right angles ● *123*.

PLAZA MAYOR

"The town of Mérida, built with the materials of the Indian city, is, like all Spanish towns in the New World, little more than a vast checkerboard of straight streets and perfectly square buildings. The large central plaza has today been transformed into a modern square."
Désiré Charnay
Voyage au Yucatán et au pays des Lacandons (1882)

The Cathedral (pictured in the 19th century, above, and today, left) and the bishop's residence were built on the east side of the Plaza Mayor. The Palacio Montejo, built for the conquistador, originally occupied the entire south side, but the building was subsequently divided up and is today flanked by a number of other buildings. To the west is the Palacio Municipal and, to the north, the Palacio del Gobierno and other official residences. These buildings have been modified over the years, with the bishop's residence being replaced by the offices of the federal authorities, which have in turn been replaced by the MUSEUM OF MODERN ART. Other late 19th-century "modernizations" have replaced some of the older buildings, and arcades have been built along the north side of the square. Although it has undergone some major modifications over the centuries (it has been open, enclosed by grilles, and has had a central kiosk and a flagpole) the Plaza has retained its essentially park-like atmosphere where visitors and inhabitants can walk or sit in the shade of the Weeping Figs (*Ficus benjamina*).

CASA DE MONTEJO. Built between 1543 and 1551, the Casa de Montejo is one of the oldest residences in Mérida. All that remains of the original structure is the sculpted Plateresque façade (19th century, far left, and today, left). Its entrance depicts the Montejo coat of arms flanked by two armed conquistadors with their feet standing on grimacing heads (the symbol of the Conquest). The scene is completed by several other figures and motifs. Today the residence has been transformed into a bank.

CATHEDRAL. The cathedral, built between 1562 and 1598, was the first to be completed on the American continent. It was based on a basilican layout, with three naves and twelve pillars, and its distinctive dome is the oldest in Mexico. In the center of the austere façade, with its two Renaissance-style towers and three entrances, a huge blazon bore the Spanish coat of arms. This was replaced, after Independence, by the Mexican eagle. Its layout and decoration were partly modified as a result of the damage sustained in 1915 during the Revolution ● 40. The two side chapels on the south side were destroyed, while venerated sculptures such as the *Christ of the Blisters*, the altar, the organ and other works of art and furnishings were burnt. The Cathedral houses important archives and a collection of ancient paintings.

PALACIO MUNICIPAL. The palace (below) stands on the site of an ancient pyramid from which materials were used to construct the Cathedral, the Casa de Montejo and other buildings in the town. The original 17th-century structure has undergone several transformations, including the addition of a tower completely out of harmony with the architectural style of the town.

PALACIO DEL GOBIERNO. The present Palacio del Gobierno – a two-story building with a central courtyard, built on the site of the former "royal residences" – was opened in 1892. It is famous for the paintings (which trace the region's history) decorating its corridors and a so-called "history" room. They are the work of one of the last great Mexican mural artists, Fernando Castro Pacheco.

MONASTERIES

During the colonial era the town was divided into "ethnic" districts. The Spanish occupied the town center while the *barrios* (outlying districts) were inhabited by the Maya, Blacks and Mexicans (Atzcapotzalco Indians who accompanied the Spanish troops). The original layout was gradually modified and by the 17th century the town occupied a vast square area delimited by stone arches, three of which still exist (Arcos de los Dragones, del Puente, de San Juan). Several monasteries were built in the town.

MONASTERY OF SAN FRANCISCO. The huge Monastery of San Francisco was built on the ruins of an ancient pyramid. The site was chosen to construct a fortification which would protect the town against attack by marauding pirates. A defensive wall enclosed the monastery, but it was not strong enough: it was abandoned and plundered in 1820 when its archives were destroyed.

MONASTERY OF LA MEJADORA. This beautiful 17th-century complex (Calles 59 and 50) today is occupied by a church, an architectural college and the MUSEO DE ARTES POPULARES.

THE STREETS OF MÉRIDA
The streets of Mérida are all numbered. With the exception of a few squares, none of the city center's main thoroughfares has a name. The streets running north–south have even numbers, while those running east–west have odd numbers. The residential districts to the north of the town, with their shady avenues and brightly colored *Delonix regia* and cascades of golden *Cassia fistula* flowers are a great advertisement for life in the tropics. In spite of its city-center traffic jams and the deafening noise of traffic, Mérida is a delightful town which still bears the marks of its secular history.

THE MUNICIPAL MARKET
The central market (above) was built on the site of the ruined monastery of San Francisco. Calles 65 and 67, opposite Calle 56, are reserved for local crafts.

MONASTERY OF NUESTRA SEÑORA DE LA CONSOLACIÓN. The monastery, known today as Las Monjas, was founded in 1633 as a residence for the Sisters of the Immaculate Conception. It has a distinctive arcaded tower. The church is still open to the public although the monastery is occupied by a workshop and CULTURAL CENTER.

CHURCHES

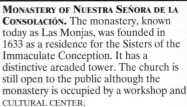

Although many of the original buildings in Mérida were subsequently converted, the churches (each *barrio* had its own church and square) tended to be preserved.

HERMITAGE OF SANTA ISABEL. The Hermitage of Santa Isabel (19th century and today, opposite) is situated on the outskirts of Mérida, on the old Campeche road. This elegant but modest, single-nave structure, which stands alone in its garden (a converted square), is today a refuge for walkers.

Iglesia de Jésus and its square in the 19th century and today.

Many churches are reminders of the colonial era: the Iglesia de Jésus (left), built by the Jesuits in the 17th-century; the 18th-century Iglesia de San Cristóbal; Santa Lucia, which stands opposite a tiny arcaded square where public musical evenings are held every Thursday; Santa Ana, Itzimná, San Sebastián, La Candelaria, Santiago and, finally, San Juan Bautista, where the first liberals met on the eve of Independence to develop a political system more favorable to the Indians.

UNIVERSITY OF YUCATÁN

The Colegio de San Pedro de la Real y Pontificia Universidad de San Francisco Javier, founded by the Jesuits in 1624, used to occupy the land between the Iglesia de Jésus and the present site of the Teatro Peón Contreras (opposite). In 1711 the seminary of San Pedro was founded on the site of the present university. The university closed long before the Jesuits were expelled in 1767. After Independence in 1824, the seminary buildings were occupied by the Literary University until it was closed in 1861.

It reopened in 1864 as the Real Universidad Literaria and became a Literary Institute in 1867. It lost its university status in 1869, but had it restored in 1922 by decree of the governor Felipe Carrillo Puerto. In 1984, it became the autonomous University of Yucatán. The old Jesuit building was transformed by the addition of an upper story and the entrance porch on the corner of Calles 60 and 57.

❝Yucatán... is covered by a vast underwood... you can try climbing to the top of the pyramids, but you will still see the same continuous, unbroken, desolate horizon. But Yucatán is favored by travelers, for it is a land rich in memories: extraordinary monuments, beautiful women, picturesque costumes... things that leave a lasting impression. It appeals

to the heart, soul, imagination and mind. Anyone who can leave Yucatán with indifference, has never been an artist and will never be a scholar.❞
  Désiré Charnay
  Un Voyage au Yucatán
  (1860)

OLD CORN EXCHANGE. The old corn exchange (Calles 65 and 56), built beneath the arcades which today are occupied by small businesses, has retained all the atmosphere of the old colonial markets.

URBAN DEVELOPMENT

PASEO DE MONTEJO. The town expanded rapidly and, from the early 20th century, the main avenue – the Paseo de Montejo – was enhanced by palatial residences such as the

one which today houses the MUSEO DE ARQUEOLOGIA (on the corner of Calle 43), built by General Francisco Cantón, the then governor of the state. A number of these beautiful edifices were subsequently replaced by modern buildings of somewhat dubious taste. At the end of the Paseo de Montejo, a monument by the Colombian sculptor Romulo Rosso gives an account of the country's history in bas-relief.

AVENIDA ITZÁ. During the same period, a number of buildings were erected at the western end of the town along the Avenida Itzá which today leads to the airport. They included the Benito Juárez prison complex and the hospital. Some of these buildings have been converted into the CULTURAL INSTITUTE. Opposite the Institute is the EL CENTENARIO ZOO AND PARK, created to mark the centenary celebrations of Independence.

PARKS AND SERVICES. After the 1910 Revolution the town underwent further development, this time in the field of public services and parks. The Parque de las Américas has many fountains and an open-air theater, built in a neo-Mayan style typical of the 1940's and 1950's.

TEATRO JOSÉ PEÓN CONTRERAS
With the boom in sisal production, Mérida experienced a remarkable period of development during the second half of the 19th century. The colonial houses with their austere façades were demolished or renovated. A new wave of European-style buildings appeared throughout the town. A European-style theater (left), with marble columns, a large dome and frescos, was built on the site of the university.

STUCCO MASK
This lithograph by Frederick Catherwood depicts a stucco mask on a pyramid at Izamal, with an imaginary jaguar hunt in the foreground. Today, unfortunately, jaguars are rarely seen in northern Yucatán.

IZAMAL ★

● *118*

Izamal (above and right), the most beautiful colonial town in Yucatán, lies about 12 miles north of Kantunil (on the Mérida-Cancún road). Before the Conquest it was a prosperous, ancient city which had been occupied from the Preclassic period onwards and had the largest pyramids in Yucatán. The temples were dedicated to the worship of Itzamná – "Lizard House", patron of learning and the sciences and inventor of writing – and to Kinich Kakmo, the Sun God. Several pyramids survive today and are currently being restored, including the small pyramid behind the arcaded plaza built by the Spanish (above), and the pyramid dedicated to the Sun.

BUILDING THE MONASTERY. Until the Spanish occupied the region, Izamal was a place of pilgrimage for the Maya. The friars saw it as their religious duty to convert the Indians to Christianity. Diego de Landa ● 55 demolished one of their temples – the Popolchac, dedicated to the Rain gods – so that a monastery could be built on its vast platform (570 yards long by 470 yards wide and 40 feet high).

Work on the monastery began in 1553 under the direction of the Franciscan architect, Juan de Mérida, who designed and built the most important monasteries in the region. The monastery, church and atrium were completed by 1561, while the additional buildings and arcades were not finished until the first half of the 17th century.

AN IMPRESSIVE COMPLEX. The Izamal complex is the largest of its kind in America. Three ramps on the sides of the atrium give access to the complex. The principal ramp was

surmounted by a magnificent triumphal arch. The arch opened on either side onto the arcades surrounding the atrium where a chapel with a pyramidal roof was built in each of the four corners. In 1880 a small, rather unprepossessing tower was added to the simple but robust original façade of the church, while the former open chapel was converted into the chapel of La Tercera. The venerated statue of the Virgin of Izamal (left) – the patron saint of Mérida and Yucatán – still stands behind the chancel. The statue, as well as a copy, were commissioned in Guatemala and destined for Mérida and Valladolid, but on leaving Izamal the porters felt that the statue was growing heavier and heavier the further they got from the town. Instead of proceeding to their destinations, they returned to Izamal with the statue and installed it in the sanctuary which soon became a place of pilgrimage. The original statue, destroyed by fire in 1829, was replaced by a copy.

❝The third pyramid, to the east, supported a temple dedicated to Ytzamat-ul, Itzamna or Zamna, described as the founder of Izamal. According to the 17th-century writer, Lizana 'This king or false god was represented by the Indians in the form of a hand ... and they say that the sick and the dead were brought to him and that the god cured them by touching them with his hand; and that is why the temple is called Kab-ul, which means the industrious hand, the miraculous hand.' The temple, where so many miracles were performed, was the object of numerous pilgrimages...❞

Désiré Charnay
Voyage au Yucatán et au pays des Lacandons

"CENOTES" ■ *16*
● *114*
The *cenote* of Zaci
(above), at
Valladolid, lies in a
garden. Its vaulted
depths and dark
waters are extremely
impressive. The
cenote of Dzitnup
(top), one of the most
beautiful in Yucatán,
lies about 3 miles
from Valladolid, in
the direction of
Chichén Itzá.

Plaza Principal in
Valladolid. The twin
towers of the church
were a common
feature of colonial
religious architecture.

BALANKANCHÉ CAVES

The Maya venerated all caves and these
dark and mysterious places are still the
sites for secret acts of worship today. The
Balankanché Caves, about 10 miles from
Valladolid, were discovered in 1959. A
rocky passageway leads to the
underground chambers where objects
from the Toltec period, presented as
offerings, can still be seen as they were
left. At the end of the passage is a pool,
lost in the darkness. There is a botanical
garden near the entrance.

VALLADOLID

After Mérida, Valladolid is the most
important town in Yucatán. It was
founded in 1543 by Montejo ▲ *198* on the
ruins of ancient Zaci (pronounced Zaki) and, with Mérida,
Campeche and Bacalar, was one of the four main Spanish
towns on the Yucatán peninsula. Valladolid was badly
damaged by fire during the Caste War ▲ *186* and will never
recover its former splendor.
SISAL CONVENT. When the Spanish occupied ancient Zaci,
they built a church and convent on the outskirts of the town,
in the neighborhood of Sisal, in order to preach the Gospel to
the Indians. The convent was deconsecrated in 1755 and
gradually abandoned until restoration work began in the
1970's. Sisal is a distortion of the Maya word *sis-ha* meaning
"cold water" and the convent was so called because it was
built near a *cenote*. The convent, church and open chapel,
designed by the architect Juan de Mérida, were completed
in 1560. Strangely, the open chapel was built onto the
side of the church rather than the façade of the
convent. Its palm-leaf roof still existed at the
beginning of the 19th century. It is now known as
the chapel of San Marco.
CONVENT CHURCH OF SAN BERNADINO
This single-nave church is 50 yards
long by 11½ yards wide, and has
a vaulted apse, decorated
with Gothic-type ribs. The
cloister is 22 yards square, the
largest in Yucatán after that
of Izamal (23 yards square).
Of the seven surviving
retables, that of San Antonio
is one of the most beautiful
examples of the early 18th
century. The chancel retable
is still attached to the wall
with reeds dating from the
18th century. The church had
a statue of the Virgin of
Guadalupe and was the first in
Yucatán to worship the
Mexican Virgin.

CHICHÉN ITZÁ ★

● *34, 112*

HISTORY. Chichén Itzá is one of the most famous and spectacular of the Mayan sites. At the end of the Classic period it was a small town, possibly even then called Itzá, which was soon subjected to Putún influence or occupation. The term "Putún" (or "Chontal") is used to designate various "Mexicanized" Maya groups of merchants and warriors who had settled along the coast of the Gulf of Mexico and who, at various points throughout history, introduced "Mexican" characteristics to Yucatán. These are already noticeable in the Puuc ▲ *220* architecture of Chichén Itzá. The strength of Puuc influence varied across the north and center of the Yucatán Peninsula and was very noticeable in the Uxmal region. In the 10th century a group of Putún Maya, almost certainly with the assistance of Toltec warriors, established a new capital at Chichén Itzá. Their chief bore the Mexican title of Quetzalcoatl, the Feathered Serpent, translated into Mayan by Kukulcán. This Putún occupation lasted for more than two centuries, confining itself to Chichén Itzá and demanding tributes and allegiance from other Mayan provinces.

DECLINE. According to Mayan chronicles of the colonial period, the circumstances surrounding the abandonment of Chichén Itzá were never fully understood. It is probable that Toltec domination ended as a result of the repeated attacks of a group of Mexicanized Maya from Tabasco who belonged to

Valladolid (above) and the Christ of San Bernadino (below), whose church dates from the 17th century.

the tribe of the Itzás. This group took up residence in the city and called it "well of the Itzás", a name that it retained up to the time of the Conquest. The pilgrimage involved throwing offerings into the *cenote*, a manifestation of the Rain God. This ritual continued to exist after the Toltecs left and the cult was secretly maintained throughout the colonial period.

CHICHÉN ITZA
1. El Castillo
2. Temple of the Warriors
3. Group of the Thousand Columns
4. Temple of the Jaguar
5. Ball Court
6. Sacred *Cenote*
7. El Caracol
8. Nunnery
9. Tzompantli
10. Tomb of the High Priest

▲ CHICHÉN ITZÁ

Chichén Itzá, mid-way between Mérida and Cancún, is undoubtedly the best-known of the Mayan sites. It was originally a small Puuc town which, as a result of direct Putún and indirect Toltec influence from the 11th to the 13th centuries, became the most important city in Maya territory and the "Mecca" of Mayan pilgrimages. Unlike other Mayan cities, which remained forgotten for centuries, Chichén Itzá was quickly discovered by the Spanish during the Conquest.

ARCHEOLOGY

The site has always been well known. In the 16th century its *cenote* ● 117 made it a place of pilgrimage and Diego de Landa described it in his *Relación de las Cosas de Yucatán*. The first archeological research, undertaken in 1841–2 by Stephens and Catherwood ● 56, was continued in the late 19th century by Maler, Maudslay and Holmes. In c. 1900 Edward Thompson, the United-States consul in Yucatán, bought and took up residence in the Chichén hacienda from where he carried out excavations and dragged part of the *cenote* on behalf of the Peabody Museum. Large-scale excavations were begun in 1924 by the Carnegie Institution team, under the direction of Sylvanus Morley, but although the larger edifices were excavated and restored, the cultural chronology of the site still had to be compiled, since various structures could not be dated precisely.

NUNNERY
On the Puuc-style entrance to the Nunnery, the jaws of the terrestrial monster are represented by a row of teeth above the lintel. Higher up, in the recess of the monster's forehead, is an image of a seated sovereign. The rest of the façade is covered in frontal masks.

PUUC STYLE ▲ 220
Chichén Itzá's Puuc-style edifices, attributed to the Terminal Classic period, are found in the southern section of the site, while the Early Postclassic structures, with their characteristic "Mexican" additions, are located in the northern section.

TEMPLE OF THE JAGUAR

Behind the huge ball court, this low temple, decorated with warriors in bas-relief, was partially covered by the pyramid of the upper temple.

The temple's façade is decorated with Toltec-inspired friezes, showing a procession of jaguars and shields.

EL CASTILLO ● 108

El Castillo stands in the center of the great, square plaza, in the northern section of the site. It consists of two superposed temple-pyramids dating from the Early Postclassic period. The first, consisting of nine, sloping terraces and a single staircase, was surmounted by a two-roomed temple with vertical walls and no serpent-columns ▲ 210, and a single entrance to the north. The Mexican decorative elements were interspersed with a procession of jaguars, round fringed shields and a *chacmool* ▲ 211. The second pyramid also had nine sloping terraces with rectangles in relief, becoming increasingly thin towards the top to emphasize the overall effect of height, and four staircases, each of 91 steps, with handrails in the form of serpents. The 364 steps, added to the step of the temple entrance, symbolize the 365 days of the solar year.

At the top is a temple with four entrances. The main entrance, to the north, is flanked by serpent-columns. The central sanctuary is preceded by a vestibule and surrounded by a passageway.

▲ CHICHÉN ITZÁ

BALL COURT
The ball court (180 yards long by 75 yards wide) is not only the largest of the thirteen courts ● *112* discovered at Chichén, but also the largest in the whole of Mesoamerica. It has markers on the vertical walls on either side of the central

aisle. At the foot of the walls a sloping bench is covered with bas-reliefs representing two teams witnessing the decapitation of the captain of the losing team. Certain elements of the ball game, which dated from the Postclassic period, were the result of Central Mexican (walls and rings) and Gulf coast (bas-reliefs of Tajín) influence.

CASA COLORADA
This reconstruction (below) by Tatiana Proskouriakoff ● *60* shows the *Casa Colorada* ("Red House"), a rather austere, Puuc-style edifice, on which all the decoration appears above roof level on the façade and on the projecting ridge. Beyond the house, to the right, is El Caracol. Tatiana Proskouriakoff imagined the site as it must have been when it was occupied, with a few inhabitants and priests officiating at an imagined ritual.

EL CARACOL

This circular structure, which stands on two superposed, rectangular platforms, was built during different periods: the *caracol* itself is more recent than its platforms. Round edifices, which appeared in Yucatán (there is one at Uxmal ▲ *219*) during the Terminal Classic, were "imported" from central Mexico where they are traditionally associated with Quetzalcoatl in the form of the Wind God. In the center a spiral staircase (*caracol* is the Spanish word for "snail") leads to a small room pierced with square openings, whose directions appear to have some astronomical significance. El Caracol (below) in the 19th century and in its present, restored state.

HUMAN SACRIFICE

According to the chroniclers, victims were thrown into the *cenote* at daybreak. If they were still alive at noon, they were pulled out and asked to make predictions for the forthcoming year ● *46*.

SACRED "CENOTE"

The *cenote* is reached along a 300-yard-long specially built causeway or *sacbé*. Archeological excavations have confirmed the account of Diego de Landa concerning the human sacrifices and offerings of precious objects thrown into the *cenote* at the north end of the site, where some fifty skulls and numerous long bones have been discovered. Contrary to the persistent legend that the Maya threw only maidens into these sinkholes, bones from skeletons of both sexes and all ages have been retrieved. Rustic pots were also found which still contained incense, but the most beautiful objects were in copper and gold: disks with repoussé decorations, necklaces, masks, pendants, rings, ear ornaments, bells and beads. While most came from central America, Oaxaca and the Mexican Valley, the repoussé disks

were made locally and illustrate scenes of battle and sacrifice. Fragments of burnt cloth, jade beads, sacrificial knives and bone and shell ornaments were also found.

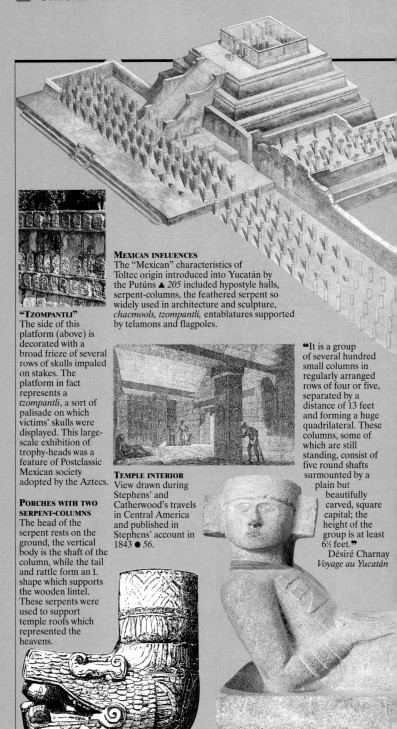

"TZOMPANTLI"
The side of this platform (above) is decorated with a broad frieze of several rows of skulls impaled on stakes. The platform in fact represents a *tzompantli*, a sort of palisade on which victims' skulls were displayed. This large-scale exhibition of trophy-heads was a feature of Postclassic Mexican society adopted by the Aztecs.

PORCHES WITH TWO SERPENT-COLUMNS
The head of the serpent rests on the ground, the vertical body is the shaft of the column, while the tail and rattle form an L shape which supports the wooden lintel. These serpents were used to support temple roofs which represented the heavens.

MEXICAN INFLUENCES
The "Mexican" characteristics of Toltec origin introduced into Yucatán by the Putúns ▲ *205* included hypostyle halls, serpent-columns, the feathered serpent so widely used in architecture and sculpture, *chacmools, tzompantli,* entablatures supported by telamons and flagpoles.

TEMPLE INTERIOR
View drawn during Stephens' and Catherwood's travels in Central America and published in Stephens' account in 1843 ● *56*.

"It is a group of several hundred small columns in regularly arranged rows of four or five, separated by a distance of 13 feet and forming a huge quadrilateral. These columns, some of which are still standing, consist of five round shafts surmounted by a plain but beautifully carved, square capital; the height of the group is at least 6½ feet."
Désiré Charnay
Voyage au Yucatán

210

WALL PAINTINGS

Wall paintings discovered by Stephens in 1841 (of which only traces remain today) decorated the interior walls of the Temple of the Warriors and Temple of the Jaguar. The paintings in the first temple include scenes of battles fought by the sea.

TEMPLE OF THE WARRIORS AND GROUP OF THE THOUSAND COLUMNS

The Temple of the Warriors, whose layout is very obviously inspired by Structure B at Tula ● *34*, is named after the sculptures of Toltec warriors on the pillars of the front portico and those supporting the temple roof. The Thousand Columns are the remains of a series of vast hypostyle meeting halls. The bonded columns have square or round drums and are often sculpted in bas-relief. The exact nature of the roof they supported is not known. It was probably flat and made of beams covered with mortar or thatch, or a corbeled vault.

The frescos in the Temple of the Jaguar show crowded battle scenes dominated by two chiefs. One has the solar disk as his emblem, while the other has the feathered serpent. There is also a village on the edge of a forest populated with animals (reproduced, above, and re-touched by Maudslay ● *56* at the end of the 19th century).

"CHACMOOL"

The *chacmool* is a sculpture representing a reclining man, holding an offerings vessel or tray.

Warrior sculpted in bas-relief on a column (below) and Quetzalcoatl, the Feathered Serpent, in the guise of Venus, the Morning Star (Temple of the Warriors).

TECOH
The village of Tecoh has a 16th-century Franciscan monastery and an 18th-century church (detail of the remains of a window gable, right). The single nave is flanked by side chapels. The baptismal fonts are 16th century, while the three gilt and polychrome retables are 18th century.

MAYAN CITIES
Mayapán was surrounded by a wall and had a population of fifteen thousand. The city's dwellings were constructed partly in stone and preferably on high ground. Thoroughfares were the result of the fairly arbitrary arrangement of the houses and were not based on the grid system used in the towns of the Mexican Valley.

RELIGIOUS STELES
The (thirteen sculpted and twenty-five smooth) steles of Mayapán represent divinities and not, as was the general rule ● 110, political figures.

ACANCEH

Acanceh means "the cry of a stag" in Maya. The church in the center of the village, dedicated to the Virgin of Guadalupe, was built in the 16th century and subsequently modified. The 17th-century façade has an entrance with twisted columns and an entablature at the dividing point between the two parts. Above the entrance, the chancel window is surmounted by a curved pediment. Next to the church are the ruins of a pyramid with four tiers and a central staircase (above) and, about 300 yards further on, the ruins of another, monumental pyramid. The façade of the so-called "Stucco Palace" is decorated with an extremely rare, Late Classic cosmological composition whose main figures are symbolic animals.
TIMUCUY HACIENDA. About 6 miles from Acanceh is the Timucuy hacienda with its central porticoed residence, machine room, chapel and outbuildings. The hacienda is open to the public.

MAYAPÁN ● 35

This important archeological site (Mayapán was one of the Maya capitals) has still not been restored although the Carnegie Institution of Washington have been researching it for five years.
HISTORY. The Mayapán chieftains belonged to the Cocom lineage, descended from a certain Hunac Ceel who captured and destroyed Chichén Itzá ▲ 205 at the beginning of the 13th century. With the decline of Chichén Itzá, Mayapán's importance increased and the city underwent significant changes (due to a new wave of Mexican influence) in the fields of structural and decorative architecture, as well as the birth of a new religion. Just before 1450, one of the noble houses of Mayapán – the Xiú – rebelled against the Cocoms. Shortly afterward Mayapán was plundered and abandoned, leaving the way open for a number of "warring kingdoms" in a state of permanent conflict.
REMAINS. Mayapán has a temple comparable to El Castillo at Chichén Itzá, complete with serpent-columns, serpent handrails, flagpoles and small telamons. But the *chacmools*, ball courts, *tzompantli* and evidence of the worship of jaguars and eagles have all disappeared. The monster-masks and the two- and three-part moldings inherited from the Puuc tradition ▲ 220 can still be seen on a few façades.
RELIGIOUS BUILDINGS. There are two types of ceremonial complex found in Mayapán. One type has a hypostyle hall, a sanctuary and an oratory, while the other has a right-angle temple with a hypostyle hall, an oratory on the vertical side of the temple, a sanctuary

UXMAL AND THE PUUC SITES ★

"RUTA PUUC". The inland road to the region's capital, Campeche, is marked "via ruinas". The excavated and restored sites form a circuit known as the *Ruta Puuc* (Puuc route) which covers the finest examples of Puuc architecture: Uxmal, Kabáh, Sayil and Labná (the four most important), as well as Kiuic, Xlabpak, Oxkintok, Xul, Chamultún and Bakná. These sites, today largely restored, experienced their golden age between AD 800 and 1000. They are characterized by large, elongated structures with sculpted decoration. The Puuc cities collapsed with the arrival of the Toltecs in Yucatán, particularly at Chichén Itzá ▲ *205.* Further south, on Route 261, the Puuc-style ruins of Itzimté lie near the road just before Bolonchén.

HOCHOB AND DZIBILNOCAC. These two accessible and virtually unexplored sites near Hopolchén are fine examples of the splendor of the Chenes style. At Hochob, (the better restored of the two) the façade of the temple, to the right of the plaza, represents the terrestrial monster. Most of the ruins on this vast site are as yet unexcavated and still keep the secrets of the people who lived there. After Dzibilchén and Vicente Guerrero, a track leads to the site of Dzibilnocac. Here the first two temples are disappointing, but the delicacy of the architecture, and the fineness of the frescos and sculptures of the third pyramid make the journey worthwhile. From the top of the temple there is a spectacular view of the surrounding ruins. At Cayal, about 25 miles from Hopolchén, a road leads to Edzná, the most important Maya site in Campeche. Rejoin the road at Cayal and continue to Campeche (32 miles).

Detail of the decoration on the arch of Labná.

UXMAL
1. Nunnery Quadrangle
2. Pyramid of the Magician
3. Ball Court
4. Cemetery Group
5. Palace of the Governor
6. The Turtle House
7. The Pigeon House
8. Great Pyramid

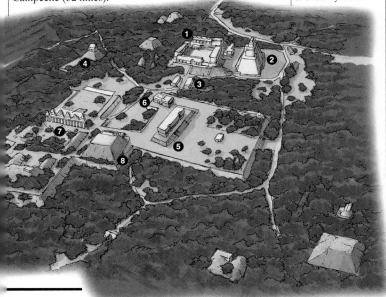

The *Codz pop* of
Kabáh.

The Puuc style takes its name from the range of hills running
northwest-southeast across the north of the Yucatán peninsula,
but its influence extends much further. It made its appearance in
the 8th century and reached its height during the second half of
the 9th century. The style is distinguished by decorative
techniques, which include stone veneering and the inclusion of
mosaics in relief on the upper portion of façades.

ORIGINS

Many of the
characteristics of
central Yucatán ▲ *190*
began to emerge from
770 onwards. These
elements included
basal moldings
decorated with groups
of small drums,
beveled moldings and
small engaged
columns (first single
and then attached).
Terrestrial monster
masks, adopted from
the Chenes tradition,
formed doors and ran
riot over façades.

DOORS

Doors became wider as
columns with capitals
were used to support
the lintel. Labná
(above) and
Sayil (right).

DEVELOPMENT OF THE PUUC STYLE

Early monumental
columns enabled
doors to become
wider, and had a
simple lower molding.
Then engaged
columns with masks
appeared (above, at
Kabáh). Finally, after
870, mosaic
decorations
triumphed over a
limited area
combining engaged
columns with
openwork and fret
motifs.

MOSAIC DECORATIONS

The Puuc style often
used sculpted stone
mosaics composed of
prefabricated
elements. The
decoration
consisted of
openwork, multiple
(keyed or non-keyed)
columns, step-and-fret
motifs and frontal
masks on façades or
superposed on the
corners of buildings,
all geometrically
arranged and repeated.
The mosaic decoration
in relief on the upper
part of the façade of
the Nunnery
Quadrangle at Uxmal
(above), illustrates this
very distinctive style.
The lower parts of
buildings are smooth
and stucco is very
rarely used. The
mosaic is bordered by a
broad molding below
and a cornice above.

VAULT

While the vault
retained its corbeled
shape, the stones
which formed it did
not support anything
and were purely a
veneer.

ARCH OF KABÁH

The arch, in the
Early Puuc style,
stands at the south end
of the causeway linking
Kabáh to Uxmal.

ARCH OF LABNÁ

The palace has three terraced stories, each resting on a stone base, with a broad central staircase (above). The first story is also the oldest. Pillars have been used to widen the doorways and the decoration is limited to a single frieze. The numerous openings on the second story alternate with panels of small, engaged, keyed columns (detail above), while the

Unlike the arch of Kabáh, the arch of Labná (today, below, and drawn by Catherwood, bottom) is not a monumental or triumphal arch but the vaulted passageway of a

quadrangle; a square or rectangular courtyard surrounded by buildings and closed off, apart from a gateway. On the courtyard side, the principal decoration consists of miniature

thatched huts, forming niches that originally contained statues. On the outside the frieze, bordered by the same moldings decorated with broken, zigzag lines and step motifs, comprises two step-and-fret motifs joined edgewise against a background of small, engaged columns. The motif represents the jaws of the terrestrial monster, the symbolic access to the underworld. Monster masks (above).

frieze on the upper part of the wall has masks of the terrestrial monster. The third story, in late Puuc style, was decorated much more soberly with a full-length stucco figure of a man

(strengthened by stone tenons) standing above each door.

Uxmal is one of the best-known and most frequently visited of the Mayan sites due to its relatively good state of preservation (a number of structures are still standing) and the quality of its Puuc-style stone mosaic decorations. Little is known of the origins and development of this important political and economic center which was at its height between AD 800 and 1000. Uxmal's many (mostly undated) steles have revealed the existence of Lord Chac who probably reigned in the early 10th century. The city is characterized by its quadrangles in which large, elongated, multi-roomed edifices form a closed complex around a rectangular or square courtyard.

RESEARCH

In 1836 Waldeck published the first, brief description of the site, visited a few years previously. Although extensive restoration work was begun in 1928 and again in 1938, the site has never been systematically excavated.

PALACE OF THE GOVERNOR

The Late-Puuc palace (9th-10th century) comprises a main building and two wings. It is almost 110 yards long by 13 yards wide, and 28 feet high. Thirteen doors give access to twenty rooms. It has been estimated that the stone mosaic decoration of the façade has some twenty thousand sculpted parts. The two largest rooms, aligned in the central building, are 22 yards long and are connected to the outside by three doors.

DECORATION

The main entrance to the Palace of the Governor is surmounted by an image of the king seated on his throne against a background of two-headed serpents, decorated with celestial symbols (like those on the east building in the Nunnery Quadrangle). Other dignitaries are represented emerging from the open jaws of the terrestrial monster. The decoration is completed by step-and -fret motifs and frontal masks against a background of lattice work (top of page). The main figure represented in the heavens is probably the founder of the dynasty. (Top to bottom and left to right): general view of Uxmal; jaguar throne and Palace of the Governor; two details of façades; and two views of the Palace of the Governor, drawn by the architect Frederick Catherwood ● 58, 130 during his travels with Stephens.

NUNNERY QUADRANGLE

The name of the quadrangle was coined by ancient travelers who compared the closed complex to that of a monastery (above). The courtyard is surrounded by buildings, each with a double row of rooms. The building on the north side of the courtyard (top) appears to be the most important. The eleven-doored façade is decorated with superposed masks of the terrestrial monster and pseudo-Tlaloc masks which alternate with images of huts surmounted by two-headed serpents (detail below). The decoration on the east building consists of several groups of rigid, two-headed serpents which

decrease in length towards the base. On the south façade, huts are surmounted by a mask of the terrestrial monster. The decoration becomes more complex on the west side: as well as the usual superposed masks, there are enthroned figures beneath a dais and warriors in relief, the whole encircled by plumed serpents. Detail of the west façade (below) by Catherwood.

THE PIGEON HOUSE

This residential palace (above) was built between AD 700 and 800 in a style which pre-dates that of the Nunnery Quadrangle. In spite of its rather poor state of preservation, it is known that the exterior walls were once lavishly covered in stucco elements and ornaments. It was named after the long. elaborate roofcomb reminiscent of European dovecotes.

PYRAMID OF THE MAGICIAN

The visible temples represent the two final stages in the construction of the pyramid. On the west side is a Chenes-style temple, an imitation of an earlier, Puuc-style structure. The most recent temple was built at the top of the pyramid. The sculpture (right) is from the first stage of construction of the temple and shows a man's head emerging from a serpent.

A king of Uxmal's head emerging from the jaws of a serpent; Pyramid of the Magician.

THE TURTLE HOUSE

The Turtle House is remarkable for its proportions and simplicity. The frieze consists of an uninterrupted decoration of small, engaged columns between two characteristically Puuc-style dovetail moldings with a central cordon. On the upper cordon is a row of realistically carved, regularly spaced turtles (above). In Maya culture the turtle is one of the creatures that symbolizes the Earth.

MONUMENTS

As well as its quadrangles and the Pyramid of the Magician, Uxmal also has the Great Pyramid, a small ball court and various temples, some of which are still hidden in the undergrowth.

TWO GROUPS
The ancient
structures of Edzná
form two groups,
linked by a *sacbé*
(causeway). The
eastern Group of the
Ceremonial Center
consists of buildings
overlooked by the
Great Acropolis. The
unrestored, western
group is dominated
by a large structure
called La Vieja.

EDZNÁ ★

URBAN CENTER. Edzná is a fine example of the organization of
Mayan society. In 600 BC a group of Maya settled in the
valley, isolated from other population centers, where they
lived continuously until the 10th century. In the 3rd century
AD an urban center developed, which provided a focal point
for the region's surplus agricultural products. Trade links were
established with the region of Petén, in Guatemala ▲ *317,* and
the influence of that area can be seen in the period rituals,
crafts and art of Edzná. The local aristocracy controled the
valley's rural population ordering them to find and build
magnificent temples and palaces.
After the 6th century other
neighboring provinces (Río
Bec ▲ *190*, Chenes and
Puuc) developed to
the east and north,
opening up new
commercial
possibilities.
These may have
included a
community of
merchants from the
Puuc region acting as a
trading post in Edzná.

The
Puuc-
style site of
Iturbide, to the north
of Edzná, drawn by
Catherwood.

NEITHER PUUC NOR CHENES. Edzná,
sometimes included in the Chenes and sometimes the Puuc
region, appears to have retained a certain autonomy and
individuality. Although it was not altogether impervious to the
influence of its powerful neighbors, it remained a tiny,
independent kingdom amidst all the cultural changes
affecting the region. Lubná is the only other site of any
importance recorded in the valley. After the collapse of the
great Maya civilization in the 9th century, Edzná declined in
importance and was abandoned like all the other such towns
and cities. The peasants retreated, probably in the interests of
safety, to the foothills of the valley where they built the
villages of Tixmucuy, Nohyaxché, Hontún and
Bolonchencahuich which still exist today. It is believed that
Lubná may have been another of these villages.

ANNEX OF THE KNIVES
The partially
excavated annex
consists of a central
plaza (44 yards
square), surrounded
by structures dating
from different
periods. An arch links
the plaza to a *sacbé*.
Southwest of the
annex the great
structure known as
the Nohol Na, with
its 394-foot wide
façade, has not yet
been restored.

GROUP OF THE CEREMONIAL CENTER. The group around the
vast Plaza Mayor is largely dominated by the partly restored
Great Acropolis to the east, the Nohol Na to the west, the
Annex of the Knives (Cuchillos) to the north and the Temple
of the House of the South (Casa del Sur) to the south. A
sacbé leads from the Great Acropolis toward a
group of dwellings, situated between the Annex of
the Knives and the Nohol Na, and surrounded
by other structures. This complex is based on
those of Petén and Tikal ▲ *322*.

SMALL ACROPOLIS
A small acropolis, to
the south of the
Great Acropolis,
consists of a 246-foot
square platform on
which four structures
surround a central
courtyard. At the foot
of a ruined temple on
the west side of the
courtyard, steles
dating from 672 to
810 were discovered
on the platform.

PLAZA MAYOR. The rectangular
(185 yards by 105 yards) Plaza Mayor,
formerly covered in stucco, slopes
slightly downward to the south to allow
any rainwater to drain into the canal.

GREAT ACROPOLIS. The impressive Great
Acropolis (its overall height is 100 feet)

> "REGARDLESS OF THE CIRCUMSTANCES THAT CONTRIBUTED TO THIS CLASSIC [PERIOD] BLAZE OF GLORY, NOTHING SO REFINED OR SO VARIED WAS EVER PRODUCED DURING THE PRE-COLUMBIAN ERA."
>
> PAUL GENDROP

stands on a platform (175 yards by 162 yards and 20 feet high) on the east side of the Plaza Mayor. Each of the four (15 foot high) pyramidal tiers of this five-story building consists of rows of cells, while the temple on the top is surmounted by a 20-foot-high crest.

A path links the plaza to a courtyard, in front of the temple-pyramid, which used to contain an altar. From here a central staircase (some of the steps bear glyphs) leads up to the temple. At the entrance to the seven first-story rooms (one beneath the staircase) are the remains of Río Bec-style, cemented stone pillars, while the monolithic columns on the fourth story are in the Puuc style ▲ 220.

The five-story temple-pyramid partly covers an older, Petén-style temple.

To the south of the courtyard a temple, reached via a 57-foot wide staircase, stands on a platform measuring 44 yards by 33 yards. This edifice also covers an older structure. At the southwest corner of its platform stands a temple influenced by the Petén style and a later annex which partly blocks the central staircase.

A similar structure existed at the other end of the staircase, leaving only a narrow access into the courtyard.

Other structures on the Great Acropolis include the Temazcal (steam bath), the northwest temple, the Puuc platform and the north platform.

EXCAVATION
It will take many more years to explore, excavate and restore Edzná, and discover the carefully guarded secrets that lie beneath its stones.

▲ WESTERN YUCATÁN
CAMPECHE

PLUNDER
Yucatán was constantly exposed to attack by pirates, buccaneers, corsairs and enemy warships which sought refuge along its coast and plundered villages to replenish their supplies. Campeche, the only port on the peninsula, was plundered by French pirates in 1559.

Campeche, founded in 1540 by Francisco de Montejo, alias El Mozo ▲ *198, 204* is the oldest Spanish town on the Yucatán Peninsula and the only import and export point for the region's products. Situated on a flat coastline, with no natural land or sea defenses, it was an easy target for pirates. Accordingly, a 26-foot-high enclosure wall was built around the town, with protective bastions and coastal batteries. The wall was opened up toward the end of the 19th century to allow the town to expand more freely. Today, vast areas of land have been reclaimed outside the old wall and modern buildings have totally altered the landscape of Campeche's golden age.

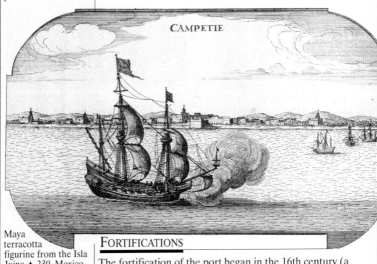

CAMPETIE

Maya terracotta figurine from the Isla Jaina ▲ *230,* Mexico National Museum of Anthropology.

FORTIFICATIONS

The fortification of the port began in the 16th century (a tower was built and equipped with a small artillery) and was completed in the 19th century. The defenses were built slowly, modified, demolished and rebuilt. Despite being captured and burned by pirates on several occasions during the 17th century, Campeche remained without any effective defense until the fortifications proper were built in the 18th century.
VAUBAN IN AMERICA. Following the sack of the port in 1685, Martín de la Torre's idea of building a wall around the city, like those of Havana and Santo Domingo, was accepted by the Spanish king and work was begun during the early 18th century under the direction of the German, Johannes Franck. The peace signed between France and Spain at Ryswick made collaboration between the two nations possible and the French engineer, Louis Bouchard de Bécour, suggested certain modifications as well as additional protective measures. In this way the Vauban-style fortress was introduced to America. Minor modifications and additions were made up to the early 19th century without the fortifications being significantly altered. They formed an irregular hexagon, with a bastion (*baluarte*) at each corner, another in the center of the rampart overlooking the sea, and another in the center of the landward-facing rampart. The wall, which was over a mile long, became

Maya statuette from the Campeche region.

superfluous and was gradually demolished from the 19th century onward. Today, only the *baluartes* remain and have been converted into museums.

MUSEUMS AND GARDEN. The Puerta del Mar, overlooking the sea, was protected by the Baluarte Soledad, which is now an archeological museum containing Mayan steles. To the west the Baluarte de San Carlos, now the town museum, was used to protect the town against attacks from the sea. On the landward side the Baluartes de Santa Rosa (now the tourist office) and San Juan (center for traditional dance) protected against attack from the south, as did the Baluartes de San Francisco, near the Puerta de Tierra (*son et lumière*), and San Pedro (center for regional handicrafts). The northern Baluarte de San José, was demolished, while the partly ruined Baluarte de Santiago is now occupied by the Xmuch Haltún botanical garden. The marshes to the northeast of the town did not provide sufficient protection and several forts were built to watch for intruders from the Isla Jaina including San Matías, situated on the hills above the beach, and San José El Alto, overlooking the coast and the sea.

PLAZA MAYOR DISTRICT ★

CATHEDRAL. The Catedral de la Concepción, the oldest church on the Yucatán Peninsula, was built between 1540 and 1705. One of its towers is known as the Spanish tower while the other, completed after Independence, is known as the Campeche tower.

COLONIAL RESIDENCES. Behind the cathedral, the Mansión Carbajal (bottom) which has been converted into an office and craft shop, is a fine example of a wealthy colonial residence with its marble floor, columns and Mozarabic arches. The exteriors of other colonial houses can be seen on Calles 55, 57 and 59.

REGIONAL MUSEUM. Another interesting colonial residence, that of the king's lieutenant, has been converted into a regional museum where Mayan objects are on display.

MONASTERY OF SAN JOSÉ. Like all colonial towns Campeche had a monastery: San José, built by the Jesuits in 1700. The monastery's beautiful Baroque church, used as a barracks during the town's turbulent history, is now a craft center.

OTHER CHURCHES. There are two other ancient churches of interest to visitors: that of the demolished monastery of San Francisco, founded in 1546, which still has its magnificent open chapel, and San Román, built in 1565 to the south of the

BASTIONS
All the ports on the peninsula were fortified during the 18th century and remains of forts can still be seen at El

Carmen, Champotón, Lerma, Sisal, Mérida and Bacalar, the last having also been converted into a museum. To the south of the town, the battery of San Luís (above, foreground), with its guns pointing out to sea, was protected by the fort of San Miguel (above, background).

CATHEDRAL
The cathedral (below) dominates the town's central plaza where a band plays on Sundays.

229

Cemetery of Champotón.

Fort of Champotón (below) and Ciudad del Carmen (bottom).

city walls in the Indian districts, where a black Christ, sculpted in Guatemala, is worshipped. The fair of San Román is held from September 14 to September 28. The Church of San Roque, built in 1654, has five beautiful wooden retables.

ENVIRONS OF CAMPECHE

ISLA JAINA. The island, famous for its ancient cemetery dating from the Classic period, was originally a coral reef. The Maya raised its surface by transporting limestone (*sascab*) to the island as a base for their architectural structures. Jaina was described in 1886 by Désiré Charnay ● *57*. The island (just over ½ mile long and 820 yards wide) lies about 18 miles north of Campeche and is separated from the mainland by a narrow channel between 88 and 109 yards wide. Among the treasures found there are the wonderful polychrome statuettes, often referred to as "American Tanagras," for which the island is famous. They represent various types of figures, clothed and

"Our water ran out. We had to go ashore near the town; it was Sunday, St Lazarus' Day, so that is what we called the place, although we later found out that the Indians called it Campeche. In order that we could all go

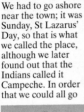

armed, and provide direct information on the costumes and ritual objects of the Classic period. A group of these Jaina statuettes is on display at the Hecelchakán museum ▲ *218*. Two partly restored complexes are open to the public, but visitors must obtain a permit from the Tourist Office in the Plaza Cohuo in Campeche.

CHAMPOTÓN. The road runs south from Campeche along the coast to Champotón, a small colonial village which still has its fort, El Moro, and a 17th-century church. Two roads run south to the state of Tabasco. The inland road passes through Escárcega where it joins the road from Chetumal ▲ *188*.

SILVITUK. About 18 miles east of Escárcega, the ruined complex of Silvituk – where two Classic steles were discovered – lies near Lake Noh. To the south of the road, which leads to Chicanná, Becán, Hormiguero, Xpuhil and Río Bec ▲ *190*, the thick jungle conceals largely unexplored Mayan ruins such as the vast complex of Calakmul. This site covers an area of several miles and is one of the largest of the Mayan sites. Currently being excavated it has already revealed some wonderful structures and extraordinary items. From Escárcega the road runs south, direct to Palenque ▲ *243* and Villahermosa.

together, we decided to take our smallest ship and the three rowing boats, keeping a good lookout.... We left our ships at anchor a good league from the shore and landed near the town by a freshwater course that the natives used for drinking water."
Bernal Díaz del Castillo
The True History of the Conquest of New Spain

CIUDAD DEL CARMEN. From Champotón a scenic coastal route runs south to Ciudad del Carmen, an island at the entrance to the Laguna de Términos and linked to the mainland by the 2-mile-long Puente de la Unidad. Today Ciudad del Carmen is a commercial center and fishing port, but its economy depends mainly on oil. The fort of San Felipe is the only reminder of the colonial period and the struggle to resist the English occupation ● *38*. Across from the island the Xicalango peninsula marked the western limit of Maya territory and several small sites have been excavated in the region, yielding interesting objects. The road continues westwards into the state of Tabasco.

CHIAPAS

ME JTZ'ETIK TE'E.ME JTIK'BETIK
SK'AK'AL TE'TIKE ¡ MULIL !
(Talar bosques y provocar incendios está penado por la ley)

¡ MU XAPAS JECH !
(¡ Evita Incendios !)
CONTRIBUCIONES SON OBRAS   TESORERIA GENERAL DEL ESTADO

Sign in Tzotzil
in San Cristóbal.

GULF OF MEXICO

PACIFIC OCEAN

CHIAPAS
This southern
state, dissected by
the 17th Parallel, has
had a turbulent
history. Its colonial
past has had a lasting
effect upon its inter-
ethnic relations which
are still very tense
and confrontational.

A COLONIAL TOWN
San Cristóbal is
situated on a plain
surrounded by
mountains, the
setting for many
colonial towns ● 122.

The
southern
border of colonial
Mexico (New Spain)
was formed by the
Isthmus of Tehuantepec.
Until Independence in 1821,
Chiapas was the gateway to a
less important province,
corresponding to modern Central
America, whose capital was Guatemala
● 39, 40. Its geological formation –
essentially Jurassic (karstic relief) and Cretaceous
(oil deposits) – dictated its geography: the Sierra Madre,
which reaches its highest point with the
Tacaná volcano (13,450 feet), marks the
beginning of the long volcanic chain
running along the Pacific coast; the
highlands, with their highest point at
Tzontehuiz (9,840 feet), extend into the
Cuchumatanes ▲ 284, whose foothills are
formed by the great arc of middle-range
mountains in the north and east. The
Lacandón Forest ▲ 258 marks the
beginning of the great tropical forest of

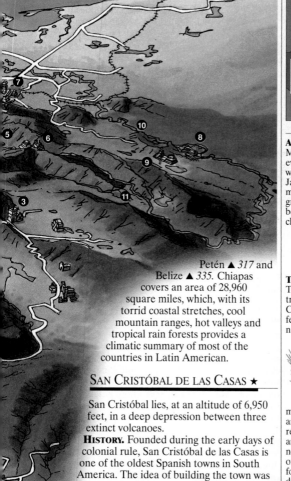

⏲ Four days

A MOUNTAIN CLIMATE
Mornings and evenings are cool. In winter (December–January) early morning mists or ground frosts are the best guarantee of a cloudless blue sky.

TEREBINTH
The terebinth (*ocote*) tree is widely found in Chiapas above 2,600 feet and has given its name to several villages in the state, for example Ocosingo. Its wood is used to make much of the furniture and many of the retables in Chiapas and Guatemala. Its needles are scattered on the ground to form a scented carpet during festivals. An ink used for the codices ● 42 was made from this conifer.

Petén ▲ *317* and Belize ▲ *335*. Chiapas covers an area of 28,960 square miles, which, with its torrid coastal stretches, cool mountain ranges, hot valleys and tropical rain forests provides a climatic summary of most of the countries in Latin American.

SAN CRISTÓBAL DE LAS CASAS ★

San Cristóbal lies, at an altitude of 6,950 feet, in a deep depression between three extinct volcanoes.

HISTORY. Founded during the early days of colonial rule, San Cristóbal de las Casas is one of the oldest Spanish towns in South America. The idea of building the town was first conceived in 1524 by Bernal Díaz del Castillo ● *152*, during his long battle against the rulers of Chamula, who occupied the territory at the time. Captain Diego de Mazariegos turned this idea into a reality in 1528. The town was torn between the fear of Indian uprisings (two occurred in 1712 and 1869) and the need to come to terms with its Indian population (today 35 percent of the inhabitants). This dichotomy was resolved by establishing a two-tiered society, with the town developing within the human shield of its *barrios* ▲ *237* of loyal Indians. The inhabitants were gradually "de-Hispanicized" and the new Creole population severed ties with Spain in 1821, initially hesitating between the statute of a free and sovereign country, and allegiance to Mexico. They voted to join Mexico in 1824, but later had to fight frequent battles to maintain their federal status.

233

The town was named after Bartolomé de
las Casas, protector of the Indians
(painting by Félix Paira, 1875).

Chiapas has fought constantly for its identity within
the Mexican Constitution. Under the leadership
of Joaquín Miguel Gutiérrez until 1838, and
then Angel Albino Corzo (1854–64), it
struggled to resist the centralism advocated
by the Conservatives and the Emperor
Maximilian. Later, under Miguel Utrilla it
pressed for free and open elections
(1866–76). In each case, armed struggle
was involved. The choice of San Cristóbal
by the AZLN – Zapata's National
Liberation Army – as the seat of the
uprising of January 1, 1994, was partly in
line with this tradition of insurgence. The
social influence of the town's stockbreeders
and landowners, who had blocked the 1910
Revolution, caused the marginalization of San
Cristóbal, with the majority of the population
reaping no benefit from the wealth generated by the
area's agriculture, oil, hydroelectric
dams, coffee or tourism. The anarchists
built new towns to the north and south, in
the shadow of the historic town. Between
1982 and 1992 the population of San
Cristóbal de las Casas doubled and today
stands at almost 100,000.

"ZÓCALO"

CATHEDRAL ★. The cathedral, which
dominates the central plaza (*zócalo*), has been renovated
many times. In the 16th century, it was a large chapel whose
entrance (to the south) opened onto the present square. Still
surviving are two huge gargoyles, adorning the west side, and
the square Mudejar bell tower whose height has been reduced
by several earthquakes and which was originally separate
from the main structure. The west façade was completed in
1696. The restoration (in 1993) of its original colors
(produced using natural colorings, lime, salt and cactus sap)
have recreated the effect of an architectural *huipil*: the
dominant colors – yellow ocher from the soil of Chamula and
red ocher from Cuxtitali – provide the
"cloth", while the white "embroidery" is
rendered by the stucco (lime, sand and
egg-white moldings) and highlighted by
two black panels and columns (Chamula
wool).
CHURCH OF SAN NICOLÁS. San Nicolás
has served as the church of the town's
Negro slaves (when the Indian
population was in decline due to
epidemics), a canonical church (chapter-
house), a prison during the Reform wars and finally a parish
church. Access is via a Baroque porch, which was formerly the
entrance to the bishop's palace gardens. It has a typically
Mudejar façade.
"PORTALES". According to Thomas Gage, during the 17th
century idlers would pass the time under the *portales* (arches)
on the east side of the *zócalo*, rebuilt after the conflict of 1836

LAYOUT OF THE TOWN
● *122*
San Cristóbal is built
along a north-south
axis and is dominated
by three architectural
complexes: the
monumental complex
of Santo Domingo in
the north, the *zócalo*
in the center, and El
Carmen in the south.
The former Calle
Hidalgo links all
three together. The
secondary centers
which developed
around this axis were
interspersed with
beautiful residences.
Beyond these lie the
barrios (former
Indian districts).

Further out still and
in line with the four
points of the compass
are the mills which
once supplied the
town.

Detail of a retable in the cathedral, which represents a dark-skinned "Indian" cherub. The angel has a blond wig and a pre-hispanic pectoral as well as quetzal-feather wings.

● *40*. An 18th-century manuscript tells how messengers from the haciendas came to conduct business. They would sing out: "How much for a black slave, how much for each of my donkeys, my mares or my plots of land."

RESIDENCES. The east façade of the hotel Santa Clara, a 17th-century residence, has Plateresque motifs; the hotel Ciudad Real is neoclassic in style; the Bancomer bank, with its French-style façade, is reminiscent of the Diaz period. ● *41*.

PALACIO MUNICIPAL. Built as the governor's palace by Carlos Flores, a local engineer, the Palacio Municipal was intended to familiarize masons with the designs and proportions of the neoclassic style. In 1895 the building was completed after which its Doric and Ionic windows, denticles, cornices and pediments were frequently reproduced as part of a new urban design trend.

SANTO DOMINGO DISTRICT

This historic church and monastery complex in the northern part of the town dispersed its monuments in the gardens of La Alameda when, in 1863, it was used as part of the fortifications during the Reform wars ● *40*. The two-headed, Austrian Habsburg eagle on the façade of Santo Domingo encouraged supporters of Maximilian ● *41* to seek refuge in the church.

MONASTERY. The monastery was established in 1546 by the monks of Las Casas who made it into an "Indian house".

CATHEDRAL
The Baroque interior has cedar retables, made and assembled at the time of the Indian bishop Moctezuma (1754–66). The two pine retables, at the top of the side aisles, and the pulpit supported by a Mexican eagle (1708) were brought from the Jesuit church. The carved wood ceiling has been restored, but without the gold which made the cathedral famous in the 17th century.

CHURCH OF SANTO DOMINGO
The damaged statues are a reminder of the days of conflict, when General Utrilla opened fire on the Imperialists from the Calle Real de Mexicanos.

Its most famous prior was Fray Matías de Córdoba, author of the "cry" of Independence (1821). Remodeled before 1712, the monastery houses a museum of regional history and a cloister.

CHURCH OF SANTO DOMINGO ★. The construction of the church, adjoining the monastery, began with the façade at the end of the 17th century. The interior was still being built in 1735.

The market in San Cristóbal.

CHURCH OF SANTO DOMINGO

TEMPLO DE LA CARIDAD. On the lower south terrace the Templo de la Caridad (Charity), built in 1714, is the memorial to the repression of the Indian rebellion of Cancuc (1712) ● 38 when the Tzeltals' patron saint, Our Lady of the Rosary, was defeated by the Spanish equivalent, Our Lady of Charity (or the Presentation). After the victory of San Cristóbal on November 21 (the festival of the Presentation), Our Lady of Charity was proclaimed "general" (after 1747 a field-marshal's baton was added to her statue) and protectress of the town. The church's façade is a more sober but equally animated expression of colonial Baroque architecture.

CHAPEL OF THE SOTANO. Adjoining the Templo de la Caridad, the Chapel of the Sótano (Christ in the Dungeon) was built between 1831 and 1839 by local Indians in response to the construction of the rebellion memorial. The masons working on the chapel had restored the cathedral in 1815 and imitated its gargoyles and neoclassic south entrance.

KIOSK WITH NEOCLASSIC DOME. The kiosk was built by the government of General Miguel Utrilla (1879–83), the first peace-time government of the 19th century, to glorify the federalist liberal constitution of the Reform in 1857.

In the 18th century the church was literally lined with gold, silver and the paintings of its thirteen retables. Today it has eight intact retables. To create an effect of uninterrupted continuity, the retables in the nave are set between vertical carved giltwood panels whose motif repeats to create an overall effect of rhythm and unity (above).

EL CARMEN DISTRICT

CHURCH OF EL CARMEN. El Carmen, damaged by a fire in 1993 when its retables and ancient paintings were destroyed, has retained its double, right-angled façade (1744 and 1764). Currently being restored, the edifice is a fine example of vernacular, polychrome Baroque. Nearby is the ruined nunnery of the Franciscan Sisters of the Incarnation, who played an important part in the life of the town's female population during the colonial period, and subsequently during the struggle for Independence, when they supported the rebels.

TOWER-PORCH. An anarchistic restoration of the roof of El Carmen mistakenly attached the church to the tower-porch of 1677, obscuring the latter's west façade. The tower-porch's former status as a city gate and its style of geometric Mudejar, stucco arabesques and naive polychromy beneath the arch combine are a valuable reminder of the early urbanization of San Cristóbal.

RETABLE IN THE CHURCH OF SANTO DOMINGO
Detail of a retable in the Chapel of the Rosary, representing a Baroque figure.

CULTURAL CENTER. The cultural center is housed in the former farm (*casa de labor*) which supplied the convent. The 17th-century building, with its extensive gardens and broad *corredor* is a particularly fine example of the local style of living.

GRAND RESIDENCES ★

HOTEL MAZARIEGOS. This 18th-century residence stands one block north of the *zócalo*. The building has a broad, wood *corredor* while an annex on the other side of the street has stucco moldings and friezes. This was the residence of Bishop Moctezuma (1754–66), a descendant of the last Aztec king.

PLAZA REAL. Built at the end of the 18th century, this stands half a block east of the *zócalo*. In the 19th century it housed the offices of the local representatives. Today it is a busy shopping arcade.

PASAJE MAZARIEGOS. The Pasaje Mazariegos, next to the Plaza Real, is lined with patioed shops and a café.

HOTEL FRAY BARTOLOMÉ. In the 19th century the Hotel Fray Bartolomé housed the bishop's court. It has an attractive patio surrounded by a beautiful *corredor*.

LA ENSEÑANZA. This residence, on the corners of Calles Belisario Domínguez and Adelina Flores, is an experiment in "neoclassic adobe" by Carlos Flores, the town's architect between 1880 and 1920.

HOTEL CASA MEXICANA. The former residence of the fathers of San-Juan-de-Dios, who ran the hospital, has been converted into a luxury hotel. The patio has a bronze sculpture by Zuñiga.

CASA NA BOLOM. This late 19th-century residence with its ecological garden, library, museum and neoclassical chapel (1903), stands at the top of Calles Chiapa de Corzo and Comitán. It was owned by the anthropologist, Frans Blom.

THE "BARRIOS"

The adobe town is best appreciated in the old Indian districts: Mexicanos; Cerrillo; San Antonio with its hill; Cerrito, the *mirador* of the town and its valley, and Cuxtitali with its colonial toll bridge (tiled roof and benches), *El Peje de Oro* and "Miguel Utrilla" mill. The districts were identified by ethnic origin (Aztec, Tzotzil, Zapotec, Quiché), the religious order responsible (Dominicans, Franciscans) and traditional specialties, such as wood, wrought iron, fire-crackers, cloth and wool dyeing and cooked meats. The streets often have no windows as the traditional houses usually only open onto a patio. They are very different from the streets of the "enlightened" town center where neoclassic modernization pierced impressive windows with adobe edicules. To the south of the valley, the Hotel de la Alborada offers a splendid view of the mill, the town and its natural setting. Footpaths lead to the other mills. In the forest to the east, about 3 miles beyond the so-called "la Garita" district, is the natural arch of the Arco Tete. It is possible to continue with a guide as far as the Quintana de los Obispos, a small, 18th-century Baroque building which was the bishops' country residence and the farm hospital.

"GALERIA"
Built for the town's founder in 1528, this is San Cristóbal's oldest residence. Situated in the Calle Hidalgo (no. 7), it is now used by businesses.

Other churches (below) are open to the public including: Santa-Lucia, San-Felipe Ecatepec, San Francisco and El Carmen.

"ENEMIES"
During the rituals of the Carnival of Chamula, the village is invaded by "enemies": Jews (responsible for the death of the Sun-Christ), Spanish conquerors, Ladinos and monkeys (who represent the forces of darkness and evil). Ritual battles, interspersed with bouts of trading, drinking and eating, are fought by the "enemies" and *pasiones* (traditional authorities responsible for overcoming or taming them) which end with the participants running over a bed of hot coals. This is a rite of purification made necessary by the contact with evil creatures, as well as a representation of the rise of the new sun and its triumph over the powers of darkness and death.

RANCHO NUEVO

The site became a battlefield in January 1994 during the Zapatista rebellion ● *40* and is now closed to the public. However, about 50 acres of the forest are still open to hikers (access is about 6 miles from San Cristóbal, on the right in the direction of Comitán). The only river in this high valley (7,500 feet) is a dry channel. During the rainy season (June–September) this becomes a torrent which "disappears" into the caves which run into the hollow mountain range (*Cerro hueco*) closing the San Cristóbal valley to the south. Approximately the first 500 yards of the caves are lit and are open for public viewing.

A NATURAL SITE. This limestone site, characteristic of the region's Jurassic landscapes, is scattered with karstic landslides, covered with conifers and pierced by small, funnel-shaped water sinks which "feed" the water table that in turn waters the forest. The forest is populated by ibex and other rare species of deer, badgers (*zorrilla*), armadillos, squirrels, green woodpeckers and snakes.

TZOTZIL VILLAGES ★

Chamula and Zinacantán, in the vicinity of San Cristóbal de las two of the most visited Tzotzil authorities have introduced in an attempt to limit tourism, to churches, and additional charges to photograph certain ceremonies. The ceremonies for which a small charge is made Year, the festivals of San Juan, Domingo, and the Carnival As well as being occasions for important rituals, strengthen ties the parent

immediate Casas, are villages. The local severe measures such as entrance fees permits and special

are those for the New San Lorenzo and Santo (*k'in tajimoltik*) ● *74*. the performance of they also serve to between members of community and its migrants (settlers in the Lacandón Forest), who today constitute an important diaspora. These villages are still the scene of bitter conflicts between Catholics and Protestants (especially in the village of Chamula, where large numbers of Protestants have had to leave for the new shanty towns around San Cristóbal). The communities have developed amidst conflict, either as the innocent victims of regional or national politics, or because the religious and administrative pressures exerted by the colonial authorities became an unbearable assault upon their very existence.

INDIAN REBELLIONS ● 38. These same communities were the seat of the great, early 18th-century rebellions, a reaction against the extortionate tributes exacted by the conquerers and the efforts of the Spanish clergy (especially Bishop Francisco Nuñez de la Vega) to eradicate idolatry and destroy the power of sorcerer-priests (or shamans) who perpetuated traditional Indian religious practices. With their idols condemned and destroyed by the priests, the Indians turned to the Catholic Christs, Virgins and Saints to represent their claims and defend their concept of a more just and equitable alternative society. The appearance of a Saviour-Virgin at Zinacantán in 1708, and then at Santa Marta in 1711, were the early signs of the great 1712–13 uprising, which spread across a large part of Chiapas from Cancuc. A total of thirty-three Tzotzil, Tzeltal and Chol communities rebelled and swelled the ranks of the "soldiers of the Virgin", but they were soon subjected to the most terrible repression, followed by years of poverty and famine. Hopes of an alternative society were not entirely destroyed; they merely took on other less spectacular means of expression. In 1994 they re-emerged in a well-organized form and for the first time in history, they attracted international attention.

CARNIVAL OF CHAMULA. The carnival period corresponds to the five transitional days of the ancient Mayan calendar and involves the ritual presentation of a series of historical events involving invaders and enemies whose intrusion represents the disorder of the world and the threat to Mayan society (opposite above).

The church of Chamula as it is today.

San Juan Chamula in the early 20th century. The crosses and grazing land have been replaced by a square, surrounded by buildings, where the local market is held.

▲ Chiapas
Toward Guatemala

"CHINKULTIC" DISK
The so-called "Chinkultic" disk is in fact one of the aisle markers ● *112* from the ball court of a minor site in the Chinkultic region. It is in sculpted limestone and dates from AD 590.

A WALK THROUGH THE RAIN FOREST
In the region of the Montebello Lakes, at altitudes of between 650 and 2,300 feet,

the early morning jungle mists lift as the sun rises and fall again during the afternoon as the air temperature cools. The eastern exposure of the site and its altitude (4,600 feet) form a barrier against the trade winds and create the conditions necessary for a high-altitude rain forest. The most commonly found species of trees are sweet-smelling conifers, oaks (with epiphytic bromeliads and orchids) and sweet gums (with their maple-like sap and leaves). They grow above a dense undergrowth of flowers, aromatic plants, giant ferns and shrubs.

TEOPISCA

In 1626, the size of this church-cemetery and the sound of its constant music had already attracted the attention of the English traveler Thomas Gage. In an attempt to control the Mayan funeral rites that were still being practiced in the 17th century, the nave of the church was designed for receiving the dead rather than for worshippers. During services, the parishioners gathered in the chancel. Of the ten Baroque retables which once decorated the church, only three remain. Two of these, transferred in the 19th century, came from the Jesuit church of San Cristóbal ▲ *233*. Behind the recently restored giltwood retable in the chancel (1706), the polychrome remains of another retable installed in 1688 were discovered.

TENAM PUENTE

About 6 miles beyond Comitán, a track on the right leads for 3 miles to the site of Tenam Puente. Current excavation work has revealed a large Late Classic site on one of the hills bordering the plateau of Comitán (which offers a magnificent view extending from the range of the Tzontehuitz to the Cuchumatanes ▲ *284*). This Mayan city is built on three levels, each with a ball court and several pyramids, often arranged around a sunken patio. Its architecture, which is sometimes superposed, represents two successive stages of the Late Classic period. With the exception of one dated stele in bas-relief (on display at the museum of Tuxtla Gutiérrez ▲ *260*), the steles discovered on the site were smooth.

MONTEBELLO LAKES

About 9 miles south of Comitán, take the left fork just before La Trinitaría and follow the road for about 18 miles. At an average altitude of 4,900 feet, the road crosses a long plateau sloping gently toward the lakes. This plateau is bordered on the right by the central mountains of Chiapas and, on the left, by the hills running along its southern edge before the land plunges down into the jungle and the central depression. All the tracks along this road lead to historical *fincas* (today mostly communal land) which initially belonged to the first inhabitants of San Cristóbal, and these then passed in some cases to the Dominicans before finally, in the 19th century, they were embraced by Comitán. They are situated in a key area: on the edge of Lacandón territory, which was unsubjugated during colonial rule ▲ *258*, and on the border of Guatemala, which was a refuge for the fighters of the civil

wars of the Reform (1855–64) ● *40*. Several of these estates were the scene of battles, either to occupy a strategic position or replenish supplies of corn, beans, livestock and dairy products.

THE SITE ★. The lakes form overflow "sinks" for the rivers of the valley of Comitán. Their color varies according to the composition of the lake floor – sand (blue-green) or rocks (chalky) – and their orientation – shadow (deep blue-black) or sun (opal-blue). A series of pools begins about 12 miles before the lakes. The water pours into the river basins and then plunges into the jungle which begins at La Cañada (in the foothills of the Cuchumatanes) about 12 miles to the east. For those traveling by road, the fork about half a mile before the first lake leads to several other lakes, including the lake at the border village of Tziscao. Don't go too close as its shores are quicksand.

CHINKULTIC

To reach the site of Chinkultic (above), take a left turn about 4 miles before the Montebello Lakes. A track (about half a mile) leads to the ruins. The site covers a long period of history as there is evidence of a connection with Toniná ▲ *242* (for which the last known date is AD 909), while colonial manuscripts refer to its occupation in the 16th century. The most interesting sculptures, although in a poor state of repair due to long neglect, are near the ball court. They bear the Mayan symbols for war and death. Higher up the mountain, on the other side of the stream, is a monumental complex with two small platforms: one at the foot of the pyramid, and the other on the edge of a deep *cenote* which, when explored, revealed several cavities containing mortuary offerings. The top of the pyramid offers a panoramic view of the series of lakes (Lake Chinkultic, left) and the valley's dense vegetation and orchids.

The Mayan site of Toniná is still being excavated by the Mexico National Institute of Anthropology and History.

The first part of the route runs through the Ocosingo fault which separates two tectonic plates: the Central American plate (highlands) to the south and the North American plate (northern mountains) to the north ■ 16. These plates move about three-quarters of an inch every year. Beneath the fertile pastures of the valley floor are the alluvial deposits of the fossil meanders of a river whose course is often altered by earth tremors.

OXCHUC

This Tzeltal village is the focal point of an agricultural pilgrimage held on the festival of Santo Tomás (December 21), which is also attended by the Tojolabals ● 63. Its church is one of the few whose atrium still has three of its four *capillas posas* (repository chapels) where traces of paintings can still be seen. In the chancel (south window) a sculpture with a pre-Hispanic motif was discovered embedded in the wall. It represents three shells, the distinctive symbols of both the name of the village in Tzeltal and of Quetzalcoatl. In 1687 Bishop Nuñez de la Vega confiscated all Mayan calendars and codices and demanded that all worshippers should repeat the *credo*. Today Oxchuc is still a seat of Maya resistance.

TONINÁ ★

Toniná, at an altitude of 2,950 feet, lies on the border of the Mayan highlands and lowlands, but belongs to the lowland tradition.

HISTORY. Although the Ocosingo Valley and the site were occupied from the Late Preclassic, Toniná experienced its golden age during the Late Classic period. This border town probably resisted the collapse of the Maya civilization ● 34 better than most because of its geographical position. It was here that the most recent stele was erected (AD 909). Although its statues and inscriptions were destroyed during the Early Postclassic, the ruined city was inhabited intermittently and its Classic tombs re-used. The center of Toniná, built on the side of a hill in seven terraces, produced the overall form of a pyramid. The site was briefly described and some of its statues illustrated by an expedition from the University of Tulane in the 1920's but it was only during the 1970's that the French researchers, Pierre Becquelin, Claude-François Baudez and Eric Taladoire devoted several campaigns to the excavation of Toniná.

SCULPTURES. A naked and decapitated captive in relief, a colossal trophy-head and numerous panels of scenes depicting capture and sacrifice decorated the temples and pyramids. The sculptures on the stucco-work structures were also based on the themes of war and sacrifice. A huge relief, discovered at the foot of the sixth terrace, presented one of the most terrifying images in the Mayan culture. It depicted

STATUARY OF TONINA
Life-size (or smaller) statues in the round have a vertical tenon which was set into a socket in the wall. The altars of Toniná are thin disks, usually sculpted with inscriptions. Sovereigns are depicted wearing a long cloak and either holding a ceremonial staff or with their hands resting on their belts. Their headdresses consist of superposed masks.

scenes of a hellish underworld, scattered with skulls, and severed heads and fearsome mythical creatures.

CHOL TERRITORY

Before the Spanish Conquest the Chol groups ● *63* occupied the vast territory of the lowlands between the Usumacinta ▲ *333* and Lake Izabal ▲ *313*. In the 16th century they were deported to the highlands where they were decimated by cold and disease and assimilated into other groups. Other members of this linguistic group are found in Tila, Tumbalá and several villages near Palenque, where they settled as a result of tradition or coercion during the Conquest.

PALENQUE ★

Palenque is built at the foot and on the sides of a specially prepared hillside site. It has three levels – the plain at sea level, an intermediate level (about 330 feet) and an upper level (390-490 feet) – and covers an area of 6 square miles. Only the center (or Principal Group), which covers an area of 37 acres, has been cleared and is accessible to visitors. Excavations in the past, mainly carried out by Mexican archeologists, have been completed by researchers of various nationalities who have analyzed the images, carved inscriptions and natural relief of the site.

AGUA AZUL
Before Palenque, a road leads to the Agua Azul Cascades. The color of the water varies with the season.

PALENQUE
1. Palace
2. Temple of the Inscriptions
3. North Temple
4. Temple of the Cross
5. Temple of the Sun
6. Temple of the Foliated Cross
7. Ball Court

▲ PALENQUE

HISTORY
Although the site was occupied in 100 BC,
the city did not expand until the 7th
century. By the end of the 9th century its
golden age was over, and no new buildings
or inscriptions were commissioned.

Palenque was one of the earliest Mayan sites to be discovered. It is also one of the best preserved and has a remarkable royal sepulcher. The city not only had access to the most famous and imaginative architects in the Mayan civilization, but also the best scribes. It consequently has some of the most beautiful calligraphy.

WALDECK

In 1784 the governor of Guatemala ordered several people to carry out an on-the-spot enquiry into the truth of the rumors circulating about "stone houses" buried deep in the forest. In 1832 the neoclassical artist, Jean-Frédéric Waldeck ● 56, 130 (a naturalized Frenchman born in Austria), spent over a year among the ruins of Palenque where he studied the architecture, made drawings of the sculptures and carried out a few excavations. His works included this *View of the Temple of the Cross*. The results of his research were not circulated for another thirty years and it was Stephens ● 56 who published the first description of Palenque in 1841. Since then vast numbers of artists, scientists and tourists have visited the site.

The first sovereign of the Palenque dynasty, Chaacal I, acceded to the throne in 501 and the last, Kuk, ended his reign after 784. The most recent inscriptions date from the very end of the 8th century.

GROUP OF THE CROSS

The references to mythical creatures are clearly expressed. The so-called Group of the Cross consists of three pyramid-temples built around a square open to the south. The Temple of the Cross is the largest and highest placed (top left); the Temple of the Sun (center left) occupies the lowest position on a four-story pyramid; the third is the Temple of the Foliated Cross (bottom left). They were built during the reign of the sovereign Chan Bahlum, between 683 (date of the death of his father, Pacal, whose jade funeral mask is shown above) and 692, and represent a three-stage cosmic journey, each defined by a specific orientation and environment. The Temple of the Cross represents the first stage and symbolizes the place of origin of the supernatural and the world of Man. The next stage of the journey is the underworld, through which

the nocturnal sun (embodied by the jaguar) has to pass. The final stage, in the sanctuary of the Foliated Cross, involves rebirth via the fertility of the upper layers of the earth. The richness of the symbolism of the Group of the Cross lies in their different orientations and the relationship between the different stages.

"EL PALACIO"

The so-called Palace of Palenque is in fact a platform (82 yards long by 60 yards wide and about 33 feet high) supporting fifteen or so structures (usually referred to as "houses" and designated by a letter of the alphabet) arranged around three courtyards. The complex is the result of almost two centuries of architectural activity which covers at least six reigns. The first structures were built in the early 7th century by Pacal (AD 615–83). In spite of its name, the Palace was not a royal residence but a religious complex reserved for the king and his elected priests, in which the various buildings are dedicated to different ritual ceremonies.

HOUSE D

This ancient reproduction of one of the stucco bas-reliefs decorating the pillars of House D, shows a figure presenting a thunder-and-lightning serpent to the sovereign. House D is associated with agrarian rites.

TEMPLE OF THE INSCRIPTIONS ● 108

This structure is in fact the funerary monument of Pacal, the first great sovereign of Palenque. The tomb, which lies beneath the temple, at the foot of a long staircase, was discovered in 1952. Prior to this it was thought that the pyramids were merely foundations for temples. Also discovered in the pyramid were three panels carved with glyphs which constitute one of the longest known Mayan inscriptions (617 glyphic blocks).

THE SARCOPHAGUS

The sarcophagus contained the royal remains, surrounded by a rich collection of jewelry and jade. It was covered with a huge, sculpted slab (right) showing the dead sovereign falling into the fleshless jaws of the terrestrial monster. On the mask representing the "underworld" is one of the sacred trees from the four corners of the world. The two-headed serpent represents the sky, while the quetzal bird in the top of the tree symbolizes the zenith of the diurnal Sun. The ten half-figures emerging from the earth, sculpted on the sides of the sarcophagus, represented some of Pacal's royal ancestors.

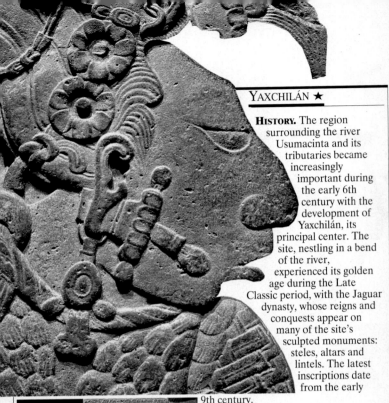

YAXCHILÁN ★

HISTORY. The region surrounding the river Usumacinta and its tributaries became increasingly important during the early 6th century with the development of Yaxchilán, its principal center. The site, nestling in a bend of the river, experienced its golden age during the Late Classic period, with the Jaguar dynasty, whose reigns and conquests appear on many of the site's sculpted monuments: steles, altars and lintels. The latest inscriptions date from the early 9th century.

MONUMENTS. Some of the structures are built on a terrace bordering the left bank of the river, while others occupy the slopes above. The majority are gathered together in two acropolises reached via long staircases (below). They are predominantly elongated, rectangular edifices with single or double rows of rooms and three entrances in the façade. Their foundations are relatively low and the large, openwork crests to their roofs are less massive than those of Petén.

SCULPTURES. The upper section of the façades is often elaborately decorated with stone mosaics as well as three-dimensional sculptures and stucco motifs. For example, the frieze of Structure 33 included statues of dignitaries seated on monster masks or appearing at inverted T-shaped window openings, while the center of the roof crest was occupied by the colossal statue of a seated sovereign. The lintels of the three doors were entirely sculpted, and a stele and altar stood before the central door. The sculptural style of the Usumacinta region, and of Yaxchilán in particular, is justly famed for its freedom of expression. The architectural sculpture and exterior monuments – steles and altars – are damaged, whereas most of the detail on the lintels

MAYAN PROFILE
The Mexico National Museum of Anthropology ▲ *376* has some fine examples of lintels from Yaxchilán. Lintel 26, dating from 719, with a detail of a face (above), offers a good impression of the typically Mayan profile of pre-Columbian sculptures and paintings. The characteristically flattened forehead was obtained by compressing the skull of newly born babies between two planks of wood, held in place for several days.

has been preserved. The iconography highlights the rites performed by the sovereign and a member of his immediate entourage: wife, mother, sons or lieutenant. Scenes of self-sacrifice, such as a woman passing a cord of thorns through her tongue, are explicitly depicted ● 46. Sometimes the ritual is evoked by its result, represented by a basket of sacrificial instruments (stingray spines, sharp knives and cords of thorns) and accompanied by strips of bast paper on which the victim's blood was offered to the beneficiaries of the sacrifice. The sculptures also show several scenes of capture in which the names of the victor and vanquished are inscribed, sometimes on their thigh. Other rituals involve objects which are rare or unknown in other regions. Apart from the famous figurine, depicting a high-priest holding a sceptre which is half-man, half-serpent ● 52, the sovereigns of Yaxchilán and their entourage are shown holding scepters in the form of a directional tree surmounted by a bird, torches, long rods extended by a wickerwork structure, and others which are wider and decorated with partly mobile crosses, jaguar paws and sacred packages.

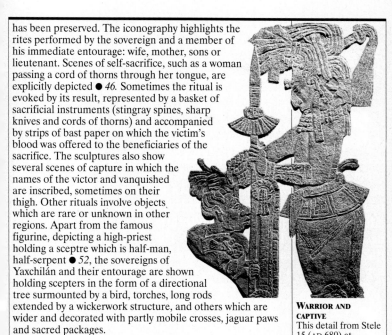

WARRIOR AND CAPTIVE
This detail from Stele 15 (AD 680) at Yaxchilán shows a warrior seizing his prisoner by the hair.

BONAMPAK ★   ● 128

It is highly probable that the interior walls of the more prestigious edifices on all Mayan sites were covered with paintings which complemented the carved or sculpted decoration of the exterior. The damp, tropical climate has meant that most of these paintings have not survived to the present day.

MONUMENTS. When it was constructed, Bonampak was a site of average importance, but today its comprehensive collection of Mayan painting provides historians with vital information. Discovered in 1946, it is situated a few miles south of the Usumacinta and Yaxchilán Rivers, on the edge of the Lacandón Forest ▲ 258. The center of the site consists of an Acropolis (a terraced hill with several small temples) overlooking a square bordered by structures on three sides. The stone sculpture, in the form of steles and lintels, is very well preserved. The edifice containing the paintings (Structure 1) and the three steles dates from the reign of Chaan-Muan, who acceded to the throne in 776 and was still in power in 790.

PAINTINGS ▲ 250. Structure 1, on the first terrace of the Acropolis, comprises three non-connecting rooms whose walls and vaulted ceilings have retained most of their paintings. The lintels of the three doors depict scenes of capture in which a sovereign seizes his fallen enemy by the hair. The paintings in the three rooms illustrate three stages of the same story: before, during and after a battle.

.ACROPOLIS OF BONAMPAK
In the foreground is the first terrace of the Acropolis and a stele protected against the weather. Beyond and to the right, Structure 1 still has its famous paintings.

▲ FRESCOS OF BONAMPAK

The first room depicts dignitaries standing inside an edifice (shown by a red background), at the foot of the royal throne. The sovereign, pictured above the door, is dressed for a dance being performed in the lower register (blue background) in the open air. To the left of the dancers is a procession of musicians and masked figures and to the right a crowd of dignitaries watching the ceremony. Opposite the entrance to the second room another fresco depicts a battle in which the armed and richly dressed warriors of Bonampak triumph over their unarmed and almost naked adversaries. The judgement and torture of the prisoners is described on the lintel of the door. The principal scene in the third room is a dance, accompanied by music, performed at the top and foot of a pyramid. The vaulted ceilings in Rooms 1 and 3 are decorated with images of the celestial cosmic monster, while those in Room 2 are decorated with captives and the symbols of constellations.

FERTILITY DANCE
A group of six dancers, wearing masks and costumes and flanked by musicians (playing trumpets, turtle shells and rattles) and fan bearers, prepare to perform. One of the dancers is dressed as a crab and raises his claws. There is also a seated crocodile. The other figures, apart from one, are wearing the masks of imaginary reptilian creatures. The dancers probably represent spirits associated with water and vegetation and are about to perform a fertility dance.

"This art is inspired by a spirit which sweeps aside all theocratic and aristocratic artistic convention. It is not afraid to depict brutality, the cruelty of scenes of war, but also likes to portray scenes of everyday life, clothing and finery."

Jacques Soustelle

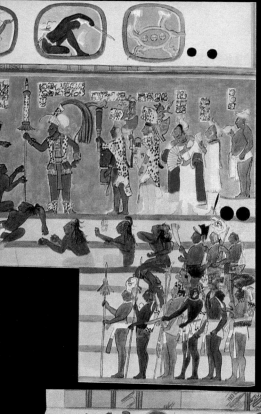

JUDGEMENT OF THE PRISONERS ● 128

The battle ends with the defeat of the enemy, their judgement and torture. Chaan-Muan appears in the center of the composition, at the top of the pyramid, accompanied by dignitaries, captains, courtiers and women of the court. The conquered enemy have been stripped of their jewelry and clothes (except for a loincloth) and their hair is loose. A dead prisoner lies at the king's feet. Everywhere tortured prisoners awaiting execution hold out bloodstained hands. On the far left an executioner holds his victim by the wrist. A severed head rests on a bed of leaves. Other warriors watch the scene at the foot of the pyramid.

LACANDÓN FOREST
The Lacandón Forest (Selva Lacandona) lies in east Chiapas, in the part of Mexico which on the map seems to project into Guatemala. It covers an area of around 1,900 square miles to the south of Yaxchilán and Bonampak. The region, classified as the Montes Azules Biosphere Reserve, has only recently been protected against the aggressive policies of land development companies who have been exploiting the forest's valuable mahogany reserves since the 19th century.

Lacandón village (right) photographed in the early 20th century.

THE LACANDÓNS

The four hundred or so surviving Lacandóns who live in the forests of Chiapas have found themselves, unwittingly, at the center of a scientific controversy which has not yet been entirely resolved. For a long time they have been thought to be the direct

descendants of the Maya of the Classic period, heirs of the architects of Yaxchilán ▲ 248 and the artists of the temple frescos of Bonampak ▲ 250. Ethnological and historical studies have shown that the Lacandóns of today are in fact descended from populations who migrated from the south of the Yucatán Peninsula and Petén during the 18th century. Although they refer to themselves as *Hach Winik* ("the True Men"), they are also referred to somewhat pejoratively as *Caribes* (cannibals) and *Lacandones*.

The term *Lacandones* is probably derived from Acam Tun, the name of an island in Lake Miramar applied, during the 16th century, to the whole of the forested region of East Chiapas, then inhabited by groups who remained unsubjugated by Spanish authority and were feared by the Christianized Indians of the highlands.

TOWARD OBLIVION? Whole areas of Lacandón mythology and ceremonial practices have been forgotten and only a few fragments of a complex pantheon dominated by Hachakyum the Creator, of the worship of censers, of the ritual use of *balché* (a fermented drink), and of the complex skills linked to hunting and fishing have survived. These people are mere shadows of their ancestors, caricatures of the last of the "noble savages". They are still exploited, nowadays by a lucrative tourist trade. In only a few years the fervor of evangelical pastors, the greed of hardwood extraction companies, and the brutal colonization of the Lacandón Forest by thousands of landless peasants have got the better of this original culture. In the words of Didier

ANIMAL SPIRITS
The little terracotta figurines made by the Lacandóns represent the animal spirits of the forest. They are both worshipped and feared, like the forest itself which is a source of life and danger for those who live there.

Boremanse: "[The *Hach Winik*] are the survivors of a lost world, an age that has disappeared for ever during which [they] lived free and at one with nature, lost and forgotten in the depths of the virgin forest. Their way of life may indeed have been harsh, and even cruel; but the tropical forest is kinder to Man than industrial civilization. And if one had to compare their past life with the life they lead at present and are likely to lead in the future, it would not be an exaggeration to say that the 'True Men' have been driven out of Paradise." (*Contes et mythologie des Indiens Lacandons*, 1986).

CENSERS. Only the Nahá Lacandóns still practise this form of worship. The clay censers bear the modeled effigy of a god and are arranged in a sanctuary separate from the people's dwellings. They are considered to be the permanent representatives of the gods among Man. During ceremonies they are placed in a row on a mat of palm fronds and offerings of incense and *balché* are made in support of a request or to repay a beneficent act on the part of the gods concerning agriculture, health or a birth.

THE "BALCHÉ" RITUAL. *Balché*, prepared in a dugout canoe, is fermented from the sap of sugar cane or honey diluted in water in which strips of bark are left soaking for twenty-four hours. It is prepared and drunk for a number of different reasons and not on specific occasions. The *balché* ritual is performed to entreat or thank the gods, individually or collectively, and as such provides frequent opportunities for the men in the *caribal* (Lacandón community) to get together without their womenfolk and talk, drink and sing all day long. This propitiatory and communal ceremony is also seen as a test for those who may have transgressed certain common rules or codes of ethics. Vomiting as a result of drinking too much is not only thought of as an indication of guilt, but also is believed to be a process of purification.

❝They all wore the same garment; a sort of wide tunic with short sleeves made of a very coarse but supple cotton cloth, spun and woven by the women. These tunics were marked with red stains which I took to be mud; but they had been made deliberately as a form of decoration, using the berries from a bush whose name I do not know.❞
Désiré Charnay
Voyage au Yucatán et au pays des Lacandons, 1882

▲ CHIAPAS
SAN CRISTÓBAL TO TUXTLA GUTIÉRREZ

CHIAPA DE CORZO

An Olmec engraving dating from 36 BC was found on this site, which was occupied in c. 1000 by the Chiapanecs and, at the beginning of the 16th century, by the Aztecs. Chiapa de Corzo was the first town in the region to be conquered by the Spanish and remained the most important town in the province until the 18th century. The former agricultural wealth (sugar cane, livestock, tropical fruits) produced by the *fincas* has been replaced by intensive industrial activity.

DOMINICAN MONASTERY. The monastery's two cloisters represent two successive structures. On the first floor, a stucco mural (Dominican shields and pairs of hounds) evokes the order of the brotherhood (the so-called "hounds of God"), protectors of the faith and Indian rights.

CHURCH OF SANTO DOMINGO. This huge edifice was originally the monastery chapel. The 16th-century church was seriously damaged by natural catastrophes and badly restored during the 1960's.

CHURCH OF SAN SEBASTIAN. The remains of the church, abandoned during the 19th century, can be seen on the hill of Atalaya. Its adobe colonnades and walls were flattened by a tornado in 1989.

FOUNTAIN OF CHIAPA DE CORZO
The fountain was the result of the extensive hydraulic work carried out during the colonial period. The monumental Mudejar fountain with its diamond-shaped bricks was built in 1562 by the Dominican friar, Fray Rodrigo de León. Today it is more of a kiosk than a fountain.

CAÑON DE SUMIDERO
Leave Tuxtla via the north bypass in the direction of Sumidero. The road winds steeply through the shanty town of La Granja and then on up the mountainside. It comes to a dead-end at 4,265 feet. The second route (25 miles) from Tuxtla follows the north bypass west as far as a summerhouse and then turns off right towards Chacona, San Fernando and Chicoasen. Beyond the tunnel the road overlooks the dam.

TUXTLA GUTIÉRREZ

Originally Olmec territory and then an Aztec garrison ● 37 this colonial town was relatively unimportant until 1892 when it became the capital of Chiapas ● 40. A regional museum traces the region's pre-Columbian history. Joaquín Miguel Gutiérrez (1796–1838), the son of a Spanish immigrant, born in Tuxtla, who became a militant of the federalist cause and was a representative, governor and then *guerillero*, made the town into a liberal center and a "mapache" alternative during the Revolution ● 41. With its 300,000 inhabitants, Tuxtla is the only town in Chiapas with modern urban developments: parks, bypasses and 20th-century monuments built by famous contemporary Mexican architects. The Zoological Gardens with characteristic lowland vegetation contains fauna from Chiapas.

CAÑON DE SUMIDERO ★ ● 36. The canyon, situated to the north of Tuxtla Gutiérrez, can be visited by road from Tuxtla or by boat from Chiapa de Corzo or Cahuaré. Its rocky walls rise to a height of 4,900 feet. Three huge hydroelectric dams have been built to control the Grijalva, Mexico's second largest river, which used to constantly change its course.

HIGHLANDS
OF GUATEMALA

▲ HIGHLANDS OF GUATEMALA

🕐 Four days

Guatemala covers an area of 42,000 square miles and lies on the same latitude as central India and the Philippines. The southern half of the country is separated from the

Guatemala remains an agricultural, rural and traditional country. The Indian people refuse to accept the regime imposed by the *Ladino* authorities. They claim the right to their own essential, and vital, individuality. The situation is complex and often confrontational.

Pacific by a coastal plain and crossed from west to east by a mountain chain (Sierra Madre) forming part of the Andean system and incorporating thirty-six volcanoes ◆ *370*.

In the north, the plain of Petén, the southern extension of Yucatán, is separated from Mexican Chiapas ▲ *231* by the great Usumacinta river. Guatemala lies on the point of convergence of three tectonic plates – the Pacific, North American and Caribbean plates – whose movement causes regular earthquakes.

CLIMATE. Guatemala has a hot, wet climate in the lowland areas and a more temperate climate in the highlands where its major towns and cities are located.

POPULATION. The population of Guatemala currently stands at ten million and is increasing at a rate of 2.9 percent per year. Its very unequal distribution – a sort of ethnic "mosaic" – is the legacy of the country's history. The Indian half of the population, concentrated mainly in the

GUATEMALA AEREO Q.0.50

TRAJE TIPICO DE COBAN, ALTA VERAPAZ
FESTIVAL FOLKLORICO NACIONAL
Cobán, Alta Verapaz
TALLER NAC · GRABADOS EN ACERO · GUATEMALA

10. CHICHICASTENANGO
11. SANTA CRUZ DEL QUICHÉ
12. TOTONICAPÁN
13. QUETZALTENANGO
14. HUEHUETENANGO
15. ZACULEU
16. SIERRA DES CUCHUMATANES
17. RETALHULEU
18. MAZATENANGO
19. FINCA EL BAÚL
20. SANTA LUCÍA COTZUMALGUAPA
21. LA DEMOCRACIA
22. PUERTO SAN JOSÉ
23. SALAMÁ
24. COBÁN

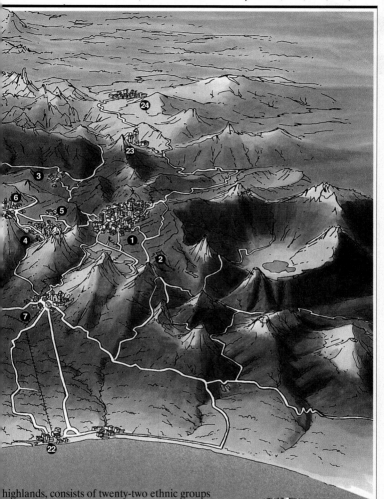

highlands, consists of twenty-two ethnic groups
● *62*. The other half is made up of mestizos or
Ladinos, either people of mixed race or
accultured Indians who have left their
native communities for the capital, the
large towns or the settlement areas of
Verapaz ▲ *292* and Petén ▲ *317*. The
whites (3 percent) are directly descended
from Spanish and European stock.

ECONOMY. Guatemala has a predominately
agricultural economy based on coffee, sugar cane,
bananas, cotton and livestock. Remaining exports consist of
industrial products sold to the countries of Central America.
Other important resources, such as a wide range of semi-
precious stones, lead and marble, are still relatively
unexplored and unexploited. The only resource which is
currently being exploited is oil. It has been extracted in
Verapaz and Petén since 1978.

After
centuries of colonial
domination, the
Indians are still a long
way from achieving
full citizenship in a
country dominated by
a form of
"apartheid".

263

The official name of Guatemala's relatively new capital is Guatemala-de-la-Asunción, but is more often referred to as "the capital", "Guate" or "Guatemala-Ciudad" (Guatemala City). As it does not have any major attractions of its own, it is best incorporated into another visit, such as an excursion to Petén ▲ *317* or, better still, seen just before leaving Guatemala when its museums will complement earlier visits to the archeological sites.

The coat of arms of Guatemala City: three volcanos and a horseman.

HISTORY

FOUNDATION. The city was officially founded during a mass held on January 2, 1776 and placed under the patronage of the Virgin. While adopting the traditional layout of colonial towns ● *122*, it retained a neoclassic architectural style which broke with that tradition. After the 1871 Revolution, the French architectural style dominated but was largely erased by the earthquakes of December 1917 and January 1918.

The plaques showing the old Spanish street names are still there, but the names have been replaced with numbers ◆ *361* (right).

MAJOR CONSTRUCTION WORK. The Belle Epoque style of which the Museo Nacional de Historia, the offices of the Banco Agricola Mercantil and the Hotel Fénix are fine examples, lasted for some time before it, too, was swept aside. A wave of major construction work produced public buildings which can still be seen today: the Palacio Nacional, the Central Post Office, Police Headquarters, the State Museums in Aurora Park ▲ *267* and, next to the museums, the more austere buildings of the General Directorate of Highways and Ministry of Communications. There are also examples of Art Deco influence, for example the Lux cinema (6 Avenida), the

PALACIO NACIONAL
On the façade the national coat of arms shows a quetzal bird perched on the top of a parchment bearing the date of Independence (September 15, 1821). The parchment is framed by olive branches and rifles, the respective symbols of peace and national defence. The building is designed in composite style, but the interior patios are of Andalusian inspiration – their fountains and faience tiles add a touch of lightness to the stately grandeur of the palace.

building of the Directorate of Public Health (9 Avenida) and the official presidential residence, behind the Palacio Nacional.

HAPHAZARD DEVELOPMENT. The type of building that predominates today is fairly uninteresting. The urban structure maintained during the 18th century – a plateau surrounded by ravines, which create a natural barrier against earth tremors – has burst wide open. One fifth of the city's estimated population of two and a half million, lives in the shanty towns built on the side of the ravines (*barrancos*).

PARQUE CENTRAL

PALACIO NACIONAL. The Palacio Nacional (president's palace), built between 1938 and 1943, stands on the north side of the central square. Today it houses the presidential office and several ministerial offices. On the second floor the reception rooms are decorated with stained-glass windows and the parquet floor is made from some of the most resistant tropical hardwoods. The huge crystal chandelier is

Mosaic on a public bench.

surmounted by bronze quetzals indicating the four points of the compass. The banqueting hall overlooking the central square has Mudejar-style paneled ceilings, two tapestries depicting the arrival of the Spanish and stained-glass windows celebrating the four cardinal virtues.

CATHEDRAL. The Baroque-style cathedral, built between 1782 and 1865, stands on the east side of the

> **"A COLONIAL TOWN. IN ITS SANDY STREETS, THE VOICES OF CLERICS MUTTER AVE MARIAS, WHILE THE VOICES OF HORSEMEN AND CAPTAINS ARE RAISED IN ANGER, CALLING GOD AS THEIR WITNESS."**
> MIGUEL ANGEL ASTURIAS

Mercado en día de Corpus, Guatemala, C. A.

MERCADO CENTRAL
The Mercado Central lies below the central square. Its three levels include a craft section, a fruit and vegetable section and an underground section which sells traditionally made objects for everyday use and is well worth a visit. Early 20th-century views of the capital (left, top to bottom): the open-air market, the entrance to the covered market, the Calle Oriente and the Palacio del Centenario.

PRESIDENT BARRIOS
The Torre del Reformador (tower of the reformer) is a 245-foot iron tower, inspired by the Eiffel Tower in Paris, which straddles the 7 Avenida in Zona 9. It was built in 1935 in honor of General Barrios who undertook numerous reforms at the end of the 19th century.

PRINCIPAL THOROUGHFARES
Today, the parallel avenues, 6 and 7 Avenida, cross the city from one end to the other. The Pasaje Rubio, between the shopping arcade and 6 Avenida, was built at the end of the 19th century and based on the Parisian "galeries".

RELIEF MAP ★
This huge, open-air model of Guatemala and Belize, built in 1905, stands on a stone base and covers an area of 2,150 square yards. Its orientation exactly matches that of the country. The relief has been reproduced using 13 tonnes of cement and all the 550 yard contour lines have been marked. The railway lines are in nickel-plated lead and the water for the rivers comes from a reservoir below the peak of Xemal, the highest point in the Cuchumatanes range.

The central square of Guatemala City has been dominated by the cathedral since the 19th century. It stands opposite the Palacio Nacional.

central square. It was damaged by the earthquakes of 1917 and 1976. As well as sculptures and altars decorated with gold leaf, it also has a statue of the Virgin, Our Lady of Mercy, the oldest statue made in Guatemala. To the left of the entrance is a replica of the black Christ of Esquipulas ▲ *298*.

CITY CENTER

CHURCH OF SAN FRANCISCO. The church is built in a neoclassic, Italianate style, with a domed glass roof. It has a small museum with paintings of various martyrs. A black wood statue of Saint Benoît of Messina is the object of popular worship.

FORMER UNIVERSITY OF SAN CARLOS. The present neoclassic structure, opposite the Congreso de los Diputados (House of Commons) on 7 Avenida, is the result of several major building phases (in 1810, 1850 and 1870 and repairs between 1918 and 1925). Although it was built as a university, the buildings were appropriated between 1823 and 1831 by the National Assembly of the United Provinces of Central America ● *39* and then by the Cámara de Representantes (House of Representatives) of the Republic of Guatemala. The National University was subsequently divided into several independent faculties and the building was occupied by the Faculty of Law and in the 1960's the University moved to a campus south of the city.

MUSEO NACIONAL DE HISTORIA. This modest museum, housed in a period building in the city center, has an old-fashioned, provincial charm. It is the only museum to provide general information, presented anecdotally, on events that the Guatemalans consider the high points of their history. There are objects and furniture from the colonial period and reminders of Independence (1821).

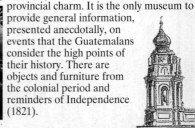

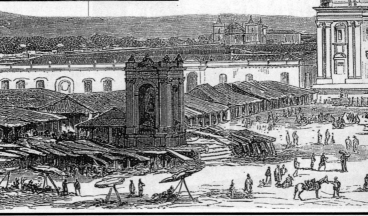

There is no shortage of public transport in the capital. "Recycled" school buses ◆ *354* from America are a common sight in Guatemala.

SOUTHERN DISTRICT

POLYTECHNIC. The buildings formerly occupied by the War Office, with their medieval-style crenellations, date from the end of the 19th century. On the same side of the street, past the intersection, the residence of the Minister of Defence is a similar blend of neo-medieval, neo-Renaissance architecture.

MUSEO IXCHEL ● *89.* The Museo Ixchel, named after the Mayan goddess of weaving, opened its new building in early 1994. Only part of its collection is on display as its spacious new accommodation is still being completed. Exhibitions provide a valuable complement to the rich overview of traditional Guatemalan textiles. Also on display are paintings of Mayan clothes and textiles by Carmen Petersen.

MUSEO POPOL VUH ★. The museum, named after the sacred book of the Quichés ● *146*, has an exceptional collection of painted Mayan funerary urns from Nebaj ▲ *289* and a fine collection of ceramic pieces. There are also sections on ethnological and colonial religious art.

LA AURORA DISTRICT

MUSEO NACIONAL DE ARQUEOLOGÍA Y ETNOLOGIA ★. The museum is housed in a 1930's, neo-colonial style building. Two of the museum's three wings have collections of the most beautiful pieces from the country's different archeological sites, while the third presents ethnological collections, particularly textiles. An attractive, central patio contains Classic steles from Petén.

MUSEO NACIONAL DE ART MODERNO. With only a few exceptions the best examples of modern art are found in private galleries.

CENTRO CÍVICO
Built in the 1960s, the Centro Cívico houses various government ministries, the tourist office (INGUAT), the central bank and the national building society, as well as the fairly unprepossessing city hall.

TEATRO NACIONAL
The Miguel Angel Asturias cultural complex (above) was the last large-scale building project to be completed (1978) in the capital.

PINULA AQUEDUCT
The aqueduct was built by the Spanish towards the end of the 18th century to bring water to the new capital. Remains can still be seen in the La Aurora district, to the south of the city.

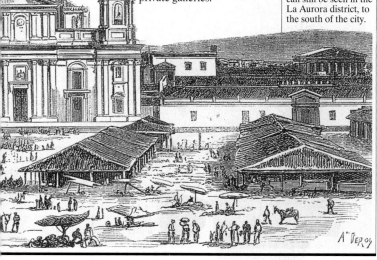

▲ HIGHLANDS OF GUATEMALA
AROUND GUATEMALA CITY

PLACE NAMES
Place names in
Guatemala are
usually composite,
with the name of a
saint (imposed by the
Spanish) preceding
the Indian name. A
commonly found
suffix is -tenango
which means "the
place of" or "the
place where ...
abounds". Names
therefore tend to be
long and difficult to
remember and there
is a tendency to
abbreviate them. So
the city of Guatemala
becomes "Guate" or
"la ciudad" (the city)
or "capital".
Chichicastenango is
shortened to "Chichi",
Panajachel to "Pana"
and Totonicapán to
"Toto". The Indian
place names are used
by the various
ethnic groups.

KAMINALJUYÚ

The valley of Guatemala City lies on the traditional route
from the north and has experienced a series of occupations.
The remains of Kaminaljuyú, now covered by the city's
northern suburbs, are evidence of the importance of the site
during the Preclassic period. Kaminaljuyú was at its height at
the same time as Teotihuacán ● *33* during the early centuries
AD, when it served as a staging post between the great
civilizations of central Mexico and the lowlands of Petén
▲ *317*. The few surviving remains of this period have been
covered by haphazard urban development. Here and there a
mound, the ruins of an ancient pyramid, rises incongruously
between the houses, while an abandoned public garden can
offer an opportunity to explore what was once a great Mayan
city. On the outskirts of the modern city (30 Avenida, Zone
7), the area around the largest of these mounds is now geared
toward tourists. Many objects found at Kaminaljuyú,
including this 5th-century vase (below), are on display in the
Museo Nacional de Arqueología ▲ *267*.

MIXCO VIEJO

SAN PEDRO AND SAN JUAN SACATEPÉQUEZ. The
Sacatepéquez region has become an important
flower-producing area, growing roses,
carnations, chrysanthemums and
gladioli for export. The road
winds between greenhouses
covered with black plastic.
The inhabitants of
these villages, the most
"Indian" near the capital,
also weave baskets and
make pottery and
wooden furniture.
San Juan has a daily market
and is a hive of commercial
activity.
MIXCO VIEJO ★ ● *117*.
Mixco Viejo dates from the
Late Postclassic period (also
known as the Protohistoric)
and was the Pokomam
capital at the time of the
Conquest ● *36*. This
defensive site comprises at
least twelve groups of
structures built on leveled
hilltops or on rocky spurs
surrounded by deep ravines.
The village population lived
on the slopes and withdrew to
the hilltops during times of
emergency. The site consists of
edifices arranged around large,
well-paved squares with a central
altar; elongated, rectangular
structures with several

> "OUR PEOPLE WILL NEVER BE DISPERSED. THEIR DESTINY WILL TRIUMPH OVER THE DISASTROUS DAYS THAT WILL OCCUR AT AN NKNOWN POINT IN THEIR HISTORY. THERE WILL ALWAYS BE A SPECIAL PLACE ON THIS EARTH THAT WE HAVE OCCUPIED." POPOL VUH

rooms; twin temples built on top of the same pyramidal base and reached via a broad staircase flanked by large balustrades and divided by a central, sloping ramp which becomes vertical just before the summit; and platforms designed to support several temples, which stood side by side and were reached via a number of staircases. Large earthenware storage jars were found buried beneath the floors of the houses. The Pokomams cremated their dead and the ashes were placed in large, triple-handled, polychrome (white decoration on a red ground) or monochrome earthenware jars.

CHINAUTLA

This Pokomam village, to the north of the capital, produces a type of low-fired, unpainted, red or cream pottery decorated with lozenges and inlaid work. Articles include large and small plant-pot holders in the form of birds and the Nativity scenes popular in Guatemala.

ESCUINTLA

AMATITLÁN. The "place of the Amates" (fig trees) is the name of both the town and the lake. The lake (5 square miles) is the nearest to Guatemala City and has for a long time been a popular resort for relaxation with the city's inhabitants. In spite of an alarmingly high level of pollution (sewage works do not exist in Guatemala), on Sundays its beach and inexpensive restaurants are completely engulfed by crowds of people from the capital. To the north and west, the altitude (4,260 feet) and climate favor the cultivation of coffee, tobacco and sugar cane (processed in the nearby refineries).

VOLCAN PACAYA ★ ◆ 370. Several of the young cones in this complex volcanic range are still active, particularly the 8,530-foot cone to the southwest. Although Volcan Pacaya is easily reached by two hours of fairly unstrenuous walking from the village of San Francisco de Sales, potential visitors to the volcano should always exercise extreme caution. Sudden resurgences of volcanic activity often lead to the frequent evacuation of the surrounding villages and the release of toxic gases is regularly recorded.

PALIN ★. The Pokomam village of Palín is famous for its vast and beautiful silk-cotton tree ● 64, dating from the early days of colonial rule. Its spectacular branches provide shade for the market held in the square.

ESCUINTLA
Escuintla lies on the Pacific plain ▲ 290, at the foot of the mountains (above). Its status as a leading commercial center is reinforced by its position at the intersection of the Pacific Highway (running to Mexico and El Salvador) and the main road linking the capital to the ports of San José and Puerto Quetzal. Escuintla is also an important railway junction, with one branch running westwards and the other south to service the ports. To the south of the town is the country's only mineral oil refinery (Texaco), while several other refineries in the vicinity produce cotton seed oil.

MIXCO VIEJO
A marker with a horizontal tenon was found in one of the I-shaped ball courts ● 112, of Mixco Viejo. Part of the marker was sculpted with a human head in the open jaws of a serpent.

▲ Highlights of Guatemala
Antigua Guatemala

A QUIET RESORT
The damage caused by earthquakes over the last two hundred years has probably changed Antigua less than the construction of the freeway in 1983. This small town is now easily accessible and attracts large numbers of the more affluent members of the Guatemalan population as well as retired North Americans, who spend large amounts of money on decorating their houses. Wandering through the streets of this town provides an ideal opportunity to step back in time and enter the mysterious world of the so-called *panzas verdes* ("green stomachs"), the nickname given to the Antigueños who are great avocado eaters. Antigua was recognized as a "national monument" in 1944 and since 1979 has been on UNESCO's cultural heritage list.

STREET SCENES
Indians selling their wares, the paved streets, the monuments and the colors of the houses all contribute to creating the special atmosphere of Antigua.

Antigua Guatemala stands in the center of the Panchoy valley, at an altitude of 5,000 feet, surrounded by mountains and volcanos: Agua (12,300 feet), Acatenango (12,990 feet) and Fuego (12,470 feet). This former capital of the Captaincy General is a fine example of colonial urban architecture, a little too artificial for some tastes. Once the seat of the colonial metropolitan, religious and civil authorities, today Antigua is a city of some 25,000 inhabitants and, although quiet during the week, is a popular place for weekend visits. Originally called Santiago de los Caballeros, Antigua Guatemala was founded in 1543 and remained the capital of Guatemala for 232 years, until the transfer of power to Guatemala City following the 1773 earthquake ▲ *264*.

History

ADMINISTRATIVE CAPITAL.
The administrative district that lay between the vice-royalties of New Spain (Nueva España) in the

north (now Mexico), and New Granada (Nueva Granada) in the south (modern Colombia), was known variously as the kingdom of Guatemala (Reyno de Guatemala) or the Captaincy General. It was administered by a Captain General, a governor whose powers were equivalent to those of a viceroy, but which were tempered by two influences. One was the presence of a royal tribunal, the Audiencia de los Confines ● *37*, a legislative and judicial body created in 1543; the other was the local power of the *criollos* – white Guatemalans of Spanish stock.
RELIGIOUS POWER. The bishops played a key role in the political, economic, social and cultural life of the colony. There was no shortage of religious orders in Antigua: Franciscans, Dominicans, Mercedarians and Jesuits, as well as Carmelites, Franciscan nuns, nuns of the order of St Clare (Clarisses) and Capuchins. In 1773, there was a total of thirty-eight monasteries and convents, fifteen chapels and oratories and several hermitages. The University of San-Carlos-Borromeo (1676) was the third to be founded on the continent after those of Mexico and Lima. By 1773, the population had reached sixty thousand (*intra muros*) with thirty thousand in the surrounding villages.

Architecture ★

The city's architectural development can only be understood when put in context with the earthquakes that shake it periodically. The effects of those which followed its

foundation between 1590 and 1650 meant that little building was done during this period. Designs and techniques were always based on the need for solidity. In view of its turbulent history, it is extremely difficult to establish an exact chronology of the construction, destruction, renovation and reconstruction of the city's monuments. Paradoxically, the earthquake of 1773 and subsequent transfer of power probably helped to save the city from a development that would have totally destroyed its character.

PLAZA MAYOR

In 1543 the Italian architect Antonelli designed the city's checkerboard layout around the Plaza Mayor. Although its gardens were redesigned in 1993, the so-called Fountain of the Sirens (1739) still stands in the center.

CITY HALL. The City Hall, officially opened in 1743, has a freestone façade and a double arcature. There is a splendid view from the balcony.

MUSEO DE SANTIAGO. The museum, situated on the first floor of the City Hall around a central patio and fountain, has exhibits from the colonial period, paintings, and weapons, some of which were used during the 1871 Revolution, while others are from the Castillo of San Felipe ▲ *312*.

MUSEO DEL LIBRO ANTIGUO. This building once housed Central America's first printing press, imported by Bishop Payo Enríquez de Riviera in 1660. The museum has a replica press and printing examples from the 16th to 19th centuries.

ARCHBISHOP'S PALACE. All that has survived of this two-story palace (access via the cathedral), built between 1706 and 1711, are the remains of the cloister and a few columns. The see was made an archiepiscopacy by Benoît XIV in 1743. A restored room on the façade houses the cultural center.

CATHEDRAL. The cathedral, consecrated in c. 1565, was badly damaged by several earthquakes. After the 1773 earthquake, only the façade (restored in 1986–7), with its carved spandrel and numerous saints' niches, and the first three bays could be saved. Today it is used as a parish church.

PALACE OF THE CAPTAINS GENERAL. The residence and offices of the Captain General also housed the royal tribunal, the Mint, the offices of the military authorities, the dragoons' quarters, the royal chapel and prisons. Built from 1549 onward, it was renovated and extended several times. The buildings, restored in the mid-19th century, today serve as the tourist office, the police headquarters and the administrative offices for the region of Sacatepéquez, of which Antigua is the capital.

MERCHANTS' AND BAKERS' GALLERY. The gallery, on the west side of the square, once symbolized the prosperity of the merchants of Antigua.

FIVE PERIODS
The architectural history of Antigua can be divided into five main periods. During the first period (16th century), which was interrupted by earthquakes and the eruption of the Volcán Fuego (1581), the buildings were in adobe and the double sloping roofs were covered with thatch and later with tiles. Spanish masons and

architects introduced an adaptation of the masonry vault, with a lowered outline forming a more resilient basket-handle arch. During the second period, following the 1651 earthquake, monasteries, churches and the cathedral were built. The third period (1680–1717) was characterized by the construction of more ecclesiastical buildings including the archbishop's palace, while the fourth (1717–51) involved intensive architectural activity: churches, convents and the City Hall. The final, twenty-year period was the golden age of Baroque.

OTHER MONUMENTS

MUSEO DE ARTE COLONIAL ★.
Antigua prided itself on having the third university founded in Spanish America: San Carlos (1676). Initially it occupied the Colegio de Santo Tomás Aquino before this building was completed in 1763. Although the earthquakes of 1773 did not really affect its thick walls, it had to move in 1776. Four galleries surround a single, central courtyard whose composite arches are reminiscent of the Mudejar style. The Museo de Arte Colonial took up residence in 1936 and has a collection of Guatemalan paintings and polychrome sculptures from the city's churches.

CONVENT OF SANTA CATALINA.
Founded in 1613, the convent was the smallest of the eleven religious complexes existing at the time, and the second convent for women. In 1694 an arch was built across the street to link it with newly acquired land on the other side. The church was completed in 1647.

CHURCH OF LA MERCED. The Mercedarian order were the first to build a monastery after the Conquest. They settled initially in Ciudad Vieja ▲ 275, remaining there for two hundred years before their monastery was built in Antigua. Having observed the effects of the 1751 earthquake, the architect constructed a squat building, with particularly thick walls and small, high-placed windows. Inaugurated in 1767, six years later it was badly damaged by earthquakes. Today the restored church is flanked by two low towers and has a lavishly decorated, stuccoed façade. All that remains of the monastery is a huge pool and fragments of walls.

MONASTERY OF SAN JERONIMO (ROYAL CUSTOMS HOUSE).
Because it had not been granted prior royal authorization, the vast two-story college, built by the Mercedarians between 1739 and 1745, was confiscated in 1761 and converted into a customs house, then a barracks.

CONVENT OF LA MONASTERY. All that remains of this monastery, restored in 1978, is a kitchen, fountain and refectory. It may have been used as an infirmary or orphanage.

JESUIT MONASTERY. This included an entire block of houses inhabited, among others, by Bernal Díaz del Castillo. Beyond the square, cluttered with stands displaying traditional crafts, the façade still bears traces of painted floral and geometric motifs.

MONASTERY OF SAN AGUSTIN. This church and monastery was founded in 1657, destroyed by an earthquake and rebuilt in 1735.

HOLY WEEK
Holy Week celebrations are particularly spectacular in the colonial setting of Antigua. As well as the Antigueños, they also attract crowds of visitors ● 74. Magnificent carpets of colored sawdust and flower petals cover the ground along the route of the processions ▲ 271, which advance to the sound of funeral marches. Palm Sunday is celebrated amidst a forest of palm branches. The processions begin on Maundy Thursday.

CROSS AND FOUNTAIN OF LA MERCED
The cross stands opposite the church of La Merced and bears two dates: 1688, inscribed in a heart-shaped escutcheon, and 1765, on the base. A fountain (probably 17th century) to the right of the façade used to belong to the Franciscan cloister.

PEDRO DE BETANCOURT

Pedro de Betancourt (1626–67), buried in the transept of the
church of San Francisco, is one of the most revered religious
figures in Central America. He led an exemplary life of
devotion and charity and was beatified in 1981. The votive
offerings around his former sepulcher are evidence of the
degree to which he is venerated.

SAN JOSÉ EL VIEJO. This hermitage,
completed in 1761, is a fine example of
earthquake-resistant architecture. Its low
walls are strengthened by small, low
towers incorporated into the façade.

MONASTERY OF SANTA CLARA. The
monastery was begun in 1700 and
completed in 1715. The then Captain
General provided the funds for the
church which was consecrated in 1734
and, unusually, opens onto the monastery
rather than onto the street.
Unfortunately there is not enough room
to stand back and admire its sculpted
façade as an inn has been built on the
church square. The two-story cloister is
one of the largest in the city.

MONASTERY OF SAN FRANCISCO. This
Franciscan monastery, which has stood
on the site since 1543, was completed in
1625. The church has been rebuilt several
times. Its façade is decorated like a
retable, with stuccoed columns, and is
flanked by two massive towers. The altars
near the side entrance illustrate scenes
from the Old Testament. The retables
and the cherubs on the ceiling are fine
examples of local Baroque.

MONASTERY OF SANTO DOMINGO. Built in
1642, this monastery was the largest and
wealthiest in the city, as well as the
intellectual center. Its ruins have been
turned into a hotel and restaurant (Casa
Santo Domingo) where some of its
furnishings and works of art remain.

A RELIGIOUS CITY
From top to bottom:
the churches of San
Francisco, a
neighboring village
and Los Remedios,
the arch of Santa
Catalina, the church
of La Merced and
Antigua cathedral.

CONVENT OF LAS CAPUCHINAS. This was
the last convent to be built in Antigua.
The increasing influence of the Capuchin
order was interrupted by the earthquake
of 1773 and the vast buildings were
occupied by only twenty-eight nuns.
Beyond the main cloister, with its massive
columns and pointed segmental arches,
the Torre del retiro consists of eighteen
cells for spiritual retreats and novices. A
staircase leads to an underground room
whose central pillar supports the floor of
the circular courtyard. It is thought that it
may have been used as a pantry although
it is the only known example (cellars were
no more common during the colonial
period than they are today).

CHURCH OF EL CARMEN. The church's
two-story façade is one of the most
beautiful in the city and is best admired
in the morning light. In places the brick is
visible beneath the stuccoed geometric
motifs on the pairs of pillars. The church
was consecrated in 1728.

▲ HIGHLANDS OF GUATEMALA
AROUND ANTIGUA GUATEMALA

Antigua has a number of shops to interest visitors, including art galleries and jade workshops which sell jewelry and jade ornaments.

COFFEE "FINCAS"
You only have to visit the environs of Antigua to realize just how much coffee is grown on the floor and slopes of the valley. The occasional owner's residence can be seen nestling amidst the vast *fincas*, beneath the trees whose shady foliage shelters the coffee shrubs. Industrial activity is limited to the Nestlé fruit-processing plant on the outskirts of Antigua toward Ciudad Vieja, and the Hunapú cotton mill in the city.

"CASAS" OF ANTIGUA GUATEMALA ★

Although they may not have the grandeur of the religious buildings, Antigua's private residences owe their charm to their single stories, their pastel-colored façades and high, often whitewashed walls, literally overflowing with flowering shrubs. The urban landscape is characterized by massive car gateways, pinnacle turrets and high windows with iron or turned-wood grilles. Inside patios are often converted into gardens, bordered with galleries and wooden pillars. Antigua has much in common with San Cristóbal de las Casas ▲ 233.
CASA DE LOS LEONES. A beautiful door, with an entablature flanked by lions, has been added to this late 17th-century aristocratic residence. Today it is one of three restored residences functioning as a hotel.
CASA POPENOE. Built during the first half of the 17th century, this private house has been restored and authentically furnished. It is open to the public.
CASA K'OJOM (MUSIC MUSEUM). The museum has a small display of pre-Hispanic instruments including conches, whistles and turtle shells, as well as Spanish musical instruments from marimbas (a kind of xylophone) to calabash (*tecomates*) and simple sound boxes● 78. There is also a reproduction of the Maximón of Santiago Atitlán ● 72 ▲ 281.

CERRO DEL MANCHÉN (CERRO DE LA CRUZ)
An equestrian statue of Santiago, the patron saint
of the Reconquest, the Conquest of America and
the city, stands on top of this hill which offers a
splendid view of the Antigua valley. The statue
was a gift from Spain.

AROUND ANTIGUA

SAN JUAN DEL OBISPO. Lying at the foot
of the Volcán Agua, this village developed
around the 16th-century residence built for Bishop
Marroquín. The church and monastery complex has retained
its original appearance.

SANTA MARIA DE JESÚS. This village was founded at the end
of the 16th century by the Indians brought from
Quetzaltenango ▲ 282. The inhabitants used to transport
wood from their forests to the town, which earned the village
its original name of El Aserradero (the sawmill). The village
is the departure point for the ascent of Volcán Agua.

SAN ANTONIO AGUASCALIENTES. This village is famous for its
weaving. The cloth used to make its *huipiles* ● 94 is decorated
on both sides with geometric bird and flower motifs.

ALOTENANGO. The Pipil dialect is still spoken in the village. It
used to be situated on the road which ran between the Agua
and Fuego volcanos and linked the colonial capital with
Escuintla ▲ 269. The Baroque church dates from the end of
the 17th century.

SAN FELIPE DE JESÚS. The village church, founded in 1430,
was rebuilt in 1850 in neo-Gothic style
with stones re-used from the church of
La Merced ▲ 272. It houses an
anonymous recumbent Christ.
Pilgrims come here on the first Friday of
Lent and throughout Holy Week.

CIUDAD VIEJA
There is still
disagreement over
the exact site of the
first Spanish town.
According to one
theory Ciudad Vieja,
at the foot of the
Volcán Agua, stands
on the site of the
former capital
(1527–41). However,
recent excavations
tend to suggest that it
lay about a mile to
the east, at San
Miguel Escobar.

ANTIGUA TO CHIMALTENANGO

A secondary road leaves Antigua via the
Calle Ancha de los Herreros toward
Chimaltenango. It goes through the village of Jocotenango
where the square has a fine late-17th-century baroque church.

SAN ANDRÉS ITZAPA. About 2 miles from the road,
the village of San Andrés Itzapa has a
sanctuary dedicated to Maximón ● 72,
▲ 281 who is venerated by Indians and
Ladinos alike. Families visit the
sanctuary to offer candles, incense
and cigarettes and ask for help,
a cure, or forgiveness.

PATZÚN
When the Franciscans settled here in 1540 they brought with them a statue of Saint Bernardino of Siena, who became the patron saint of the village. During the Corpus Christi festival the streets of Patzún (below) are covered with flowers and colored sawdust arranged in wonderful patterns. Arches of vegetables are erected at the intersections.

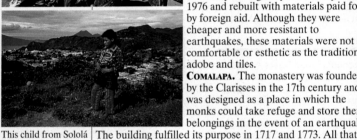

This child from Sololá is wearing the local costume: striped trousers, a woollen apron and "western" style shirt.

SUMPANGO
The 16th-century parish church was badly damaged in the 1976 earthquake – its square shape, large buttresses and low towers and pediment were not enough to protect it. It has since been restored. On November 1, the inhabitants of Sumpango, like those of Santiago Sacatepéquez, fly huge kites.

SANTIAGO SACATEPÉQUEZ. This village of five thousand inhabitants is famous for its All Souls' Day (Day of the Dead) celebration ● 74. The ancient tradition of making and flying huge kites on November 1 is thought to be based on a legend which tells of demons invading the cemetery and disturbing the sleep of the dead. An old sage from the village suggested that the demons could be frightened away by the noise of rustling paper, so the decision was taken to fly kites in the rising winds of November and the custom began. Other explanations take into consideration the astronomical knowledge of the Maya, the traditional use of bright colors in clothing, art and crafts, and the climatic changes that take place in the highlands of Guatemala at the end of October. These changes are characterized by the end of the rains, strong winds, clear skies and a drop in temperature. The kites are made several weeks in advance by families and groups of friends, Indians and mestizos, using bamboo for the ribs and paper for the sails. Their diameter can be anything from 6 to 26 feet.

CHIMALTENANGO ▲ 275. Chimaltenango means the "town of the walls" in Nahuatl, while its Cakchiquel ● 63 inhabitants call it Bocob, (meaning shield). Like all the villages on the high central plateaux, it was badly damaged by the earthquake of 1976 and rebuilt with materials paid for by foreign aid. Although they were cheaper and more resistant to earthquakes, these materials were not as comfortable or esthetic as the traditional adobe and tiles.

COMALAPA. The monastery was founded by the Clarisses in the 17th century and was designed as a place in which the monks could take refuge and store their belongings in the event of an earthquake. The building fulfilled its purpose in 1717 and 1773. All that remains is the church with its beautiful Baroque façade, badly damaged in 1976 and subsequently restored. A tradition of primitive painting ● 132 depicts the traditions and customs of everyday life in the village. These works can be seen in the village or in the galleries of Antigua and Guatemala.

IXIMCHÉ. For three years (1524–7) following the truce agreed with Alvarado ● 36, the Cakchiquel capital was also the Spanish capital. The Mayan site, an example of the Postclassic ceremonial center, was restored in the 1960's by the Guillemin. The site occupies a narrow promontory between two ravines. The promontory was dissected by an artificial moat which separated the ceremonial and aristocratic center in the east from the large area occupied by the "commoners". A series of four ceremonial squares, constituting separate groups, occupies the upper part of the promontory. Two of the groups have a ball court. Little remains of the structures, as the columns and walls were made of adobe. Polychrome paintings on a layer of stucco have been discovered on some of the surviving remains. A sacrificial stone used for tearing out hearts and an offering of skulls from decapitated victims provide evidence of human sacrifice ● 46.

SANTA APOLONIA. Beyond this small pottery-producing village, the road winds through the valleys and along the rocky slopes of the Sierra Madre before climbing (mirador of Lake Atitlán) towards the major intersection of Los Encuentos (78 miles). Here a road to the right leads to the Quiché region ▲ *286* and about 2 miles further on is the road to Sololá and Lake Atitlán.

SOLOLA. Situated on the border of the Cakchiquel and Quiché regions, Sololá constitutes an important link between the mountain economy and the tropical production of the Pacific coast ▲ *290*. As well as the usual food crops, potatoes, carrots, radishes, beetroot, peaches and apples are grown. The large covered market is organized in sections – utensils, industrial items, meat, basic products and clothes – and gives a clear picture of the consumer habits of the rural population.

A great variety of motifs appear on the All Souls' Day kites. They may be inspired by Mayan symbols and divinities, depict scenes of everyday life or even bear images of modern-day personalities.

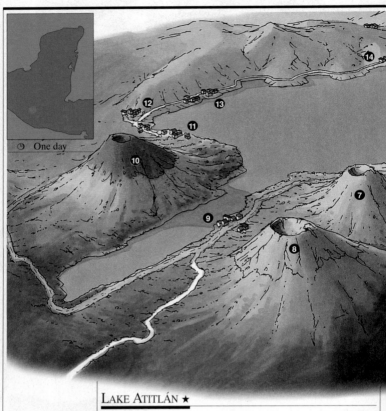

⏱ One day

LAKE ATITLÁN ★

ORIGINS. According to some geologists, the lake was formed as a result of the appearance about eighty thousand years ago of a volcano to the west of the present depression. Three volcanos (**7, 8, 10**) emerged from the water in its crater, giving the lake its characteristic kidney-bean shape. They were followed, at the foot of Tolimán, by the smaller Cerro de Oro (**6**), a volcano in the process of being formed and where, according to legend, the Tzutuhils hid their treasure when the Spanish arrived. Although the depth of the lake shown on maps is in the region of 1,050 feet, surveys carried out in the 1960's estimated the depth near San Lucas Tolimán to be 1,970 feet. It is thought that the water drains by underground seepage toward the Pacific plain. The 1976 earthquake caused the faults at the southeastern end of the lake to widen and the water level to drop by 16 feet.

CLIMATIC CHANGES. The prevailing wind on the lake – the *xocomil* – blows in the afternoon from the southeast. Toward the end of the year cold north winds clear the sky, giving it the purity so sought-after by photographers. *Tumberías*, whirlwinds caused by winds blowing from opposite directions, can form dangerous troughs

BLUE CLOTHES
The clothes of the inhabitants of Santa Catarina Palopó are predominantly in shades of blue, which is fairly rare in Mayan textiles ● *89*. It would seem that this development is due to new techniques and artificial materials.

1. Sololá
2. Panajachel
3. Santa Catarina Palopó
4. San Antonio Palopó
5. San Lucas Tolimán
6. Volcán Cerro de Oro
7. Volcán Tolimán
8. Volcán Atitlán
9. Santiago Atitlán
10. Volcán San Pedro
11. San Pedro La Laguna
12. La Laguna
13. Pablo La Laguna
14. Santa Cruz La Laguna

FISH AND BOATS

Although there is an abundance of fish in the lake, there is little variety. The carnivorous blackbass, introduced in the 1960's, has wiped out all other species except the mojarra, a small fish with white flesh and very fine bones, served grilled or fried in restaurants. Fishing is done with a line, early in the

up to 6 feet deep on the lake and are much feared by fishermen. Among the many legends relating to these meteorological phenomena is that of a wicked giant who could only be destroyed by the combined strength of the villagers. The limbs of the dismembered giant were shared out and displayed in the public squares of the villages. The village which had the head grew tired of the trophy and threw it into the lake. Since then, every afternoon the giant is said to take his revenge by blowing fiercely from the watery depths and endangering the small fishing boats.

ECONOMY. The villages on the lake's eastern shore lie on the border of the Cakchiquel ● 63 region. Like their Tzutuhil counterparts in the south and west, they are prevented from producing large food crops by the steepness of the slopes and the shortage of land. Families limit their own food consumption so that they can sell more and make the additional income necessary to buy indispensable industrial products. The drop in the level of the lake has in fact released fertile land along its shores. Onions, introduced in the 1960's, are now widely cultivated and complement the traditional fishing industry, with mojarra and blackbass, being sold at market or direct to the restaurants of Panajachel. Another important source of income is tourism, either in the form of wages paid to hotel and restaurant staff or for the production of traditional craft items ● 84 sold on the stands lining the streets of the villages, in the capital or abroad.

morning, from *cayucos*, small dugout canoes whose sides are raised with five lateral planks (top). The handles at the back are used to haul them up onto the beach, and a small bench about mid-way along gives the fisherman somewhere to sit. These boats can be seen along the lake shores, their bottoms filled with leaves to maintain humidity.

Doing the washing at San Lucas Tolimán (above).

279

TRADITIONAL CRAFTS
The *huipiles* and trousers of Santiago Atitlán are embroidered with animal motifs (birds, rabbits and fish), arranged between vertical and horizontal lines against a white ground (top, opposite page).

Many of the inhabitants are versed in the art of painting primitive portraits and scenes of everyday life (the market, picking coffee beans and cotton, the village streets). The master of this distinctive "school" of painting was Juan Sisay, assassinated in 1992 for taking too much interest in the development of his village community and the life of its inhabitants. The more recently developed art of wood carving produces figures of fishermen, weavers, porters or women cooking *tortillas*, birds, fish and crabs (*jaiba*), and elegant and unusually shaped little boxes with mysterious drawers.

LAKE CIRCUIT
It is possible to complete a circuit of the lake on foot. Various guides and travel agents organize excursions ◆ 366.

ON THE SHORES OF THE LAKE

SAN JORGE LA LAGUNA. During the 19th century the inhabitants took corn and vegetables down to the Pacific plain where they bartered them for cocoa and sugarcane molasses. The village still has its Maximón ● 72.

PANAJACHEL. Those interested enough to climb to the market and church (below), in the village center, will discover the traditional face of the Cakchiquel village of Panajachel. The other "Pana", decried by the very visitors who contribute to its artificiality, has indeed become a tourist center. There are

boats available for hire to take tourists across the lake.

SANTA CATARINA PALOPO AND SAN ANTONIO PALOPO. Onion crops and irrigated gardens occupying tiny parcels of land are the main forms of agricultural activity. Most of the buildings are orientated in the same way, with a door on the north or south side and a small window overlooking the lake. The other main activities are weaving, for both domestic use and the local tourist industry, fishing and producing mats and cushions (*petates*) woven out of reeds (*tul*).

SAN LUCAS TOLIMAN. This important village has the advantage of being linked both to the *altiplano* road network and to the Pacific coast, which makes it the gateway to Santiago Atitlán.

SANTIAGO ATITLÁN. Santiago Atitlán, whose name means "flower of the nations", is the main town in the Tzutuhil region and successor to the capital of the ancient kingdom which shared its name. Today nothing remains of ancient Chuitinamit, which was situated on the far side of the bay. Although the village itself has become a much-visited tourist center, it is still possible to appreciate the richness and diversity of its traditional crafts. The local divinity, Maximón ● 72, has the upper hand over the Catholic Church, although he did not make his first appearance until the end of the 18th century. There are several founding myths concerning his creation. For a long time he was shrouded in mystery, only appearing to the faithful during Holy Week and always eclipsing Christ during the spectacular village ceremonies. Maximón has provided a considerable source of income for the members of the Santa Cruz brotherhood who display him between a recumbent Christ and crucifixes (below). Santiago is a real hotbed of Indian resistance and, like many other villages in the region,

SAN MARCOS LA LAGUNA
This lakeside village, divided in two by the football pitch and the school, lies partly on a fairly large plateau and partly on the hillside. The old adobe church has just been demolished, no doubt to make way for a new place of worship. The rows of pine and avocado seedlings on the shores of the lake are part of a reforestation project. There is also a scheme to revive the use of medicinal plants among the villagers.

has suffered from violent repression during recent years. This spiritually rich village has about thirty chapels. There are more than ninety, often fundamentalist, sects in Guatemala, not to mention the original traditional beliefs, while catechization is often underpinned by fairly unsubtle forms of indoctrination.

SAN PEDRO LA LAGUNA. The village of San Pedro is very similar to Santiago. It has the same houses, built of volcanic rock with corrugated iron roofs; the same steam baths (*temascal*) in the yard, where the family washes in a way which is both hygienic and ritualistic; the same two-story houses belonging to the *nouveau-riche* merchants, carriers and emigrés who have made money abroad; and, finally, the same population which is gradually opening up to outside

influences, both national and foreign. San Pedro is also popular with hippies, who consider Panajachel far too polluted by tourism.

SAN JUAN LA LAGUNA. This sleepy village is like an extension of San Pedro. In fact many of San Juan's peasants rent land from the village of San Pedro. There is a modern church which has little aesthetic appeal, but the adjoining town hall is charming and has retained its old, individually hand-carved, wooden pillars. The landscape surrounding San Juan la Laguna is dotted with coffee-drying "patios" dominated by nearby pulpers and hoppers.

SAN PABLO LA LAGUNA. This is a strange little village with no weekly market. Most of the houses still have their original adobe walls and thatched roofs. The agave (sisal) grown on the hillsides is the raw material for the main activity of San Pablo: rope-making.

NAHUALÁ
A few miles northwest of the lake, the inhabitants of Nahualá quarry the basalt used to make millstones (*metates*). The villagers also make simply decorated pine furniture and painted wood sculptures reminiscent of the colonial era.

TOTONICAPÁN

San Miguel Totonicapán is a large, busy village situated at an altitude of 8,200 feet. It is the main town in the region of Totonicapán and lies in the center of a very densely populated valley. Its main activities are traditional crafts ● *84* and commerce. The church of San Cristóbal Totonicapán prides itself on its 17th-

CUATRO TERMINOS
This major intersection services Totonicapán 9 miles to the north and Quetzaltenango and its valley to the west. The road continues west to Huehuetenango ▲ *284* and the border post of La Mesilla (Mexico), and into Chiapas ▲ *231*. Fruit-growers' stalls sell organically grown apples, pears, small peaches (*duraznos*) and sweet candied fruits.

century paintings. Like all the *huipiles* in the Totonicapán basin, the local *huipil* has retained the lace collar added by the Spanish ● *97*. The houses of San Andrés Xecul, nestling at the foot of the hill, still have adobe walls and tiled roofs. The church has a multicolored dome and its naive painted enamel façade, decorated with cherubs, tropical fruits and the lions of the Spanish crown (above) is one of the village's main attractions. However, the paved streets leading up to the chapel and calvary, which stand next to a Mayan sanctuary ● *66*, are also worth a visit. In the forest beyond, the mouth of a sacred cave where Indian priests officiate, can be seen mid-way up the hillside. Maximón is also venerated at San Andrés ● *72*, ▲ *281*.

QUETZALTENANGO

Quetzaltenango's Quiché name, Xelajú, is still used but is usually abbreviated to Xela (pronounced "chéla").
THE SECOND REGIONAL TOWN. Quetzaltenango has no major attractions but is nonetheless a charming place. There is a contrast between the impressive volcanic stone and freestone architecture of the monuments in its main square (including the city hall, the museum of history and natural history and the Banco de Occidente), and the modesty of the neighboring streets which are often still paved and lined with tiny adobe houses. The opulent structures built during the late 19th-century coffee boom are still characterized by a certain rural traditionalism.

SALCAJÁ
The village of Salcajá is situated between San Cristóbal Totonicapán and Quetzaltenango. Its church, the first to be founded in Guatemala, stands off the main street, to the right, in a pretty square. Although it has been renovated, the façade still has its original naive decorations.

HISTORY. The town was founded by Pedro de Alvarado ● *36* on May 15, 1524. After the declaration of Independence and the brief attachment of the newly created

states to the Mexican empire of Agustín de Iturbide, in 1828–40 western Guatemala formed the Estado de los Altos, the sixth state in the Federation of Central America. Towards the end of the 19th century the production of coffee led to the development of roads and ports, and the country's oldest bank, the Banco de Occidente, was founded in Quetzaltenango in 1883 (view of the town in 1896, below). **MONUMENTS.** The beautiful Parque de Centroamérica (central square) is surrounded by neoclassical buildings (cathedral, city hall and cultural center) built in volcanic stone. Opening onto the square is the Pasaje Enríquez, designed in 1900 using the Parisian *passages* as a model. The six-domed cathedral, rebuilt in 1899, has retained the façade (only slightly offset) of the former Catedral del Espíritu Santo, built in 1535 and destroyed by an earthquake. The Casa de la Cultura houses a small history museum on the first floor and a natural history museum on the second. The neoclassical theater has a beautiful, colonnaded façade.

ALMOLONGA
Almolonga, known locally as the "orchard of Central America", is a major center for vegetable growing. Its daily market is characterized not only by the scents of the mountains ("volcanos" as they are called here), but also by the colors of the *huipiles*, embroidered with orange, yellow and red zigzag motifs ● *94*, and the *sotto voce* negotiations so typical of Indian markets ◆ *374*.

AROUND QUETZALTENANGO

CERRO EL BAÚL. This hill offers a splendid view of Quetzaltenango and the valley.
ZUNIL. In the chancel of this town's huge church, the silver repoussé tabernacle and altar front date from the colonial period. Crops, predominantly onions, are grown in the river bed which is littered with huge basalt rocks spewed out by the Volcán Zunil. The impressive Cerro Quemado and Santa María volcanos can be seen from the valley when it is not shrouded in mist. Maundy Thursday procession in Zunil (below, opposite).
FUENTES GEORGINAS. One of the springs rising on the slopes of the Volcán Zunil has been channeled and harnessed. However, the formerly high temperatures of the source are decreasing and today do not exceed 95°F. Bathing is permitted and accommodation is available.

TOWARD SAN MARCOS

SAN JUAN OSTUNCALCO. The village, the home of Jesús Castillo who composed music for the marimba ● *78*, specializes in wicker furniture.
SAN MARTÍN SACATEPÉQUEZ. This Mam village, at the foot of the Volcán Chicabal, was once quite an important center. In 1902 San Martín and its neighbor, Concepción Chiquirichapa, suffered the worst natural disaster of their history. An earthquake in April was followed, on October 24, by the eruption of the Volcán Santa María which buried the surrounding arable lands under three feet of pumice.
VOLCAN CHICABAL. The summit of this squat volcano, to the south of San Martín Sacatepéquez, can be reached on foot in two hours with the help of a guide.

CANTEL
The Cantel textile factory, founded in 1883, is the oldest industrial installation in Guatemala. It has employed as many as several thousand workers. The village also has a glass workshop, which produces attractive functional and decorative items.

SAN PEDRO SACATEPÉQUEZ AND SAN MARCOS. The towns of San Pedro (Indian) and San Marcos (predominately mestizo) are linked by a broad avenue and form a single urban center.

QUETZALTENANGO TO HUEHUETENANGO

SAN FRANCISCO DE ALTO. The Friday market is the highlight of the week for this sleepy village, which specializes in home-produced traditional crafts. On October 4 the largest livestock market of the *altiplano* is held here, on the vast esplanade overlooking the square.

MOMOSTENANGO. Momostenango (bottom, center) is an important center for sheep and wool: blankets (*colchas* or *frazadas*), ponchos, jackets and shirts in white, gray or brown wool are mass-produced in its workshops and sold at markets throughout the country.

CUCHUMATANES

HUEHUETENANGO. Huehuetenango, at the foot of the Cuchumatanes range, is the successor to the ancient Mam capital, Zaculeu ("white land"), and the last major town on the road to La Mesilla and the Chiapas ▲ 231 border. Its market provides an opportunity to meet inhabitants from all parts of the region.

ZACULEU. The archeological site of Zaculeu (top, left) was built on an easily defendable plateau surrounded by

ravines. It was inhabited from the end of the Preclassic period, but did not reach the height of its glory until the second half of the Postclassic period when it became the Mam capital until the arrival of the Spanish in 1525. After 1,000 the temples were built in stone rather than adobe. Structure 1 was built during the Early Postclassic and consists of a single, rectangular room with a stone altar built against the back wall. Most of the other Late Postclassic temples also had a single room, although there are exceptions (Structure 4 has three rooms). There are nearly always three entrances each with two columns placed in a long opening. The bases, which are usually square, consist of large vertical steps and have staircases on one, three or four sides flanked by ramps. Other elongated structures were built on low platforms. The ball court, like the one at Mixco Viejo ▲ 269, is in the form of an I. The decision taken by the restorers of Zaculeu to cover all the restored buildings with stucco has been much criticized. Although the present appearance of the buildings (with the exception of the colors) is probably quite close to their original state, it is unpopular because it does not correspond to the general preconception of ruins: with exposed stonework and lush green vegetation climbing all over on the walls.

CHIANTLA. Pilgrims come here from the neighboring regions to worship the silver-cloaked Virgin of la Candelaria.

SIERRA DE LOS CUCHUMATANES. The Cuchumatanes range was thrown up from the depths of the sea by powerful geological forces. It reaches its highest point with the peak of Xemal (12,795 feet) where marine fossils are found in abundance. This karstic causse, the so-called "terraced cordillera", is characterized by its stark relief, valleys, folded slopes, rocky ledges and tangled, rocky peaks. The conifers that once covered it have been replaced by a stunted vegetation of thistles and dry grasses where coyotes, pumas, a few jaguars and birds of prey manage to survive. The villages lie in the warmer, but often wet, lateral valleys.

TODOS SANTOS ★. The 90 percent Mam ● *63* village of Todos Santos nestles in a north-facing valley which, throughout the year, is shrouded in mist from the early afternoon. In recent years it has experienced significant changes, due as much to a northward population migration as to the increase in tourism. The men of Todos Santos wear one of the most interesting costumes in Guatemala: striped shirts with long, embroidered collars; black woollen over-trousers, to keep their thighs warm, and red and white striped trousers ● *98*. Both men and women wear rigid straw hats. The village is dominated by the Postclassic ruins of Tecumanché which are still used as a place of worship. Turkeys are sacrificed around two crosses – the cross is also a Mayan symbol representing the crossing of the four ways, (the four points of the compass) ● *66*.

MOUNTAIN VILLAGES ★. The isolated village of San Juan Atitlán can only be reached after a very steep climb in a four-wheel drive vehicle, or on foot (about six hours). San Pedro Soloma, situated in a valley, has experienced every imaginable disaster. It was destroyed by earthquakes in 1773 and 1902 and by fire in 1884. A year later its population was decimated by smallpox. San Mateo Ixtatán is perched on the side of a desolate valley.

The marimba, the national instrument of Guatemala, is played at all Indian and mestizo festivals ● *78*.

The central square in Huehuetenango.

SACRED SPRINGS
Deep in the valley of San Mateo Ixtatán, salt springs have been harnessed and are worked every afternoon. The collection of the water is considered a sacred event and is authorized by supernatural powers. The descent to the entrance of the mines is preceded and concluded by ritual ceremonies on the altars (*quemaderos*). The water is carried back to the village in large earthenware jars and evaporated in huge cooking pots.

285

"POPOL VUH" ● *146*
The *Popol Vuh* manuscript was discovered in the Franciscan convent next to the church of Santo Tomás by Father Ximénez. One of his successors, the

Abbé Brasseur de Bourbourg, took the manuscript to Spain in 1860 and published it in Paris in 1866 ▲ *292.*

SANTO TOMÁS
The church of Santo Tomás was built in c. 1540 by the Dominicans. Its vault was rebuilt after the 1976 earthquake but the parishioners refuse to have its smoke-damaged retables cleaned. The high walls are newly whitewashed for the festival of the patron saint.

CHICHICASTENANGO

In spite of the influx of tourists, Chichicastenango has not only retained its outward appearance of a mountain village, with its mudbrick walls, but also its own sense of identity as a village community ● *64, 68.*
MARKET ◆ *374.* On the day before the market the square is invaded by traveling merchants setting up the frames of their

stalls. At night the trading families sleep on their bundles, wrapped in old blankets, giving the place a ghostly appearance. After all this chaos the market, which offers a good sample of crafts from all over Guatemala, comes as something of a surprise as all the negotiations are conducted in low voices. It is advisable to make your way through the outer barrier of crafts of doubtful quality, which have been made specifically for tourists, to the center of the square. The villagers do their trading in the Indian market, held around the fountain.
CHURCH OF SANTO TOMÁS. The great stairway leading into the church (pictured above, during the festival of Santo Tomás) was built on top of an older place of worship, and Indian priests burn incense on an altar at the foot of the steps. Other *chuchkajau* incessantly swing censers ● *70* in front of the door. It is courteous to respect the sacred nature of the place and avoid parking on the church square or using the main entrance.
INDIAN RITUALS. The architectural and artistic interest of the church is eclipsed by the rituals performed there. Families first present their bundles containing offerings of rose petals, candles, alcohol and sometimes corn at the foot of the central altar before distributing them on the altars along the main aisle. They are accompanied by an Indian priest who, kneeling on one knee, murmurs prayers addressed to the divinities, although a request sometimes involves a discussion aloud. These devotions express the complex and multi-faceted faith of a nation that has been converted willingly or by force. It is probable that the Indians are more receptive to the dialogic and sacrificial aspects of the imported religion than to the abstractions of the great mysteries of a totally alien theology.
RELIGIOUS SYNCRETISM. The priest is only in charge of the church during the bilingual services (accompanied by a marimba, flutes and drums), or during collective christenings.

> **"WE HAVE ALWAYS LIVED HERE: IT IS ONLY JUST THAT WE CONTINUE TO LIVE IN THE PLACE THAT WE LOVE AND WHERE WE WANT TO DIE. FOR IT IS ONLY THERE THAT WE CAN BE RESTORED TO LIFE."**
>
> POPOL VUH

CEMETERY
The attractive cemetery of "Chichi" reflects the social structure of the village. Near the entrance there are impressive mausoleums, simple colored tombs and many children's tombs. In the chapel at the far end, the tomb of Father Rossbach, the village priest in the 1930's and founder of the little archeological museum, lies alongside the tombs of the region's Spanish priests, assassinated during the violence of the 1980's.

DIVERSE CULTURES
The highlands, with their mainly Indian population, are a mixture of ethnic groups, traditions and colors. Rigoberta Menchú (above), winner of the 1992 Nobel Peace Prize, comes from the village of Chimel, near Chajul ▲ 289.

PASCUAL ABAJ
On one of the hills overlooking Chichicastenango is the altar dedicated to Pascual Abaj, a local "saint". People travel long distances to receive his blessing, to ask for favors and good fortune and to be healed
● 70.

MAYAN REMAINS
Excavations carried out in the east of the Quiché region led to the discovery of a number of objects, including two Late Classic funerary urns (above and right), a ceramic vase in the form of a human skull (below), an Early Classic ceramic piece representing a monster (center) and a carved jade plaque (top, opposite).

UTATLÁN
The Mayan city of Utatlán, built on a rocky spur, is one of the late defensive sites of the Guatemalan highlands. The ruins lie several miles west of Santa Cruz del Quiché, the regional capital.

The cemetery of the Ixil ● 63 village of Chajul, with its whitewashed tombs, is typical of the cemeteries of the region.

The sanctuary belongs to the community and when priests tried, on more than one occasion, to rid it of pagan rites, they were themselves driven out. More recently the priests in charge, Indian in some cases, have been much closer to their flock and supported their rights and interests.

EAST QUICHÉ

SAN ANDRÉS SAJCABAJA, LA LAGUNITA. These mixed villages, occupied by Indians and *Ladinos*, are in the center of a region which was dramatically affected by the political violence of the 1980's. Franco-Guatemalan archeological excavations carried out under the direction of Alain Ichon at La Lagunita, a few miles from the regional capital, led to the discovery of thirty or so steles and sculpted stones, ceramic urns with lids, an effigy of the jaguar (symbol of the nocturnal sun) and four monolithic sarcophagi. Offerings, including three hundred pieces of pottery, were found in a vast artificial cavity beneath the central plaza, surrounded by four pyramids. Their date of AD 400 corresponds to La Lagunita's golden age. The site was occupied between 600 BC and AD 600.

ZACUALPA AND JOYABAJ. The intense mauves and reds of the *huipiles* ● 95 of Zacualpa are now used in huge bedspreads. The blouses of Joyabaj have a mauve background and broad, embroidered collar, decorated with rosettes of stylized flowers. The village, whose patron is the Virgen de la Asunción, celebrates its saint's festival on August 15. The pre-Columbian *palo volador* ● 77 is still performed under the Christianized name of Saint Michael's dance.

North Quiché

SACAPULAS. The first inhabitants of the village came from the north, following the Río Negro (or Chixoy) upstream. Sacapulas, where the Río Negro flows east-west before turning north, has for a long time been a crossroads.

CUNEN AND USPANTÁN. These villages are situated in the valley of the Río Chixoy and lie on the road linking Huehuetenango and Quiché with Verapaz ▲ 292. Uspantán was on the edge of the northern region held by the guerillas between 1979 and 1983 and was caught in the cross-fire between the rebels and the army. Rigoberta Menchú ▲ 287, from the isolated village of Chimel, to the north of Uspantán, gave an account of daily life in these rural areas and of the fierce repression brought to bear on the population during those terrible years. These accounts, together with her action to promote the rights and identity of the Indian people, won her the 1992 Nobel Peace Prize.

IXIL REGION. Nebaj, Chajul and Cotzal are three mountain villages which share the same language and are traditionally known as the Ixil Triangle. During the 1970's rebellion, this area was used as an army outpost and suffered as a consequence. It was also at the heart of the "reconquest by force" initiative of 1980–2, which employed a scorched earth strategy combined with the idea of "civil self-defence patrols" and "model villages". Once again its people found themselves caught up in a conflict which made day-to-day living conditions unbearable. There were more refugees from this region than anywhere else, with people fleeing to Mexico (almost a hundred thousand went in 1985) or the high mountain ranges. With the military maintaining an influential role, the return to a so-called civilian government in 1985 did nothing to allay fears. The CPR (communities of the population in resistance) of the Sierra, more than ten thousand people, were to all intents and purposes surrounded by the army and unable to reach the areas that were ready to receive them until March 1994, under international control. During this time, the survival of the Ixil population and the reconstruction of the region were supported, at arm's length, by foreign aid and organizations.

The church of Chajul in the Ixil region.

The Late Classic Mayan remains in the *Ladino* village of Canillá (below), near La Lagunita and San Andrés, have been restored.

289

Indian woman from the highlands picking coffee.

HOSTILE COASTLINE
A stretch of gray sand shelving steeply beneath the water, violent breakers, currents running parallel to the shore, powerful ebb tides and sharks constitute the "charms" of the Pacific Ocean. Bathing is ill-advised.

Sculpture dating from AD 700–900, from the region of Santa Lucía Cotzumalguapa.

COFFEE "FINCAS"

The Quetzaltenango-Retalhuteu-Mazatenango triangle produces 90 percent of Guatemala's coffee. The country is the fifth largest exporter of coffee in the world and, in spite of fluctuations in the exchange rate, coffee (with an average income of three hundred million dollars), combined with tourism and the money sent home by those working abroad, accounts for most of Guatemala's foreign currency revenue. Although Brazil and Colombia are larger producers, Guatemala has the largest private coffee plantations in Latin America.

SEASONAL WORK. In the Pacific coastal region coffee is picked from August to November and requires a large additional workforce (known as *cuadrilleros*). These seasonal workers, usually Indians, come from the villages of the *altiplano*. The big landowners employ them for a few weeks and pay a derisory wage.

PACIFIC PLAIN AND COAST

The benchland proper (*boca costa*), characterized by low altitude, tropical vegetation, is succeeded by wet grassland. The road known as the Pacific Highway (CA-2) runs along the benchland at an average distance of 25 miles from the coast. The plain is intersected by rivers which are dry for part of the year and torrential for the other part.

A NATURAL HIGHWAY. The corridor formed by the alluvial plain bordering the Pacific Ocean has been a natural highway since the continent was first inhabited. All the groups that populated South and Central America crossed the continent from west to east. The inhabitants of the southern coast of Mesoamerica were simple hunters and gatherers until the Olmecs ● *31* introduced their "parent culture".

AGRI-EXPORT MODEL. For a long time after the arrival of the Spanish the mountain villages had vast communal lands on the plain. From the early 20th century the region was occupied by banana plantations. United Fruit ▲ *307*, for example, owned plantations around Tiquisate. During the 1950's and 1960's a more diverse form of agriculture was introduced. After sugarcane (shown top, opposite page), the main agricultural products today from the border of Mexico to El Salvador ▲ *314* are cattle, cotton and, to a lesser degree, sesame and soya.

RETALHULEU. This small town is the coastal counterpart of Quetzaltenango ▲ *282*. The histories of the two towns during the coffee boom of the late 19th and early 20th centuries show striking similarities. The splendid Palacio del Gobierno, which houses the town's administrative offices and city hall, is a reminder of this golden age.

ABAJ TAKALIK. In the district of EL ASINTAL, the vast site of Abaj Takalik ("the standing stone" in Quiché) extends across an area now

covered by several *fincas*. A number of archeologists have explored the remains since the end of the 19th century. The site is thought to have been occupied from the Middle Preclassic period. This is indicated by the structure of the main square, which is characterized by a form of mudbrick architecture found at Kaminaljuyú ▲ 268. A second phase of Mayan-style construction, during the Middle and Late Preclassic, extended into the Classic period. In-depth excavations have been carried out since 1987 by the National Institute of Anthropology, but analysis has been hampered by the poor state of preservation of these fragile structures, which have been subjected to heavy rainfall.

SANTA LUCÍA COTZMAGUAPA. Like the neighboring communities of La Gomera and Nueva Concepción, which were the product of the division of state territory, Santa Lucía is a "mushroom town" which developed during the 1970's.

"FINCA" EL BAÚL. The owner of a sugarcane *finca* has gathered together the sculptures found on his land and placed them under one roof. Among the sculptures, which date from the beginning and the end of the Classic period, a stele with two ball-players wearing animal skins, and a stone jaguar are of particular interest.

"FINCA" EL TARRO. On a hill rising out of the fields of sugarcane, a head sculpted from a large stone (c. AD 300) is set into the ground next to a stele. It has a headband decorated with geometric disks. Mayan rituals are regularly performed here to ask for good harvests.

BILBAO. Some fine sculptures decorate the flat surfaces of enormous stones which lie scattered among the sugarcane. They are too heavy to move.

"LAS ILUSIONES". Monoliths representing figures and serpents have been placed in the courtyard of this farm where a small, private museum is open to the public.

LA DEMOCRACIA. Huge stones from several farms in the vicinity have been gathered together in the village square. Others, too big to move, are still *in situ*. The small village museum has pieces of similar origin, but of more modest dimensions (10–13 inches), as well as other objects found in the region.

PUERTO SAN JOSÉ AND PUERTO QUETZAL. Since Puerto Quetzal was built, between 1978 and 1982, the old port of San José has been virtually abandoned. However, the beaches of San José, the most easily accessible for Guatemalans, are totally engulfed at weekends and on public holidays. The sea along the entire length of the Pacific coast is extremely dangerous and unfortunately drownings are frequent. To the east is the Monterico Nature Reserve, dominated by beautiful mangrove planations ■ 20.

MAZATENANGO
Mazatenango is a fast-developing town at the center of a stockbreeding and cocoa- and hevea-producing region. One of the area's few carnivals, which includes dancing and cock fights, is held here in February.

MONOLITHS
The Late Preclassic sculptures of La Democracia (center) use the natural shape of the rock. This style of sculpture, found as far afield as El Salvador, is derived from the Olmecs. The sculptures include large-scale human heads and big-bellied men known as *Dioses Gordos* (fat gods). They are probably trophy heads and statues of sacrificed enemies. Statue (below) found at La Concepción (300 BC–AD 250).

ABBÉ BRASSEUR DE BOURBOURG (1818–74)

↻ The French *abbé* was the priest of Rabinal in 1855. He learned the Quiché language and translated the *Popol Vuh* ● *146* and the *Rabinal Achi* ● *148*, described by the 1862 French edition as "a scenic presentation of the town of Rabinal, transcribed for the first time by Bartolo Ziz, an elder from that same town". Brasseur later became priest of San Juan Sacatepéquez where he discovered the text known as *Memorial de Soledad* or *Anales de los Cakchiqueles*. The accounts descend from the oral tradition and were written after the Conquest. They are among the rare sources providing a basis for the study of kingdoms that existed before the arrival of the Spanish.

"TORITO"
This ritual, still performed in villages during the festival of their patron saint, is part of the Paabanc festival.

HISTORY

Between 1524 and 1530 the Spanish subjugated all the kingdoms that lay in their path, from Chiapas to the central highlands of Guatemala ● *36*. After 1530, their attempts to continue north and east proved more difficult. The region to the east, which for half a century had been subjected to the expansionist pressures of the Quiché kingdom, became known as the "battlefield" and until 1537, this was where the Conquerors encountered fierce resistance from the Kekchis and Chols ● *63*.

EVANGELICAL CONQUEST. In 1537 the bishop Marroquín and the governor Maldonado reluctantly signed an agreement with Bartolomé de Las Casas ▲ *234* giving the Dominicans the exclusive right to represent the Spanish presence in what was to become Verapaz. They adopted a similar evangelical policy to that used a few years earlier in the north and east of Quiché ▲ *286* and, from 1542, concentrated on converting merchants and, more especially, local chieftains (*caciques*). The Church promised to allow the latter to retain their power over the people. In 1545 seven villages, including Rabinal, Cobán and Chamelco, were converted to Christianity. Conflicts arose subsequently between the population and the overseeing religious authorities who wanted to regain control of a region which had become too free for their liking.

BAJA VERAPAZ

SIERRA DE LAS MINAS. The sierra, which straddles the regions of Alta and Baja Verapaz, El Progreso, Zacapa and Izabal, owes its name to its relatively unexploited mineral wealth. Although the ancient Maya extracted jade, the tradition was lost during the colonial period and it is only during the last twenty-five years that jade has been reintroduced into the workshops of Antigua. Some marble is mined and exported. The forest, on the other hand, is being gradually destroyed by over-exploitation, a situation which led to the sierra being declared a nature reserve and subject to the 1989 law governing protected regions.

SALAMA. The church has a 17th-century central altar, retable and statues. The neighboring village of San Jerónimo has a 17th-century church and will soon have a museum of popular traditions and arts. It will be housed in one of the earliest sugar mills in South America, currently being converted.

RABINAL. Gourds and *morros* (fruit with a thick, hard skin) made into carved or painted receptacles (*guacales*) are one of the local specialties, along with pottery and candle making.

KAJYUB. The territory of the Rabinaleb, who themselves succeeded the Poq'omab in the valley, was threatened by the expansionist ambitions of the Quichés during the fifty years prior to the arrival of the Spanish. About a mile

north of Rabinal, the stone enclosure of the old fortified town of Kajyub stands at an altitude of 4,130 feet. Various entrances give access to a courtyard

PAABANC
The region's traditional festival is held at Cobán on or around July 4. For the past twenty years it has opened with a folk festival.
Although the event tends to be limited to the presentation of certain external aspects of the Indian identity, it still arouses a degree of interest among the communities.

containing a temple-pyramid which covers an area of 393 square feet. Pyramid staircases lead to the temple above built of flat stone slabs.

BIOTOPO DEL QUETZAL ■ *24*. This nature reserve (2,840 acres rising to an altitude of 7,545 feet) is in the heart of the Sierra de las Minas, which forms the eastern extension of the Cuchumatanes range and is a favorite haunt of the quetzal. The reserve's primary concern is the preservation of the high-altitude rain forest. Constant temperatures and levels of rainfall throughout the year maintain biological conditions making this a unique genetic "reservoir". Although the chances of seeing a quetzal are slim (dawn is the best time), there is plenty of opportunity to enjoy a walk through the forest with its varied flora and fauna.

ALTA VERAPAZ

SALAMÁ TO COBÁN. The village of Tactic makes a variety of traditional wares (silver jewelry, straw hats, dairy products) but is especially famous for the quality of its embroidery and weaving. The women here wear characteristic wide skirts caught in at the waist and red coral necklaces. The village is dominated by the sanctuary of Chixim (with its Cristo de la Misericordia), a place of pilgrimage on January 15. Santa Cruz Verapaz, founded in 1543, has a church with a rare exterior apse. Further west San Cristóbal Verapaz is famed for its Good Friday celebrations.

QUETZAL
The length of its tail plumes forces the quetzal to build tunnel-shaped nests in rotten tree trunks, between 10 and 16 feet above the ground. The male's green tail plumes (up to 3 feet long) are extremely decorative and used as ornamentation. Imported by the lowland Maya, they are highly prized and have long been the subject of a well-established trade. Today the quetzal (*Pharomachrus moccino*) is threatened as much by the disappearance of its natural habitat as by the trade in its feathers.

HIGHLANDS OF GUATEMALA VERAPAZ

EMBALSE CHIXOY
Between 1978 and 1983 a huge, hydro-electric dam was built on the borders of Quiché and Baja and Alta Verapaz. The resulting reservoir filled the valley of the Chixoy and its tributaries (Salamá, Quixal and Carchelá). The five Quixal turbines (300 megawatts) now provide virtually all the region's electricity. The archeological survey carried out before the valley was flooded revealed an ancient and relatively dense population in the area during the pre-Hispanic period.

CUBULCO
Cubulco, to the west of Rabinal, is one of the few villages in Guatemala where the traditional dance of the *Palo volador* ● 77 is performed on July 25. A broad flight of steps leads to the Iglesia del Calvario.

Mayan cemetery in the highlands.

VALLEY OF COBÁN.
Situated at 4,330 feet in the heart of the Sierra de Chamá the valley of Cobán has high levels of rainfall. Its orchid nurseries (the climate is ideal ■ 28) are open to the public. But this is above all a region of cardamom and coffee. The cultivation of coffee shrubs, encouraged in the central regions from 1845, was extended into Verapaz in 1860 with the arrival of German immigrants ● 88 fleeing from the crisis in Europe. Cobán, founded by the Dominicans, was granted the status of "imperial city" and received its coat of arms from Charles V in 1558. The central square is dominated by the Baroque façade of the cathedral of Santo Domingo. The village of San Pedro Carchá is famous for its tanneries, wooden masks and goldsmiths. The Verapaz regional museum is housed in the Don Bosco college. To the east the caves of Lanquín have some remarkably shaped stalactites.

TOWARD IXCÁN AND PETÉN

To the north of the Sierra de Chamá, the mountains subside and give way to the *Franja Transversal del Norte*, the setting for

a vast agricultural development project which took place in the 1970's. The idea was to relieve the pressure on the densely populated high plateaux by settling the under-populated areas of the north, using the offer of free property rights on state territory.

RIVER AND CAVES OF LA CANDELARIA. The complex, discovered in 1971, was studied by the archeologist Patricia Carot in 1975. The river disapppears and resurges many times along a 7-mile network eroded into the limestone hills. The biggest of La Candelaria's underground chambers is almost 220 square yards with a 196-foot high vaulted ceiling. These caves were not used as dwellings or defensive sites but had a religious function. As symbols of life they were dedicated to the worship of the Earth and Rain gods, and as underground caves, they were the domain of the dead and the "other world".

IXCÁN. This isolated region is particularly well known as the rear-line guerrilla base of the 1970's. The ensuing violence and repression caused more than a hundred thousand peasants to seek refuge in Mexico. Since the establishment of a constitution and the return of a civilian government in 1985, the situation is gradually becoming more stable.

LAKE OF LACHUA. This circular lake (720 feet deep) lies in the center of a national park (24,700 acres), a paradise for tropical flora and fauna.

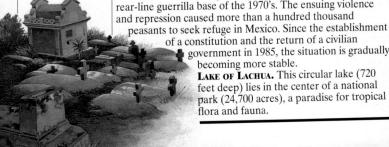

SOUTHEASTERN MAYA

▲ SOUTHEASTERN MAYA
TOWARD THE CARIBBEAN COAST

1. GUATEMALA CITY
2. SALAMÁ
3. JALAPA
4. MOTAGUA VALLEY

M aya territory extends into eastern Guatemala and as far as Honduras and El Salvador, where several archeological sites can still be seen today.

⊙ Four days

PACIFIC OCEAN

MOTAGUA FAULT
At the 140 kilometer (87 mile) mark, the road between Guatemala City and Esquipulas crosses the fault separating the North American from the Central American (tectonic) plate. A violent earthquake in February 1976 caused the plates to move to such a degree that the central line of the road was displaced by about three feet. On the right is a monument to the disaster which claimed 24,000 lives.

This area includes eastern Guatemala (Oriente) from the Pacific coast to the shores of the Caribbean, the extreme west of Honduras, which has one of the most remarkable Mayan sites (Copán ▲ 299), and the western half of El Salvador, the smallest country in Central America. Together they cover the southeastern section of the Route of the Mayas.

MOTAGUA VALLEY

The main highway (CA-9) linking Guatemala City to the Atlantic Ocean was built in the 1950's under the government of President Arbenz. It replaced the old colonial road (Río Dulce–Lake Izabal–Verapaz–Antigua), which ran parallel to the north and fell into disuse following the construction of the large Atlantic port of Puerto Barrios ▲ 310 and the

296

development of the late 19th-century banana plantations. The new road was intended above all to break the transport monopoly held by the IRCA railway company, a subsidiary of the banana producers, the United Fruit ▲ 307.

TOWARD ORIENTE. At Chayal, on the 24 kilometer (15 mile) mark, the road crosses a hill made out of obsidian, a type of rock formed from natural volcanic glass and used by the Maya to make tools.

Debris lies below the road at the foot of the rock face. Before reaching the floor of the Motagua Valley, the road follows the rugged relief of the sierra, whose desert hillsides positively bristle with cereus cacti. At the 136 kilometer (84 mile) mark, a road leads to Zacapa, Chiquimula, the track to Honduras and Copán, and finally Esquipulas.

ORIENTE

LAKES AND VOLCANOS. Oriente – a term used to designate the regions situated to the east of Guatemala City, towards El Salvador and Honduras – has tended to be neglected by short-term visitors because its mestizo population appears less "typical" than the Indian population of the western *altiplano*. It is nevertheless a region of grandiose and varied

Growing cocoa (below) in Oriente.

INDUSTRIAL PROJECTS
To the right of the bridge across the Motagua River are the remains of a huge paper factory. This was never put into

production because of a political and financial dispute between Spain and Guatemala. It was part of a wave of great infrastructure projects in the 1970's which also included the Chixoy hydro-electric dam ▲ 294, the oil pipeline to Santo Tomás and the new port on the Pacific coast ▲ 291. A little further on, the Guatemalan cement company, *Cementos Progreso*, stands to the left of the hairpin bends around the 40 kilometer (25 mile) mark on the CA-9. The company is now promoting the reforestation of the region, having first devastated it to maintain its industrial activity.

▲ SOUTHEASTERN MAYA
TOWARD THE CARIBBEAN

The town of Esquipulas is famed for its worship of a black Christ, sculpted in orange wood by the Portuguese sculptor Quirio Catano in 1549, which stands in the basilica.

ESQUIPULAS II

un paso firme hacia la paz

AEREO GUATEMALA Q.0.40

TALLER NAC. GRABADOS EN ACERO·GUATEMALA

ROAD TO COPÁN
Turn left in the village of Vado Hondo at the 178 kilometer (110 mile) mark on the CA-9. Copán is very

landscapes, where volcanos alternate with mountain lakes.

"ROSARIO PARK". Near Chiquimula and the village of Ipala, which is dominated by a volcano with a crater lake, paleontological deposits have been under excavation since April 1994. Although the bones are, unfortunately, damaged (they were either used as foundations for houses or ground into powder to fatten cattle), the deposits have nevertheless revealed some very large bones belonging to mammoths. Others came from the ancestors of today's bears, some of which reached heights of almost 10 feet, and to the contemporaries of the first American bears of 30,000–8,000 BC.

ESQUIPULAS. Esquipulas lay within the orbit of Copán during the Classic period, and then of the Payaqui kingdom under the influence of Mitlán. By the time the Spanish conquerors arrived, Esquipulas was politically and militarily weakened and was finally subjugated in 1530. The river Lempa runs through the valley and crosses El Salvador on its way to the Pacific Ocean. Dominated by the distant, high peak of Miramundo (5,560 feet), the town is the official seat of the Central American Parliament, a consultative tribunal created after the 1986 Esquipulas agreements and based on the European Parliament. Few sessions are held here, however. The town is also the capital of the *Trifinio*, a zone which covers the borders of Guatemala,

badly signposted, so you will need to use a map. Make sure you don't confuse the site of Copán, shown as "Copán Ruinas", with Santa Rosa de Copán (both are in Honduras) as this will result in a very long detour, albeit on a very pretty mountain road. It takes about two hours to cover the 31 miles between Vado Hondo and the frontier post at El Florido. The site of Copán lies about 8 miles across the Guatemala-Honduras border. Crossing the border to visit the site is not a problem: the authorities issue a special 48-hour visa for this purpose
◆ *356.*

Honduras and El Salvador, and deals with tri-national development projects. A vast neoclassic basilica (above), completed in 1795 after twenty years' work, is visited by worshippers from the surrounding regions and literally invaded around January 15, the date of the annual pilgrimage in honor of its black Christ. One distinctive feature of the event is the iridescent garlands (*toquilla*) wound around straw hats or decorating vehicles. If you continue beyond the attractive 17th-century parish church, you will come to the Franciscan monastery, perched on the hill of Belén opposite the town, from where there is a magnificent view of the town and valley.

TOWARD COPÁN

ESTANZUELA. A small museum of paleontology has a collection of bones of prehistoric animals discovered in the region, including a fine mastodon skeleton and various items found locally. There is also a reconstruction of a pre-Columbian sepulcher.

ZACAPA AND CHIQUIMULA. The main activities of these two fairly unprepossessing and extremely hot towns are stockbreeding and, more recently, the cultivation of crops in glasshouses situated at the bottom of the valley where they cannot be seen from the road. A little further on, the landscape of the Oriente gives way to vast estates, the ancestral fiefs of *Ladino* families.

TOWARD HONDURAS. The track leading to the frontier post of El Florido and then on to Copán, passes through the Chorti villages of Jocotán ("the place where plums grow") and Camotán ("the place where sweet potatoes grow"). Here the peasants wear characteristic white shirts and trousers. The land is divided into small, individual properties devoted to raising livestock and producing food crops, sometimes using irrigation.

COPÁN

The floor of the Copán valley, in Honduras, is carpeted with tobacco plants, interspersed with wooden drying houses which are gradually being replaced by breeze-block structures. The local cigars are renowned for their quality. Coffee is the region's other famous source of wealth and at harvest time beans can be seen drying by the roadside and in courtyards. The village has preserved its traditional character, with its whitewashed walls, tiled roofs and checkerboard streets around the central church square. A delightful museum effectively displays ceramics and other small objects of interest found during the excavations.

SITE OF COPÁN ★
The ruins lie just outside the village, in a dry deciduous forest. Beyond the site is the Copán river whose course is followed by the road from Zacapa. A museum houses the monumental sculptures that have been replaced on the site by replicas.

1. Great Plaza
2. Ball Court
3. Court of the Hieroglyphic Stairway
4. Temple 22
5. East Court
6. West Court

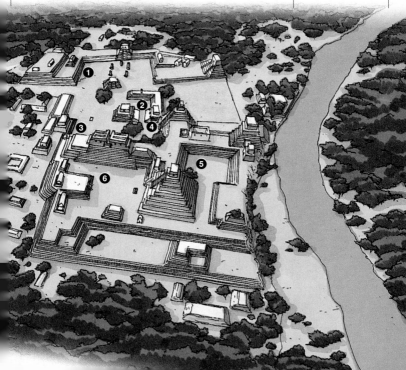

▲ COPÁN

The archeological site of Copán lies close to the Guatemalan border and is one of the few Mayan sites in Honduras. The wealth of its monuments, and particularly its many elaborately decorated steles, make it one of the most important cities in Maya territory. In competition with Quirigua, about 30 miles to the north, Copán reached the height of its glory between the 5th and 9th centuries AD.

BALL GAME ● *112*

The I-shaped ball court near the Great Plaza is open to the south and closed by steps surmounted by a stele to the north. The court proper is divided by three markers placed on the central axis of the aisle. Three macaw heads, the winged symbol of the diurnal sun, are placed at the top of each of the slopes on either side of the court. The game, played by two teams, was more of a ritual than a sport and symbolized the victorious struggle of the forces of life over the forces of death.

RESEARCH

The ruins were described for the first time in 1576, in a letter written to the Spanish king by a senior colonial magistrate, Diego de Palacio (published 1860). But it was Stephens and Catherwood ● *56* who brought them to the attention of the world in 1841. In

1885 Maudslay ● *56* photographed the site (right, the east face of the collapsed Stele C, since restored). Copán has been the subject of much research and, with Tikal, is the most excavated and best known of the Mayan sites. Head of one of the *bacabs* (above) which supported the sky on the façade of Temple 11.

SCULPTURE

Sculpture appears on architectural elements as well as independent pieces such as steles and altars. Most of the steles bear a full-length portrait of the king on one of the main sides, while the rest of the monument is carved with intricate hieroglyphic inscriptions. The most ancient steles, slightly wider towards the top, are sculpted in bas-relief. The relief becomes more pronounced towards AD 700. Stele P, dated AD 623, and Stele C, AD 782 (left).

ALTARS ● 110

With the exception of the most recent, altars usually accompany the steles. The sixteen kings of the Copán dynasty are represented round Altar O. AD 776 (above).

HISTORY

The Copán valley was inhabited at least from the beginning of the first millennium BC, although it did not become a Mayan site until c. AD 400. The Copán dynasty, founded at about this time, came to an end at the beginning of the 9th century with the death of the sixteenth sovereign.

STELES ● 110

Stele H, dated AD 721 (front view, above), was among the several Copán steles drawn by Frederick Catherwood ● 130. Stele B ▲ 304 (detail, right) represents the accession to the throne of king Eighteen Rabbit as an emergence from the jaws of the terrestrial monster, thus comparing the young sovereign with the rising sun. The entire structure represents the earth in the form of a two-headed monster. On the east face is the first head, seen from the front, from which the king is emerging (right). On the west face the second head is represented as a mask seen from above. Other masks are superposed on the smaller north and south faces of the stele which form the body. Frame of the inner door of Temple 22 and Stele D, preceded by its sculpted altar in the form of a two-headed monster (left).

Copán
Stele B

East face

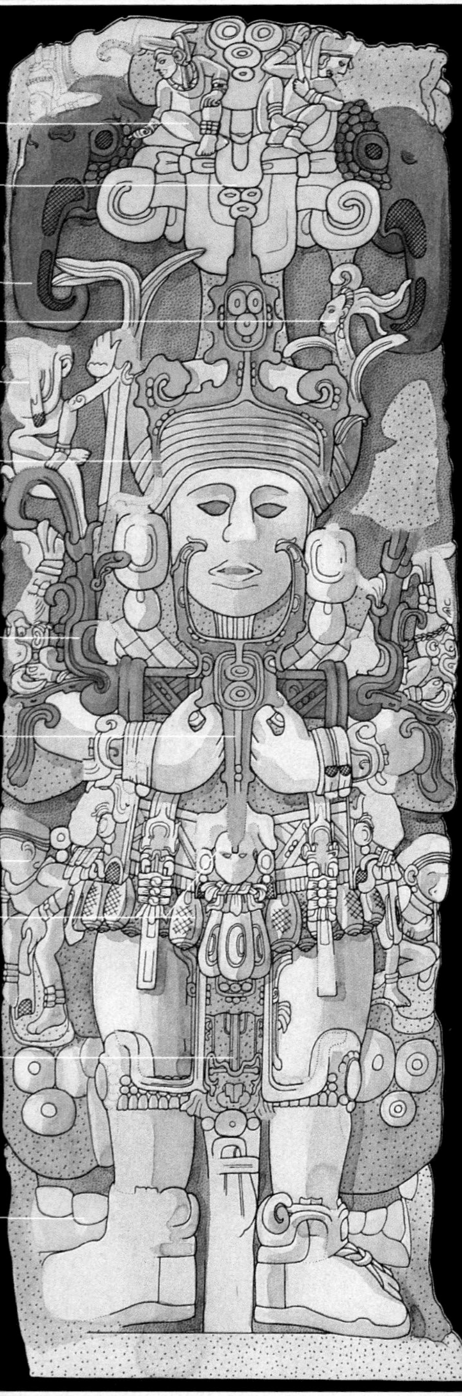

First head of the terrestrial monster from which the king Eighteen Rabbit is emerging.
Ancestor
Terrestrial monster
Macaw, symbol of the diurnal sun
Personified corn
Ancestor
Royal headdress with turban
Scepter in the form of a two-headed serpent whose jaws are open on a supernatural creature marked with various sacrificial symbols
Symbolic sacrificial object
Ancestor
Belt and shells
Loin cloth with solar image
Lower jaw of the terrestrial monster

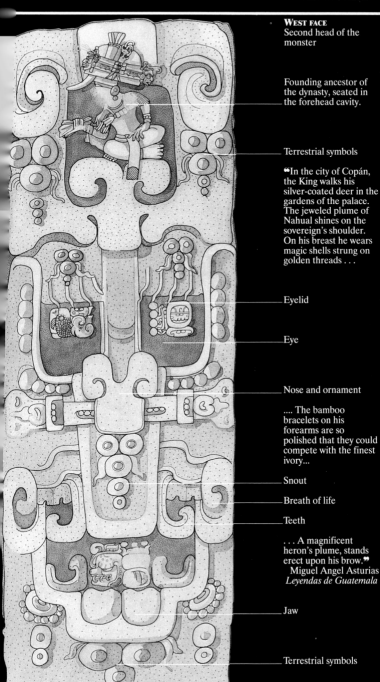

"CARVED DIRECT, IN THE ROUND, [THE SCULPTURE] TAKES ON A BAROQUE LUXURIANCE AND A REFINEMENT WHICH HAVE AROUSED ADMIRATION AND EXERTED AN IRRESISTIBLE ATTRACTION OVER ARCHEOLOGISTS." HENRI STIERLIN

WEST FACE
Second head of the monster

Founding ancestor of the dynasty, seated in the forehead cavity.

Terrestrial symbols

"In the city of Copán, the King walks his silver-coated deer in the gardens of the palace. The jeweled plume of Nahual shines on the sovereign's shoulder. On his breast he wears magic shells strung on golden threads . . .

Eyelid

Eye

Nose and ornament

.... The bamboo bracelets on his forearms are so polished that they could compete with the finest ivory...

Snout

Breath of life

Teeth

. . . A magnificent heron's plume, stands erect upon his brow."
Miguel Angel Asturias
Leyendas de Guatemala

Jaw

Terrestrial symbols

▲ SOUTHEASTERN MAYA
TOWARD THE CARIBBEAN

THE STELES OF QUIRIGUA ● 110
These steles are not accompanied by altars, and the few round sculptures that have been designated as such appear, because of their shape and size, to have been used for other purposes. It is also obvious that the zoomorphs cannot be described as altars. These huge sandstone blocks, between 10 and 13 feet long, represent a mythical animal while partly conserving the original shape of the rock. The two-headed terrestrial monster is often depicted with the sovereign emerging from its open jaws, symbolizing his accession to the throne. Zoomorphs O and P have a flatter rock at their base which continues the inscription of the principle monument. It also bears the image of a dancing figure wearing a jaguar mask (and thus identified with the nocturnal sun) who is about to disappear into the bowels of the earth. Together the two monuments celebrate a dynastic succession: the dead sovereign disappears into the earth while his successor, in the form of a bird (the embodiment of the diurnal sun) emerges from it.

QUIRIGUA ★

Despite its small size, Quirigua has some of the most original and beautiful sculptures in the Mayan world. Situated in the lower Motagua valley, the site lies about 25 miles from Copán ▲ 299 as the crow flies, and the history of the two sites is indissociable. The huge steles and enormous carved rocks (called zoomorphs) were briefly described by Stephens. At the end of the 19th century Maudslay ● 57 photographed, drew and made molds of them. The site has been excavated by several expeditions, the most important being that of the University of Pennsylvania in 1974–9.

HISTORY. The city was founded during the Early Classic period, as evidenced by two dated 5th-century steles. The early occupations of the site are today buried beneath several feet of alluvial deposits. Quirigua, for a long time dependent on Copán, freed itself when its king, Cauac Sky, captured and put to death the king of Copán, Eighteen Rabbit, in 737. This marked the start of a period of glory for Quirigua which lasted more than a century. The last date carved on the site (810) appears on the façade of one of the buildings of the king Jade Sky.

THE LARGEST MAYAN STELE. The layout of the principle group is like a smaller version of the Copán group, with an Acropolis to the south and a Great Plaza to the north containing a number of monuments. The steles on this site (left and center) are of impressive dimensions: the 35-foot high Stele E, erected in 771 is the largest monument of this type. The sovereign is shown from the front of these steles, standing on the mask of a terrestrial monster or a jaguar and holding

306

a thunder-scepter and a round shield. His headdress consists of one or more helmets, crowned with a mask and a panache of plumes. The quality of the calligraphy is superb. One cannot but admire the elegance of the text of Stele F (dedicated in 761) and of the complete glyphs of Stele D (766) ● *44*.

UNITED FRUIT COMPANY

Until the 1960's the banana plantations that stretched from Quirigua to the Caribbean coast were the property of the *Frutera* (United Fruit) company. In 1880, the government granted a land concession to a Boston company which, as a result of mergers and consolidation, became the United Fruit Company (UFCO). This company gradually gained control over all areas of economic activity to the point of becoming, with the help of successive governments, a state within a state. In 1904, Estrada Cabrera empowered it to take over the railways, under construction since 1884 by various companies under the direct influence of North

"The heavy magnificence of the architecture of Quirigua evokes the towns of the Orient. The air of the tropics lightly brushes the impalpable delights of lovers' kisses. Balms which weaken. Mouths are hot, full and moist. Warm waters where lizards sleep on virgins' bodies. The tropics are the erogenous zones of the world! In the city of Quirigua, women wait at the door of the temple, their ears adorned with beads of amber. Tattooed, their breasts left free. Men painted in red and wearing a strange obsidian ring in their noses. And young girls painted in a raw clay wash symbolizing the virtue of grace. The priest arrives and the crowd moves aside. The priest knocks at the door of the temple with his golden finger. The crowd kneels and licks the ground to bless it."

Miguel Angel Asturias
Leyendas de Guatemala

Sacrificial stone among the ruins of Quirigua.

▲ Southeastern Maya
Toward the Caribbean

EXPORTING BANANAS
The Bandegua factory, situated a few hundred yards from the entrance to the site of Quirigua, offers an opportunity to see inside a banana packaging plant. The bananas are conveyed on ropes and sorted: those rejected are kept for local consumption and loaded loose into lorries, sometimes bearing El Salvador number plates. Once they have been washed and weighed (top, opposite page), the fruit is packed under chemically protected conditions into cases bearing different quality labels: United Brands for the best quality and Chiquita for inferior quality. The cases are taken by rail or lorry to the banana quay at Puerto Barrios which has just been privatized.

America. This led to the formation of an economic and financial network involving almost 217,450 acres of banana plantations, 152 miles of IRCA (International Railways of Central America) railway tracks, the quay at Puerto Barrios ▲ 310 and the maritime transport of bananas by the "great white fleet". The entire operation was exempt from export duties and harbor dues.

THE "GREEN OCTOPUS". In 1924, the "Green Octopus", as United Fruit became known in Guatemala, obtained legal authorization to grow bananas along the banks of the Motagua river, subject to the payment of $14,000 to rent this state land, plus 1 cent per bunch of bananas exported. In 1928, war almost broke out between Guatemala and Honduras when the rival Honduran Cuyamel Fruit Company tried to extend its territory by extending the border. In the same year the Compañía Agrícola de Guatemala, a subsidiary of the UFCO, began its operations on the Pacific coast, near Tiquisate. The IRCA came under United Fruit control in 1933.

LAND REFORMS. The land reforms (the famous decree 900) were decided by the Árbenz government, voted on June 17, 1952 and introduced in January 1953. They mainly involved confiscating uncultivated land from the banana company and other big landowners and redistributing it among the peasants. The UFCO lost around 173,000 acres (80 percent) of its land at Izabal and 217,450 acres on the south coast. In 1951, the banana company, the country's largest corporation, led an attempt to destabilize the government, which was being accused of communism. With a US Secretary of State as a shareholder (John Foster Dulles, whose brother was head of the CIA) the banana company had no difficulty in protecting its own interests.

REGAINING CONTROL. Árbenz refused to yield to injunctions from Washington and the country was attacked from Copán in June 1954 by a small band of armed mercenaries under the command of Colonel Castillo Armas. The government lost the support of the army and collapsed within a few days. The rebel colonel seized power and the confiscated land was returned to the *Frutera*.

END OF AN ERA. In 1971, the plantations were

sold to Del Monte which later merged with the UFCO and became United Brands. Meanwhile the banana company, which, according to the US Ministry of Justice, controlled 85 percent of all the land suited to growing bananas on the continent, was condemned in the United States for monopolistic practices and had to sell off the IRCA. United Brands, by now a multinational food company with extremely diverse interests, redeployed its fruit-growing operations in Central America, moving into Panama, Costa Rica and Honduras and withdrawing from Guatemala after the fruit there was attacked by disease. Today United Brands buys bananas from individual properties, companies and cooperatives, packages the fruit and transports it to Puerto Barrios for export.

TOWARD PUERTO BARRIOS

SANTO TOMÁS DE CASTILLA. The road that forks to the left, just before Puerto Barrios, leads to the modern Atlantic port Santo Tomás de Castilla. Founded in 1604 in the shelter of the Amatique Bay, Santo Tomás de Castilla was modernized during the 1950's to compete with the banana port of Barrios, then owned by United Fruit. It gradually took over the merchandise traffic from Puerto Barrios and was equipped with cranes in the 1970's.

CERRO SAN GIL NATURE RESERVE. The nature reserve of Cerro San Gil, at the eastern end of the Montaña del Mico, is administered by the private foundation Fundaeco. It has an impressive range of tropical rainforest fauna: three hundred species of birds, salamanders and other native amphibians, and twenty-eight species of mammals, including jaguars, tapirs, spider monkeys and howler monkeys ■ 24.

> "As the train climbed the Motagua valley, the luxuriant strip of coastal vegetation gave way to a parched, dusty landscape. The river flowed between great, arid mountains, tawny gold except where they were tinged violet-blue by the shadow of the clouds. Here and there the landscape was tufted with brown, leafless shrubs or still bearing withered leaves hanging from their branches. Beneath the burning sun, the landscape was strangely wintry. On the bare slopes, immediately above the river, cereus cacti rose stiffly towards the sky. Not a shadow: the dust rose in clouds as we passed. "
>
> Aldous Huxley
> *Winter Cruise in Central America*

Puerto Barrios has many examples of Caribbean-style architecture. The houses are wooden with wide verandas and balconies.

Chapel of Santo Tomás de Castilla, 19th century.

House in Puerto Barrios

PUERTO BARRIOS. As an epigraph to his novel, *Le salaire de la peur* (*The Wages of Fear*), Georges Arnaud wrote: "Guatemala is a country that doesn't exist; I know, I have lived there." The port, founded by the liberal president Justino Rufino Barrios ▲ *265*, has developed considerably since Arnaud's apocalyptic description. Although no place names are mentioned, the novel, which describes the oil wells of Petén during the 1950's, is extremely well documented. Like the towns on the Pacific plain, Puerto Barrios experienced an extremely rapid demographic and economic development. Although its black population is tending to decrease, the town and its seafront have retained certain Caribbean characteristics. Puerto Barrios has many unusual features. For example, the little monument that stands

The Wages of Fear (1953), directed by Henri-Georges Clouzot and starring Yves Montand and Charles Vanel.

CULINARY SPECIALTY You really must sample Livingston's *tapado*, a fish soup made with coconut milk and eaten with plantain.

on a brackish canal at the edge of town, inscribed with a poem exalting the noble feelings, self-sacrifice and courage of the plantation worker, active from dawn to dusk; or the funerary mausoleum in the form of a maharajah's palace, probably the tomb of a Hindu immigrant; in the center of the town, the cinema–hotel–restaurant–wash house *A sus ordenes*, whose wooden walls also house many other small businesses; or, finally (and the list is by no means complete), the *Hotel del Norte*, the silent – and haunted – reminder of the "good old days" of the rail transport and merchant navy of yesteryear.

LIVINGSTON

Although situated on the mainland, Livingston can only be reached by boat from Puerto Barrios or along the Río Dulce, or by light aircraft (it has a short landing strip). The town is known locally as La Buga (the mouth), a reference to the fact that it stands on the Río Dulce estuary. Its black population, originally from Jamaica, settled here around 1800 and named the town after Jamaica's governor, Louisiane Edward Livingston, the author of a code abolishing slavery. These Garinagus ● *88* are related to the Garinagus of southern Belize ▲ *343*, a region with which they have much closer family, commercial, smuggling and all other forms of

The Río Dulce (below) flows into the Caribbean at Livingston. Main street (right).

trading ties than with the rest of Guatemala. The language spoken is Garifuna: a mixture of island Creole, English and Kekchi, interspersed with a few words of French, particularly those related to counting.

A MATRIARCHAL SOCIETY. The influence of the women, who are often in charge of matters of education, religion and politics, is a fundamental part of Garinagu society. Women interpret dreams and maintain the relationship with the ancestors. The matrilineal tradition is reinforced by the fact that the men often emigrate to the United States or Canada, both countries with large Garinagu communities. The new breeze-block and two-story houses have been built by the *nouveaux riches* with dollars earned in the North.

END OF THE WORLD. The small township has only four streets – the main street leading from the jetty and three others running at right angles to it – and as many vehicles, two of which are used to distribute two internationally famous brands of fizzy drinks to local retailers. The merchants tend to be Kekchis and the Blacks fishermen, although it is their wives who sell the fish in the village or the *barrios*. The festival of San Isidro, the patron saint of these excellent fishermen, coincides with Yurunen which commemorates their arrival on the continent. Livingston's attractions are modest, but can be highly enjoyable. In the evening the streets are alive with swaying, rhythmic dancing to the sound of reggae and calypso music, while sea breezes cool the air. The nearby Siete Altares waterfall (non-existent in the dry season) is well worth a visit. It can be reached on foot, but journeying by boat is much more comfortable. Village artists devote themselves to various styles of painting, and make locally inspired jewelry, while the local gastronomy should not be missed.

LEIDEN STONE
For a long time the jade Leiden stone (owned by the Leiden Museum in the Netherlands) gave the earliest known Mayan date (AD 320). It was discovered at Puerto Barrios but most probably came from Tikal ▲ *322*.

RÍO DULCE ★

Whereas Livingston has a mainly black population, the banks of the Río Dulce are inhabited by Kekchis who live in thatched huts on the water's edge. The river (below), whose bridge lies 32 miles from Livingston, is the only communications route and, as public transport (a dugout) only "runs" once a week, on Tuesdays, each family has its own craft (*cayucos* with oars or an outboard motor). Immediately above its mouth the Río Dulce flows between two steep, limestone walls and forms numerous meanders. Beyond that it winds between two lower banks, from which hot springs emerge, before opening up into a lake, El Golfete, which is 3–4 miles wide, over 12 miles long and bordered by mangroves.

BIOTOPO CHOCÓN MACHACAS. The nature reserve on the north bank, named after the two rivers that flow through it, belongs to Guatemala's San Carlos University. Its 17,800 acres cover a region of tropical rainforest, mangroves, lakes and slow-flowing rivers. A few manatees still exist in this aquatic maze which is their natural habitat. Commonly known as the "sea cow" this marine mammal is probably the source of the myth of the siren. It has a slender body, thick skin covered with short hair, a spatula-shaped tail and dense, resilient bones. As a vegetarian it controls the growth of aquatic plants and shares the same habitat as turtles, dogfish and many other species of fish. A short nature trail enables visitors to admire mahogany trees, American cedars, sapodilla and custard-apple trees, as well as large numbers of parrots, toucans, golden orioles and green woodpeckers.

MANATEE
Although the Maya believed that the manatee had supernatural powers, they were not averse to butchering them for important ceremonies. Christopher Columbus sighted three of these "sirens" in January 1493: "They were as pretty as their descriptions, even though there was something human about their faces." With the arrival of the Conquerors manatees, which abounded in the region at the time, were increasingly widely hunted. The 17th-century (date of the engraving, above) chronicler Fuentes y Guzmán recorded that: "they can be hunted all year round, not only in Lake Izabal and the Río Dulce, but along the entire coast from Mexico to Nicaragua".

CASTILLO DE SAN FELIPE

From the beginning of the 16th century, goods being traded between the captaincy and the Spanish metropolis were

transported via what was then known as the Golfo Dulce. Pirates had been making constant attacks along the Gulf of Mexico and the coast of Belize, and their increasing incursions up to the Río Dulce and into Guatemala, led to the fortification of the entrance to Lake Izabal at the point where warehouses received merchandise on its way to and from Spain. In 1595 a tower was built, subsequently destroyed, and rebuilt in 1604. During the 1640's pirate attacks were intensified and the building was again damaged. The fort was rebuilt by the magistrate Lara in 1651 who called it the Castillo de San Felipe de Lara, in honor of the reigning Spanish sovereign and so that his own name would not be forgotten.

MULTIPLE RECONSTRUCTIONS. As the threat of pirates diminished, in 1655 the building became a prison. It reverted to its former use ten years later, however, when the "coastal fraternity", based on Turtle Island, resumed their attacks. A drawbridge and ramparts were added to the original tower, which had a thatched roof and damaged beams. Over a period of several decades pirates and Spanish fought numerous battles, many of which prompted further architectural alterations to the fort. In the 18th century its defenses were considerably improved by the military engineer Andrés Ortiz de Urbina who extended the ramparts and increased the number of guard posts to one hundred. Although it has since fallen into ruins, the fort has retained this final layout.

LAKE IZABAL ★

The origin of the lake's name is uncertain. According to one of two current theories, "Izabal" is a Mayan word meaning "where you sweat continuously", while the other maintains that the lake was named by the Spanish conquerors in honor of the sovereign of Castile, Isabella la Catolica. The lake is fed by the Río Polochic and is the largest lake in Guatemala, with an area of 250 square miles. Between 1978 and 1979, the nickel on its northern shores was mined by the Exmibal company, a subsidiary of the big Canadian company, INCO. Following the highly costly construction of an ore-refining plant, world prices collapsed due to over-production and the factory was forced to close within six months. After this, tiny boats took the concentrate to the loading terminal whose metal structure at Livingston is still used by roosting seagulls. There has always been a suspicion that the INCO was interested in these deposits because of the presence of more strategic metals than nickel. Near the lake, the cave of San Antonio is open to the public.

Port of Izabal, 19th-century engraving.

TOURIST SITE
The ruined Castillo de San Felipe (below) was reconstructed as a tourist attraction in 1955–6 by the architect Francisco Ferrus. It is situated at the entrance to Lake Izabal, on the northern shore, and is easily reached by boat from the bridge. The surrounding grounds have been planted with coconut palms.

RÍO DULCE BRIDGE
The Río Dulce bridge (opened in 1979) spans the river at its narrowest point. Secondary residences are springing up on the approaches to the bridge, which has become an extremely popular area among wealthy city dwellers from the capital; boatmen are keen to point out the residences of former presidents. It is also a popular place for sailing, speedboats and water skiing. The oil pipeline from Rubelsanto (Verapaz) crosses the Río Dulce below the bridge.

▲ SOUTHEASTERN MAYA
EL SALVADOR

At the entrance to the town, past the craft market (below), the statue of Salvador del Mundo (Saviour of the World), the capital's patron, celebrated on August 4 to 6, blesses this martyred country.

TOURIST RESORTS
Many of the villages along El Salvador's 200-mile coastline have become tourist resorts. Visitors can enjoy fishing for tuna, groupers, swordfish and sailfish, or watersports such as surfing on the oceanic race and windsurfing. To the west, from the beach of Zunzal to Mizata, the rocks of the jagged coastline abound with oysters and shellfish. Further on, near the Guatemalan border, is the modern port of Acajutla, the most important in Central America.

SAN SALVADOR
In the city center, devastated by the 1986 earthquake, the beautiful neoclassical architecture of the Palacio Nacional (inaugurated in 1911) in the Plaza Libertad (top, right) contrasts with a concrete cathedral built in the 1970's. The relatively elegant Teatro Nacional (1917) was restored in 1978 and has a fresco on the ceiling of the auditorium.

One pseudo-Gothic cathedral (right), built between 1905 and 1936, is dedicated to Santa Ana, whose festival is celebrated from July 18 to 25.

El Salvador occupies the ancient territory of Cuzcatlán ("land of jewels") the home of several ethnic groups: the Pipils ▲ *316* on the coastal plain, the Chortis to the west of the Río Lempa, the Lencas and the Uluas to the north and the Pokomams on the present border of Guatemala. When Pedro de Alvarado first attempted to conquer the territory in 1524 he was wounded and defeated by Chief Atlacatl. The second attempt, led by his cousin Diego in 1528, proved more successful. El Salvador did not regain independence until 1821, following the "call" to rebellion issued by the priest José Matías Delgado on November 5, 1810. Since then the country's political development has been regularly punctuated by *coups d'état* and civil conflict ● *40*.

ROCKY TERRAIN. El Salvador has the same physical characteristics as the southern regions of Chiapas and Guatemala: from south to north, a coastal plain, three mountain ranges reaching a height of 7,930 feet, a high central plateau and interior mountain chains. The cordillera includes a line of twenty-five volcanos. The Río Lempa, whose waters have been harnessed by four hydro-electric power stations, flows through the country for a distance of 217 miles. The colonial village of Suchitoto lies on the shores of Lake Suchitlán (52 square miles). Several nature reserves, Cerro Verde, El Bosque, El Imposible, Montecristo (rainforest), El Jocatal lake and the Parque Walter Deininger, as well as signposted walks and other modest sites (rivers, lakes, hot springs and pools) offer a range of varied and interesting excursions.

SOCIETY. This densely populated country (5.5 million inhabitants in an area of 8,110 square miles) has an entirely mestizo population (in the cultural sense of the word) and an extremely polarized social structure. El Salvador is emerging from a long period of civil war with the firm intention of putting its recent and bloody past behind it and adopting a positive approach to its problems, with a view to moving toward a more equitable social and political development.

> **"THE AMERINDIAN CIVILIZATIONS ALL EXPRESS THIS SANCTIFICATION OF THE EARTH. FROM THE NORTH TO THE SOUTH OF THIS VAST CONTINENT, THE EARTH-MOTHER IS THE SOURCE OF ALL LIFE."**
>
> JEAN-MARIE LE CLÉZIO

ECONOMY. Coffee (65 percent), sugar, cotton and prawns are El Salvador's main exports. The currency transfers of emigrant workers (there are over one million in California alone), American financial aid (although decreasing) and income from tourism are invisible but very real resources. El Salvador's industrial economy, which deals mainly with the processing of agricultural products, did well during the boom years following the creation in 1963 of the Central American common market, and is now the second largest on the isthmus, after that of Guatemala.

SAN SALVADOR

San Salvador was one of the Spanish regional capitals during the Conquest. The capital epitomizes the national contradictions: its fashionable districts on the hills to the north (Escalón, Miramonte) contrast with the neglected city center where the after-effects of the 1986 earthquake can still be seen. Demobilization has merely added to the latent problem of delinquency created by social deprivation. The ever-present fear of attack, kidnapping and burglary does not prevent the wealthy and middle classes doing their shopping on the Boulevard de los Héroes or enjoying themselves at the weekend in the terraced restaurants and night clubs of the Zona Rosa.

JOYA DE CERÉN ★

This small site, discovered by chance in 1976, lies in the Zapotitán Valley, not far from the ceremonial center of San Andrés ▲ *316*. The village was buried by volcanic ash following the eruption of Volcán Caldera in c. AD 600, which is why it became known as the "Pompeii of Central America". The main interest of the ruins, which have been extremely well-preserved by the lava, is that they have revealed various aspects of the daily life of Mayan peasants at the end of the 6th century. The modest adobe and mud dwellings, surrounded by fields of corn and beans, were buried beneath the first layer of lava. The ash (1067° F) which then covered the lava was accompanied by toxic gases which asphyxiated the villagers. Using radar, archeologists were able to uncover the remains of dwellings divided into several rooms with beaten-clay floors and roofs thatched with palm branches. Domestic equipment retrieved included corn mills, terracotta plates and dishes, obsidian utensils and benches, as well as food remains. The most important discovery was a codex found in a cupboard which is still being studied. Although fairly unspectacular, the site is of great historical and archeological interest.

CHALCHUAPA

Santa Ana, situated in the heart of the coffee-growing region, is the country's second largest town but has nothing of any particular interest to attract visitors. However, a little further west is Chalchuapa, a vast site

▲ SOUTHEASTERN MAYA EL SALVADOR

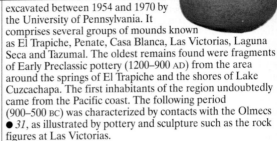
Vase found in El Salvador.

SITE OF SAN ANDRÉS
The interest of Joya de Cerén far outweighs a visit to the ceremonial center of San Andrés (below), where fifteen 8th-century structures have been outrageously restored.

A DRAMATIC PERIOD
The 1980's will go down in the history of El Salvador as the period of murderous civil war when two guerrilla movements opposed the junta groups supported by the United States. Negotiations, headed by President Duarte, ended in agreement in 1987, within the context of a peace plan for Central America, signed in Guatemala. After a shaky start El Salvador is trying to forget this dramatic period and look toward development and tourism.

excavated between 1954 and 1970 by the University of Pennsylvania. It comprises several groups of mounds known as El Trapiche, Penate, Casa Blanca, Las Victorias, Laguna Seca and Tazumal. The oldest remains found were fragments of Early Preclassic pottery (1200–900 AD) from the area around the springs of El Trapiche and the shores of Lake Cuzcachapa. The first inhabitants of the region undoubtedly came from the Pacific coast. The following period (900–500 BC) was characterized by contacts with the Olmecs ● *31*, as illustrated by pottery and sculpture such as the rock figures at Las Victorias.

EL TRAPICHE. Dating from about the same period is the first version of the pyramid of El Trapiche, which was at the time one of the largest (at 65 feet) in Mesoamerica. It is likely that, at this stage in its history Chalchuapa was an Olmec trading center responsible for providing supplies of cocoa, hematite and obsidian to the Gulf region. During the Late Preclassic period (400 BC–AD 200) Chalchuapa, like Kaminaljuyú, was part of the Mayan highlands. Along with other monumental structures, the pyramid of El Trapiche was reconstructed with new platforms on its summit and adobe access ramps. Monument 1 has a long, somewhat eroded, hieroglyphic text with a calendric glyph, which once again demonstrates the precocity of the southeastern Maya in this field. During the 3rd century the site was rendered uninhabitable for several generations by the eruption of Volcán Ilopango, 46 miles away.

TAZUMAL. During the Late Classic period the small center of Tazumal was dominated by Structure 1 (49 feet high) which consisted of two superposed pyramidal platforms. There is barely any trace of the temple on the summit. Excavations have revealed six phases of construction for the lower platform and three for the upper platform. The temple was reached on the west side by a staircase flanked by ramps. The platforms were built of adobe bricks or stones, set in clay and covered with stucco. The group also includes a ball court with two parallel mounds running east–west and with its west end closed by a low wall. In spite of these efforts there is no doubt that the Late Classic site of Chalchuapa is relatively insignificant when compared with the Preclassic version.

PIPILS. After the year 1000 the Postclassic period was marked by the arrival of the Nahua-speaking Pipils. Their presence is evidenced by a range of characteristics of central Mexican origin in both architecture and sculpture such as stone *chacmool* and the life-size statue of Xipe Totec, the Mexican god of the springtime. During the Late Postclassic period, the groups of Laguna Seca and Tazumal were abandoned and occupation was limited to the Penate group which included, in particular, some low mounds. At the time of the Conquest, the region was predominately occupied by Pokomam-speaking populations ● *62*.

PETÉN

▲ PETÉN

1. FLORES
2. LAKE PETÉN ITZÁ
3. TIKAL
4. UAXACTÚN
5. RÍO AZUL

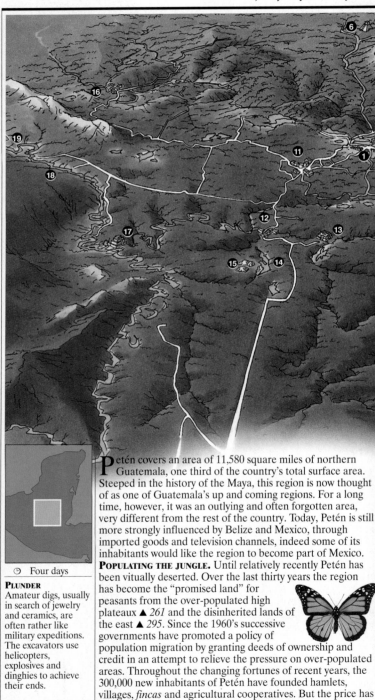

⊕ Four days

PLUNDER
Amateur digs, usually in search of jewelry and ceramics, are often rather like military expeditions. The excavators use helicopters, explosives and dinghies to achieve their ends.

Petén covers an area of 11,580 square miles of northern Guatemala, one third of the country's total surface area. Steeped in the history of the Maya, this region is now thought of as one of Guatemala's up and coming regions. For a long time, however, it was an outlying and often forgotten area, very different from the rest of the country. Today, Petén is still more strongly influenced by Belize and Mexico, through imported goods and television channels, indeed some of its inhabitants would like the region to become part of Mexico.
POPULATING THE JUNGLE. Until relatively recently Petén has been vitually deserted. Over the last thirty years the region has become the "promised land" for peasants from the over-populated high plateaux ▲ *261* and the disinherited lands of the east ▲ *295*. Since the 1960's successive governments have promoted a policy of population migration by granting deeds of ownership and credit in an attempt to relieve the pressure on over-populated areas. Throughout the changing fortunes of recent years, the 300,000 new inhabitants of Petén have founded hamlets, villages, *fincas* and agricultural cooperatives. But the price has

318

"EL MUNDO MAYA" In 1988 the National Geographic Society proposed to the governments of those countries which share the territory of the ancient Mayan empire a common tourist development project designed to preserve their natural and cultural wealth.

been the "ecological assassination" of the continent's second largest area of tropical forest. The virgin forest has been relentlessly felled, cleared and burned so that corn and beans can be cultivated. After two or three years the fragile layer of soil, often less than a foot deep, becomes exhausted. Yields fall and the area is converted to use for cattle breeding ■ 22.

ECONOMIC INTERESTS. Small farmers are often "relieved" of their property deeds by large landowners or unscrupulous members of the military. The region, which was wealthy under ancient Mayan rule, dreams of a return to that golden age of prosperity based on the felling of rare tropical trees, the collection of chewing gum (chicle ▲ 330) or, more recently, the cutting of ornamental tropical plants and palms (xate) for export. The market for rare woods brings in an annual revenue of two million dollars ($7,000–10,000 per mahogany tree) at the cost of 123,550 acres of forest being destroyed.

TOO LITTLE, TOO LATE. Despite the power and influence of private economic interests, the authorities have finally responded to pressure from conservationists to protect this fragile and

threatened environment. With the advent of a civilian government in 1985, measures have been initiated to classify parks and reserves in parts of the Petén region. A list of nature reserves administered by CONAP (National Commission for Natural Regions), where programs for reforestation and the protection of resources are a priority, has been added to the list of archeological sites already drawn up by the Institute of Anthropology and History. Any form of construction is theoretically prohibited in these areas.

THE MAYAN BIOSPHERE. This region, covering a vast rectangle of 3,706,575 acres across the northern third of Petén, is protected by a statute drawn up in 1990. Under it, any form of economic activity must receive prior official authorization. However, a lack of political motivation makes enforcing controls and sanctions impossible.

Polychrome vase with bird decoration from Petén, on display in the Museo Popol Vuh ▲ 267 in Guatemala City.

LAKE PETÉN ITZÁ ★

With increasing levels of rainfall recorded over the past fifteen years, the inhabitants of this area face a worrying situation that can only be resolved by digging an artificial canal to drain water from the lake into the Río San Pedro to the northwest. Neither the local authorities nor the government appear to have the funds to finance the project. In the long term the nearby airport is under threat, but here, as elsewhere, it is hoped that international aid will save the day. The causeway between Flores and Santa Elena is periodically raised, the riverside houses are gradually being abandoned and the main street is undergoing resurfacing. In some areas, planks are used as sidewalks. The lake is still well stocked with fish and species such as the *blanco,* with its delicious white meat, and the *aletón* are especially popular.

EL REMATE
Lake Petén Itzá (below and above right). El Remate, to the east of the lake, is the starting point for the road which runs round the northern shore of the lake, toward the Cerro Cahuí and San Andrés reserves ▲ 329.

FLORES ★

Flores, surmounted by its small cathedral, is an island in Lake Petén Itzá. Since the 1970's Flores and the mainland villages of Santa Elena and San Benito have undergone major, if somewhat haphazard, development. However, Flores, the regional capital since the 19th century, is threatened by the

waters of the lake. It is an attractive town of single-story dwellings, with adobe or brightly painted wooden walls (although an aerial view reveals an expanse of corrugated iron roofs). The central square is decorated with steles from the surrounding area. As a result of international interest in the protection of the tropical forest, a number of conservation agencies have set up bases on the island.

TAYASAL. The site of the ancient Itzá capital, Tayasal lies opposite Flores and at the western end of the peninsula which cuts the lake in two. It was here, in the heart of Petén, that the long Itzá migration came to an end. The Itzás, originally from central Mexico, settled in Yucatán in the 10th century (during the renaissance of Chichén Itzá ▲ 205) and remained there for more than two hundred years before continuing southwards. According to tradition, Hernán Cortés ● 36 passed through the region in 1525, on his way to Honduras and left his wounded horse at Tayasal. The Itzás, who had never seen such an animal, deified it and offered it delicacies such as flower petals. The horse couldn't resist these choice offerings and died. The Indians made an effigy in its honor, which scandalized Franciscans later destroyed. Remote from Spanish influence and hidden in the forest, the Indians survived at Tayasal until the end of the 17th century. Their defeat by Martín de Ursula on March 13, 1697 marked the end of the last Indian kingdom. The terrified Itzá warriors fled in panic into the lake and were drowned. According to one theory, the high limestone content of the waters of the lake may have petrified their skeletons. The mirador at the tip of the peninsula, named after the last Itzá king, Canek, offers a splendid view of the lake.

CAVE OF ACTÚN CAN. Underground erosion caused by the penetration of rainwater into the karstic hills (*mogotes*) to the south of Flores has created caves. Nearest to Flores is the cave of Actún Can on the southern edge of Santa Elena. The large rocky chambers are evocatively named after the striking shapes of the many stalactites and stalagmites that adorn them.

THE ROAD TO TIKAL

This road, tarmacked in 1983, is the only surfaced road in Petén. It crosses green pastureland and even an archeological site, Ixlú, whose ruined pyramids can be seen to the right. About 18 miles from Flores, a road turns off toward Melchor de Mencos ▲ 334 and the border of Belize ▲ 335. Craftsmen in the village of El Remate, on the eastern shore of Lake Petén Itzá, work in tropical woods such as American cedar (*jobillo*).

CERRO CAHUÍ CONSERVATION PARK. This 1,600-acre warm subtropical rainforest is a conservation area dedicated to this type of natural habitat and its flora and fauna, administered by the research and conservation department of Guatemala's San Carlos University.

POACHING
Rainforest covers between 10 percent and 15 percent of the total area of Central America and contains 10 percent of the world's species. The jaguar and ocelot are still hunted shamelessly for their beautiful skins, while coati and rare breeds of deer are served in the restaurants of Flores.

ISLAND OF PETÉNCITO
The island's zoological gardens contain alligators, jaguars, coatis, weasels, peccaries, macaws and parrots. It is easily reached by boat.

SANTA ELENA AND SAN BENITO
On the mainland, opposite the island of Flores, the two villages of San Benito and Santa Elena form a single center, linked by an avenue which crosses them from east to west. The international airport lies to the east, on the road to Tikal. Near San Benito are the caves of Nojojnaj. Large pre-Hispanic steles stand in Santa Elena's central square.

HERITAGE
In 1979 the site was declared a monument and placed on UNESCO's international cultural heritage list.

TIKAL ★

With Copán ▲ *299*, Tikal is one of the best-known Mayan sites. Many of its monuments were photographed at the end of the 19th century by Alfred Maudslay (such as that below) and Teobert Maler ● *56*. Later, plans were made of the site and its inscriptions studied. In 1956 a team from the University of Pennsylvania began a series of systematic excavations. Their work was continued in 1970 by Guatemalan excavation and restoration teams.

HISTORY. Tikal was occupied from the Middle Preclassic period (900–600 BC) and reached the height of its glory during the Late Classic period (AD 550–950). The earliest stele on the site (Stele 29) bears a date equivalent to AD 292, while the latest (Stele 11) is dated AD 869. It has been estimated that, during its peak, Tikal had around ten thousand inhabitants within a radius of thirty minutes walk from the center. However, defensive moats and embankments, as well as other remains, have been found even further afield. The town was situated almost at the center of Maya territory, on the route between Campeche and Belize, which could be the reason for its extraordinary development.

LAYOUT. The city has some of the highest temples in Maya territory, comparable to those of El Mirador ▲ *329*. Temple 4 (230 feet) is the tallest of Tikal's temples which are characterized by the steepness of their staircases and, above all, by their roof crests decorated with stuccoed relief ● *108*. The monuments are organized around the Great Plaza, bordered by Temples 1 and 2 and the North Acropolis. A number of perfectly restored groups of structures, scattered in the forest, are linked by paths or broad

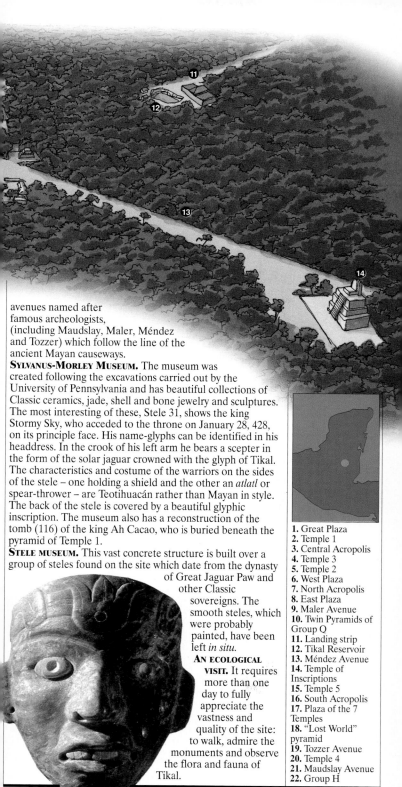

avenues named after
famous archeologists,
(including Maudslay, Maler, Méndez
and Tozzer) which follow the line of the
ancient Mayan causeways.

SYLVANUS-MORLEY MUSEUM. The museum was
created following the excavations carried out by the
University of Pennsylvania and has beautiful collections of
Classic ceramics, jade, shell and bone jewelry and sculptures.
The most interesting of these, Stele 31, shows the king
Stormy Sky, who acceded to the throne on January 28, 428,
on its principle face. His name-glyphs can be identified in his
headdress. In the crook of his left arm he bears a scepter in
the form of the solar jaguar crowned with the glyph of Tikal.
The characteristics and costume of the warriors on the sides
of the stele – one holding a shield and the other an *atlatl* or
spear-thrower – are Teotihuacán rather than Mayan in style.
The back of the stele is covered by a beautiful glyphic
inscription. The museum also has a reconstruction of the
tomb (116) of the king Ah Cacao, who is buried beneath the
pyramid of Temple 1.

STELE MUSEUM. This vast concrete structure is built over a
group of steles found on the site which date from the dynasty
of Great Jaguar Paw and
other Classic
sovereigns. The
smooth steles, which
were probably
painted, have been
left *in situ.*

**AN ECOLOGICAL
VISIT.** It requires
more than one
day to fully
appreciate the
vastness and
quality of the site:
to walk, admire the
monuments and observe
the flora and fauna of
Tikal.

1. Great Plaza
2. Temple 1
3. Central Acropolis
4. Temple 3
5. Temple 2
6. West Plaza
7. North Acropolis
8. East Plaza
9. Maler Avenue
10. Twin Pyramids of
Group Q
11. Landing strip
12. Tikal Reservoir
13. Méndez Avenue
14. Temple of
Inscriptions
15. Temple 5
16. South Acropolis
17. Plaza of the 7
Temples
18. "Lost World"
pyramid
19. Tozzer Avenue
20. Temple 4
21. Maudslay Avenue
22. Group H

The center of the city is built on a series of hills, at an altitude of around 165 feet above the swampy depressions that lie to the east and west of the site. Most of the structures date from the Late Classic period, the golden age of Tikal, but there are some older structures which were not renovated during this period. These include the so-called "Lost World" pyramid, from the Late Preclassic, and a number of Early Classic pyramids in the North Acropolis. Tikal also has architectural groups known as the Twin Pyramid Groups, a feature peculiar to this site and that of Yaxhá. They were the setting for the celebrations of the end of the *katun*.

TWIN PYRAMIDS
Each group consists of four structures surrounding a central plaza (1): to the north, an enclosure sheltering a stele and its altar (2); to the east and west, a pyramid with four staircases (3); and to the south, a long, rectangular building pierced by nine doors (4). The Group A E-4 formerly known as Group Q (above), was built by the king C to celebrate the end of the seventeenth *katun* (AD 771) ● *44*.

The northern enclosure contains Stele 22 and its altar ● *111* (above and opposite). These elements are almost all sculpted.

JADE MASK
The many objects, including masks, figurines and jewelry, found in the tombs of Tikal include this jade, pyrites and shell mask dating from the Early Classic period (AD 527).

A MULTITUDE OF STRUCTURES

Tikal consists of a great many structures, from the temples in the central plaza to the groups linked by *sacbeob*. The largest structures in the center of the city are grouped around the triangle formed by the Maler, Maudslay and Tozzer causeways.

NORTH ACROPOLIS

When the site was abandoned, this vast platform (109 yards by 87 yards) supported eight funerary temples, which were the result of three hundred years of architectural activity. Beneath the platform older remains were discovered, some dating from the 3rd century BC.

THE MEANING OF THE TWIN PYRAMIDS

These complexes were built to celebrate the end of the *katun* ● *44*. They undoubtedly had a cosmological significance since the various structures always follow the same layout and are always found in the same place and facing in the same direction. Thus although the exact use of this group of buildings is not known (nor the nature of the rituals performed or the identity of the participants), it is reasonable to assume that the complex represented a microcosm visited by the king or his representatives to summarize the passage of time. These ambulations guaranteed universal order before embarking upon a new period of uncertainty.

RITUAL

Stele 22 shows the king C during the celebration of the end of the *katun*. With his right hand he is scattering pearls or seeds while in his left hand he is holding a scepter. A supernatural creature is hovering above his head.

SOVEREIGNS OF TIKAL

...rl-Nose is depicted on
...ele 4 (below).

The glyph Stormy Sky represents the element "sky" and is surmounted by a smoking axe, flanked with two arms (yellow glyphs).

The earliest known Tikal steles already bear the portrait of the sovereign accompanied by an inscription in which his name appears as the principle subject. The first identified sovereign is Great Jaguar Paw who ruled in the first half of the 4th century and whose successor is still unknown. Then came Curl-Nose (AD 379–426) and his son Stormy Sky (426–57). The principle face of Stele 31 (AD 445) bears a portrait of Stormy Sky surmounted by the protecting figure of his father. A long inscription on the back of the monument establishes his line of descendance and mentions, as well as his own name, those of Curl-Nose and Great Jaguar Paw.

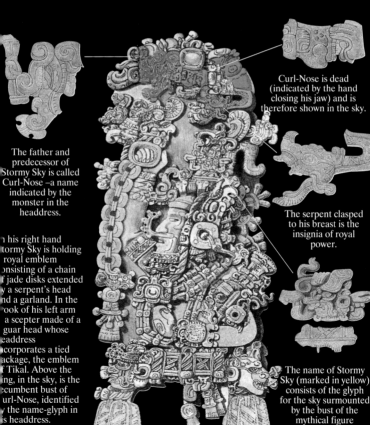

Curl-Nose is dead (indicated by the hand closing his jaw) and is therefore shown in the sky.

The father and predecessor of Stormy Sky is called Curl-Nose –a name indicated by the monster in the headdress.

The serpent clasped to his breast is the insignia of royal power.

...n his right hand ...tormy Sky is holding ...royal emblem ...onsisting of a chain ...f jade disks extended ...y a serpent's head ...nd a garland. In the ...ook of his left arm ...a scepter made of a ...guar head whose ...eaddress ...ncorporates a tied ...ackage, the emblem ...f Tikal. Above the ...ing, in the sky, is the ...ecumbent bust of ...url-Nose, identified ...y the name-glyph in ...s headdress.

The name of Stormy Sky (marked in yellow) consists of the glyph for the sky surmounted by the bust of the mythical figure representing lightning with his distinctive symbol: a smoking axe embedded in his forehead.

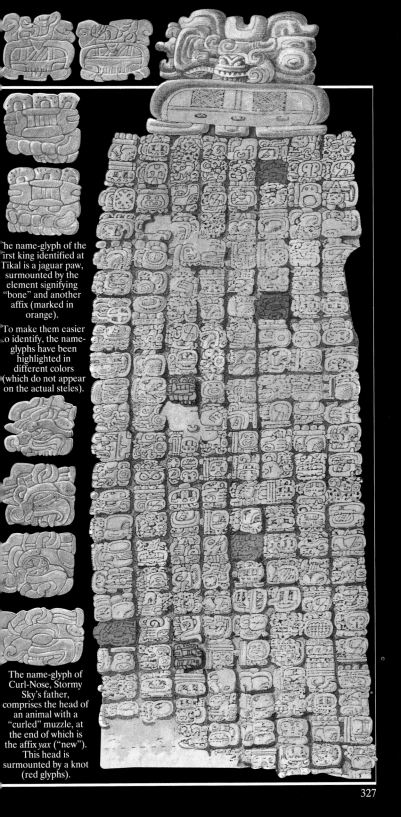

The name-glyph of the first king identified at Tikal is a jaguar paw, surmounted by the element signifying "bone" and another affix (marked in orange).

To make them easier to identify, the name-glyphs have been highlighted in different colors (which do not appear on the actual steles).

The name-glyph of Curl-Nose, Stormy Sky's father, comprises the head of an animal with a "curled" muzzle, at the end of which is the affix *yax* ("new"). This head is surmounted by a knot (red glyphs).

327

WALL PAINTINGS
Reproduction
(below), painted in
1959 by Antonio
Tejeda Fonseca
● 128, of the wall
paintings at Uaxactún
(above).

UAXACTÚN ★

Like Tikal, 18 miles to the south, Uaxactún (meaning
"eight stones") was inhabited during the Middle Preclassic
period and finally abandoned during the 10th century.
Early research undertaken by the Carnegie Institution
between 1926 and 1937 laid the foundations of the archeology
of the central Mayan lowlands. Uaxactún's chronology was
established by means of the dates on its inscriptions, and the
historical evidence supplied by its ceramics and
architecture.

FIVE HILLS. Groups of stone structures built on five
hills constituted the heart of the city. These were
surrounded by scattered platforms for houses.
Archeological surveys of the land around the
ceremonial and political center have revealed that
the major Mayan sites were veritable cities with a
large, permanent population.

MONUMENTS. The step pyramid in Group E dates
from the Late Preclassic period. Like the "Lost
World" pyramid at Tikal, it has a staircase on each
of its four sides and masks of cosmic creatures. A
structure made of perishable materials, indicated
today by stake holes, was built on this stucco-
covered base. The entire structure was covered
during the Classic period by a new pyramid
which has not survived, faced on the east side
by a rectangular platform supporting three
small temples. From the top of the pyramid it was
possible to see the sun rise behind the central
temple on the spring and autumn equinoxes. The sun
rose behind the left-hand temple on June 21 (the
summer solstice) and behind the right-hand
temple on December 21 (the winter solstice). These
remarkable astronomical positions were undoubtedly
celebrated by rituals held on the pyramid. A wooden
tower in Group A offers a splendid view of the ruins
of Structure A-5.

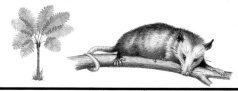

Hummingbird, tree fern and an opossum: three examples of the widely varied flora and fauna of Petén ■ 24.

RÍO AZUL

About 28 miles east of Dos Lagunas, the site of Río Azul, which can be reached only by four-wheel-drive vehicle, has been plundered several times since it was discovered in 1962. Even so, between 1983 and 1987, a team from the National Geographic Society and the University of Texas discovered some magnificent items which yielded valuable information on the Early Classic period. More than five hundred edifices, the tallest of which is 154 feet high, cover an area of just over a square mile.

BURIED TREASURE. Among the many sepulchers of Río Azul, thirty-two of which have been plundered, Tomb 1 (AD 417) was undoubtedly one of the richest. Tomb 12 is decorated with painted glyphs in which the symbols representing the four points of the compass are in their exact position and are accompanied by their respective patrons: the Sun (east), Venus (south), Darkness (west) and the Moon (north).

A CITY IN DECLINE. Río Azul seems to have been abandoned in c. 535, probably following a civil war. It was reoccupied in the 8th century, under the control of a family bearing the same name as that which had ruled two hundred years earlier. The city would soon have re-established itself as the frontier post for Tikal, but in c. 830 Río Azul was the victim of a raid from the Puuc region and the city once again became a military outpost.

TOWARD EL MIRADOR

The road that skirts round Lake Petén Itzá to the west passes through the village of San Andrés, the last surviving pocket of the Itzá language ● 62. From here the road continues round the lake, offering some splendid views *en route*, while a track heads 56 miles due north to Carmelita (the journey on this track takes at least four to five hours).

EXPEDITION. Carmelita is the departure point for an excursion to the ruins of El Tintal, El Mirador and Nakbé. This trip should only be attempted between February and April. Hiring a mule is less tiring than walking and a more leisurely way of appreciating the forest and its remarkable flora and fauna ■ 24.

EL MIRADOR ★. The site of El Mirador is thought to date from the Late Preclassic period. Its huge pyramids (the eighteen-story Tigre pyramid stands 197 feet high) were built before the oldest stone structures of Tikal ▲ 322 and Uaxactún. Public art was designed to consolidate the social order. At El Mirador it was

A WILD REGION
The two roads leading north from Flores (toward Tikal ▲ 322 and San Andrés, on the shores of Lake Petén Itzá, above) enter the Mayan biosphere, the wildest region in Petén. This is the world of the *chicleros* ▲ 330, *xateros* and the grave robbers.

Vase with glyph and number (below, left) and vase depicting an audience scene (below), from Uaxactún.

DOS LAGUNAS
This "jewel" of the Mayan biosphere is situated 31 miles north of Uaxactún. Many non-governmental organizations involved in conservation programs for the tropical environment are based at Dos Lagunas.

CHICLE
The *chicleros* set off into the forest at the height of the rainy season, between September and January, when the sap of the sapodilla tree is at its most plentiful. They build a basic camp of huts made of branches to shelter beds, cooking pots and heating facilities for the latex. Moving outward from these temporary camps, the peasants (left to right, top) climb the sapodilla trees to make incisions in the bark and then make regular collections of the liquid that is exuded. It is heated to solidify it and molded into white latex bricks. The

the impressive size of the architecture which was important and not, as would later be the case, the glorification of great deeds and rulers.

Climbing to the top of the Danta (Tapir) pyramid, the taller twin of the Tigre, is an experience which is hard to describe. Like the temples of Tikal, it offers a magnificent view across a vast expanse of the forest.

NAKBÉ

The site of Nakbé was identified during a reconnaissance flight in the 1930's by archeologists from the University of Pennsylvania. It lies about 8 miles southeast of El Mirador and is linked to that site by a Mayan causeway (*sacbé*) built during the Middle Preclassic period (between 1000 and 400 AD). In 1962 Ian Graham of the University of Harvard plotted the first plan of the site which he called Nakbé ("on the way" in Yucatecan Maya). The ruins were dated in 1987. The monumental platforms and structures that can be seen today, built between 500 and 300 BC, cover structures built several hundred years earlier. The tallest temple in the West Group is

147 feet high, while the tallest in the East Group is 98 feet high. The stone buildings have no interior rooms and stand on solid rock bases.

FOUR GIANT MASKS. One of the major archeological discoveries was the four huge masks, carved in stone and decorated with stucco, found at the foot of Structure 1 in the West Group. Three were covered up again, due to the absence of any means of preserving them,

bricks are then transported from the camp by pack mules which return with food supplies. In spite of the development of synthetic gums there are still export outlets for the natural chicle gum, primarily in Japan.

but the one that is still visible is remarkable for its size and craftsmanship. The mask is 36 feet wide and 16 feet high and represents a head with a 5-foot long muzzle.

"CORAL" GROUP. The group consists of five structures, two of which are surmounted by three rooms, furnished with stone benches and decorated with wall paintings. Places of worship and dwellings were discovered beneath numerous small mounds. A complete ball court ● *112*, one of the three Preclassic courts in Petén, is though to have covered an earlier court dating from 500 BC making it the earliest court known to date.

> "THE DOORS HAVE CLOSED ON AN ENCHANTED TREASURE. THE FLAME OF THE TEMPLES HAS BEEN EXTINGUISHED. EVERYTHING IS AS IT WAS BEFORE. LOST SHADOWS AND VACANT-EYED PHANTOMS WANDER THROUGH DESERTED STREETS." MIGUEL ANGEL ASTURIAS

SOUTHWEST OF FLORES

The other route to the highlands, besides the one linking Petén with the Río Dulce ▲ 312, follows the track maintained by the oil companies to take the crude oil extracted in the Río San Pedro region south via La Libertad, Sayaxché and Yalpemech (the "northern transversal fringe"), before climbing the foothills of the Sierra de Chamá to Cobán ▲ 294. From Sayaxché a fleet of small craft travel up and down the rivers.

SAYAXCHÉ. The town of Sayaxché developed as a result of the waves of migration from the north which affected southwest Petén. It has become a small regional capital, particularly with the transport of crude oil from the fields of El Naranjo. It stands at the confluence of the Ríos Pasión and Petexbatún and on the only road between Petén and Verapaz ▲ 292. It is also the departure point for excursions to the sites of El Ceibal, Aguateca and Altar de los Sacrificios. Apart from the spectacle of a transporter ferry moved by a ridiculously small dugout canoe, the only local item of any interest is the stele in front of the town hall.

CEIBAL ★

HISTORY. The site of Ceibal (Structure A-3, left) lies at the heart of the Río Pasión region and was relatively unimportant during the Classic period. It experienced its golden age from 830, probably after the arrival of the Putúns who followed the Usumacinta upstream. Ceibal is the historic site of Chakanputún, founded by the Itzás, a Putún Maya group who adopted a number of Mexican characteristics. Its architecture and sculpture reveal Yucatecan traits and the new sovereigns of Ceibal were certainly foreigners judging from the characteristics of the figures on the steles. The role played by Ceibal in the 9th century as the most important city in the southern lowlands is indicated on

A NEW STYLE
Putún influence can be seen on the steles of Ceibal. The principle figures on Steles 10 and 11 (AD 849) do not have the usual cranial deformation in which the forehead extends the line of the nose, ▲ 248 and they also have a moustache. After 870, monuments moved even further from the Classic tradition. The sculpted figure on Stele 13 has long hair and is not wearing the characteristically high and complicated Mayan headdress.

Early Classic tetrapod vase (center) and bowl (below) from Petén.

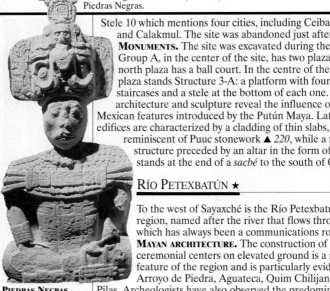

Torso of figure on Stele 6 (AD 687) at Piedras Negras.

Stele 10 which mentions four cities, including Ceibal, Tikal and Calakmul. The site was abandoned just after 900. **MONUMENTS.** The site was excavated during the 1960's. Group A, in the center of the site, has two plazas. The north plaza has a ball court. In the centre of the south plaza stands Structure 3-A: a platform with four staircases and a stele at the bottom of each one. The architecture and sculpture reveal the influence of the Mexican features introduced by the Putún Maya. Later edifices are characterized by a cladding of thin slabs, reminiscent of Puuc stonework ▲ 220, while a round structure preceded by an altar in the form of a jaguar stands at the end of a *sacbé* to the south of Group A.

RÍO PETEXBATÚN ★

To the west of Sayaxché is the Río Petexbatún region, named after the river that flows through it which has always been a communications route. **MAYAN ARCHITECTURE.** The construction of ceremonial centers on elevated ground is a recurring feature of the region and is particularly evident at Arroyo de Piedra, Aguateca, Quim Chilijan and Dos Pilas. Archeologists have also observed the predominance of a plaza layout consisting of a group of three or more rectangular structures, arranged symmetrically round a central court. Contrary to those in central Petén, however, there is no ritual structure on the east side. This type of layout relates particularly to groups of dwellings, although it has also been employed in districts reserved for the elite. Ball courts are rare and are only found at Dos Pilas, Punta de Chimino and Ceibal ● 112.

PIEDRAS NEGRAS
It is a two-day voyage from Sayaxché, along the Ríos Pasión and Usumacinta, past the Mexican border, and Yazchilán ▲ 248. Piedras Negras lies downstream past several sets of rapids (whose crossing on

the return journey is hazardous), and can only be reached by dinghy. There are few remains on the site – most have either been bought by collectors or are in the archeological museum in Guatemala City ▲ 267.

The ocelot (above) is one of the protected species in the Mayan biosphere.

DOS PILAS

HISTORY. Dos Pilas dominated a vast area since its territory lay in the rectangle delineated by the Ríos Pasión and Salinas and which also included the towns of Cancuen and La Amelía. The city was founded by a member of the Tikal royalty, exiled in c. 600. Although the three successive sovereigns ruling from 698–760 successfully consolidated the military power of the city, Dos Pilas was nevertheless defeated by the satellite town, Tamarindito, during the reign of the last sovereign. This reversal of fortune provoked the collapse of the metropolis which was abandoned in 760. The two concentric defensive walls with stakes on their summits were not resistant enough to prevent the fall of the city.

MONUMENTS. The unfinished hieroglyphic stairway was interrupted in c. 700. The sculpted motifs depict a crouching hostage, but the end of the text is missing. It is thought to represent the capture of the sovereign of Ceibal who was sacrificed seventeen years earlier. Funerary enclosures with walls made of thin stone slabs and covered with stones to form a flat roof were discovered, as well as two tombs, one of which was not found until 1991 and contained the remains of the second sovereign. Also concealed in this sepulcher was a jade, shell and mother-of-pearl headdress, pottery decorated with glyphs and thousands of slivers of obsidian.

USUMACINTA
Below the site of Altar de los Sacrificios the Río Pasíon flows into the Usumacinta (above, 19th century) which forms the border with Chiapas ▲ 248.

AGUATECA

Aguateca (right) stands on a cliff overlooking the Río Petexbatún. After an initial period of occupation during the Late Preclassic it probably experienced a renaissance. The structures and steles that can be seen today are products of this second era. The royal family occupied a sort of acropolis situated to the east of the central plaza but, because the city was in a permanent state of conflict, moved to a more strategically secure structure, built to a new design and with new materials. Linear defense walls were constructed with greater care than those at Dos Pilas and were thicker around the area occupied by the royal family. The city center represented the deified sovereign, and the protection of his person was of paramount importance. An acropolis which stood on a platform on the west side of the central plaza is one of the few examples of this type of complex in the region. The sculpture on the steles depicts some of Aguateca's rulers: the sovereign Shield Turtle is featured on a sculpture dated 640; Stele 8 (750) shows a sovereign with jaguar paws for hands and feet; Stele 13 (860) is decorated with seven serpents; Stele 17 shows a jaguar at the feet of the principle figure; Stele 4 (800) bears a motif of a monkey or a man dressed in a monkey skin. Like the whole of southwest Petén, the town was invaded in the early 10th century. The finest pieces can be seen in the archeological museum in Guatemala City ▲ 267.

CONSTRUCTION TECHNIQUES ● 106
Hieroglyphic stairways and sculpted panels flanking flights of access steps are one of the region's architectural characteristics. They are present on the major sites of Dos Pilas, Tamarindito and Ceibal, while at Aguateca smooth panels occupy the same position next to the steps. After the fall of Dos Pilas, Aguateca and Ceibal used larger stones sculpted on several sides, as well as employing similar techniques and layouts to those used in central Petén for structures built for the elite.

STELES OF PIEDRAS NEGRAS
Stele 40 (center), dated 746, and Stele 12 (left), dated 795.

▲ PETÉN

Corn cobs drying in a village in Petén.

YAXHÁ
The temples and steles in Plaza C (broken stele, below), built in the 3rd and 4th centuries, are astronomical monuments for observing the solstices.

"As for Mayan architecture . . . it is a collection of pyramids, flat walls divided into rectangular panels, and broad, regular flights of stairs. As such, it is a materialization of the most characteristically human imaginings of Man, and the most unnatural."
Aldous Huxley
Winter Cruise in Central America

LAKE YAXHÁ
Mid-way between Flores and Belize, a track leads to Lake Yaxhá (below), a favorite haunt of crocodiles. Its limestone bottom gives a gray tinge to its waters.

FLORES TO BELIZE

Beyond Tikal the road running eastward from Flores toward Belize becomes a track. During the rainy season muddy potholes often make it impassable.

YAXHÁ. The archeologist Teobert Maler ● *56* was the first to explore the ruins of this site in 1904 and published his discoveries in 1908. Few Mayan cities have revealed such an urban network of streets, side streets and sidewalks. Its nine acropolises with a total of five hundred structures are still largely unrestored. In Plaza B, Structure 90, a promontory supporting the remains of six pillars, is original. To the east of the plaza, Temple 216 stands on an acropolis and offers a spectacular view of the forest, the lakes of Yaxhá and Sacnab and the island of Topoxté.

Plaza A is a complex with twin pyramids, like those of Tikal ▲ *324*. A huge, ten-tonne stone lies mysteriously abandoned on its side.

TOPOXTÉ. The island can be reached by boat or on foot in the dry season. Built during the Postclassic period, three main structures are aligned on a meridional axis: a pyramid with a platform and no temple to the south, the principle pyramid, with a staircase visible on its west face, in the center, and a smaller pyramid to the north. Facing the pyramids and to the west are the altars and steles decorated with small circles.

BIENVENIDOS SITIO Arqueológico **YAXHA**

NAKUM. Nakum, about 12 miles north of Yaxhá, is reached via a track running across swampy depressions (*bajos*), which are flooded during the rainy season. Its buildings, used for astronomical observations, bear the dates 771, 810 and 849. Palace D, positioned on a vast plaza bordered by massive structures, is unusual in that it has forty-four rooms. The monoliths opposite Temple A were erected to celebrate solstices and equinoxes. They were built of limestone which is now badly eroded. The plaza and the other buildings, to the east and west, form the group known as the "Solstice observatory", and are built along similar lines to the astronomical mounuments at Yaxhá and Uaxactún.

NARANJO. The ruins cover a large area. Thirty-six of its forty-seven steles are sculpted.

MELCHOR DE MENCOS AND THE BELIZE BORDER. The border zone is deeply indicated in the illegal trade of rare tropical woods. The inhabitants of Melchor de Mencos, the last village in Guatemala (39 miles from Flores), report periodical incursions by soldiers from Belize trying to move the border markers.

BELIZE

In 1981 British Honduras became independent and joined the Commonwealth as Belize (national flag, below).

"Walking through the streets [of Belize City], there was little evidence of the terrible catastrophe of 1930, when a hurricane unleashed the full force of a huge tidal wave upon the city. It is true that a pile of bricks was all that remained of the principle house of God; but Mammon, Caesar and the Penates had been raised, fresh and shining, from their ruins. Nearly all the dwellings, all the government buildings, all the shops and warehouses had been rebuilt or repaired. On the whole the city looked remarkably clean and well kept. Even a tidal wave has its good side: at least it clears away the slums fairly effectively. Our governments and local authorities are less brutal; but they are also, unfortunately, considerably less effective."

Aldous Huxley
Winter Cruise in Central America

Belize, bordered to the north by Mexico and to the west by Guatemala, extends for 180 miles along the Caribbean coast. The country has an average width east to west of just 68 miles and a total surface area of 8,866 square miles, not including its two hundred or so islets and reefs. While the northern and coastal regions are flat, the mountains in the south and west reach heights of above 3,300 feet (Victoria Peak rises to 3,680 feet). The climate varies slightly from one district to another and the rainy season takes place between June and September. Between September and December, the north winds can become violent hurricanes, like those which destroyed Belize City in 1930, 1955 and 1961, causing the capital to be moved to Belmopán. A number of rivers cross Belize from west to east: the most important are the Río Hondo, which forms the border with Mexico ▲ 188, and the Belize and Sarstún Rivers.

ECONOMY. During recent years the chicle gum market ▲ 330 has declined, and Belize has had to diversify its economy. It exports mahogany, pine, cocoa, fruit and tobacco as well as lobsters, prawns and oysters. It also produces corn, rice, bananas and cattle. Tourism is an important source of income

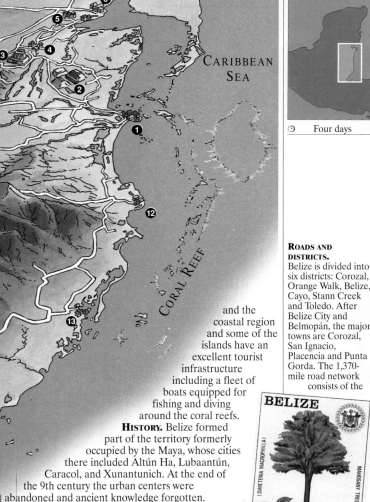

CARIBBEAN
SEA

CORAL REEF

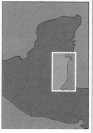

⏱ Four days

**ROADS AND
DISTRICTS.**
Belize is divided into
six districts: Corozal,
Orange Walk, Belize,
Cayo, Stann Creek
and Toledo. After
Belize City and
Belmopán, the major
towns are Corozal,
San Ignacio,
Placencia and Punta
Gorda. The 1,370-
mile road network
consists of the

and the
coastal region
and some of the
islands have an
excellent tourist
infrastructure
including a fleet of
boats equipped for
fishing and diving
around the coral reefs.
HISTORY. Belize formed
part of the territory formerly
occupied by the Maya, whose cities
there included Altún Ha, Lubaantún,
Caracol, and Xunantunich. At the end of
the 9th century the urban centers were
abandoned and ancient knowledge forgotten.
A renaissance during the Postclassic period was little
more than a prelude to the final collapse provoked
by the arrival of the Spanish. Enforced migrations,
territorial incursions and imported European
diseases decimated the last remaining survivors of
the great Mayan civilization.
Until the 17th century
missionaries
based at Bacalar
▲ 185 paid sporadic
visits to Tipu,
the most
important
village in the
region.

BELIZE

(SWIETENIA MACROPHILLA)

MAHOGANY TREE

INDEPENDENCE 21 SEPTEMBER 1981

$1

BELIZ

Western Highway
(toward Guatemala),
the Northern
Highway (toward
Mexico), the
Hummingbird
Highway and the
Southern Highway.
The international
airport is 10 miles
from Belize City.

337

TOWARD THE REEFS
From Belize City, the principal areas
of interest along the coast can be
reached by sea. Amateur divers
should visit the Cayes.

AN ETHNIC MOSAIC

THE LAST OF THE MAYA. The corsair and pirate vessels that scoured the côast forced the last of the Maya to seek refuge in the forests of the interior where they were joined during the Caste War ▲ *186* by groups of Maya fleeing from Yucatán. In modern Belize the Maya form three different linguistic groups: the Kekchis, from Guatemala, who have come to work in the sugarcane plantations in the south of the Toledo district; the Mopáns, in the upper valley of the Belize River; and the Yucatecs in the district of Corozal to the north of Orange Walk. Altogether, they represent 10 percent of the population ● *62*.

A SECOND LINGUISTIC GROUP. The first British settlers on the coast of Belize came to exploit its hardwoods. They brought with them black African slaves and Carib Indians from the Antilles. The descendants of the black slaves, known as Creoles, speak the Creole language, which is a mixture of English, African dialects, Mayan, Carib and Spanish, as well as English. They represent 60 percent of the population and are concentrated in Belize City. The Spanish-speaking mestizos, are of mixed Spanish–Mayan descent. The rest of the population consists of refugees from the Caste War and emigrants from Guatemala and Central America.

A MULTICULTURAL SOCIETY ● *88*. The descendants of workers imported from the West Indies (between 1844 and 1917) to work on the sugarcane plantations still live in the districts of Toledo and Corozal. They usually speak Spanish, Creole and English. Merchants from India settled in Belize City (Hindu temple, left) and Orange Walk. They no longer speak Hindi and so have lost contact with the country of their forebears. In the early 20th century Chinese emigrants settled in Belize and were followed by Syro-Lebanese who formed a tightly knit group of traders. The last group of immigrants were German-speaking Mennonites, now   farmers and stockbreeders.

GARINAGUS ● 88
▲ *342*
African slaves shipwrecked in the Antilles formed an independent group on the island of St Vincent and adopted the language and customs of the Caribbean. These Garinagus (who

spoke Garifuna) supported the French republican rebellion and were exiled by the British to Roatán in 1797. From there they settled along the coast of Honduras, Nicaragua, Guatemala and Belize (in the Stann Creek district). Driven back by the Bay Men, who feared their rebellious and libertarian spirit, they were not officially acknowledged by the community until November 19, 1832. This date has now become a national festival.

Port of Belize City, late 19th century.

BELIZE CITY

Belize City stands on the estuary of the Belize River and is dissected by Haulover Creek. For a long time it was the capital of a country with a population of around 200,000, but was replaced by the centrally located city of Belmopán due to the frequent hurricanes which threatened the inhabitants and administrative infrastructures. Today it has 50,000 inhabitants and is still the country's main economic and cultural center.

FORT GEORGE. This former British fort was built on an island separated from the mainland by a narrow channel. This was filled in during the 1920's when a monument to the memory of Baron Bliss, one of the country's benefactors, was also erected. Today the Fort George Hotel stands on the site. It was built after World War Two and is one of the city's best hotels.

SOUTHERN PART OF THE CITY. The most characteristic part of the city lies south of the Swing Bridge. It is an old district of narrow streets, wooden houses and small shops. A fresh produce market is held there every Saturday. Regent Street and Albert Street, the only streets to have survived from 18th-century Belize, house large companies and the business sector. The town clock, on its metal scaffolding, shows a different time on each of its four faces. A flea market now occupies the site of the former Court House, which was destroyed by fire in 1918.

GOVERNMENT HOUSE. The building was abandoned following the Hurricane Hattie disaster and the foundation of Belmopán. The wooden edifice was built on the Southern Foreshore between 1812 and 1814 by the British architect Christopher Wren and is now used as a VIP visitors' residence.

HOTEL MONA LISA
The hotel (above) was used in Peter Weir's film, *Mosquito Coast* (1986), starring Harrison Ford.

BRIDGES IN BELIZE CITY
Belize City is linked to the mainland by Belcan Bridge upstream, and the old Swing Bridge at the mouth of the river. On the other side of the Swing bridge, the Fort George district offers a splendid view of the port.

JAMAICANS
Rastafarians have mainly settled in Belize City. They believe in the redemption of the Black Race and its return to Africa, and worship the Negus Haile Selassie I, under the name of Ras Tafari. They can be recognized by their long hair (dreadlocks) that their religion forbids them to cut.

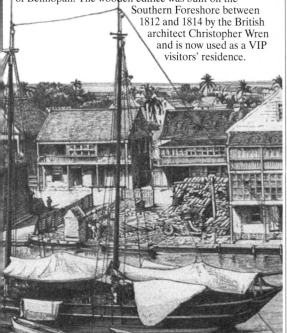

339

▲ Belize

NORTHERN ARCHEOLOGICAL SITES

LAMANAÏ ★
Of all the Mayan sites, Lamanaï was occupied for the longest period: 500 BC to the 19th century. The site is unmaintained and is reached by following the New River upstream from Orange Walk for about 18 miles. During the dry season there is also a track from San Felipe. The oldest pottery shards on the site date from 500 BC. Four centuries later the tallest Mayan pyramid

A lack of roads makes it difficult to reach the many archeological sites discovered, but as yet relatively unexplored, in the northern region of Belize. Only seven sites are open to the public and none of them have any facilities, so it is essential to take drinking water. As these visits often involve crossing areas covered with high grass, visitors should wear boots, trousers tucked into socks, long-sleeved shirts and a hat as protection against the tropical sun.

SANTA RITA. The present town of Corozal, in the extreme north of Belize, is built on part of the site of Santa Rita, occupied by the Maya when the Spanish arrived. The surviving Mayan structures are about one mile from the town. Stucco decorations and two sepulchers have been found dating from the Early Classic period. The buildings are from the Late Postclassic period (1350–1530). In 1985 Diane and Arlen Chase discovered a tomb and a skeleton covered with pieces of jade and mica. One of the buildings has been reconstructed and is the only one which can be visited.

CERROS. The site of Cerros lies across the bay from Corozal. It can be reached by boat and, in the dry season, by road via Chunos, Progreso and Copper Bank. Cerros was an important site during the Late Preclassic period (350 BC–AD 250). Stucco masks nearly 8 feet high flanked the staircases of two structures. The tallest edifice stands 72 feet high, but the residential area is often flooded. During its prime, Cerros controlled the trade along the Río Hondo and the New River and a canal was dug around the town to facilitate the traffic of large dugouts.

(108 feet) of that period was constructed. There is a Late Classic ball court, as well as houses built over ceremonial structures and Postclassic temples over Classic houses.

NOHMUL. Situated about a mile from San Pablo, in the direction of Orange Walk, this major site consists of two groups linked by a *sacbé*. It was occupied at the end of the

ALTÚN HA
Archeologists from the Ontario Royal Museum in Canada, who excavated the site (right) between 1964 and 1971, translated the name Rockstone Pond into Mayan: Altún Ha.

Preclassic period, and then at the end of the Classic period (600–900). There are less significant sites, such as San Esteban and San Antonio, near Orange Walk.

ALTÚN HA ★. The Mayan city of Altún Ha, which lies about 28 miles north of Belize City and 7 miles from the coast, can be reached via the Northern Highway. Restored in the 1970's, this is the most explored site in Belize. It was occupied from the Early Preclassic period (c. 1000 BC), but most of the visible structures date from the Late Classic period. Altún Ha must have had a population of about ten thousand. The center consists of two adjoining plazas, one to the north and the other to the south. Its water came from a huge, clay-lined reservoir with a stone and clay dam at the southern end to prevent water escaping into the swamps. In the stone Temple of the Altars, which is covered by a later structure, broken pieces of carved jade were discovered, while excavations of a tomb unearthed almost three hundred jade objects and the decomposed remains of a codex. Like Lubaantún ▲ 343, Altún Ha has no steles or monolithic altars.

CHAN CHICH. Chan Chich lies near the Guatemalan border and can be reached by road or charter aircraft from Belize City. The site is ideal for observing tropical flora and fauna, especially birds ■ 26 or for simply relaxing in its chalets or restaurant-bar. The complex, which dates from the Classic period, consists of two large plazas surrounded by structures. When they were discovered, the temples had already been partially plundered. In the south of Orange Walk, between Lamanaï and Chan Chich, the sites of Las Milpas, El Infierno, Kakabish and San José have also been found, but are difficult to get to. They date from the same period and have not yet been excavated.

XUNANTUNICH
The site (left) was occupied in the Classic period (150–900). The 147-feet-high Castillo, opposite the central plaza, is a monumental Mayan structure. On its south face, a stucco frieze, restored in 1972, is a cosmological composition on several levels representing the earth and the sky in the form of a celestial band supported by *bacobs* (detail above).

Lemboglossum rosii orchid.

KINICH AHAU
A royal tomb at Altún Ha contained the largest piece of sculpted Mayan jade ever discovered: the head of Kinich Ahau, the Sun.

▲ BELIZE

AN IMPORTANT SITE
One of the special features of Caracol are the giant inscriptions with dates carved on circular altar stones. Like other major sites, such as Tikal, huge reservoirs were hewn out of the rock to store water, and a vast network of terraces made intensive agriculture possible. Every day the research carried out on the site brings new discoveries to light and confirms the fact that Caracol was one of the most important centers of the Mayan civilization.

XUNANTUNICH. The Western Highway runs from Belize City to Flores ▲ *320* in Guatemala. Near the border it crosses a region which was densely populated until the 18th century. Xunantunich is situated about 8 miles from San Ignacio, the most important town in western Belize. Three carved steles stand in Xunantunich's central square. In 1959 Evan Mackie proved that the site, which consists of three plazas surrounded by structures, had been partially destroyed by an earthquake during the Late Classic period. From the top of the Castillo there is a splendid view of the Petén jungle ▲ *317*, the Mayan mountains and the district of Cayo. Several other sites can be visited near San Ignacio, including Barton Ramie, El Pilar and, to the south of the Western Highway, Tipu and Mucnal Tunich. To date, they are all relatively unexplored and overgrown.

CARACOL. The Mayan city of Caracol, also in the district of Cayo in western

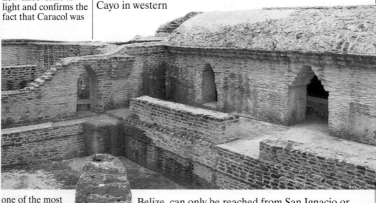

Belize, can only be reached from San Ignacio or Georgeville. A track enters the Pine Ridge nature reserve and runs south to Caracol via Augustine and San Luis. Prior authorization must be obtained from the Department of Archeology or the Forestry Department Western Division before visiting the area. The site of Caracol, probably the largest site in Belize, stands on the Plateau of Chiquibil in the Chiquibil Forest Reserve, at the heart of the region. The tallest temple on the site is slightly taller than the Castillo at Xumantunich, and its base is slightly larger than that of the temples of Tikal ▲ *322*. Caracol and Tikal, about 43 miles away, were both Classic sites and were constantly at war with each other. Following a conflict in 562, Caracol dominated the region for more than a century.

CAHAL PECH
The ruins of Cahal Pech lie on a hill overlooking the town of San Ignacio. The palace has unusual vaulted doorways (above). Some of the recent reconstructions at Cahal Pech have been strongly criticized by experts.

TOWARD THE SOUTH

DANGRIGA, A GARINAGUS VILLAGE ● *88* ▲ *338*. A poorly maintained mountain road, the Hummingbird Highway, runs from Belmopán into southern Belize and the village of Dangriga (opposite) which means "stagnant waters" in Garifuna. In 1802 a Garinagus community was founded at the mouth of Stann Creek River and was later augmented by runaway slaves. In 1823 other Garinagus from Honduras,

342

The Caribbean influence can be seen in the cuisine of the Garinagus. Thin pancakes, known as cassava bread, are a specialty and are made by grating manioc and passing the flour through large cylindrical sieves made from plaited palms.

under the command of Alejo Bani, settled in southern Belize. They grew crops and sold their vegetables in Belize City where they were only allowed to stay for forty-eight hours at a time. The Garinagus still preserve certain African traditions, especially music, dancing and food, and continue to practice their animist religion called *obeah*. On November 19 they celebrate the anniversary of their recognition by the Belize authorities. The festival, a cultural feast is extremely popular.

UNEXPLORED WEALTH. There are a number of unexplored sites in the forests around Dangriga. The Southern Highway passes the sites of Pomoná and Kendal and, further south, Alabama, all in the Stann Creek district, as well as Kuchil Balum in the Cockscomb Basin Forest Reserve.

INVADERS. South of Dangriga the track enters the district of Toledo and continues to Punta Gorda. The region – which has numerous remains of its former Mayan inhabitants and no direct communications routes with its neighbor, Guatemala – was invaded by American Confederates who came to buy weapons from the British during the Civil War. After the defeat of the South, some confederates set up sugarcane plantations here, but, unused to the climate and living conditions, soon returned to the United States. Their lands were taken over by newcomers of every ethnic origin: Garinagus and Hindus, Kekchi and Mopán Maya, Chinese, Europeans and mestizos.

PUNTA GORDA. Punta Gorda lies at the southern end of Belize and can be reached by plane from Belize City and Dangriga and by boat from Livingston and Puerto Barrios in Guatemala ▲ *309*. Punta Gorda has a Saturday market, remarkable for its colors and the variety of the products sold, and where the colored cloth ● *89* of Guatemala has

pride of place. The departure point for visiting the archeological sites in this district is San Pedro, about 11 miles north of Punta Gorda. The inhabitants of San Pedro, San Antonio, Santa Cruz, Aguacate and others are Kekchi and Mopán Maya ● *62* refugees from the Guatemalan coffee plantations. They have preserved their Indian languages and traditions, including weaving. Guides are available, offering conducted tours of the Hokeb Ha and Blue Creek caves. The ruins of Hokeb Ha, Pusilha and Uxbenka can only be visited on horseback.

LUBAANTÚN ★. Work on the site of Lubaantún ("place of the fallen stones"), about a mile from San Pedro, was carried out by a series of mainly British archeologists between 1903 and 1970, from Thomas Gann to Norman Hammond. The latter

Tropical forest near Lamanaï.

CAVES OF SAINT HERMAN
About 11 miles from Belmopán in the direction of Dangriga, the caves of Saint Herman form a remarkable underground network once occupied by the Maya. These labyrinthine caves, where narrow passages open onto huge chambers several dozen yards high, offer an extraordinarily beautiful and spectacular display of stalactites and stalagmites, underground rivers and "windows" where rays of light penetrate into the very bowels of the earth.

KINKAJOU
This Central American monkey is mainly active at night, eating fruit, eggs, several varieties of insects and honey.

discovered that the site was founded just after AD 700 and abandoned less than two hundred years later. Its architecture is extremely original and consists of pyramidal platforms, with staircases, on which edifices were built in perishable materials. The tallest structure on the site is 36 feet high. The Mayan vault was not used here and there doesn't appear to be any form of stone decoration. The stonework was entirely dry, without mortar, and usually consisted of small elements, perfectly adjusted and arranged to create the best esthetic effect. Terraces were also built using large blocks known as megaliths. No sculpted steles have been discovered at Lubaantún. The site consists of over one hundred structures grouped around twenty plazas. There are three concentric zones: a central religious zone, a belt of ceremonial structures including ball courts and edifices whose function is unclear, and a residential zone. The ceramic figurine-whistles discovered on the site are extremely varied and include a unique figure wearing a sort of helmet with a single vent opening. The site is not maintained and visitors are advised to go suitably equipped and wearing boots and trousers.

UXBENKA. Uxbenka, near Santa Cruz, was not discovered until 1984. The site has yielded twenty dated Early Classic steles, seven of which were sculpted.

NIM LI PUNIT. Midway between Punta Gorda and Dangriga, near Indian Creek, Nim Li Punit was discovered in 1970 not far from Xnaheb. Architecturally, the site can be linked with Lubaantún. Among the twenty-five steles, (dated between 600 and 800) discovered here one was 10 feet high; the largest stele yet found in Belize. Although, like most of the other sites, Nim Li Punit had been plundered, the tomb excavated in 1986 by R. Leventhal was intact. There are probably several dozen undiscovered sites, hidden in the jungles of Belize. Each new discovery enriches the archeological map of this tiny country.

344

PRACTICAL INFORMATION

◆ USEFUL INFORMATION

A trip to Central America should be organized carefully. To avoid any disasters or a premature return, it is best to make the following arrangements: firstly, contact your doctor and find out which vaccinations you will need and when you will need to have them, then apply for any necessary visas, and finally decide what to pack; be well prepared if you are traveling during the rainy season.

HEALTH

Before traveling to any tropical country, you will need to take certain health precautions. The elderly, young children, pregnant women and those with a medical condition are advised to take particular care, as emergency medical treatment may not always be available outside the major cities.

VACCINATIONS
Vaccinations are not compulsory although you are recommended to have vaccinations against tetanus, typhoid-paratyphoid and polio, meningitis, hepatitis A and B, malaria, cholera, yellow fever and rabies. You will usually need a course of vaccinations starting a minimum of one month before you travel. Missing any of these vaccinations by even a day can lead to a three-month delay.

MALARIA
The parasite responsible for malaria is transmitted by a mosquito bite and can cause repeated attacks of malaria accompanied by high fevers. Preventative treatment is indispensable and is taken either daily or weekly throughout your stay (it is usually commenced one week before arriving in the affected area and continued for several weeks on returning). Anti-malarial tablets are only available on prescription. You are recommended to protect yourself against mosquito bites as much as possible by wearing long sleeves, long trousers and insect repellent at all times.

FIRST AID KIT
Take a first aid kit with you: diarrhea tablets, anti-malarial pills, insect repellent, disinfectant and cotton wool, antiseptic ointment, pain killers, eye drops, water purification tablets, motion sickness tablets, adhesive bandages, total-block sunscreen and lip-balm.

TIME DIFFERENCES
The time in four major cities at midday in Mayan countries

summertime *am*
• *the following day*

wintertime *am*

summertime *pm*

wintertime *pm*

ON ARRIVAL
Should you need to purchase any medication after you arrive, always buy it from a pharmacy and not a market. *Lemotil* is for stopping attacks of diarrhea and *Entocid* for upset stomachs (a bottle costs around $2). Insect repellents are often more effective than imported products.

TREATMENT
If you are undergoing a course of medication remember to bring prescriptions with you stating clearly the actual scientific name of the drugs you are taking, as the commercial name often varies from one country to another.

AIDS
As in other tropical countries, the Aids virus has been slowly spreading throughout central America.

WATER
Drink bottled liquids where possible – mineral water, beer, soft drinks – and avoid drinking any tap water (when ordering drinks always ask for them without ice, as it may have been made from tap water).
Belize City has a modern water purification system and many hotels in Cancún and Belize also have their own purification systems.
Avoid salads as these may have been rinsed in tap water and eat only cooked vegetables and thick-skinned fruits that you peel yourself.

INGUAT

VISAS AND PASSPORTS

MEXICO
There are no visa requirements for US or UK visitors. US citizens do not require a passport, although proof of citizenship is needed.
US:
EMBASSY OF MEXICO
1911 Pennsylvania Avenue, N.W.
Washington, DC 20006
Tel. (202) 728 1600
MEXICAN CONSULATE GENERAL
8 East 41st Street
New York, NY 10017
Tel. (212) 689 0456
UK:
MEXICAN EMBASSY
60/61 Trafalgar Sq
London WC2N
Tel. (0171) 839 6586
EL SALVADOR
US citizens require a visa (available free from the consulate). There are no visa requirements for UK visitors.
US:
EL SALVADOR EMBASSY
2308 California Street
Washington, DC 20008
Tel. (202) 265 9671
SALVADORAN CONSULATE
46 Park Avenue
New York, NY 10016
Tel. (212) 889 3608
UK:
EL SALVADOR EMBASSY AND CONSULATE
1st Fl, 5 Gt James St
London WC1N
Tel. (0171) 430 2141
GUATEMALA
All visitors from the US and the UK require a valid passport and a visa.
US:
CONSULATE GENERAL OF GUATEMALA
57 Park Avenue
New York, NY 10016
Tel. (212) 686 3837
GUATEMALA EMBASSY
2220 R. Street, N.W.
Washington,
DC 20008
Tel. (202) 745 4952
UK:
GUATEMALAN EMBASSY
13 Fawcett Street
London SW10
Tel. (0171) 351 4042

BELIZE & HONDURAS
All visitors must have a valid passport. There are no visa requirements for US or UK citizens.
US:
EMBASSY OF HONDURAS
3007 Tilden St, N.W.
POD 4-M Washington,
DC 20008
Tel. (202) 966 7702
EMBASSY OF BELIZE
2535 Massachusetts Avenue, N.W.
Washington, DC 20008
Tel. (202) 332 9636
UK:
BELIZE HIGH COMMISSION
10 Harcourt Houses
19a Cavendish Sq.
London W1M
Tel. (0171) 499 9728
HONDURAN EMBASSY
115 Gloucester Pl.
London W1H
Tel. (0171) 486 4880

WHAT TO PACK

Whatever the season, do not forget that the nights can get extremely cold in places of high altitude.
Take a bathing-costume, t-shirts, shorts, lightweight trousers, a light sweater or jacket, sunglasses, a hat, a raincoat for the wet season, good hiking boots, plastic sandals (for showers where you have doubts about the level of cleanliness, and also in case you need to walk in or through water). Pack a flashlight with extra batteries, a pocket knife, a money belt and toiletries (cosmetics can be very expensive). It is preferable to use a waterproof bag or case that can be padlocked. Leave jewelry or valuables at home.

PHOTOGRAPHY

possibly an isothermal box to protect your films.
Make sure you take the correct film and filters (ones that are designed for use in strong sunlight).
Print film (35mm) is readily available all along the Route of the Mayas, main outlets being pharmacies, hotels, and camera stores. You are advised, however, to check that the film is not out of date before purchasing.

Because of the humidity of the climate you may wish to take silica capsules to place in your camera bag to absorb damp and

MAYA TRAILS AND SPECIAL-INTEREST HOLIDAYS

Many specialist tour operators offer small-group or special-interest holidays with fixed itineraries. Some may even be prepared to design a tour specially for you. These usually last between 14 to 24 days and will take you through ancient lands of the Mayas, visiting the major highlights. Usually starting from Mexico or Cancún, they frequently include visits to Guatemala, Chichén Itzá, Antigua and Flores and often finish with several days at a beach resort.

DRIVER'S LICENSES

Should you wish to rent a car you will require a valid passport and a current driver's license. If traveling from the UK you will need an International Driver's License, which is available from the Automobile Association Haymarket London W1 Tel. (0171) 839 4355

◆ CLIMATE AND ECONOMY

If you are planning a visit to Central America, you can prevent the holiday of your dreams turning into a nightmare by taking account of the climate and customs of the countries you will be visiting. The first will help you pack your suitcase and the second ensure that you return with it.

CLIMATE

The tropical climate of the Mayan countries means that you will have good weather during your visit, regardless of the time of year. In the rainy season (June–September) it only rains in the late afternoon which does not interfere too much with visits or excursions. Temperatures tend to vary more with altitude than with season. If you visit the Caribbean coast don't underestimate the strength of the sun which is often disguised by a warm breeze.

YUCATÁN PENINSULA (MEX.)
It is always warm on the Yucatán Peninsula with temperatures often reaching 104° F. Brief but violent storms (*nortes*) can occur in the late afternoon, even during the dry season.

TABASCO (MEX.)
The low altitude of the state of Tabasco means the climate is warm and wet throughout the year. It is more pleasant during the dry season.

CHIAPAS (MEX.)
The mountainous regions of Chiapas are swept by cool winds and are cold at night, hence their name: *terra fria* (cold land).

GUATEMALA
Temperatures in the Guatemalan highlands are very cool at night and sometimes even during the day in winter. The Pacific coast and the Petén jungle have a hot, wet, tropical climate.

BELIZE
The inland climate is similar to that of Yucatán. The islands are swept by sea breezes and are extremely pleasant throughout the year.

From top to bottom: Mexico, Guatemala, Belize, Honduras, El Salvador.

RECOMMENDED
Plan your visit for November and enjoy the magnificent All Souls' Day celebrations in the highlands, relatively few tourists and a cloudless sky.

THE BEST TIME TO VISIT

	JAN.	FEB.	MARCH	APRIL	MAY	JUNE	JULY	AUG.	SEP.	OCT.	NOV.	DEC.
Weather	☀	☀	☀	☀	🌥	🌧	🌧	🌧	🌧	☁	☀	☀
Tourists	🚶🚶🚶	🚶	🚶	🚶	🚶🚶	🚶	🚶🚶	🚶🚶	🚶🚶🚶	🚶	🚶	🚶🚶

☀ Dry Season   🌧 Rainy Season   ☁ Intermediate Season   🚶🚶🚶 No. of tourists

ECONOMIC SITUATION

MEXICO
The rigorous economic policies of the Mexican government in recent years appear to be bearing fruit with inflation reduced to around 12 percent in the early 1990's. Mexico is now setting its sights on the great North American market.

GUATEMALA
After Mexico, Guatemala has the greatest wealth of natural resources especially coffee, of which it is the world's sixth largest producer. The *guerilleros* who held sway in the highlands are gradually being reabsorbed into the community.

BELIZE
Former British Honduras still maintains strong ties with Britain through the Commonwealth – Queen Elizabeth II remains the Head of State of Belize. Its Gross Domestic Product per head of population is the highest in Central America, with the exception of Mexico.

HONDURAS
This essentially agricultural country produces the traditional products of the region: coffee and fruit destined for the North American market.

EL SALVADOR
In 1992 this tiny country adopted a new presidential constitution and since then it has been making a concerted effort to maintain internal stability. After twelve years of civil war the country is experiencing its first years of peace.

SAFETY

TOWNS AND CITIES
The shanty towns surrounding the capitals, such as the narrow side streets of Belize City, have nothing to offer tourists and are best avoided during the day as well as at night. The centers of the more tourist-orientated towns (Mérida, Cancún, Antigua, Flores and San Cristóbal) are safe even at night. However, visitors are advised not to walk out after dark in Guatemala City and San Salvador.

BANDITS
Many isolated and forested regions are notorious for bandits. These places should not be visited alone and especially not after dark. Tourist offices issue warnings concerning certain excursions which could prove dangerous and these should be listened to.

POLICE
A form of "legal" highway robbery, in which drivers of private vehicles can be stopped by the more unscrupulous members of the national police force, is becoming fairly common practice. A mind-boggling list of imaginary offenses is read out which the driver is invited to "clear" by making a "voluntary contribution" (*mordida*). If this should happen to you, pay up with good grace and lodge your complaint later, but only at the tourist office or with the tourist police. Although common practice in Guatemala and Mexico, this type of incident is less frequent in the other countries on the "Ruta Maya".

PICKPOCKETS
The most common type of crime against tourists is the classic pickpocket. So take a few simple precautions: use traveler's cheques, keep photocopies of official documents (passport, plane tickets) in a safe place, and only carry the amount of money needed for a particular day or visit (leave the rest somewhere safe).

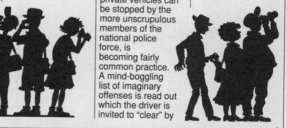

IDENTIFYING THE MAYAN COUNTRIES					
	BELIZE	**GUATEMALA**	**HONDURAS**	**MEXICO**	**EL SALVADOR**
CAPITAL	BELMOPAN	GUATEMALA CITY	TEGUCIGALPA	MEXICO CITY	SAN SALVADOR
SURF. AREA (sq.miles)	8,865	42,042	43,278	759,529	8,124
POPULATION (millions)	0.19	9.47	5.26	87.80	5.38
DENSITY (inhabitants/sq. mile)	3.3	33.5	18.1	17.3	98.8
LIFE EXPECTANCY (years)	67	65	66	70	67
LITERACY (% of population)	95	55.1	63.1	63	63

◆ TRAVELING TO THE MAYAN COUNTRIES

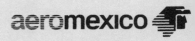

Cancún is the most common point of entry to the Route of the Mayas, although each area does have its own international airport. The cost of an air ticket can vary greatly, depending on the time of year and the particular destination. Tour operators offer a wide range of different types of holidays. For the hardened traveler or those with plenty of time it is even possible to travel from the US to Mexico by train or bus.

BY AIR
Most international flights arrive in Cancún, Guatemala City, Mexico or Belize City. From there take connections to many of the other towns and cities in Central America. Tegucigalpa and San Salvador, situated on the periphery of the Route of the Mayas, have their own international airports. For travelers with a limited amount of time it is probably best to stay based in Cancún and take trips from there. For those with more time at their disposal and who wish to explore the south of the region, most companies with flights to Central America (Taca in particular) will fly to San Salvador.

FROM THE US
American Airlines and United Airlines offer roundtrips from New York to Guatemala City and New York to Mexico City. American Airlines and

Continental Airlines offer roundtrip flights from New York to Cancún. Prices range from $1405 (business or first class) to $582 (coach class) for a ticket to Guatemala City, $1390 (first class) to $363 (coach class) for a ticket to Mexico City and $2020(first class) to $412 (coach class) for a ticket to Cancún.

FROM THE UK
British Airways and American Airways offer direct flights from London Heathrow to Mexico City. Roundtrip ticket prices range from £579 to £629 according to season. Roundtrip fare to Cancún via Mexico City costs £806 to £844, and to Guatemala City via Miami costs from £1,029 to £1,131

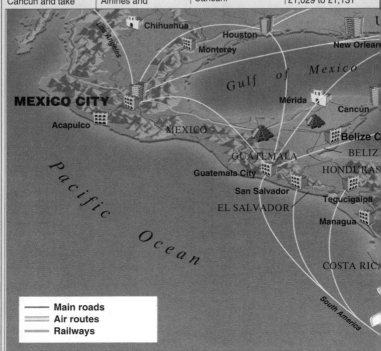

BIENVENIDOS
A LA CIUDAD DE MEXICO
CAPITAL DE LA NACION

according to season. British Airways reservations Tel. 0345 222111.

BY TRAIN
It is possible to travel to Central America by train from Mexico or the US, although as there is no American train company which travels to Mexico you will need to change at the border. Allow a minimum of thirty hours to travel from Los Angeles or Houston to Mexico City and between twenty-four and thirty hours for the journey from Mexico City to Mérida. For information and reservations contact: Ferrocarriles Nacionales de Mexico, estación central de Buenavista, Tel. (5) 547 85 45 or 547 58 19

TOUR OPERATORS
Many specialist tour operators offer different types of holidays throughout the Route of the Mayas. Tours, leisure trips, activity holidays and special interest holidays are all available.

US
AMERICAS TOUR AND TRAVEL
Tel. (800) 238 4467
ARCHEOLOGICAL TOURS
Tel. (212) 986 3054
CULTURAL TOURS OF MEXICO
Tel. (800) 487 4783
DESIGN TRAVEL & TOURS
Tel. (800) 543 7164

ELEGANT VACATIONS
Tel. (800) 451 4398
GLOBETROTTERS
Tel. (888) 824 5623
GREAT ADVENTURE TRAVEL
Tel. (800) 874 2826
GRAND CIRCLE TRAVEl
Tel. (800) 321 2835
GREAT TRIPS
Tel. (800) 552 3419
MAYA CARIBE TRAVEL
Tel. (800) 223 4084
MAYA WORLD TOURS
Tel. (800) 392 6292
QUESTERS WORLDWIDE NATURE TOURS
Tel. (800) 468 8668
SPANISH HERITAGE TOURS
Tel. (800) 221 2580
SOUTHERN HORIZONS
Tel. (800) 333 9361
UK
EXODUS
Tel. (0181) 675 7996
EXPLORE WORLDWIDE
Tel. (0125) 231 9448
KUONI WORLDWIDE
Tel. (0171) 499 8636
SOUTH AMERICAN EXPERIENCE
Tel. (0171) 976 5511
TWICKERS WORLD
Tel. (0181) 892 8164

◆ TRAVELING AROUND THE MAYAN COUNTRIES

Although travel is not always simple, the various means of transport in the Mayan countries will certainly feature among the more picturesque memories of your visit. Flying is the quickest and most comfortable way to travel. Buses are widely used by the local people and are a lively and convivial form of transport, although if you are visiting only one of the five countries you may well prefer to drive. Some isolated sites, such as lakeside villages and small Caribbean islands, can only be reached by boat.

INTERNAL AIRLINES
The Mayan countries have a highly developed internal airline network. Most flights are daily and reasonably priced. The large number of national airports in each of the five countries enables you to visit most places and make best use of your time.

ISLAND LINKS
In Belize the small planes of the local Island Air company operate daily services between the islands of Cay Caulker, Ambergris Cay (San Pedro) and Belize City international airport.
ISLAND AIR
Belize City
Tel. (2) 31 140; 31 707
Ambergris Cay
Tel. (26) 2180; 2484: 2435; Fax 2192
TROPIC AIR
Belize City
Tel. (2)45 671
Fax 32 794
Ambergris Cay
Tel. (26) 2012; 3275/77; Fax 2338
Cay Caulker
Tel. (2) 2040

"MAYAN AIRPASS"
The *Mayan Airpass* is an option offered by the airline companies Aviateca and Taca, based in Paris, Tel. (33) 1 44 51 01 64 or 1 44 51 01 65 Fax 1 40 07 12 72. It is designed to enable visitors to take advantage of the regular air services to travel quickly and at competitive prices within the Mayan countries.

HOW IT WORKS
Choose your itinerary from the selection of towns and cities serviced by the companies. Each stage costs one or two coupons. Calculate the number of coupons required for your itinerary: it must be worth at least four coupons to qualify for the *Mayan Airpass* option. Calculate the cost of your trip by multiplying the number of coupons by US$65.

0   30   60 m

Bus routes:
28 miles / 1 hr   Distance and journey time

Air services:
— — Mayan Path
——— Other routes
✈ International airport

MEXICO ◄

Veracruz
VILLAHERMOSA
94 miles 2 ½ hrs

Oaxaca

TUXTLA GUTIERREZ
53 miles 2 hrs
Oaxaca   San Cristóbal de las Casas

119 miles 5 ½ hrs

109 miles 3 hrs

Cuauhtémoc City

MEXICO

Tapachula

GULF
OF
MEXICO

CANCÚN

MÉRIDA
72 miles
2 ½ hrs
28 miles
1 hr
100 miles
2 hrs
40 miles
1 hr
Playa del
Carmen
Chichén
Itzá
Valladolid
Cozumel
128 miles
40 miles
3 ½ hrs
1 hr
Tulum

CAMPECHE
265 miles
8 hrs

Yucatán

348 miles
10 hrs
348 miles
10 hrs
(2 hrs)
(1 hr)
157 miles
4 hrs

udad del
rmen

MEXICO
CHETUMAL

100 miles
3 ½ hrs
San Pedro

BELIZE

que
BELIZE CITY

139 miles
4 ¾ hrs
CARIBBEAN
SEA

Flores
182 miles
8 hrs
212 miles
8 hrs
Roatán

hiapas
(1 hr)
(1 hr)

316 miles
14 hrs
(1 hr)
Punta Gorda
La Ceiba

GUATEMALA
192 miles
6 hrs
Puerto Barrios
124 miles
3 hrs
(1 hr)

214 miles
7 hrs
124 miles
4 ½ hrs
San Pedro Sula
278 miles
6 ½ hrs

(2 hrs)
175 miles
7 hrs
Copán
(1 hr)
(1 hr)

Antigua
hr
28 miles
GUATEMALA CITY
HONDURAS

168 miles
5 hrs

(1 hr)
TEGUCIGALPA

SAN SALVADOR
(1 hr)
EL
SALVADOR

IC OCEAN

Buses are colored and often decorated with icons and good-luck charms.

Motor boats link the Caribbean islands with the mainland.

INTERCITY BUSES

A highly developed bus network makes it possible to reach

nearly all the villages, even the most isolated ones, in the Mayan countries. Journey times vary according to the road, the vehicle and, above all, the weather. Prices vary between $4 and $6 per 100 km (62 miles).

FIRST-CLASS BUSES
The fir-class buses run by private companies are more spacious than the second-class buses run by the national bus company, although not necessarily particularly comfortable. They do, however, offer a more rapid service between the main towns and cities for virtually the same price as the public buses. Tickets are paid for in advance at the company office where you can also reserve a seat on the day before departure.

Prices and timetables are displayed. These buses often run at night, especially on long journeys.

SECOND-CLASS BUSES

Second-class buses, usually old American school buses, are uncomfortable and normally packed. Put your trust in the driver: he is in complete control of his vehicle. An extremely agile young man is responsible for taking on passengers, shouting out the destination at each intersection, and letting them out at the right "stop". He also puts heavy luggage on the roof and collects the transport tax (*tasa*) from passengers. As the cost of transport varies, ask among local passengers. These buses run mainly in the morning, from 5am onward, but are less frequent in the afternoon.

BOATS

FERRIES
A passenger ferry service operates between the Isla Mujeres and Cancún (Puerto Juárez), the Isla de Cozumel and Playa del Carmen or Puerto Morelos, and links Puerto Barrios and Livingston (Guatemala) to Punta Gorda (Belize).

"LANCHAS"
These small motor boats are a means of public transport and will take you to isolated lakeside villages and sites that can only be reached by boat (for about US$2). Regular services are often interrupted in the late afternoon. Out of season you have to negotiate on the spot for a *lancha privada*. The price, preferably return, should be agreed before you leave. It can be up to ten times the price of a public *lancha*.

TRAINS

The rail network is used more for merchandise than passengers. Trains are fairly slow and dangerous (keep an eye on your luggage) and are a far from ideal means of transport.

MEXICAN NETWORK
Mexico is the only one of the five Mayan countries to have an extensive and efficient rail network. As first-class seats are extremely reasonable, avoid traveling second class. Beware of theft during the night in sleeping compartments.

Guatemalan buses are often old American school buses.

This curious and typical tricycle is ideal for weaving through the narrow streets of Belize City.

CITY TRANSPORT

BUSES

Only large urban centers such as Guatemala City, San Salvador, Mérida and Cancún have an urban bus network. The number indicated on the front of the bus corresponds to its route (information is available from the tourist office). There are no fixed stops, although buses tend to slow down at intersections to take on or set down passengers. Just indicate to the driver that you want to get off. A journey never costs more than US$1, payable when you get on.

"COLECTIVOS"

These minibuses or light trucks carry around ten passengers and operate between airports (or ports) and the city center. This rapid service costs, on average, only a tenth of the equivalent taxi fare.

HITCHHIKING

This service is usually provided by light trucks, open at the back, known locally as pick-ups. Don't climb aboard these joyful convoys before you have negotiated the cost of the journey, and don't pay until you have reached the agreed destination.

ROAD SIGNS

Stop: *alto*
Slow down: *despacio*
Danger: *peligro*
Give way: *ceda el paso*
Parking: *estacionamiento*
Maximum height: *altura maxima*
Maximum width: *ancho libre*
No turning: *no voltear*
Cul de sac: *no hay paso*

TAXIS

The famous Mexican "beetles" and other cars sporting a taxi sign have two things in common: they are rare and it is unusual for them to have a meter. Make sure you agree the cost of the journey before you set off.

CARS

Cars can be hired in all the large towns and cities and at the international airports (where they are more expensive) of all the five Mayan countries.

HIRING A CAR

Make sure you have

an international driving license ◆ *346*. If you pay by

banker's card (accepted everywhere) allow for an additional charge of 5 percent. A supplement is charged to leave a car in a town other than the place of hire. Hire vehicles may not be taken into Petén, in northern Guatemala, except to the Flores/Santa Elena airport.

AGENCE KOKA
Tel: 50 12 33 or 50 05 26.
It is also forbidden to cross borders in hire vehicles unless they are from the Dollar and Avis agencies who, subject to a supplement (US$20), allow you to cross from Guatemala into Honduras.

DRIVING ON THE "RUTA MAYA"

Once you leave the main roads, road surfaces are poor (especially in Guatemala) and signposting often non-existent. Good maps are available from the American Automobile Association (AAA) in Texaco and Esso gas stations. Do not leave valuable items in the car. If you are driving in town, avenues have priority over streets. The maximum speed is 50 km/h (30 mph). Gas is extremely cheap in all five countries (around $1.50 per gallon). Gas stations are few and far between off the main roads.

Crossing borders between the Mayan countries can be an adventure in itself. It is prohibited, and dangerous, to cross a border in a hire vehicle so public transport is the only option. A number of airline companies operate daily services between the main towns of the various countries. Unlike the first-class buses, economy-class buses do not cross borders. Once the customs formalities are over, you can continue your journey by bus or pick-up in the next country.

LOCAL TRANSPORT: BUSES, BOATS, TRAINS AND PLANES

GUATEMALA/MEXICO

◆ INTERCITY BUSES
A number of border posts allow buses to cross between Guatemala and Mexico. The border towns (and their Mexican counterparts) of Tecún Umán (Ciudad Hidalgo), El Carmen (Talisman) and La Mesilla (Ciudad Cuauhtemoc) have the best service.

◆ BOATS
It is also possible to cross directly from Petén (in the north of Guatemala) into Chiapas (Mexico) by *lancha* ◆ 354 (prices and frequency variable) along the Río San Pedro and the Río de la Pasión. This is a long and physically demanding trip, best undertaken in a group.

◆ TRAINS
The railway line which links Puerto Barrios–Guatemala City–Tecún Umán (Mexican border) and continues toward the United States along the Mexican Pacific coast is currently out of service.

EL SALVADOR / GUATEMALA

◆ BUSES
There is a direct, first-class bus service between San Salvador and Guatemala City: from SanSalvador, the King Quality bus from the Hotel Presidente and the Comfort Lines bus from the hotel El Salvador; from Guatemala City, there is a bus from the hotel Las Americas. There is also a daily, economy-class service from San Salvador's Occidente terminal. Some buses only go as far as the border where you can catch a Guatemalan bus to Guatemala City. Others go to Puerto Barrios (Guatemala) and the Guatemalan–Mexican border.

GUATEMALA / BELIZE

◆ FERRIES
A boat leaves Puerto Barrios (Guatemala) on Tuesdays and Fridays at 7.30am, stopping at Livingston (Guatemala) at about 9am before continuing to Punta Gorda (Belize). It makes the return trip on the same day, leaving at 2.30pm. Tickets can be bought on the day of departure before boarding. Get there at least two hours beforehand to be sure of a seat and to allow enough time for customs and immigration formalities.

◆ BUSES
There are direct daily links between Flores (Guatemala) and Chetumal (Mexico) via San Ignacio, Belize City and Orange Walk (Belize). The bus leaves Flores at 5am (reservations at the Hotel San Juan, Santa Elena).

EL SALVADOR / HONDURAS

◆ BUSES
The border post of El Amatillo, in the east of El Salvador, is the most frequently used and the safest for Honduras. The buses for El Amatillo arrive and leave from the Oriente terminal in San Salvador. For passengers in the south of the country, a more direct route takes them to Copán (Honduras). However, it is advisable to ask for information on safety at tourist offices as there is still the possibility of disturbances in the region.

MEXICO / BELIZE

◆ BUSES
Chetumal (Mexico) is the departure and arrival point for buses to and from Belize. Batty Brothers and Venus operate a daily return service from Belize City to the north: Chetumal–Belize City via Corozal and Orange Walk.

◆ AIR LINKS
There are daily services from Belize City to Cancún and Mérida.

VISITING COPÁN (HONDURAS) FROM GUATEMALA

The quickest way is to go direct from Guatemala City to Chiquimila (105 miles) by first-class bus: Rutas Orientales (19 Calle 8–18, Zona 1, Guatemala City). Take the Transportes Vilma bus from the Chiquimila terminal to the border, in the direction of El Florido. The last bus that will enable you to cross the border (which closes at 5.30pm) leaves at 2.30pm. To cross the Guatemala–Honduras border (open 6am–5.30pm), take the minibus (the last bus is at 3.30pm) to Copán. If you miss the last minibus, you can take a pick-up.

Loading luggage: an extremely picturesque operation.

El Salvador welcomes you at the border with Guatemala.

CROSSING A BORDER

Customs formalities are carried out at the border post. This involves showing your passport, having it stamped by the customs official for the country you are leaving

	CUSTOMS DUTIES	AIRPORT TAX
BELIZE	$B 1 (US$ 0.5)	US$ 10
GUATEMALA	10 Quetzals (US$ 2)	US$ 10
HONDURAS	10 Lempira (US$ 1.5)	US$ 10
MEXICO	6 Pesos (US$ 2.5)	US$ 17
EL SALVADOR	15 Colones (US$ 2)	US$ 17

and paying an exit tax. The procedure is repeated at the customs post of the country you are entering where you pay customs duty. You will also be asked how long you plan to stay in the country (maximum length of stay is 3 months). The time taken by these formalities varies according to the number of people crossing (allow 20 minutes on average) and the time spent waiting for the bus to continue your journey.

PRINCIPLE AIRLINE COMPANIES IN THE TOWNS AND CITIES OF THE MAYAN COUNTRIES

	CANCÚN	CHETUMAL	MÉRIDA	VILLAHERMOSA	GUATEMALA C.	BELIZE CITY	SAN SALVADOR	TEGUCIGALPA
AÉROCARIBE	84 20 00		28 18 17	56 00 84				
AÉROMEXICO	84 35 71	215-76	27 90 00	14 16 75				
AÉROCOZUMEL	84 20 20		28 18 17					
AVIACSA	87 42 14	2 76 77	26 90 87	14 57 80				
AVIATECA	86 01 55		25 80 59		334 7722		298 5055	31 5047
LACSA	87 31 01		20 01 04		334 7722		298 5055	31 5047
MEXICANA	87 44 44		24 66 33	16 43 16				
TROPIC AIR						2 45 671		
TAESA	87 33 26		20 20 17					
AÉROLITORAL				14 36 14				
AÉROVIAS					332 5686	2 75 445/6		
AVCOM					331 5821			
COPA					361 1567		271 2333	36 5760
TACA					334 7722		298 5055	31 2469
TAPSA					331 4860			
TRASLADOS					334 7783			
TIKAL JETS					332 5070			
ISLAND AIR						2 31 140		
MAYA AIRWAYS						2 35 794		
SKY BIRD						2 32 596		

◆ CURRENCY

Years of soaring inflation have taught the inhabitants of the Mayan countries to be extremely cautious where money is concerned. It is a region where the dollar rules and European currency is only changed in the large towns and cities.

MEXICAN PESO

On January 1, 1996, following a period of high inflation, the "new peso" (N$), divided into 100 *centavos*, replaced the "old peso" ($) which is still in circulation. A new peso is worth 1,000 old pesos. The new coins are bi-colored, and smaller and lighter than the old ones. Since January 1996, both coins and notes are called pesos, with old notes marked "nuevos pesos" and recent notes "pesos". The

denominations of 10,000, 20,000, 50,000 and 100,000 old pesos are no longer in circulation. Prices are marked in new pesos (N$) and cheques and credit card slips must be made out in new pesos.

DOLLAR AND PESO

The symbol for the US dollar (S with two bars) and the peso (S with one bar) are very similar. Look carefully at prices for the big hotels, luxury goods, etc. as they are often marked in US dollars, especially in Yucatán.

QUETZAL

The local currency of Guatemala is named after the quetzal bird which is also the national emblem. The quetzal is divided into 100 *centavos*.

Coins are rarely used.

	LOCAL CURRENCY	EQUIV. US$ 1
BELIZE	Belize Dollar	B$ 2
GUATEMALA	Quetzal	Q 6.85
HONDURAS	Lempira	£ 11.05
MEXICO	Peso	N$ 7.40
EL SALVADOR	Colón	C 8.72

BELIZE DOLLAR

The currency of Belize is the Belize dollar (B$).

Unlike its neighbors, where the rate of exchange fluctuates fairly significantly, Belize operates a "one for two" rate, where US$1 is equivalent to $B2.

LEMPIRA

The currency of Honduras is the lempira, divided into 100 *centavos*.

COLÓN

Like the other currencies, El Salvador's colón is divided into 100 *centavos*.

358

SOME PRICES

1 MEAL AT A MARKET: US$ 1

1 DOUBLE ROOM: US$ 50

A ONE-WEEK SPANISH COURSE: US$ 65

ONE DAY'S CAR HIRE (4x4): US$ 70

ENTRANCE TO A MAJOR MAYAN SITE: US$ 6

GOOD QUALITY "HUIPIL" (EMBROIDERED INDIAN TUNIC): US$ 30

1 ROOM WITH HAMMOCK: US$ 5

1 DIVING EXCURSION (INCLUSIVE): US$ 50

EXCHANGE

The US dollar is the most easily exchanged form of currency (bank notes or traveler's cheques). These can be exchanged in banks (Monday–Friday 9am–1pm), in Bureaux de Change (most numerous in Mexico and open at night), or in most big hotels (poor exchange rate but useful in the evening or at weekends).

BLACK MARKET EXCHANGE
It is possible to exchange money and traveler's cheques on the black market, in the city-center streets of the capitals and at border posts. Although the rate of exchange is poor, it is one way of getting rid of the currency of the country you are leaving since banks in the neighboring country do not necessarily accept it.

METHODS OF PAYMENT

US DOLLAR
In Belize you can pay for purchases with US dollars. In the other Mayan countries the dollar is the only foreign currency accepted, but it can't be used for small purchases.
CREDIT CARDS (*tarjeta de crédito*) Automatic cash dispensers accepting international credit cards are few and far between and it is difficult to withdraw money after the banks have closed. Cards are readily accepted in major

hotels, restaurants and stores but usually involve an additional charge of about 5 percent. Visa, American Express and Diner's Club cards are the most widely accepted.

TIPPING

Tips in restaurants are usually in the order of 10 percent. You are expected to fill in the *Tips* or *Propina* section and write the total at the bottom of the invoices and checks given to you. If you want, the proprietor or storekeeper will do it for you. In hotels tips are calculated on the basis of length of stay. Give at least US$1 to the cleaner, the chamber maid and the child who has patiently watched over your car without you asking.

COST OF LIVING

The cost of a holiday in Central America varies from country to country. Holidays in Mexico are the least expensive due to the collapse of the peso. They cost slightly more in El Salvador, Honduras and Guatemala. Belize is the most expensive country of all. Prices on the sites and in major towns and cities tend to be higher than in the rest of the country. Prices for leisure activities and hotels are between 15 percent and 25 percent lower during the rainy season. The cost of your holiday will depend on how you travel.

VAT

When paying checks don't confuse tips and VAT (*IVA*). The latter is 15 percent (10 percent in Guatemala) on standard consumer products (including all hotel and restaurant expenses) and 20 percent on luxury products.

6a. Avenida

Patience and discretion are two of the qualities required, and always rewarded, during a journey through the Mayan countries. Allow at least one hour to make a call from an international telephone center and two to four weeks for a letter to reach Europe. Communications are not only slow and laborious but also expensive – international telecommunications charges in Central America, and especially Guatemala, are among the highest in the world.

TELEPHONE

International calls (*larga distancia*) are extremely expensive from Central America (on average US$25 for three minutes). Collect calls (*por cobrar*) can be made from Mexico (dial 09) and Belize (dial 115) but are not so easy from Guatemala, El Salvador and Honduras. In some cities you can use AT&T's US Direct which accesses you

to an AT&T operator who will help you place a call to the US, or you can call directly with the use of a calling card (Belize 555, Guatemala 190, Honduras 123, El Salvador 190, Mexico 95 + 800 + 462 + 4240). All towns have telecommunications centers where you can make national and international calls, send telegrams, telexes and faxes (sending a one-page fax costs half as much as a three-minute telephone call). Opening hours are usually very convenient with most centers staying open until midnight.

MEXICO
Only Mexico has phone boxes that take phone cards (blue for international calls and orange for national calls). Cards cost 10 or 30 pesos.

FROM THE US
Calls to Central America cost from $1.00 to $2.46 per minute.

FROM THE UK
Calls to the region cost from £1.14 to £1.39 per minute.

MAIL

RECEIVING MAIL
The most reliable method is to have mail sent *poste restante* to the main post office of the relevant town (preferably a capital or major center) where it will be easiest to collect.

SENDING MAIL
The Central American postal service is extremely slow and unreliable. It is best to send mail from the main post offices in the capitals or large towns. Have it weighed before you send it so that any additional tarifs may be paid in advance, avoiding extra delay.

STAMPS

The stamps from the five Mayan countries are among the most beautiful in the world. Collectors will find a wide range of stamps on sale in the central post offices of Guatemala City and Belize City in particular.

ELECTRICITY

The current is 110 volts and sockets need flat American plugs, so take an adapter. Only the large hotels have 220 volts. Some regions (e.g. Honduras, Guatemalan highlands and Tulum in Mexico) have frequent restrictions on the use of electricity.

TELEPHONE CODES FROM AND TO THE US AND UK				
	FROM US	**FROM UK**	**To US**	**To UK**
BELIZE	011-501	00-501	00-1	00-44
GUATEMALA	011-502	00-502	00-1	00-44
HONDURAS	011-504	00-504	00-1	00-44
MEXICO	011-52	00-52	98-1	98-44
EL SALVADOR	011-503	00-503	0-1	0-44

8a. Calle

5a. Avenida Arco Gucumatz

FINDING YOUR WAY AROUND

Most of the towns are built around a central square (Plaza Mayor or Zócalo) and crossed from north to south by avenues (avenidas) and from east to west by streets (calles).

STREET SIGNS
Streets and avenues have either a name or number, and sometimes both. Street names may be indicated on two superposed plaques: one in Spanish and the other in Maya.

STREET LAYOUT
In El Salvador, Honduras and Antigua Guatemala, streets and avenues are numbered in relation to the central square. Streets to the east of the square are called Calle Oriente, and to the west Calle Poniente. Similarly, avenues to the north are Avenida Norte, and to the south Avenida Sur. For example: 3 Calle Oriente, no. 10 is the address of no. 10 on the third street to the east of the central square.

IN BELIZE
Most of the towns in Belize do not conform to this grid layout and use the English terms street, avenue, lane, etc. to designate the winding streets which often follow or lead to the coast.

ADDRESSES IN GUATEMALA CITY
The capital is divided into over twenty zones (zonas), each with the same street and avenue numbers. First locate the zone in question. The first figure after the (numbered) street indicates the nearest avenue; similarly, the first figure after the (numbered) avenue indicates the nearest street. The second figure indicates the distance in meters between the place you are looking for

and the intersection with the nearest avenue or street. For example, the INGUAT tourist office:
7a Avenida 1–17
Zona 4
is situated in zone 4, on 7th avenue, 17 meters from the intersection with street no.1.

TAKING PHOTOGRAPHS

Taking photographs on the "Ruta Maya" is, first and foremost, a continual process of tact and respect. A telephoto lens is invaluable since it avoids disturbing the local inhabitants, although it is always preferable to ask their permission. In certain Maya villages and during certain ceremonies, photographs are strictly prohibited. Do observe these restrictions which are always clearly indicated. On some sites a charge is made for the right to take photographs and this is paid at the entrance. A charge is always made for movie cameras on archeological sites in Mexico.

GOING OUT

Bars close just after midnight. In Mexico, where the night life is more lively, many bars have "happy hours" when they offer two drinks for the price of one. On the Atlantic coast, in Cozumel, Playa del Carmen and Livingston, there are sometimes open-air discos. In Guatemala it is an offense to drink alcohol in the street. The national police forces are totally unsympathetic toward cannabis smokers: abstinence is the simplest and best form of precaution.

NEWSPAPERS

Local newspapers are in Spanish, except in Belize where they are in English. The dailies (below) are thick and heavy and usually provide good coverage of international events. You will find the Herald Tribune in the big hotels and you can read national newspapers in the relevant embassies.

Markets are a feast for the eyes as well as a source of snacks throughout the day.

On the coast buy fish direct from the fishermen when they return to shore.

Corn, chicken and black beans form the basis of a local cuisine deeply rooted in the Mayan culture. Although it cannot be described as gourmet cooking, it is sufficiently varied to be enjoyable. Bear in mind, however, that food is the prime carrier of a number of infections so it is essential to take a number of basic precautions.

CORN AND "TORTILLAS"

Corn is the basis of the local cuisine and is found in a large number of dishes: the *tortilla,* for example, is a flat maize pancake which serves as bread, plate, spoon and serviette. This unique dish is served filled with cheese or mince (*enchiladas*), covered with melted cheese (*quesadillas*), or filled and fried (*tacos*). It can also be rolled up and dipped in *guacamole* (a thick puree of avocado, chilies and onions, and flavored with coriander). El Salvador has a variation on the *tortilla*: the *pupusa* is a smaller pancake

filled with cheese, sausage and black beans.

BEANS AND CHICKEN

Red and black beans (*frijoles*) and white rice (*arroz*) are served with most dishes. Beef is rare in the region and poultry is the only meat eaten in any quantity. Chicken (*pollo*) and turkey (*guajolote*) are served in a brown, chocolate-based sauce (*mole*), which has an incredible twenty different ingredients and is seasoned with hot spices.

FISH AND SHELLFISH

Very much in evidence in the coastal regions are shrimps and prawns (*camarones*) and oysters (*ostiones*) from September to April, and lobsters (*langosta*) from June to February. A salad of raw fish (*ceviche*) marinated in lemon juice is also a classic dish. Shark and barracuda are among the deep sea fish on the menu.

BREAD

Although introduced relatively recently, a wide variety of breads are available including: bread rolls (*bollilos*), wholemeal or black bread (*pan negro*), coconut bread (*pan coco*) sweet bread (*pan dulce*) and salted bread (*pan frances*).

DESSERTS

Dessert often consists of a fresh fruit salad: grapefruit, oranges, bananas, melon, mangos and papaws all grow in abundance in the region. Restaurants offer a variety of different flans and ice creams (*helados*). Don't be caught out by *tortas*: in Central America (Mexico) they are filled sandwiches, not pies.

Local beers are light. The rum, on the other hand, should be treated with caution and drunk in moderation.

"Mercados de la comida" are a pleasant and inexpensive alternative to "tourist" restaurants.

DRINKS

Don't drink tap water. Always ask for bottled mineral water, which will be opened when served. Some hotels leave a carafe or container of drinking water in the rooms for guests. The delicious fruit juices, sold in the

street and squeezed while you wait, are perfectly alright, although the same cannot be said for the local drinks made from freshly squeezed fruit, water, corn juice or coconut milk. You can always use water purifying tablets, but it takes several hours before the water is drinkable. Ironically in these great coffee-producing countries, the black coffee is often mediocre: thin and very sweet. You need to specify if you drink coffee without sugar (*sin azúcar*).

SPECIALITIES

Barbaco: a piece of mutton or goat's meat wrapped in banana leaves and cooked on charcoal.
Carnitas: little pieces of fried pork, eaten hot.
Chicharron: fried pork rind, eaten cold. *Ciles rellenos*: peppers stuffed with meat, fish or cheese. The *tamales* eaten in Mexico are made from polenta (ground corn) and meat.

SOMETHING DIFFERENT

Poc-chuc consists of strips of fillet pork marinated in orange juice and served with a sauce and spicy onions.
Pollo pibil is a dish consisting of chicken pieces marinated in a non-spicy sauce (annatto seeds, orange juice, garlic, salt and pepper), wrapped in banana leaves and cooked in the oven.

PRECAUTIONS

Raw vegetables and fruit sold in the street should be peeled or washed before eating. If possible only eat pre-cooked pork: locally prepared dishes are ideally suited to the potential problems associated with some foods. Only take water, ice creams, sorbets and ice cubes in the big hotels. Only buy milk in sealed bottles with a "pasteurized" label (*pasterizada*). In this tropical climate food is spicy. Very spicy food is described as "hot" (*calientes*) and less spicy food as "moderate" (*templados*).

Although chilies are recognized as having antiseptic properties, a western palate can find them hard to handle. You can always make it clear when placing your order that you want dishes without spices (restaurants are used to such orders).

MEAL TIMES

Breakfast (*desayuno*), served until 10am, is a very rich meal consisting of a choice of several different egg dishes, including *huevos rancheros* (fried eggs in a chili sauce, served on a *tortilla*) and *huevos a la mejicana* (scrambled eggs with tomato and chili). Lunch (*comida* or *almuerzo*) is served up to 3pm and dinner (*cena*) up to 10pm. Dinner is often replaced by a tea (*merienda*) consisting of sweet bread and coffee. If you decide to adopt the local eating habits you will snack throughout the day and only eat one full meal at lunchtime.

WHERE TO EAT

Every village has a *mercado de la comida* where you can eat on the spot, up to 3pm, at ridiculously low prices (around US$1 for a hot dish, a drink and a coffee). To ring the changes, you can eat Italian or Mexican food in most of the larger towns. Belize has a number of Chinese restaurants and El Salvador has several vegetarian restaurants.

363

◆ TOURS AND ITINERARIES

When you have exhausted the secrets of local, everyday life, why not try a tour designed to reveal the main Mayan sites or some of the more original aspects of the Mayan countries. These tours can be organized and combined to suit your particular needs. The minimum time indicated should be extended during the rainy season. The cost varies according to the regions visited, the means of transport and the type of accommodation.

CLASSIC TOUR
(2 WEEKS)
Leaves from and returns to Cancún, stopping at Chichén Itzá, Mérida, Uxmal, Palenque, Chichicastenango, San Cristóbal de las Casas, Panajachel, Antigua, Tikal and Belize City. The tour enables you to see the major Mayan sites and three countries: Mexico, Guatemala and Belize. It can be extended by any of the following options.

DIVING EXTENSION
(+ 5 DAYS)
Leaves from Belize City with accommodation on the island of Ambergris Cay and/or Cay Caulker and various excursions to, for example, the underwater caves of the Blue Hole or the depths of the Marine Reserve.
The tour is designed for diving and leisure enthusiasts, who will discover one of the most beautiful coral reefs in the world on the Caribbean coast of Belize. Prices in San Pedro (Ambergris

Cay) are high and you should avoid staying there if you want to spend your money on diving.

EL SALVADOR EXTENSION
The tour leaves from Guatemala City and visits the site of Joya de Cerén. The two-day trip into El Salvador can be made from Honduras (border incidents are minimal since the end of the civil war).

COPÁN–LIVINGSTON –POPTÚN EXTENSION
(+ 7 DAYS)
This tour enables you to visit the site of Copán (Honduras), discover the village of Livingston with its Caribbean atmosphere, and visit the Ixobel *finca* at Poptún (Guatemala) where you can help to pick coffee beans at harvest time. The tour takes a minimum of one week but the time spent in each place can vary. For example, it is possible to go from Guatemala City to Copán, visit the ruins and return to Guatemala in one day ◆ 356. However, to avoid having to rush, it is better to allow two days for this trip, staying overnight in Copán.

ADVENTURE TOUR
(21 DAYS)
Leaves from and returns to Cancún, passing via Tikal, Sayaxché, Bonampak, Palenque and Mérida. This demanding and original (and rather costly) route is ideal for would-be adventurers. It takes you through the jungle in a dug-out and enables you to visit the more inaccessible sites. It can be undertaken individually but is rather difficult to organize.

YUCATECAN SITES TOUR
(1 WEEK)
The tour leaves from and returns to Cancún, crossing Yucatán via Chichén Itzá, Mérida, Uxmal and Palenque (Chiapas). It is ideal if you are short of time and want to visit the major Mayan sites in Mexico and enjoy the beaches of the Caribbean coast.

GULF OF MEXICO

CANCÚN

MÉRIDA
Dzibilchaltún
Chichén Itzá

Mayapan

Uxmal
Kabah
Sayil

Cobá

Tulum

CAMPECHE
Labná
Muyil

Edzna
Yucatán

Balamku
Xpuhil
Becan
Kohunlich
CHETUMAL
Hormiguero
Cerros
Chicanna
Río Bec
Nohmul
Calakmul
Santa Rita
El Palmar

MEXICO
Río Azul

El Mirador
Altun Ha
Nakbe
Lamanai
Uaxactún
Chan Chich
BELIZE CITY

Tikal
Naranjo

Piedras Negras
Yaxhá
Xunantunich
Cahal Pech

xchilan
Flores
onampak
BELIZE
Caracol
CARIBBEAN

ultic
Ceibal
Dos Pilas
SEA

Altar de
Lubaantun
Nim Li Punit
Sacrificios
Aguateca

PUERTO BARRIOS

GUATEMALA

Zaculeu
Utatlán
Quiriguá

a
d
r
e
Mixco Viejo

Kaminaljuyu
Copán
HONDURAS

GUATEMALA
CITY
El Baúl

La Democracia

Tazumal
San Andres
SAN SALVADOR

Joya de Ceren
EL SALVADOR

OCEAN

The many lakes in the Mayan countries provide an ideal focus for walks and excursions.

Sunset from the shores of Lake Atitlán.

The wide range of sporting opportunities offered by the volcanos, waterfalls, nature reserves, lakes and oceans of the Mayan countries are a unique way of discovering some of the many different facets of this region. Green tourism is becoming increasingly popular and specialist agencies in Guatemala and Belize are offering quality "sport-and-nature" tours.

WALKING

Walking is an enjoyable way of discovering a region at your own pace, and off the beaten track. The Mayan countries have some of the most volcanic highlands in the world. Climbing the volcanos ◆ 370 will delight any traveler, while committed long-distance walkers can enjoy the beautiful landscape of the vast plains and plateaux which stretch between the villages.

RIVERS AND WHITE-WATER RAFTING

Excursions are organized in Belize from San Ignacio and Belize City, and in Guatemala from Flores, Antigua and Guatemala City. The Usumacinta, the longest river in the Mayan countries, flows from Guatemala into the Gulf of Mexico. It used to be one of the Mayas' main trade routes, which explains why there are so many Mayan sites along its banks. Here you are far from the more easily accessible sites, with only the cries of monkeys to disturb you. The three other navigable waterways are the Grijalva, the Hondo and the Motagua.

WINDSURFING

Windsurfing enthusiasts can surf on Lakes Atitlán, Petén Itzá and Izabal in Guatemala and Lake Coatepeque in El Salvador, as well as off the coast. Equipment can be hired at each site. At Panajachel (Lake Atitlán) Luis René Portillo organizes day excursions and nautical mornings (*mañana acuatica*) on the lake as well as hiring out equipment, such as pedalos, rowing boats, windsurfing boards and canoes.

CAVING

There are a number of underground caves and rivers that were once the setting for sacred Mayan ceremonies.

POPTÚN AND ITS ENVIRONS
Visits to the caves in the vicinity of Poptún (mid-way between Flores and Río Dulce) are organized from the Ixobel *finca* (Poptún) ◆ 364 and the hotel Villa de los Castellanos in Machaquilla.

LA CANDELARIA
It is advisable to organize your visit to the caves of La Candelaria with a tour operator or La Candelaria agency. The caves and river (33 yards wide in places) form an underground network over 7 miles long. The visit lasts for at least two hours and is made partly on foot and partly by boat along the river.

Map Legend:

0 30 60 miles

≈ Beaches and seaside resorts

Diving

Fishing

Cave

Volcano

Map Labels:

MÉRIDA
Balankanche
Dzitnup
Loltun
Yucatán
Isla Mujeres
Cancún
Playa del Carmen
Cozumel
Tulum

Chiapas
Tzontehuitz
San Cristóbal de las Casas

Ambergris Cay
Cay Caulker
Turneffe Islands
Blue Hole

CARIBBEAN SEA

Isla de Roatán
Isla de Utila

Najtunich
Candelaria
Lanquin

Sierra Madre

Tapachula
Tajumulco
Santa María
Tolimán
San Pedro
Fuego
Atitlán
Agua
GUATEMALA CITY
Amayo
Cerro Verde
San Salvador
SAN SALVADOR

PACIFIC OCEAN

SPECIALIST AGENCIES

◆ **HORSERIDING, VOLCANOS, EXCURSIONS**
TURISMO EK CHUAH
3a, calle 6–24,
Zona 2
Guatemala City
Tel. 232 0745
Fax 232 4375

◆ **BUNGY JUMPING, WHITE WATER RAFTING**
MAYA EXPEDITIONS
15a, calle 1–91
Zona 10
Guatemala City
Tel. 337 4666

Fax 594 7748
◆ **SAILING (LAKE IZABAL, LIVINGSTON, BELIZE)**
VIAREAL
4a calle Oriente, no.
14 La Fuente
Antigua Guatemala
Tel/Fax 832 3228
IZABAL ADVENTURE
La Galleria, 7 Av.
14–44, Zona 10
Guatemala City
Tel. 334 0323/24
Fax 334 0341

◆ **EXCURSIONS IN PETÉN**
EXPLORE
Av. Centroamérica,
Flores, Guatemala
Tel. 926 0655/0843
Avenida la Reforma
12–51, Zona 10
Guatemala City
Tel. 331 6243
Fax 334 1179

◆ **CAVING**
STP
2 Av. 7–78, Zona 10
Guatemala City

Tel./Fax 334 6236/37
◆ **HORSERIDING, CANOEING, CYCLING (BELIZE)**
MAYA MOUNTAIN
LODGE
3/4 MI Cristo Rev
Road
PO Box 46,
San Ignacio, Cayo
Tel/Fax 92 2164 and
92 2029; Freephone:
1-800-344-MAYA

The most beautiful coral reef in the Caribbean stretches along the Atlantic coast from Quintana Roo to the Islas de la Bahia (Honduras). This 620-mile ecological paradise, dotted with islands, is a world apart which merits a visit in its own right.

DIVING
Scuba diving and snorkeling are practiced all year round along the Caribbean coast. The barrier reef, the longest in the world after the Great Barrier Reef of Australia, is a marine reserve which harbors an infinite wealth of underwater flora and fauna. It is strictly prohibited to take coral from the reef.

SNORKELING

If you don't have a diver's certificate you can hire a mask, flippers and breathing tube for about US$3 per day and admire the coral and fish at shallow depths. The Isla de Cozumel has a number of reserves for divers, such as Chankanaab Park, while day trips in a motor boat offer an opportunity to see the shoals. The skipper provides a mask and breathing tube to enable you to explore each site. Cost: around US$25.

DIVER'S CERTIFICATE

You can take your international diver's certificate while on holiday. It takes three to five days and involves five dives and a written test. Cost: from less than US$150 (the cheapest certificate in the world is at Utila, Honduras) to US$350. Average cost of two 45-minute dives (including transport and equipment): US$50.

CANCÚN AND ISLA MUJERES
The "sleeping shark" reserve is 3 miles north of the island (at a depth of 75 feet). The low level of oxygenation in the underground caves makes the sharks lethargic and, in theory, harmless.

DIVING SITES

PLAYA DEL CARMEN AND COZUMEL (MEX.)
More than twenty-five diving sites around the Isla de Cozumel and off the Playa del Carmen are remarkable for their colorful corals.

CAULKER, AMBERGRIS AND OTHER CAYS (BELIZE)
◆ Blue Hole: Plunging to a depth of 130 feet off the Turneffe Islands, this formation, studied by Jean-Yves Cousteau, is the only one of its kind in the world. By torchlight it reveals underwater caves barred by huge stalagmites and stalactites. Allow five hours to get there from Cay Caulker.
◆ Hol Chan Marine: This submerged canyon, at a depth of 98 feet, is covered with coral and teems with fish.

◆ Half Moon Cay (Lighthouse Reef): About 70 miles east of Belize City lies one of the Northern Hemisphere's only three atolls (coral islands formed by an emerged ring of land around a lagoon).

BAY ISLANDS: ROATÁN, UTILA AND GUANAJA
The diving sites of Honduras afford the same quality of underground landscape as the northern sites at a substantially lower cost.

FISHING

Underwater fishing is practiced in the rivers and sea. For those who like something more exhilarating, there is always game fishing which involves long trials of strength with deep-sea fish, such as tarpon, tuna, swordfish and porgies, before returning them to the water. The less daring may prefer to fish for prawns and shrimps in the shallows of Belize. On the islands restaurants are happy to cook the fruits of your fishing trips. The lobster-fishing season is between June 15 and March 15.

FISHING CALENDAR

	J	F	M	A	M	J	J	A	S	O	N	D
BLUE MARLIN	○	○	◗	◗	●	●	●	●	●	○	○	○
WHITE MARLIN	○	○	◗	●	●	●	●	●	◗	○	○	○
FLYING FISH	○	◗	●	●	●	●	●	●	●	○	○	○
TUNA	○	○	●	●	●	●	●	●	●	○	○	○
BARRACUDA	●	●	●	●	●	●	●	●	◗	●	●	●
BONITO	○	◗	●	●	●	●	●	●	●	◗	◗	◗
PORGY	●	●	●	●	●	●	●	●	●	●	●	●
SHARK	●	●	●	●	●	●	●	●	●	●	●	●

● large number	◗ not many	○ none

◆ VOLCANOS AND NATURE RESERVES

The high plateaux of El Salvador and Guatemala have a remarkably dense concentration of volcanos. As well as offering some magnificent views, these active giants give the most spectacular *son et lumière* display in the world.

For those who prefer less strenuous walks, the Mayan countries have nature reserves open to the public which offer the chance to encounter a wealth of wildlife.

ACTIVE VOLCANOS

PACAYA (8,373 feet) is the most famous active volcano in Guatemala. Allow a 2-hour drive by minibus and a 2½-hour walk to reach the summit. At night the boiling magma spews its lava into the cold, dark sky.

SANTIAGUITO AND FUEGO
These are Guatemala's other two active volcanos. Fuego can be reached from Antigua.

TWO GIANTS

TAJUMULCO
At 13,845 feet this is the highest volcano in Guatemala. It is popular with walkers as it is easy to climb in spite of its impressive size.

TACANA
Tacana ("the house of fire") is the second highest volcano (13,425 feet) in the Mayan countries. It lies on the border of Mexico and Guatemala and is one of the few active volcanos in the region.

CLIMBING A VOLCANO

◆ Never climb a volcano alone. You run the risk of getting lost or being the victim of one of the numerous attacks recorded every year in these dangerous places.

◆ In the towns which are the departure points for these excursions there are a number of agencies and guides available. Descents are often at night to enable you to watch the sunset from the summit and, on the active volcanos, to see the luminous lava in the dark.

◆ Take something to eat and drink and some warm clothing. It is cold in the mountains, especially at night, with the only warmth coming from the very hot ground near the active craters.

VOLCANOS OF EL SALVADOR

In El Salvador excursions to climb the Izalco, Cerro Verde and Santa Ana volcanos are organized from Santa Ana or San Salvador.

CERRO VERDE
One of the most beautiful national parks in El Salvador lies on the slopes of this huge, extinct volcano, above Lake Coatepeque. On either side of the Cerro Verde are the Izalco and Santa Ana volcanos.

IZALCO
The Volcán Izalco is still listed as an active volcano as its last eruption was in 1966. Its history is famous in El Salvador. Until February 1770 the present site of Izalco was occupied by a hole emitting a column of sulphuric steam. Then a cone began to form around the edge of the smoke, growing at an amazing rate until it reached a height of 6,135 feet. Izalco went on spewing out fire, a spectacle visible for several miles around, which earned it the name of the Lighthouse of the Pacific. In 1957 all activity suddenly ceased and the small eruption of 1966 has been its only sign of life since then. Its slopes have become fresh, peaceful and incredibly fertile.

CLIMBING IZALCO
A marked path leads from the car park at the entrance to the Cerro Verde National Park. The excursion takes 3–4 hours from start to finish.

VANTAGE POINTS
The best point from which to view Izalco is from the top of the Cerro Verde volcano which, at 6,660 feet above sea level, allows you to look down on its crater. Another famous vantage point is the Hotel de Montana, built to offer guests a unique view of an active volcano. It was completed in 1957, the year in which, after two hundred years of activity, the volcano suddenly fell silent.

Lake Izabal offers an opportunity to admire a wide variety of rare tropical species.

Hut on the banks of the Río Dulce, reached from Livingston or Lake Izabal.

DIFFICULT CLIMBS (GUATEMALA)

SAN PEDRO
The Volcán San Pedro (9,908 feet) is one of the three volcanos of Lake Atitlán. In Cakchiquel Maya it is called "Choyjuyub" meaning "volcano of the lagoon". From the summit, "El Mirador", there is a magnificent view of the lake and the other two volcanos, Tolimán and Atitlán.

TOLIMÁN
The Volcán Tolimán (10,360 feet) is covered with a profusion of dense vegetation. The difficulty experienced in finding a way through the undergrowth is outweighed by the pleasure of walking in such wild, natural surroundings.

AGUA
You can go down into the very deep crater of the Volcán Agua (12,388 feet) to a mountain refuge which can accommodate up to thirty people.

SANTO TOMÁS
The Santo Tomás volcano (11,499 feet) is one of the hardest to climb in the region. Two paths lead to the summit: allow 6–8 hours walking time if you take the *Las Georginas* path and 8–10 hours via the *Cumbre de Alaska*. Don't consider attempting it without a guide.

NATURE RESERVES

GUATEMALA
CERRO CAHUI CONSERVATION PARK
The park, on the northern shore of Lake Petén Itzá, is reached from Flores. Its fauna includes jaguars, howler monkeys and peccaries.

BIOTOPO CHACÓN MACHACA DEL MANATI
Near Livingston. The tapir and jaguar are its most impressive inhabitants.

BIOTOPO DEL QUETZAL
About 100 miles from Guatemala City, on the road to Cobán and near the village of Purulhá. The largest nature reserve for this sacred bird.

MEXICO
SIAN KA'AN BIOSPHERE RESERVE
About 68 miles of coral reefs and 1,284,950 acres of jungle and mangroves inhabited by pumas, jaguars and tapirs make this the most diverse nature reserve in all the Mayan countries. It can be reached from Felipe Carrillo along the road between Tulum and Chetumal.

CALAKMUL BIOSPHERE RESERVE
Over 180 species of birds live in the jungle and savanna of the reserve, crossed at the northern end by the Escárcega–Chetumal road.

BELIZE
COCKSCOMB BASIN WILDLIFE SANCTUARY
This 101,310-acre sanctuary has a large jaguar population. It is reached from Dangriga.

HALF MOON CAY RESERVE
This manatee sanctuary is reached

from Cay Caulker.

EL SALVADOR
CERRO VERDE NATIONAL PARK
On the slopes of the Cerro Verde volcano, this forest has many species of birds and animals. The volcano offers a great view of Lake Coatepeque and Volcán Izalco.

CLIMBING VOLCANOS				
VOLCANO	HEIGHT	DIFFICULTY	CLIMBING	POINT OF DEPARTURE
PACAYA	8,373 feet	easy	3 hours	Antigua Guatemala
FUEGO	12,346 feet	difficult	4 hours	Antigua Guatemala
SAN PEDRO	9,908 feet	difficult	3–4 hours	Panajachel (Lake Atitlán)
TOLIMÁN	10,360 feet	very difficult	5 hours	Panajachel (Lake Atitlán)
AGUA	12,388 feet	difficult	3–4 hours	Antigua Guatemala
SANTO TOMÁS	11,499 feet	very difficult	6–10 hours	Quetzaltenango
IZALCO	6,070 feet	easy	3 hours	Cerro Verde (San Salvador)

Most Mayan festivals celebrate the patron saint of the community or the founding of the village. The villagers take part in religious processions and traditional dances, wearing the magnificent ceremonial costumes of their own particular region. The Guatemalan highlands have the largest Indian community in Central America and the most authentic Indian festivals ● *72, 74, 76*.

EASTER IN ANTIGUA GUATEMALA

During Holy Week in Antigua, the Passion of Christ is re-enacted with great fervor. The paved streets are strewn with flowers and long, brightly colored ribbons. On the night of Maundy Thursday, before Easter Day, a carpet of colored sawdust is spread on the ground by the families of Antigua. They decorate it using stencils of all kinds of geometric designs, flowers and animals. On Good Friday, the sawdust carpets disappear as the procession, consisting of a hundred or so costumed participants, passes through the streets. The ensuing festival lasts until dawn.

FEAST OF THE ASSUMPTION AT SOLOLÁ

On August 15 the Indians of the Cakchiquel and Tzutuhil communities of Sololá celebrate the Assumption of the Blessed Virgin. The day begins with the traditional market of Sololá, with the women wearing red flowered *huipiles* and blue striped skirts. Mass is followed at 11am by a grand procession in honor of the Virgin Mary. The members of twelve brotherhoods, dressed in ceremonial costume, take part in the procession and perform religious rites accompanied by music and masked dancers.

ALL SAINTS DAY AT TODOS SANTOS

The festival of Todos Santos begins on October 31 with masked dances (*bailes de la Conquista*) to the sound of marimbas in the church square. A horse race is held outside the village the following day. From dawn until dusk, about fifteen horses (ridden in turn by the inhabitants) compete over a course of a hundred yards or so until they are ready to drop. On November 2, religious ceremonies are followed by a costumed procession which makes its way drunkenly to the cemetery where families give free rein to demonstrations of laughter and tears. Todos Santos, lost in the mountains of the Sierra de los Cuchumatanes (at an altitude of more than 8,200 feet), can only be reached by bus once a day from Huehuetenango. The bus leaves at 2pm but make sure you reserve your seat in the morning. The same bus does not return until 5am the following morning. Allow three days for the return journey and the visit to Todos Santos ▲ *285*.

CHRISTMAS IN THE MAYAN COUNTRIES

Christmas Day is preceded by weeks of processions, the *posadas*, that re-enact Mary and Joseph's search for shelter. The festival is celebrated in all the Mayan countries by costumed dances and music. The festivities of Chichicastenango in Guatemala, where they also celebrate the festival of the patron saint from December 13–21, are undoubtedly some of the most spectacular. The more daring can even climb the *palo volador* and "fly"

upside down around this huge pole. This spiritual rather than physical test represents the movement of the stars around the sun ● *76*.

Planning your trip to the Route of the Mayas around a particular holiday or festival is an ideal way of joining in the local spirit. Holy Week (the week before Easter) is the most important holiday. Local people have a week off work and often take a trip to a beach or resort so buses and hotels tend to be packed for the whole week. It is worth remembering too that during festivals virtually all businesses and government agencies are closed.

JANUARY

1   Día del Año Nuevo (New Year's Day)
Throughout the Mayan countries

6–10   Día de los Reyes Magos (Epiphany)
Guatemala and Mexico

7–15   Fiesta de Cristo de Esquipulas
Throughout the Mayan countries,
in particular Esquipulas, Guatemala

15-31   San Sebastián
Mexico, Honduras and El Salvador

28–31   Candalario (Candlemas)
Campeche, Mexico

FEBRUARY

1–2   Candalario (Candlemas)
Mexico, Honduras and El Salvador

1–5   San Felipe
Yucatán, Mexico

11–23   Campeche Carnival
Campeche, Mexico

21   National holiday
Mexico

Weekend preceding Lent–   Carnival
Mardi Gras
Mexico and Guatemala

MARCH

1–6   Regional holiday
Chiapas, Mexico

9   Baron Bliss Day
Belize

16–21   Festival of Spring
Quintana Roo, Mexico

19   San José
Copán, Honduras

21   Vernal Equinox, Chichén Itzá
Yucatán, Mexico

24   San Gabriel
Chiapas, Mexico

Easter   Semana Santa, Holy Week
Throughout the Mayan countries
in particular Antigua, Guatemala

APRIL

15   Ascension Day
Yucatán, Mexico

11–25   Festival of Spring
Commemoration of the foundation of the town of
San Cristobál de Las Casas,
in Chiapas, Mexico

25   San Marcos
San Marcos La Laguna,
Sololá, Guatemala

29   Festival of the Three Crosses
Yucatán, Mexico

MAY

3–10   Saint Helen of the Cross
Throughout the villages in Santa Cruz,
Mexico and Guatemala

24   Commonwealth Day
Belize

30   San Ferdinando
Honduras

JUNE

22–9   San Antonio de Padua
Yucatán, Mexico, and Honduras

22–4   San Juan Bautista
San Juan La Laguna, Guatemala

22–9   San Pedro and San Pablo
Mexico and Guatemala

24   San Juan Chamula
San Juan Chamula
Chiapas, Mexico

29   San Pedro La Laguna
Sololá, Guatemala

30   Army Day
Guatemala

End of June   Festival of Corpus Christi
Guatemala

JULY

17   Fiesta de San Cristóbal de las Casas
Chiapas, Mexico

19   Festival of the Sacred Heart of Jesus
Puerto Barrios
Izabal, Guatemala

25   Santiago Apóstolo
Throughout the Mayan countries

AUGUST

4   Fiesta de Santo Domingo de Guzman
Cobán, in Alta Verapaz,
Guatemala

4–6   Festival of the Divine Savior
Divino Salvador del mundo
San Salvador

10–16   Traditional Mexican festivals
Yucatán, Campeche
and Tabasco, Mexico

15   Festival of Guatemala
Guatemala City

20–30   San Juan Chamula, San Augustino
and San Miguel
Chiapas, Mexico

SEPTEMBER

10   National holiday
Belize

15 and 16   Independence Day
Guatemala (Sept. 15), Mexico (Sept. 16)

14–20   Civil week
Honduras

OCTOBER

4   Fiesta de San Francisco de Asisi
Panajachel in Sololá and San Francisco
El Alto in Totonicapán, Guatemala

12   Día de la Raza (Columbus Day)
Throughout the Mayan countries

NOVEMBER

1   Todos Santos, All Saints' Day
Todos Santos (Huehuetenango), Guatemala

1–30   Festival of Our Lady of the Martyrs
Honduras

2   Day of the Dead
Throughout the Mayan countries

5   Independence Day
El Salvador

13   San Diego
Yucatán, Mexico

19   Garifuna Settlement Day
Belize

30   Pilgrimage and Festival of Xmatkuil
Mexico

30   San Andrés Apóstol
Chiapas, Mexico

DECEMBER

1   Feast of the Immaculate Conception
Quintana Roo and Campeche, Mexico

7   Burning of the Devil
Throughout Guatemala

8   Saint Nicolas
Noche Buena Chiquita

10–12   Feast of Our Lady of Guadalupe
Mexico and Honduras

21   Saint Thomas
Chichicastenango, Guatemala

16–24   Processions de las Posadas
Mary and Joseph's search for lodgings
Throughout the Mayan countries

19–26   Festival of the Nativity
Throughout the Mayan countries

A profusion of colors in the fruit and vegetable markets where the women sell their produce.

The finest markets on the Route of the Mayas are, once again, found in the Guatemalan highlands. The markets of the *altiplano* are brightly colored showcases of local crafts, offering an ideal opportunity to buy traditionally made clothes, woven items and other everyday objects at reasonable prices ● *82*.

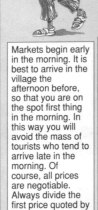

SOME GUATEMALAN MARKETS		
	TOWN	**REGION**
MONDAY	Antigua	Sacatepéquez
	Chimaltenango	Chimaltenango
	Zunil	Quetzaltenango
TUESDAY	Comalapa	Chimaltenango
	Patzún	Chimaltenango
	Sololá	Sololá
	San Lucas Tolimán	Sololá
	Santa Clara la Laguna	Sololá
	Tucuru	Alta Verapaz
WEDNESDAY	Huehuetenango	Huehuetenango
	Momostenango	Totonicapán
	Palín	Escuintla
	Patzicia	Chimaltenango
	Sacapulas	El Quiché
THURSDAY	Antigua	Sacatepéquez
	Chimaltenango	Chimaltenango
	Chichicastenango	El Quiché
	Nebaj	El Quiché
	Patzún	Chimaltenango
	Sacapulas	El Quiché
	San Mateo Ixtatán	Huehuetenango
	San Miguel Ixtahuacán	San Marcos
	Santa Cruz del Quiché	El Quiché
	Tecpán Guatemala	Chimaltenango
	Totonicapán	Totonicapán
	Tucuru	Alta Verapaz
FRIDAY	Comalapa	Chimaltenango
	Palín	Escuintla
	San Andrés Itzapa	Chimaltenango
	San Lucas Tolimán	Sololá
	San Pedro Sacatepéquez	Guatemala
	Santiago Atitlán	Sololá
	Sololá	Sololá
SATURDAY	Patzicia	Chimaltenango
	Santa Cruz del Quiché	El Quiché
	Santa Clara la Laguna	Sololá
	Santiago Sacatepéquez	Sacatepéquez
	Todos Santos	Totonicapán
SUNDAY	Chichicastenango	El Quiché
	Esquipulas	Chiquimula
	Momostenango	Totonicapán
	Rabinal	Baja Verapaz

Markets begin early in the morning. It is best to arrive in the village the afternoon before, so that you are on the spot first thing in the morning. In this way you will avoid the mass of tourists who tend to arrive late in the morning. Of course, all prices are negotiable. Always divide the first price quoted by two to give yourself a basis for negotiation.

Markets are an important part of Indian economic and social life. They provide an opportunity to meet friends and acquaintances. For many inhabitants it is the only time they come down from the mountains.

These dolls are sold by children as good luck charms.

The stylized bird appears on most embroidered textiles.

Unlike Mexican markets, the markets of the Guatemalan *altiplano* have retained their authenticity, remaining primarily Indian markets.

Seven of the most interesting are mentioned in the following list and offer a wide range of different products:
◆ brightly colored, hand-woven textiles and clothes whose motifs and materials are specific to their

village of origin;
◆ ceramics (at Santa Cruz Chinautla, Jalapa, Huehuetenango, Totonicapán, Antigua);
◆ classic Mayan jewelry in jade and carved stone, now found in many jewelers (Antigua);
◆ straw hats with colored bands (characteristic of Todos Santos, Cuchumatán, Huehuetenango);

◆ musical instruments and objects made of carved wood;
◆ ritual masks in painted wood, representing gods, devils and animals.

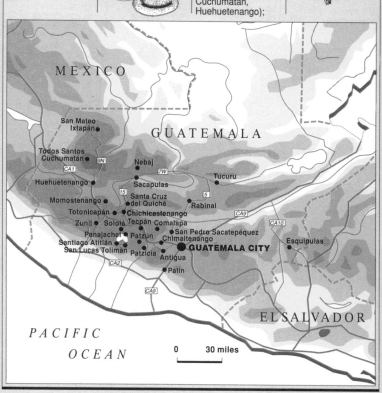

Mexico has the largest museum of pre-Columbian art in Latin America. It offers an excellent introduction to the Mayan culture for those starting their visit in Mexico City (allow at least one day). The museums of the other main towns and cities in the region are also well worth a visit. Collections of Mayan art in Europe and North America are a good starting point when preparing for your visit.

MUSEO DE ANTROPOLOGIA (MEXICO CITY)

The museum, which has the most complete collection in Latin America, offers an excellent introduction to Mayan history and culture and, more generally, to all the civilizations of Mesoamerica. At the entrance to the first floor is a relief map showing the area covered by Mayan culture as well as an exhibition of the different geographical environments in which it flourished. The first floor is devoted to archeology, while the second floor presents an ethnographic view of the richness and diversity of Mayan traditions, from the classic world of the Mayas to the present day. The archeological collection is extremely impressive.

NOT TO BE MISSED

◆ The collection of figurines from Jaina ▲ 230, an island off the coast of Campeche. These terracotta miniatures (sometimes polychrome) represent various important figures and constitute one of the most complete and realistic records of the social hierarchy and costumes of the Mayan culture. Warriors, women from the aristocracy and priests can be identified by their characteristic attire.
◆ The "stone of Jonuta" from the State of Tabasco ● 52 shows a kneeling priest presenting an offering. A macaw is perched on his shoulder. His typically Mayan profile is clearly visible.

◆ The collection of steles and lintels constitutes a major record of social and religious life. The remarkably preserved steles on display illustrate the official art form and propaganda medium of the Mayan sovereigns.
◆ The collection of funerary objects and bas-reliefs from the Temple of the Inscriptions at Palenque ● 108, includes several stuccoed sculptures, a

reproduction of the funerary chamber and its sarcophagus and the famous bas-relief of the Temple of the Cross at Palenque.
◆ In the gardens is a reconstruction of the Temple of Hochob, in the State of Campeche, with a huge mask of the terrestrial monster forming the entrance. There is also a reproduction of the Temple of the Frescos at Bonampak ▲ 249, ▲ 243, containing copies of its famous wall paintings.
◆ Finally, there is a collection of everyday items, richly decorated ceramics and musical instruments.

USEFUL INFORMATION

The Museo de Antropología: Open Tues.–Sat. 9am–7pm, Sun. and public holidays 10am–6pm. Closed Mon. Tickets are on sale until 6pm. Admission 16 pesos, free on Sun. and public holidays.
◆ Guided tours for groups (minimum five persons): 9.30am–5.30pm. These can be in English or Spanish

(no charge for Spanish). No guided tours on Sundays. For large groups it is possible to reserve a guide.
INFORMATION
Tel: 553 63 86
◆ The museum bookshop is open during museum hours. It has an excellent selection of books, Mexican crafts and reproductions of the exhibits, although its prices are rather high.

◆ The museum library is open Mon.–Fri. 9am–8pm.

HOW TO GET THERE
The museum is situated on the corner of the Paseo de la Reforma and the Calzada M. Gandhi. The nearest subway stations are *Auditorio* and *Chaputelpec*.

Central patio of the museum and the column decorated with bronzes by Chavez Morado.

The façade of the reconstruction of the Temple of Hochob in the museum gardens.

AN ARCHITECTURAL MASTERPIECE

The Museo de Antropología, designed by the architect Pedro Ramirez Vazquez, was opened on September 17, 1964. A vestibule leads into a central patio where a huge column, covered in

bronze bas-reliefs by Chavez Morado, supports a monumental roof. All the first-floor rooms open onto this central patio which enables visitors to choose the order of their visit. Modern Mexican art is renowned for its murals: the entrance hall and the introductory rooms to the anthropological and Mesoamerican culture sections are decorated with frescos by Rufino Tamayo, Jorge Gonzalez Camarena and Raúl Anguiano.

MAYAN COLLECTIONS IN THE MUSEUMS OF THE WORLD

◆ UNITED STATES:
The finest collections of Mayan art are housed in the museums of North America.
METROPOLITAN MUSEUM OF ART
5th Avenue and E 82nd Street
New York
AMERICAN MUSEUM OF NATURAL HISTORY
Central Park West
79th Street
New York
THE BROOKLYN MUSEUM OF ART
200 Eastern Parkway
New York
DUMBARTON OAKS
1703 32nd Street

Washington D.C. 20007
UNIVERSITY MUSEUM
University of Pennsylvania
33rd and Spruce Streets
Philadelphia
PA 19104
Steles from Piedras Negras ▲ 332.
PEABODY MUSEUM OF ARCHEOLOGY AND ETHNOLOGY
Harvard University
Cambridge
Massachusetts
◆ GREAT BRITAIN:
BRITISH MUSEUM, MUSEUM OF MANKIND
6, Burlington Gardens

London
The museum has the finest collection of Mayan art in Europe.
◆ SWITZERLAND:
MUSEUM FÜR VÖLKERKUNDE
Augustiner Gasse 2
4001 Basel
Wooden lintels from Tikal ▲ 320.

MUSEUMS ON THE "RUTA MAYA"

◆ MEXICO:
MUSEO LA VENTA
Av. Adolfo Ruíz Cortinez S/N
Villahermosa
Daily 8am–4.30pm. Collection of Olmec statues.
MUSEO DE HISTORIA
Corner of Calle de Juárez and 27 de Febrero
Villahermosa
Daily 9am–6pm.
MUSEO REGIONAL DE ANTROPOLOGIA
511, av. Carlos Pellicer
Villahermosa
Daily 9am–8pm.
MUSEUM OF THE MAYAN PEOPLE
Archeological area of Dzibilchatún
Closed Mon.
MUSEO DE ARTE MODERNE
Near the cathedral, Mérida
Closed Mon.
MUSEO DE ARQUEOLOGIA
Paseo de Montejo y

Calle 41
Mérida
Daily 8am–8pm, Mon. and Sun. 8am–2pm.
◆ GUATEMALA:
MUSEO SANTIAGO DE LOS CABALLEROS
Plaza Mayor
Antigua
Daily 9am–12pm and 2pm–6pm.
MUSEO DEL LIBRO ANTIGUO
Plaza Mayor
Antigua
Daily 9am –12pm and 2pm–6pm.
MUSEO DE ARTE COLONIAL
6 Calle Final, Zona 10
Univ.F. Marroquin, Antigua
PALACIO NACIONAL
Zona 1
Guatemala City
Daily 8am–4pm.
MUSEO NACIONAL DE ARQUEOLOGIA
Edificio 5, La Aurora, Zone 13
Guatemala City

Tue.–Sun. 9am–4pm. Closed Mon. and weekends noon–2pm.
MUSEO DE ARTE MODERNO
Edificio 6, La Aurora, Zona 13
Guatemala City
Tue.-Sun. 9am–4pm. Closed Mon. and weekends noon–2pm.
MUSEO IXCHEL
6, Calle Final, Zona 10
Univ. F. Marroquin
Guatemala City
MUSEO POPOL VUH
Av. La Reforma 8–60, Zona 9
Guatemala City
◆ HONDURAS:
INSTITUTO HONDURENO DE ANTROPOLOGIA E HISTORIA
Villa Roy, Barrios
Buenos Aires
Tegucigalpa D.C.
MUSEO REGIONAL
Archaeological site in Copán.

In spite of the continued survival of the Mayan languages and the increasing use of English with the development of the tourist industry, Spanish remains the first spoken language in the Mayan countries. If you have the time, why not start your visit to Central America with a Spanish course? Learning Spanish *in situ* can be combined with lodgings in a host family, which in no way restricts your opportunities of discovering the country. On the contrary, it will enhance the experience.

The towns of Quetzaltenango and Antigua, in Guatemala, and San Cristóbal de las Casas, in Mexico, are the main centers for learning Spanish. However you can learn the basics or brush up your Spanish in all the towns of Guatemala, Mexico and Honduras (there are two schools at Copán).

The average cost of a one-week, four hour-a-day private course is US$65 (or about US$100 with lodgings). If you are interested in this type of course you should allow a minimum of seven days. You will find the most highly recommended schools in the towns cited in the list of useful addresses ◆ 386–406. But there are others, so ask the local tourist office or former pupils who are still in the region.

Common expressions ◆

Yes: *sí*
No: *no*
Please: *por favor*
Thank you: *gracias*
Pardon/Sorry: *perdón*
Excuse me: *disculpe* or *con su permiso*
At your service: *a sus ordenes*
Good morning: *buenos días*
Good afternoon (evening): *buenas tardes*
Goodnight: *buenas noches*
Of course: *¡Cómo no!*

Today: *hoy*
Tomorrow: *mañana*
Yesterday: *ayer*
Allowed/Permitted: *autorisado*
Forbidden/Prohibited: *prohibido*
I am English/American: *soy inglés (a)/ norteamericano (a)*
I don't understand: *no entiendo*
Can you help me?: *¿me puedes ayudar?*
What time is it?: *¿Qué hora(s) es(son)?*
It is 3pm: *son las tres de la tarde*

Days of the week ◆

Monday: *lunes*
Tuesday: *martes*
Wednesday: *miercoles*
Thursday: *jueves*
Friday: *viernes*
Saturday: *sábado*
Sunday: *domingo*

Months of the year ◆

January: *enero*
February: *febrero*
March: *marzo*
April: *abril*
May: *mayo*
June: *junio*
July: *julio*
August: *agosto*
September: *septiembre*
October: *octubre*
November: *noviembre*
December: *diciembre*

◆ Numbers ◆

One: *uno*
Two: *dos*
Three: *tres*
Four: *cuatro*
Five: *cinco*
Six: *seis*
Seven: *siete*
Eight: *ocho*
Nine: *nueve*
Ten: *diez*
One hundred: *cien*
One thousand: *mil*

◆ People ◆

Mestizo: *ladino*
Indian: *indigena* (the term *indio* is pejorative)
Woman: *mujer*
Man: *hombre*
Surname: *apellido*
What is your name? : *¿Cómo te llamas?*
First name: *nombre*
Mother: *madre*
Father: *padre*
Daughter: *hija*
Son: *hijo*
Sister: *hermana*
Brother: *hermano*
Aunt: *tía*
Uncle: *tío*

◆ Travel ◆

To travel: *viajar*
Plane: *avión*
Airport: *aeropuerto*
Luggage: *equipaje*
Ticket: *boleto*
Change: *cambio*
Customs: *aduana*
Departure: *salida*
Arrival: *llegada*
Travel agency: *agencia de viaje*

Finding your way around ◆

Where is ...?: *¿Dónde se encuentra ...?*
Is it near here?: *¿Está cerca de aquí?*
Is it far from here?: *¿Está lejos de aquí?*
Straight on: *todo recto*
On the left: *a la izquierda*
On the right: *a la derecha*
How long by car?: *¿Cuánto tiempo en coche?*
How long on foot?: *¿Cuánto tiempo caminando?*
How many kilometers?: *¿Cuántos kilómetros son?*

Getting around ◆

Bus: *camión* (Mex.) or *camioneta* (Guat.)
Luxury bus: *camión de lujo* or *pullman*
First class: *primera clase*
Second class: *segunda clase*
Bus station: *terminal* or *central des autobuses*
Car: *coche* or *carro*
Small car: *cochecito* or *carro compacto*
Four-wheel drive: *cuatro-cuatro* or *doble tracción*
To hire: *alquilar* or *rentar* (Mex.)
Insurance: *seguro*
Unlimited mileage: *kilometraje libre*
Driving license: *licencia de conducir*
Gas station: *gasolinera*
Gas: *gasolina*
Oil: *aceite*
Tire: *llanta*
Taxi: *taxi*

Collective taxi: *collectivo*

♦ At the hotel ♦

Hotel: *hotel*
Room: *cuarto* or *habitación*
Single room: *cuarto sencillo*
Double room: *cuarto doble* or *matrimonial*
Key: *llave*
Bed: *cama*
Shower: *ducha*
Toilets: *baños* or *servicios*
Hot water: *agua caliente*
Cold water: *agua fría*
Soap: *jabón*
Bathroom: *cuarto de baño*
Towel: *toalla*
Where is the nearest hotel?: *¿Dónde se encuentra el hotel más cercana?*
I have reserved a room: *tengo un cuarto reservado*
I would like a room: *quisiera un cuarto*
I would like to see the room: *quiero ver el cuarto*
Can you wake me up?: *¿me puede despertar?*
To camp: *acampar*

♦ At the restaurant ♦

Restaurant: *restaurante*
Table: *mesa*
Plate: *plato*
Knife: *cuchillo*
Fork: *tenedor*
Spoon: *cuchara*
Glass: *vaso*
Purified water: *agua purificada*
Red wine: *vino tinto*
White wine: *vino blanco*
Beer: *cerveza*
Real coffee: *café de cafetera*
Instant coffee: *Nescafé*
Coffee with milk: *café con leche*
(Black) tea: *té (negro)*
Fruit juice: *jugo*
Diluted fruit juice: *agua de fruta*
Fruit juice with milk: *licuado con leche*
Breakfast: *desayuno*

Lunch: *comida*
Today's menu: *comida corrida*
Dinner: *cena*
Menu: *carta*
Chili: *chile*
Especially no chili: *sobre todo sin chile*
Soup: *sopa caldo* or *sopa de verduras*
Eggs: *huevos*
Scrambled eggs: *huevos revueltos*
Fried eggs: *huevos estrellados*
Toast: *pan tostado*
Butter: *mantequilla*
Jam: *marmelada*
Sandwich (meat salad, tomato): *torta*
Kidney beans: *frijoles*
Corn pancake: *tortilla*
Filled corn pancake: *taco*
Meat: *carne*
Beef: *carne de res*
Fried chicken and chips: *pollo frito con papas*
Fried chicken and rice: *pollo frito con arroz*
Pork fillet: *lomo de puerco*
Pork chop: *chuleta de cerdo*
Steak and chips: *bistek con papas*
Fish: *pescado*
Avocado puree: *guacamole*
Green tomato sauce: *salsa verde*
Vegetables: *verduras*
Salad: *ensalada*
Cheese: *queso*
Dessert: *postre*
Cake/pastry: *pastel*
Ice cream: *helado*
Ice cream made with milk: *helado de leche*
Fruit: *fruta*
Dish of fruit: *plato de frutas*
Banana: *plátano*
Orange: *naranja*

Papaw: *papaya*
The check, please: *la cuenta, por favor*
Tip: *propina*
Service included: *servicio incluido*

♦ Visits ♦

To visit: *visitar*
Open: *abierto*
Closed: *cerrado*
Ticket: *boleto*
Town: *ciudad*
Village: *pueblo*
District: *barrio, zona* or *colonia*
Street: *calle*
Avenue: *avenida*
Boulevard by the sea: *malecón*
House: *casa*
Garden: *jardín*
Theater: *teatro*
Cinema: *cinema*
Museum: *museo*
Archeological site: *ruinas* or *sitio arqueológico*

♦ At the post office ♦

Post office: *oficina de correos*
To telephone: *telefonear* or *hacer una llamada*
Collect call: *por cobrar*
Fax: *fax*
Stamp: *estampilla, sello* or *timbre*
For Europe: *para Europa*
Telegram: *telegrama*
Envelope: *sobre*
Air mail: *por avión*
Letter: *carta*
Post card: *postal*

♦ Emergencies ♦

State police: *policía federal*
Municipal police: *policía municipal*
Fire brigade: *bomberos*
Hospital: *hospital*
Pharmacy: *farmacia*
Doctor: Call the doctor please: *llama al doctor, por favor*

♦ Money shopping ♦

Bank: *banco*
Credit card: *tarjeta de crédito*
Traveler's checks: *cheques de viajero*
In cash: *en efectivo*

Price: *el precio*
How much is it?: *¿Cuánto vale?* or *¿Qué precio?*
It's too expensive: *es demasiado caro*
Receipt: *comprobante*
Packet of cigarettes: *cajetilla de cigarros*
Newspaper: *periódico*
When does the shop open?: *¿A qué hora abre la tienda?*
When does the shop close?: *¿A qué hora cierra la tienda?*
Where can I find . . . ?: *¿Dónde se puede encontrar . . . ?*

◆ ACCOMMODATION

"Cabana" with a palm roof on the beach of Playa del Carmen.

Houses on stilts, built on the beaches of the cays (Belize).

The Mayan countries tend to organize their day around the sun, which rises very early and sets around 6pm. Don't wait until it gets dark to think about accommodation. Reservations are not the best way of ensuring a room in a hotel. It is better to get there early and take possession of the room before it is offered to someone else. Only the big hotels operate a reservation system. The "Ruta Maya" offers a wide range of different types of accommodation at vastly differing prices, from the most luxurious to the most basic.

RESERVATIONS AND ADVERTIZED PRICES

There is no point in reserving rooms in advance during off-peak periods or in other than the largest hotels. Your room will be offered, with no misgivings, to the first guests to arrive. It is better to get to your destination before sunset to allow time to choose your hotel and especially your room – ask to see it first. The price of a room in a small hotel, out of season, can be negotiated.

DIFFERENT TYPES OF ACCOMMODATION

HOTELS AND MOTELS
The largest international hotels in the region are in Villahermosa, Guatemala City, Belize City and Cancún. The high prices (US$100–US$400 for a double room) are justified by the extremely high quality of service. Away from these cities the quality of accommodation

varies greatly, but prices are reasonable.

YOUTH HOSTELS (*Albergues de la juventud*)
Youth hostels are few and far between in Guatemala and Belize, but more common in Mexico. They are run by the CREA (*Consejo Nacional de Recursos para la Atención de la Juventud*) in association with the international Youth Hostel Association. Students must have an international student card to benefit from the special rates available.

CAMPING
Camping is allowed on most beaches. Supervised camp sites charge between US$1 and US$10 per night. Two camp sites well situated for visiting Mayan temples at sunrise are those at Chichén Itzá (Mexico) and Tikal (Guatemala).

"CABANAS" AND HAMMOCKS
This typical Central American accommodation consists of a hut or *cabana* with a palm roof and equipped with hooks for

suspending hammocks. This apparently very basic accommodation, with candles the only form of lighting and a sand floor, is often ideally situated – facing the sea or in natural surroundings. If you don't travel with a hammock you can always hire one on the spot. Prices per night vary from US$1 (communal accommodation) to US$10 (private *cabana* with hammock provided).

USEFUL ADDRESSES

AGUATECA ▲ 333

Guatemala
Accessible by *lancha* from Sayaxche.
Guide compulsory to gain access.

ALTAR DE SACRIFICIOS ▲ 331

Guatemala
At the confluence of the Usumacinta River and the Río de la Pasíon, 4 hours by *lancha* from Sayaxche.

ALTÚN HA ▲ 341

Belize
25 miles north of Belize City on the Old Northern Highway. Accessible to four-wheel-drive vehicles (track signposted). Open 9am–5pm

BALAMKU ▲ 194

Mexico
Not far from the village of Conhuas, 36 miles from Escarcega on highway 186.

BECÁN ▲ 191

Mexico
1½ miles from the village of Xpuhil on highway 186. Open 8am–5pm
Bus from Chetumal and Escárcega to the village of Xpuhil.

BONAMPAK ▲ 249

Mexico
A very isolated site. Tour operators can take you from Palenque or San Cristóbal by plane or by track and *lancha*. Make inquiries in advance. *Take supplies, water and a torch. Conditions at the site are very primitive.*

CAHAL PECH ▲ 342

Belize
2 miles from San Ignacio on the San Antonio road.

CALAKMUL ▲ 230

Mexico
Track restricted to four-wheel-drive vehicles, off the Chetumal-Escárcega road.
A very isolated site which can only be reached by this track.

CARACOL ▲ 342

Belize
36 miles by track from San Ignacio, restricted to four-wheel-drive vehicles
Prior permission required.

CEIBAL ▲ 331

Guatemala
From Sayaxché by a track restricted to four-wheel-drive vehicles or by river 1 hour by *lancha*.

CERROS ▲ 340

Belize
From Corozal, the last town before Chetumal by boat.

CHAN CHICH ▲ 341

Belize
20 miles north of Belmopán, by a track restricted to four-wheel-drive vehicles during the wet season.

CHICANNÁ ▲ 192

Mexico
2½ miles outside Xpupil on the Chetumal-Escárcega road.

CHICHÉN ITZÁ ▲ 205

Mexico
1 mile from the village of Piste on the Mérida-Valladolid road (no. 180). Open 8am–5pm
There are plenty of buses from Cancún and Mérida. It is possible to charter a plane in Cancún with Aerocaribe. Son et lumière every evening at 7pm in Spanish and at 9pm in English.

COBÁ ▲ 182

Mexico
25 miles from Tulum on the Nuevo Xcan road, half a mile from the village.
Open 8am–5pm

COPÁN ▲ 299

Honduras
Half a mile from the village. Open 8am–4pm.
Several buses a day from the Guatemalan border and Tegucigalpa or San Pedro Sula.

DOS PILAS ▲ 332

Mexico
Inland, on the road to Aguateca from Sayaxche.

DZIBILCHALTÚN ▲ 216

Mexico
10 miles from Mérida on the Progreso road, then take a right turn toward Conkal for 6 miles. The site is on the right-hand side, a few hundred yards from the road.

EDZNÁ ▲ 226

Mexico
From Campeche, through the village of San Antonio Caya on highway 261, soon after which is the junction with the Edzna road.
Open 8am–5pm
Bus from Campeche.

EL BAÚL ▲ 291

Guatemala
20 miles from Escuintla, coming from Guatemala City on highway 2. Turn right at the village of Santa Lucia Cotzumalguapa. The El Baúl *finca* is a few miles further on the left.
Key from the warden.

EL MIRADOR ▲ 329

Guatemala
Bus from Flores to San Andrés, from there hitch a ride to Carmelita then on foot or by mule (track accessible to four-wheel-drive vehicles).
Take supplies and water purifying tablets. Guide recommended.

HORMIGUERO ▲ 191

Mexico
A 10-mile track from Xpuhil. Restricted to four-wheel-drive vehicles.

IXIMCHÉ ▲ 276

Guatemala
2 miles from the town of Tecpán, Guatemala (30 miles from Guatemala City on the Panamerican Highway toward Lake Atitlán).

JOYA DE CERÉN ▲ 315

El Salvador
On the San Juan Opico road, 5 miles north of the Panamerican Highway. Open 9.30am–4.30pm. Closed Sat.
Bus from Guatemala City or San Salvador.

KABÁH ▲ 220

Mexico
8 miles south of Uxmal on highway 261.
The highway passes right through the middle of the site. Buses from Mérida and Campeche.

KAMINALJUYÚ ▲ 268

Guatemala
On the outskirts of Guatemala City. Accessible by public transport.

KOHUNLICH ▲ 189

Mexico
From highway 186, coming from Chetumal, just before the village of Francisco Villa, take a turning toward the south. The site is 4 miles from the village.
Open 8am–5pm
This site is difficult to get to without a rented vehicle.

LABNÁ ▲ 221

Mexico
4 miles from Sayil.
The Puuc road passes in front of the entrance to the site.

LA DEMOCRACIA ▲ 291

Guatemala
10 miles from Escuintla, coming from Guatemala City on highway 2. Turn left at the village of Siquinalá. The ruins are in the square.

LAMANAÏ ▲ 340

Belize
1½ hours by *lancha* from Orange Walk.

LUBAANTÚN ▲ 343

Belize
About 12 miles north of Punta Gorda on the San Pedro road. 1 mile outside San Pedro.
Open 8am–5pm

MAYAPÁN ▲ 212

Mexico
The ruins are 1 mile outside the village of Techalquillo, 20 miles from Mérida on highway 18.
Open 8am–5pm

MIXCO VIEJO ▲ 268

Guatemala
35 miles north of Guatemala City, 12 miles outside San Juan Sacatepequez. Buses pass the entrance of the site from the bus station in Zone 4.

MUYIL ▲ 184

Mexico
This site is also called Chunyaxche.
Half a mile from the village of Muyil.
Open 8am–5pm
8 miles from Tulum on highway 307 toward Chetumal.

NAKBÉ ▲ 330

Guatemala
In the Dos Lagunas National Park.
Guide essential. Arrange your visit through a tour operator.

NARANJO ▲ 334

Guatemala
From Melchor de Mencos, on the Flores-Belize City road, a 10-mile track accessible to four-wheel-drive vehicles.
Guide recommended.

NIM LI PUNIT ▲ 344

Belize
12 miles north of Punta Gorda (signposted).
Bus from Punta Gorda.

NOHMUL ▲ 340

Belize
2 miles north of Orange Walk on the Northern Highway

PALENQUE ▲ 243

Mexico
4 miles from the small town of Palenque.
Open 8am–5pm
Bus from Villahermosa and San Cristóbal. The Mexico–Mérida train stops at Palenque.

PIEDRAS NEGRAS ▲ 332

Guatemala
On the banks of the Río Usumacinta, accessible from Sayaxché on certain days by *lancha*.
Guide recommended. Arrange your visit through a tour operator.

QUIRIGUA ▲ 306

Guatemala
About 4 miles off the Guatemala City-Puerto Barrios road. Get out at Los Amates, from where there are taxis and frequent buses.

RÍO AZUL ▲ 329

Guatemala
By a 60-mile track from Uaxactún restricted to four-wheel-drive vehicles.
Take supplies and water purifying tablets with you.

RÍO BEC ▲ 192

Mexico
10 miles from Xpuhil by track.
Only accessible to four-wheel-drive vehicles.
To visit this site you will need a permit which you can obtain on your way through the village of 20 de Noviembre.
Guide compulsory.

SAN ANDRÉS ▲ 316

El Salvador
The site is near Joya de Ceren on highway 1 between San Salvador and Guatemala City.

SANTA RITA ▲ 340

Belize
A few miles from the village of Corozal, on the Chetumal road.

SAYIL ▲ 221

Mexico
2 miles from Kabah, turn right on the Puuc road. The site is 2 miles further on. Open 8am–5pm

TAZUMAL ▲ 316

El Salvador
500 yards from Chalchuapa, 10 miles from Santa Ana.
Open 9am–5pm
Closed Mon.
Regular buses from Santa Ana and San Salvador.

TIKAL ▲ 322

Guatemala
Tarmac road from Flores
Open 6am–5.30pm.
Many buses and taxis; plane as far as Flores from Guatemala City.

TONINÁ ▲ 242

Mexico
5 miles from Ocosingo on a good track, off the Palenque–San Cristóbal road.
Open 9am–4pm.
Accessible to all types of vehicle. Numerous buses.

TULUM ▲ 177

Mexico
Half a mile from El Crucero on highway 307.
Open 8am–5pm
Numerous buses take highway 307 throughout the day. Catch one at El Crucero for the return journey. An early-morning visit is advisable as this is a very popular site.

UAXACTÚN ▲ 328

Guatemala
By bus from Flores via Tikal or by a track restricted to four-wheel-drive vehicles.

UTATLÁN ▲ 288

Guatemala
1 mile from Santa Cruz del Quiché by car.

UXMAL ▲ 222

Mexico
35 miles from Mérida on highway 261.
Open 8am–5pm
Buses run all day from Mérida and stop at the entrance to the ruins. Son et lumière at 7pm in Spanish and at 9pm in English.

XPUHIL ▲ 190

Mexico
5 miles outside the village of Xpuhil on highway 186.
Open 8am–5pm
Track restricted to four-wheel-drive vehicles. Visits to the site require a permit which you can obtain at the Rancho San José. Guide compulsory.

YAXCHILÁN ▲ 248

Mexico
Like neighboring Bonampak, this site calls for a well-planned visit. See Bonampak.

YAXHÁ ▲ 334

Guatemala
Accessible by the Flores–Belize City road, then by a signposted track restricted to four-wheel-drive vehicles.

XUNANTUNICH ▲ 341

Belize
From San Ignacio, just before the Guatemalan border.
Open 8am–5pm
Bus from San Ignacio.

ZACULEU ▲ 284

Guatemala
On the way out of the town of Huehuetenango. Taxis or bus from the town center.

383

CAMPECHE

Dialing code 981

USEFUL INFORMATION

BANK AND BUREAU DE CHANGE
BANAMEX
Calle 10, no. 15
Open Mon.–Fri.
9am–1pm
BANCOMER
Calle 59, no. 2A
Open Mon.–Fri.
9am–1pm

TOURIST OFFICE
OFICINA DE TURISMO
ESTATAL
Pl. Moch-Cuouh and
Calle 61
Tel. 673 64

MAIN POST OFFICE
OFICINA DE CORREOS
Ave 16 de Septiembre
and Calle 53
Tel. 621 34
Open Mon.–Fri.
8am–7pm, Sat. 8am–1pm,
Sun. 8am–2pm

TRANSPORT

AIRLINES
AEROCARIBE
Ave López Portillo S/N
Tel. 129 08
AEROMEXICO AIRPORT
Tel. 658 78, 666 56
Fax 649 25

CAR RENTAL
HERTZ RENT A CAR
Baluartes Hotel
Ave Ruiz Cortínez
Tel. 633 79
JAINA RENTE UN AUTO
Ramada Hotel
Ave Ruiz Cortínez,
no. 51
Tel. 622 33
KALAKMUL
TRANSPORTES
TURISTICOS
Calle 8, no. 201
Tel. 118 71

RESTAURANTS

** RESTAURANTE IRAMAR
Calles 8 and 61
Tel. 628 83

Campeche's most renowned seafood restaurant.

* RESTAURANT AND BAR MARGANZO
Calle 8, no. 265
Overlooking the sea,
between Calles 57
and 59
Tel. 623 28
Open lunchtime and
evening (until late).
Mexican cuisine and
seafood.

HOTELS

*** RAMADA HOTEL
Ave Ruiz Cortinez, no. 51
Tel. 622 33
Fax 116 18

** HOTEL ALHAMBRA
Ave Resurgimiento, no.85
Tel. 668 22

** POSADA DEL ANGEL
Calle 12, no. 189
Next to the cathedral.
Tel. 677 18

* HOSPEDAJE TERESITA
Calle 53, no. 31
3 blocks from the
Plaza Central.

CANCÚN

Dialing code 98

USEFUL INFORMATION

CONSULATES
AMERICAN CONSULATE
Ave Náder, edificio
Marruecos, local 31,
Centro
Tel. 84 24 11
Open 9am–2pm
and 3–6pm
CANADIAN CONSULATE
Ave Tulum 200, Plaza
Mexico, suite 312,
Centro.
Tel. 84 37 16
Fax 87 67 16
FRENCH CONSULATE
Instituto Internacional
de Idiomas
Ave Xel-Ha 113
Tel. 84 60 78
Fax 87 39 50
GERMAN CONSULATE
Punta Conoco, no. 36
SM 24
Tel. 84 18 98
SPANISH CONSULATE
Edificio Oasis, Ave 4
miles from Kukicán,
Lote 1, Zona Hotelera

HOTELS (DOUBLE ROOM)

*	up to $25
**	$25 to $75
***	over $75

Tel. 841 895
Fax 83 28 70

BANK AND BUREAU DE CHANGE
CUNEX CASA DE CAMBIO
Ave Tulum, no. 13
close to Ave Cobá
Open 9am–9pm

TELEPHONE
TELMEX
Ave Cobá et Alcatraces
Ave Uxmal

TOURIST OFFICE
DELEGACION ESTATAL DE TURISMO
Ave Tulum, no. 26
Cancún Centro
Tel. 84 80 73

MAIN POST OFFICE
OFICINA DE CORREOS
At the western end of
Ave Sunyaxchén, near
Ave Yaxchilán
Open Mon.–Fri.
8am–7pm
Open Sat. and public
holidays 9am–1pm
*International money
orders can be collected
up to one hour before
closing.*

TRANSPORT

AIRLINES
AEROCARIBE & AEROCOZUMEL
Ave Coba Local B1 and
B2, Plaza America
Tel. 84 20 00
Fax 84 13 64
Airport:
Tel. 86 01 62
Fax 86 00 64
AEROMEXICO
Ave Cobá, no. 80
SM 03 Centro
Tel. 84 11 86 /
84 35 71
AVIACSA
Ave Cobá, no. 55
Centro
Tel. 87 42 11 /
87 42 14
AVIATECA
Ave Tulum, no. 200,
Plaza Mexico,
Centro
Tel. 86 01 55 /
86 01 56
CONTINENTAL
Airport
reservations:
Tel. 86 01 69
Crew:
Tel. 86 00 06
Fax 86 00 07
CUBANA DE AVIACION
Ave Yaxchilan 23
Plaza America
Tel. 87 73 73

LACSA
Ave Bonampak
and Ave Cobá
Edificio Atlantis SM 4
Centro
Tel. 87 31 01 /
87 51 01
MEXICANA
Ave Cobá, no. 13
Centro
Tel. 87 44 44 /
87 27 69

CAR RENTAL
AVIS
Airport:
Tel. 86 01 47
Fax 86 02 38
BUDGET
Reservations:.
Tel. 84 02 04 /
84 07 30
Airport: 86 00 26
Playa del Carmen:
Tel. (987) 235 54 /
235 44
Cozumel:
Tel. (987) 209 03
DOLLAR
Reservations:
Tel. 86 01 68
Airport:
Tel. 86 01 33
HERTZ
Calle Reno, 35
SM 20
Tel. 87 66 04 /
84 13 64
Fax 84 46 92
Airport: 86 01 50
NATIONAL
Ave Uxmal, no. 12
Cancún Centro
Tel. 86 44 90 /
864 492
Fax 864 493
Airport:
Sala Nacional: 86 01 52
Sala Internacional:
86 01 53

RESTAURANTS

*** LA HABICHUELA
Margaritas, no. 25
Parque las Palapas
Tel. 84 31 58
Open 1–9pm
*Interior garden in an
elegant Mayan setting.
Superb local dishes.*

*** ROSA MEXICANA
Calle Claveles, no.4
Tel. 84 63 13
*One of Cancún's largest
restaurants, built in the
style of a hacienda.
Local cuisine.*

** LA LANGOSTA FELIZ
Avenida Tulum, no. 33 C
Centro
Open 7am–10.30pm
Seafood.

** LOS ALMENDROS
Ave Bonampak
and Calle Sayil
Tel. 84 09 42 /
87 13 32
*A popular restaurant.
Specialties include "poc-
chuc" (pork with onion,
lemon and pimento) and
"papadzules" (tortillas
with an egg-and-tomato
sauce).*

** LOS BRACERITOS
Ave Yaxchilán, no. 35
Open 24 hours
Local cuisine.

** PIEMONTE PIZZERIA
Ave Yaxchilán, no. 52
*Good value Italian
specialties. Delicious
snacks.*

* 100% NATURAL
Opposite the Caribe
Internacional Hotel
Ave Yaxchilán and
Ave Sunyaxchén
Tel. 84 01 02
*Large café with
pleasant pastel-colored
surroundings. Local
vegetarian cuisine.*

NIGHTLIFE

CARLOS "N" CHARLIES
Tel. 83 13 04
Bd. Kukulcán.
*This bar-restaurant is
very popular with
American tourists.
Offers a festive
atmosphere.*

LOS PERICOS
Ave Yaxchilán 71
Centro
Tel. 87 48 84
Hale and hearty.

HOTELS

ON THE BEACH

CAMINO REAL CANCÚN ***
Punta Cancún
Tel. 83 01 00 /
83 12 00
Fax 83 17 30

*** CLUB MÉDITERRANÉE
Punta Nizuc
Tel. 85 24 09
Fax 85 22 90

*** MARRIOTT'S CANCÚN RESORT
Bd. Kukulcán
Tel. 85 20 00
Fax 85 13 85

*** SHERATON CANCÚN RESORT
Bd. Kukulcán
Tel. 83 19 88
Fax 83 14 50

TOWN CENTER

** HOTEL ANTILLANO
On the corner of Calle
Claveles and Ave
Tulum
Tel. 84 15 32
Fax 84 18 78
*One of the best value
hotels found in Cancún.*

** HOTEL MARIA DE LOURDES
Ave Yaxchilán 80
Tel. 84 47 44 /
84 17 21
Fax 84 12 42

** HOTEL PARADOR
Ave Tulum, no. 26
Tel. 84 19 22

* HOTEL UXMAL
Ave Uxmal. Just before
Ave Chichén Itzá
Tel. 84 23 55

** VILLA MAYA CANCUN
Ave Uxmal, no. 20
Tel. 84 17 62 /
84 29 18

SPORT

SCUBA DIVING
SCUBA CANCUN
PO Box 517
Cancún, QROO

PONY TREKKING AND DIVING
XCARET
25 miles south of
Cancún, on the coast.
Tel. 830 654, 830 743
Open 9am–6pm
Closes 5pm, Oct.–Mar.
*Pony trekking and
scuba diving. It is
possible to explore the
archeological
conservation area on
the coast between
Cancún and Tulum.*

CHETUMAL

Dialing code 983

USEFUL INFORMATION

GUATEMALAN CONSULATE
Obregón, no. 342
On the corner of
Rafael Melgar
Tel. 2 85 85
Open Mon.–Fri.
9am–2pm

BANK AND BUREAU DE CHANGE
BANCO EL ATLANTICO
Calle 50, no.406
Open Mon.–Fri.
9am–1pm

TOURIST OFFICE
CASETA DE INFORMACION
TURISTICA
Ave de los Heroes
and Efrain Aquilar
Tel. 2 08 55

MAIN POST OFFICE
OFICINA DE CORREOS
Plutarco Elias Calles 2 A
Tel. 2 00 57

TRANSPORT

AIRLINES
AEROCARIBE Airport
Tel. 2 66 75
AVIACSA
Hotel del Prado
On the corner of Ave de
los Heroes and
Chapultepec
Tel. 2 76 76

CAR RENTAL
AMEN RENTE
UN AUTO
Ave Carmen O.
de Merino, no. 208-A
NATIONAL RENT A CAR
Ave de los Heroes,
no. 138

RESTAURANT

* LA CABAÑA AZUL
Ave 5 de Mayo, close to
the seashore.
Local cuisine.

HOTELS

** HOTEL EL MARQUES
Ave Lázaro Cardenas,
no. 121
Tel. 229 98

** LOS COCOS
Heroes de Chaputelpec,
no. 138
Tel. 205 44

* HOTEL UCUM
Calle Gandhi, no. 4
Tel. 207 11

CHICHÉN ITZÁ

Dialing code 985

HOTELS

*** HOTEL MAYALAND
200 yards from the
entrance of the ruins
Tel. (Mérida)
23 68 51
Fax (Mérida)
24 62 90
Tel./Fax (Chichén Itzá)
101 29
*The best hotel in
Chichén Itzá.
Magnificent view of the
Caracol. Air
conditioning, gym and
tennis courts.*

** HOTEL DOLORES ALBA ★
Between the
Balankanché caves and
the ruins.
Tel. 28 31 63 (Mérida)
*Swimming pool. The
proprietor will take you
to the site in the
mornings.*

** PIRÁMIDE INN AND TRAILER PARK
Half a mile from the
west entrance to the
ruins.
*Swimming pool, air
conditioning.*

CAVES

BALANKANCHE
Two miles from Chichén
Itzá (signposted)
Hourly guided tours.
Open 9am–4pm
Closed Mon. and Sun.
1pm

COBÁ

Dialing code 985

HOTEL

*** VILLA ARQUEOLÓGICA COBÁ
Next to Lake Cobá
Tel. 420 87
*Houses an extensive
library specializing in
Mayan culture.
Swimming pool, good
restaurant.*

COZUMEL

Dialing code 987

TRANSPORT

AIRLINES
AEROCARIBE/
AEROCOZUMEL
Airport
Tel. 208 77 / 234 56
Fax 209 28
MEXICANA
Ave R. Melgar Sur,
no. 17
Tel. 201 57 / 201 33
Fax 204 05

CAR RENTAL
A. MONTEJO BUDGET
5a Ave no. 8
Tel. 209 03
ALGO RENT/AVIS
Airport
Tel. 202 19
HERTZ
Airport
Tel. 238 88
NATIONAL CAR RENTAL
AVE Juarez, no. 10
Tel. 232 63
At quay: Tel. 241 01

RESTAURANTS

*** PEPE'S GRILL
Ave Rafael Melgar
and Calle Adolfo
Rosado Salas
Tel. 202 13
*One of the best menus
in Cozumel. Seafood,
langoustines, unusual
and delicious dishes.*

** LA CHOZA
Calle Adolfo Rosado
Salas, no. 198
Corner of Ave 10 Sur
Tel. 209 58
*Reasonably priced for a
Cozumel restaurant.
Local dishes.*

* RESTAURANTE LAS PALMERAS
On the main square
Tel. 205 32
*Regional dishes served
on a charming terrace.*

* PIZZA ROLANDI
Ave Rafael Melgar
between Calles 6 and
8 Norte
*Extremely popular,
good value.*

SPORT

SCUBA DIVING
★BLACK SHARK
DIVE SHOP
5a Ave between Rafael
E. Melgar and 3 Sur
PO Box 462

TEL. 203 96 / 232 82
Fax 203 96
*Groups limited to a
maximum of seven
people. Offers diving
certificates (PADI).*
BLUE BUBBLE DIVERS
At the intersection of
5a Aveand Calle 3 Sur
Tel. 218 65 (local)
or 011 52 987 (USA)
CARIBBEAN DIVERS
39 B Melgar Av.
(Hotels *Melia Mayan
Cozumel* and *Sol
Cabanas del Caribe*)
Tel. 210 80
214 26, 211 45
DIVE PARADISE
Waterfront
601 Melgar Ave
Tel. 210 07 or 213 66
DIVING ADVENTURE
Calle 5, no. 2
PO Box 78 - Cozumel
Quintana Roo
Tel. 230 09
Fax 230 09
FREDDY CONTREAS
Adolfo Rosado Salas
and 5a Ave Sur
Tel. 241 23
SNORKOZUMEL
Melgar Ave no. 471
(Lobby of the *Soberamis*
hotel)
Tel. 241 66
For keen snorklers.

FISHING AND SCUBA DIVING
WILD CAT DIVERS
5a Ave
Between Calle 2
and Calle 4 Norte
Tel. 210 28 or 239 21
Fax 210 28

HOTELS

*** STOUFFER COZUMEL
Carretera a Chankanab,
four miles
Tel. 203 22
Fax 213 60
*Two swimming pools,
tennis courts and boat
hire.*

** HOTEL PLAZA
Calle 2 Norte 3,
San Miguel
Tel. 227 00
*Roof pool and air-
conditioned rooms.*

* HOTEL MARY-CARMEN
Ave 5 Sur 4, San Miguel
Tel. 205 81
*This hotel has a very
Spanish atmosphere
with its rooms
overlooking an
illuminated patio.*

NIGHTLIFE

CARLOS "N" CHARLIES
On the sea front
Tel. 201 91
Open noon–dusk.
Mexican-American bar-restaurant. Friendly atmosphere. Prices tend to be high.

DOS OJOS

SPORT

RAMBLING, TREKKING AND DIVING
DIVERS OF THE HIDDEN WORLDS
"Dos Ojos Jungle Adventure"
A.P.66, Tulum, Quintana Roo
Tel. 744 081

ESCARCEGA

Dialing code 982

HOTELS

** HOTEL ESCARCEGA
In the city center
Tel. 401 86
Half a mile from ADO station.

ISLA MUJERES

Dialing code 987

RESTAURANTS

** GOMAR
Madero
Specialty: seafood

*ARRIBA RESTAURANT BAR
Ave Haldigo
Tel. 704 58
Seafood and vegetarian dishes.

* CAFÉCITO
Matamorros, no. 42
Tel. 704 38

Delicious breakfasts served in unusual surroundings.

HOTELS

***NAUTIBEACH
Rueda Medina and Playa Norte
Tel. 702 59 / 704 36

** HOTEL PERLA DEL CARIBE ★
Madero, no. 2
Tel. 701 20 / 705 07
Friendly hotel with a charming atmosphere. Tastefully decorated, spacious, clean rooms.

* HOTEL CARACOL
Ave Mataoros, no. 5
Tel. 701 50

MÉRIDA

Dialing code 99

USEFUL INFORMATION

CONSULATES
CONSULATE OF BRITAIN AND BELIZE
Major A. Dutton
Calle 58-53, no. 450
Tel. 28 39 62

CONSULATE OF THE
UNITED STATES OF
AMERICA
Paseo Montejo, no. 453
and Ave Colón
Tel. 25 54 09

**BANKS AND
BUREAUX DE CHANGE**
BANAMEX
Pl. Mayor
Palacio Montejo
BANCOMER
Calle 65, no. 506,
Centro
CASA DE CAMBIO
Calle 56, no. 491
Between Calle 57
and Calle 59.
Open Mon.–Sat.
9am–5pm
*Tends to offer best rates
amongst the banks.*

DOCTOR
DOCTOR AH PUGA
NAVARRETE
Calle 13, no. 210
Between Calle 26
and Calle 28
Tel. 25 07 09
English spoken.

BOOKSTORES
SANBORN'S
Hotel Fiesta Americana
*European and US
magazines and
newspapers. Also
records, perfumes,
chocolates.*
LIBRERIA DANTE PEON
Teatro Peón Contreras
On the corner of
Calle 60 and Calle 57
Tel. 24 95 22
Open Mon.–Sun.
*Books in English,
French and Spanish.*

MAIN POST OFFICE
OFICINA DE CORREOS
On the corner of Calle
65 and Calle 56.
(between Calle 56
and Calle 56 A)
Tel. 212 561
Open Mon.–Fri. 7am–
7pm, Sat. 9am–1pm

TRANSPORT

AIRLINES
AEROCARIBE
Paseo Montejo, no. 500

Tel. 28 18 17
Airport: 46 13 61
Fax 46 16 78
AEROCOZUMEL
Paseo Montejo, no. 500
Tel. 28 18 17
Airport: 46 13 66
Fax 46 16 78
AEROMEXICO
Paseo Montejo, no. 460
Tel. 27 90 00 /
27 94 33
AVIACSA
Reservations:
Tel. 26 90 87
AVIATECA
Paseo Montejo,
no. 475-C
Tel. 25 80 59 /
25 80 62
Airport: 46 13 12
MEXICANA
Paseo Montejo, no. 493
Tel. 24 66 33
Airport: 46 13 32
TAESA
Ave Reforma 544
Local 10
Tel. 20 20 77
Airport: 46 18 26 /
46 18 27

CAR RENTAL
AVIS
Paseo Montejo, no. 498
Tel. 28 28 28 /
23 61 91
Fax 84 30 79 /
84 21 35
BUDGET
Lobby, Holiday Inn:
25 54 53
Lobby, Hyatt Hotel:
42 12 26
Airport: 46 13 80
Reservations:
46 22 55
HERTZ
Calle 60, no. 486-D
Tel. 24 28 34
Lobby,
Hotel Fiesta Americana:
25 75 95
Airport: 46 25 54 /
46 13 55
Fax 84 01 14
DOLLAR RENT A CAR
Calle 60, no. 491
Tel. 28 67 59
Fax 25 01 55
Airport: 46 13 23
NATIONAL RENT A CAR
Calle 60, no. 486-F
Tel. 23 24 93 /
28 63 08
Lobby, Hotel Fiesta
Americana: 42 11 11
Airport: 46 13 94

RESTAURANTS

*** LA CASONA
Calle 60, no. 434
Tel. 238 348
*Good Italian and
Mexican cuisine.*

*** PANCHO'S
Calle 59, no. 509
Tel. 23 09 42 /
27 04 34
*Mexican food and
atmosphere.*

***** PORTICO
DEL PELEGRINO**
Calle 57, no. 501
(between Calle 60
and Calle 62)
Tel. 28 61 63
Open lunchtime
noon–3pm, evenings
6–11pm.
*Local specialities (pavo,
poc-chuc).*

***RINCON ORIENTAL
Paseo Montejo, no. 466
Tel. 26 13 59
Good Chinese food.

**** CAFETERÍA
EL MESÓN**
In the Hotel Caribe
Calle 59, no. 500
(behind Hidalgo park).
Tel. 24 90 22
*Local dishes, self-
service.*

**LEO
Paseo Montejo,
no. 460-A
Tel. 29 65 14 /
26 64 80
Open noon–1am.

** LOS ALMENDROS
Pl. de Mejorada,
Calle 50 (between Calle
57 and Calle 59)
Open 11am–11pm
*Varied cuisine,
Yucatán specialties
often featured, good
cocktails. Very popular
air-conditioned
restaurant.*

*POP
Calle 57, no. 501
Tel. 28 61 63
Tasty, good-value food.

HOTELS

***** FIESTA
AMERICANA**
Paseo Montejo, no. 451
Tel. 42 11 11 /
42 11 12
*Luxurious, with all
facilities.*

** GRAN HOTEL ★
Calle 60
(between Calle 61
and Calle 59).
Tel. 23 69 63 / 24 7730
Fax 24 76 22
*Situated on the most
attractive plaza in
Mérida. Magnificent
colonial building with
galleries connecting two
floors of rooms,
mosaics, and a patio
covered in greenery.
American Express not
accepted.*

**** MARIA DEL
CARMEN**
Calle 63, no. 550
Tel. 23 91 33 / 23 92 90
*Pool, restaurant and
bar.*

* HOTEL COLONIAL
Calle 62, no. 476
Tel. 23 64 44 / 23 64 78
Fax 28 39 61

* HOTEL SANTA LUCIA
Calle 65, no. 508
Tel. 24 62 33
Fax 24 63 75
*Good value hotel facing
the Colonial Square.*

NIGHTLIFE

EL TUCHO
Calle 60
To the north of the Plaza
Central
Tel. 24 23 23
*Live bands and dancing
(salsa), reasonably
priced good food.*

TROVADOR BOHEMIA
Santa Lucía park
*Guitar trios featured.
Bar open from 9pm.*

CULTURE

PARC SANTA LUCÍA
On the corner of Calles
55 and 60.
*Folk dance performed
every Thursday starting
around 9pm.*

**TEATRO PEÓN
CONTRERAS**
Calles 60 and 57
*Folk dancing, Tuesdays
at 9pm.*

ARCHEOLOCIAL MUSEUM
Paseo de Montejo and Calle 41
Open 8am–8pm. Closed Mon. and Sun. from 2pm.

OCOSINGO

HOTEL

** HOTEL CENTRAL
Ave Central, no. 1
Tel. (967) 300 24

PALENQUE

Dialing code 934

TRANSPORT

CAR RENTAL
VIAJES YAX-HA
Ave Juarez 123
Tel. 507 67

RESTAURANTS

*** LA OAXAQUEÑA
At the entrance to the town coming from the ruins.
Good food, rather expensive.

*** RESTAURANT-BAR HARDY'S OR LA SELVA
On the road to the ruins 100 yards from the Maya statue.
Tel. 503 63
Regional cuisine.

** LA PALAPA DE APOHEL
Ave 5 de Mayo (between Independencia and Abasolo).
Comfortable surroundings, good food. Seafood a specialty.

* GIRASOLES
Juárez, no. 189
Open morning, lunchtime and evening.
A popular meeting place for visitors. Regional cuisine.

* MONTES AZULES
Juárez, no. 120
Generous portions, friendly welcome, music (marimba) on Fri., Sat. and Sun. Local cuisine.

HOTELS

** HOTEL LA CAÑADA
Close to Maya Tulipanes
Bungalows dotted through the forest. Spacious, clean, double rooms.

** HOTEL PALENQUE
Ave 5 de Mayo, no. 15
Tel. 504 44, 501 89
Fax 500 39

** HOTEL MAYA TULIPANES
La Cañada, no. 6
Tel. 502 01 / 502 58
Fax 510 04

PLAYA DEL CARMEN

Dialing code 987

RESTAURANTS

*** RESTAURANTE MASCARAS
Plaza Central.
The oldest and most famous city in Playa del Carmen.

** DA GABI *
Calle 12 (behind the Blue Parrot)
Good fast service. Regional, Italian and European cuisines.

HOTELS

** BLUE PARROT INN *
(by the beach to the left of the Embarcadero).
The most pleasant place in Playa del Carmen, with happy hours (two drinks for the price of one) almost all day. Original décor: the bar

seats have been replaced by swinging chairs. Good restaurant.

** MAYA BRIC
Ave 5 between Calle 8 and Calle 10.
Rooms around a flower-covered patio. Swimming pool. Very quiet.

SAN CRISTÓBAL DE LAS CASAS

Dialing code 967

USEFUL INFORMATION

TELEPHONE CENTER
BOUTIQUE
SANTO DOMINGO
Esquina Paniagua
Credit cards accepted. Reverse charge calls possible.

HOSPITAL
CROIX ROUGE
(CRUZ ROJA)
Ave Insurgentes
(close to Centro Recreativo Municipal).
Tel. 807 12
SAN CRISTÓBAL
CENTRO DE SALUD
Ave Insurgentes, no. 24
(Opposite the Fray Bartolomé Park).
Tel. 807 70
24-hour emergency service

BOOKSTORES
EL MURAL
Crescencio Rosas, no. 4
Books and magazines in English and Spanish .

Daily newspapers – enquire when you arrive.
LIBRERÍA EL RINCÓN
Diego de Mazariegos
Secondhand books – exchange two for one.
LIBRERÍA SOLUNA
24-D Real de Guadalupe, to the east of the main square.
Some English books but mostly stocks b ooks in Spanish. Possible to exchange two books for one.

MAIN POST OFFICE
OFICINA DE CORREOS
Cuauhtémoc, no. 13
(between Crescencio Rosas and Hidalgo).
Open Mon.–Fri.
8am–7pm,
Sat.–Sun., holidays
9am–1pm

TRANSPORT

CAR RENTAL
AUTO RENTA
RICCI DIESTEL
Ave 5 de Mayo, no. 6-A
On the corner of Guadalupe and Victoria
Tel. 809 88
BUDGET/AUTO RENTAS
YAXCHILÁN
Diego de Mazariegos, no. 36
Barrio la Merced
Tel. 818 71
Fax 831 00

CULTURE

CASA DE LA CULTURA
At the intersection of Hermanos Domínguez and Hidalgo (Opposite *El Carmen*).
Concerts, movies, lectures, exhibitions.

ROBERTO RIVAS BASTIDAS
Centro Bilingüe
Ave Insurgentes, no. 57
Tel. 850 14
Language courses.

UNIVERSIDAD AUTÓNOMA DE CHIAPAS
Ave Hidalgo
Departamento de Lenguas
Language courses.

HOTEL D'MÓNICA
Ave Insurgentes, no. 33
Live Latin-American music Friday evening.

RESTAURANTS

*** EL TEATRO
Calle Primero de Marzo, no. 8
Tel. 831 49
Open 11am–11pm
Magnificent view of the town. Excellent food, particularly the steak châteaubriand, wood-fire cooked pizzas and best of all the fillet steak San Cristóbal.

*** LA PARRILLA
Ave Belisario Dominguez, no. 32
Closed Sat.
Saloon-style décor, wood fire. Regional cuisine: good cheeses and grilled meats.

** TULUC
Ave Insurgentes, no. 5
Tel. 820 90
Open morning, lunchtime and evening. Breakfast served from 6.30am
Good restaurant, but rather expensive. Regional and French cuisine.

* RESTAURANT AND PANADERÍA MADRE TIERRA
Ave Insurgentes, no. 19
Open 8am–9.30pm
Regional cuisine (very good coffee).

HOTELS

*** HOTEL CASA MEXICANA
Calle 28 de Agosto, no. 1
Tel. 806 98 / 806 83
Fax 826 27
In a large renovated colonial house. Beautifully planted patio.

*** HOTEL FLAMBOYANT
Calle Primero de Marzo, no. 15
Tel. 800 54
Once a colonial house. Tends to be full of groups of tourists during high season.

** HOTEL EL PARAÍSO
Ave 5 de Febrero, no. 19
Tel. 800 85
Pleasant little hotel with modern decoration.

** HOTEL ESPAÑOL
Calle Primero de Marzo, no. 16
Tel. 804 12
To the north of the cathedral in a colonial-style building with two small interior courtyards. Each room has its own fireplace

* HOTEL FRAY BARTOLOMÉ DE LAS CASAS
Calle Niños Heroes, no. 2
Tel. 809 32
Fax 835 10
This basic hotel has a pretty flowered patio.

TULUM

Dialing code 987

RESTAURANT

* CABAÑAS DON ARMANDO ★
500 yards to the south of the ruins, on the beach.
Open 8am–noon.
*Bar and dancing every evening.
Regional cuisine.*

HOTELS

** HOTEL EL PARAÍSO
One mile to the south of the ruins.

** HOTEL EL FAISAN Y EL VENADO
Opposite the access road to the ruins.

* HOTEL CABAÑAS DON ARMANDO ★
On the beach.

TUXTLA GUTIÉRREZ

Dialing code 968

USEFUL INFORMATION

TELEPHONE CENTER
LADATEL
Ave 1 Sur and Calle 2 Or.
Open 9am–10pm

MAIN POST OFFICE
OFICINA DE CORREOS
To the east of the Plaza Central.
Open Mon.–Sat. 8am–6pm, and Sun. 9am–noon, for stamps only.

MUSEUM

REGIONAL ANTHROPOLOGICAL MUSEUM
Calzada de los hombres illustres de la Revolución
Madero Park
Tel. 344 79

TRANSPORT

CAR RENTAL
AUTO BADIA
Hotel Flamboyant
Bd Belisario Dominguez, km 1081
Tel. 108 88 / 109 99
TUXTLA RENT A CAR
Bd Dr Belisario Dominguez 2510
Tel. 506 72 / 506 83
Fax 509 71
Airport: 255 59
Other companies are based at the airport.

AIRLINES
AEROCARIBE
Bd Belisario Dominguez, no. 180
Tel. 515 30
MEXICANA
Ave Central Poniente, no. 206
Tel. 271 08
Fax 216 92

RESTAURANTS

** LA PARILLA NORTEÑA
Calle 14 de Septiembre and Calle 11 Oriente Norte
Large dining room with walls covered in frescos. Specialties: grills and kebabs.

* RESTAURANTE LAS PICHANCHAS
Ave 14 de Septiembre, Oriente 857
Open-air restaurant enlivened by marimba playing. Varied menu featuring regional cuisine.

* RESTAURANTE EL GRAN CHEFF
Ave Central Poniente, no. 226 and Calle 1 Poniente Norte.
Regional cuisine, comida corrida (fast food).

HOTELS

*** HOTEL FLAMBOYANT
Bd Belisario Dominguez, km 1081
Tel. 509 29
Comfortable rooms situated around a swimming pool. Disco, tennis courts, restaurant and bar.

** HOTEL REGIONAL SAN MARCOS
Calle 2 Or. Sur, no. 176
Tel. 318 87
Basic, air-conditioned rooms.

* GRAN HOTEL OLIMPO
Ave Sur Orientete, no. 215
Very basic.

UXMAL

Dialing code 99

CAVES

LOLTUN
Four miles to the south
of Oxkutzcab
Guided tours 9.30am,
11am, 12.30pm and
2pm. Closed Mon.

HOTELS

***** HACIENDA
UXMAL HOTEL**
500 yards from the
ruins, on the opposite
side of the road.
Tel. 471 42
*Quiet with a beautiful
patio and pleasant
swimming pool.
Generous breakfasts.*

***** HOTEL VILLA
ARQUEOLÓGICA**
*A Club Méditerrannée
hotel. Next to the site.*

** RANCHO UXMAL
Coming from Mérida,
2 miles before the ruins,
on the right.
*Rooms with hot water,
fan and mosquito net.*

VALLADOLID

Dialing code 985

CAVES

DZITNUP
Four miles from
Valladolid, taking the
road to Chichén Itzá
then the dirt track, one
mile on the right.
Open Mon.–Sun.
9am–5pm.
*Bus and taxi from
Valladolid.It is advisable
to take a torch.*

HOTELS

**** HOTEL EL MESÓN
DEL MARQUES**
Calle 39, no. 203
Tel. 630 42
Fax 622 80

*Superb, beautifully
planted patio and
extremely comfortable
rooms. No hot water in
the evening.*

** HOTEL DON LUIS
Calle 39, no. 191
Tel. 6 20 08
*Air-conditioned rooms
around a shaded
swimming pool.*

*** HOTEL MARÍA DE
LA LUZ**
Calle 42, on the zócalo.
Tel. 620 71
*Pleasant surroundings,
swimming pool in a
verdant setting.*

RESTAURANTS

**** RESTAURANTE
CASA DE LOS ARCOS**
Calle 39, between
Calle 38 and 40.
Tel. 624 67
*Perfect for enjoying a
choice of delicious
Yucatán specialties.*

* EL PAPILLON
Calle 42, on the zócalo
*Small, basic and very
popular restaurant.*

VILLAHERMOSA

Dialing code 93

USEFUL
INFORMATION

**BANK AND BUREAU
DE CHANGE**
BANCOMER
On the corner of
Zaragoza and Juárez.
Tel. 237 00
Open Mon.–Fri.
9am–1.30pm
BANAMEX
At the corner of Madeira
and Reforma streets.
Tel. 12 25 75
Open Mon.–Fri.
9am–1.30pm.
CAMBIARIA DEL CENTRO
Saenz, no. 22
Open Mon.–Fri.
8.30am–2pm and
4pm–6.30pm.

*Service tends to be
faster than the banks,
but at a cost.*

TOURIST OFFICE
SECRETARIA DE
TURISMO DEL ESTADO
Ave Paseo de Tabasco,
no. 1504
Tel. 16 36 50

MAIN POST OFFICE
OFICINA DE CORREOS
Saenz 131
Zona Remodelada
Tel. 14 26 77
Open Mon.–Fri. 8am–
5.30pm (stamps
available until 7pm)
Open Sat. 9am–noon
(stamps only available
noon–1pm)
Closed Sun.

TRANSPORT

AIRLINES
AEROCARIBE
Fco. Javier Mina, no. 901
Tel. 56 00 84
AEROLITORAL
Airport: 14 36 13
AEROMEXICO CICOM
Avenida Carlos Pellicier
Camara, no. 511
Tel. 14 16 75
AVIACSA
Fco. Javier Mina,
no. 1025-2
Tel. 14 57 80
MEXICANA
Ave de los Ríos, no. 105
Tabasco 2000
Tel. 16 31 32 to 38.

CAR RENTAL
AUTO RENT
Ave Ruiz Cortinez,
no. 1201
Tel. 12 34 69
AVIS
Juan Alvares, no. 602a
Tel. 129 214
HERTZ
Lobby, Holiday Inn
Paseo Tabasco, no.
1407
Tel. 16 44 00 ext.
Airport: 56 02 00
NATIONAL CAR RENTAL
Lobby, Hotel Viva
Calinda
Ave Ruiz Cortinez,
corner with Paseo
Tabasco.
Tel. 15 18 56
Airport: 56 03 93

MUSEUMS

HISTORY MUSEUM
On the corner of Calle
de Juárez
and 27 de Febrero.
Open daily 9am–6pm

**MUSEO REGIONAL DE
LA ANTROPOLOGÍA**
Ave C. Pellicer, no. 511
Open daily 9am–8pm

PARC DE LA VENTA
Av. Adolfo Ruíz Cortinez
S/N
Open daily 8am–4.30pm
*Collection of Olmec
statues.*

RESTAURANTS

** CAPITÁN BEULO
On the quay opposite
the Museo Regional de
la Antropología.
Departures–1.30pm,
3.30pm and 9.30pm
*Floating restaurant
which departs for a one
and a half hour tour of
the Río Grijalva. The
food is less interesting
than the cruise itself.
Regional cuisine.*

**** RESTAURANTE
LA PLAYITA**
Constitución, no. 202
Seafood.

HOTELS

***** HOTEL EXALARIS
HYATT REGENCY**
Laguna de las Ilusiones,
Juarez, no. 106
Tel. 15 12 34
Fax 13 44 44

**** HOTEL
DON CARLOS**
Madero, no. 418
Tel. 12 24 99

*** HOTEL PALMA
DE MALLORCA**
Madero, no. 516
Tel. 12 01 45

Well located, basic rooms. Often full.

XPUHIL

GUIDED WALKS

Contact Serge Riou, called Checo. Apartado Postal 27, CP 24640 Xpuhil, Campeche. Fax–Chetumal: 983 21 251
This French resident of Xpuhil is an excellent guide for visits to the sites in the Río Bec.

*Dialing codes:
2 for the capital,
9 for other towns*

ANTIGUA GUATEMALA

USEFUL INFORMATION

BANKS AND BUREAUX DE CHANGE
BANCO DEL ARGO
To the north of the Plaza Central.
Open 9am–2.30pm
Only banks are open on Saturdays.
LLOYD'S BANK
4a Ave and 4 Calle
Open Mon.–Fri.
9am–2.30pm

HOSPITAL
HOSPITAL PEDRO DE BETANCOURT
3a Ave and 6 Calle
Tel. 320 301

BOOKSTORES
LIBRERÍA MARQUENSE
5a Ave Sur, no. 9
LIBRERÍA DEL PENSATIVO
5a Ave Norte, no. 29
English and Spanish books.

★ UN POCO DE TODO
Plaza Central.
Open Mon.–Fri.
9.30am–1pm
Travel guides, books in English and Spanish, maps, postcards. English spoken

TOURIST OFFICE
OFICINA DEL INGUAT
Palacios de los Capitanes Generales
5a Calle Oriente and 4a Ave Sur
Tel. 320 763

MAIN POST OFFICE
OFICINA DE CORREOS
4 Calle Poniente
Alameda Santa Lucía
Open Mon.–Sat.
8am–noon and 2–8pm

TRANSPORT

MOTORBIKE RENTAL
MOTO-RENT
Hotel Los Capitanes
9a Ave Sur
Motorbikes to rent (Yamaha 200).

SPANISH COURSES

★ CENTRO DE ESPAÑOL "DON PEDRO DE ALVARADO"
4 Calle Poniente, no. 27
Open 8am–1pm or 1–6pm
*Cost of Spanish courses: $65 per week (four hours per day for five days).
Accommodation is*

available, with access to a kitchen, in a house with garden.

CHRISTIAN SPANISH ACADEMY (CSA)
6a Ave Norte, no. 15
PO Box 320
Tel. 323 922
Fax 323 760
Closed Sat. and Sun.
Individual Spanish tuition for four to five hours per day, Mon. to Fri. Classes held in the garden. Accommodation available with a family.

EL QUETZAL
7 Calle Poniente
Appartado Postal no. 428
Accommodation can be arranged with a family ($40 per week.)

ESCUELA DE ESPAÑOL ATABAL
1a Ave Norte, no. 6
Tel. 320 791
Small school, friendly atmosphere.

INSTITUTO ANTIGÜEÑO
1a Calle Poniente, no. 33

MAYA ESCUELA DE ESPAÑOL
5 Calle Poniente, no. 20
Cost: $70 per week. (Accommodation with a family $50 per week.)

POPOL VUH
7a Ave Norte, no. 34
Tel. 323 343

PROYECTO LINGÜISTICO "RIGOBERTA MENCHU"
5a Ave Sur, no. 11C
Tel. 322 931

PROYECTO LINGÜISTICO "FRANCISCO MARROQUÍN"
4 Ave Sur, no. 4
Apartado Postal no. 237

Tel. 320 406
Fax 320 406
Up to seven hours of classes per day. Accommodation available (with an Antiguan family). Cost: $150 per week.

QUICHÉ
3 Ave Sur, no. 15 A
(Behind the cathedral, 2½ blocks to the south.)
Tel. 320 575
Fax 320 575
Very popular with students. Friendly atmosphere.

TECÚN UMÁN
6 Calle Poniente, no. 34
Tel. 322 792
Fax 322 792
Individual tuition. A tour of local sites of interest can also be organized.

PROFESSIONAL SPANISH LANGUAGE SCHOOL
7 Ave Norte, no. 82
Tel. 320 161
*Director: Roberto King, author of "Spanish, an easy way".
Individual classes of two, four or six hours per day for a week.*

RESTAURANTS

*** CAFE OPERA
6a Ave Norte, no. 17
Café-Bar-Restaurant. Italian cuisine. Friendly atmosphere, classical music.

*** EL SERENO
6 Calle Poniente, no. 30
Tel. 320 073
Open Wed. to Sun.
noon–3pm and
6.30–10pm.
Beautiful restaurant in an old colonial-style house. Children under 8 years are not accepted. Booking recommended, particularly on Sun. Regular music recitals Mon. and Tue. Local crafts for sale. Regional cuisine.

***WELTEN
4 Calle Oriente, 21-A
Tel. 832 0630
Closed Tuesdays.
Expensive but excellent food in a pleasant setting (garden). Movies shown in the evenings.

*** FONDA DE LA CALLE REAL ★
Two addresses:
5 Ave Norte, 5 and 3 Calle Poniente, no. 7
Tel. 832 0507
Guatemalan cuisine. Good restaurant, attractive décor. Specialty: cheese fondues.

** KATOK
4 Ave Norte, no. 7
In a small patio. Guatemalan cuisine.

** QUESOS Y VINO
5a Ave Norte, no. 32A
A good pizzeria which also serves pasta and wine. Specializes in a parmesan-style cheese.

** RESTAURANTE CAFÉ
5a Ave Norte, no. 14
Within the La Casa de los Gárgolas building, this restaurant is located in a flowered courtyard with a fountain. Regional cuisine.

** DOÑA LUISA
4 Calle Oriente, no. 12 (at the east side of the square).
A large colonial residence with a patio, destroyed several times by earthquakes and completely rebuilt. Today it is a tea house and bakery. The perfect place for a delicious breakfast.

* CAFÉ CONDESA
5 Ave Norte, no. 4
Parque central
Tel. 832 3322
Open throughout the day for breakfast, coffee and snacks. Situated in a courtyard behind a bookshop on the Plaza Central opposite the church.

* RESTAURANTE ITALIANO EL CAPUCHINO
6a Ave N., no. 10
between 4 and 5 Calles Poniente
Tel. 832 0613

A small, inexpensive restaurant which serves delicious Italian food.

HOTELS

**** HOTEL ANTIGUA
Callejon San José, 8 Calle y 5a Ave esquina
Tel. 832 0288 / 832 0331

**** RADISSON VILLA ANTIGUA
9 Calle Poniente, at exit of Ciudad Vieja
Tel. 832 0011/0015

*** CASA SANTO DOMINGO ★
3a Calle Oriente, no. 28
Tel. 832 0112 / 832 0138
A former convent which has been magnificently restored. Delightful setting.

*** POSADA DE DON RODRIGO ★
5a Ave Norte, no. 17
Tel. 832 0291 / 832 0387
An impressive colonial building around an interior courtyard. Marimba band on Sat.

** HOTEL EL DESCANSO
5a Avenida Norte, no. 9
Tel. 832 0142
Small hotel in a family house. Five pleasant rooms for 2, 3 or 4 persons.

* POSADA LAS ROSAS
6a Avenida Sur, no. 8
Tel. 832 0644
Steam baths and generous breakfasts.

SPORT

SAILING
VIAREAL ADVENTURE TRAVEL CENTER
4a Calle oriente, no. 14
Tel. and fax 832 3228 / 832 0082

Organized excursions to Lake Izabal, Livingston and the Cayes of Belize.

VOLCANA EXPEDITIONS
QUETZAL VOLCANO EXPEDITIONS
Alameda Santa Lucía Sur, no. 6
Excursions to the volcanos of Pacaya, Agua, Fuego, Acatenango.

★ POPEYE TOURS
INGUAT BUILDING
4a Calle Poniente, no. 38
Take warm clothes and waterproofs for the three-hour climb to the top of the Pacaya volcano. Groups of a minimum of five people.

MUSEUMS

MUSEUM SANTIAGO DE LOS CABALLEROS
Plaza Mayor
Open daily 9am–noon and 2–6pm

MUSEUM OF ANCIENT BOOKS
Plaza Mayor
Open daily 9am–noon and 2–6pm

MUSEUM OF COLONIAL ART
On the corner of the Calle de la Universidad and de Ave Norte

NIGHTLIFE

★ BAR PICASSO
7a Ave Norte
(between 2a Calle Poniente and 3a Calle Poniente)
Open daily, 7pm–midnight. Closed Wed. Good music, very popular.

CAFÉ FLOR CINEMA
4a Ave Sur, no. 1
(Half a block from the Plaza Central)
Closed Sun.

Three screenings a day except Sun. (movies in English and Spanish).

CINE GEMINIS
5a Calle Oriente, no. 11a
Three screenings a day, four at the weekend. Movies in English or Spanish with subtitles.

CINEMALA
3a Ave Norte, no. 9
Behind Doña Luisa
Two or three screenings a day.

JAZZ GRUCIA
Cal. Santa Lucía, no. 17
Jazz bands once or twice a week.

MOSCAS Y MIEL
5 Calle Poniente, no. 6
A good place to dance or just to listen to music. Also a nightclub.

MISTRAL
4 Calle Oriente, no. 7
Bar/movie theater which is extremely popular with visitors.

RAINBOW VIDEO
7a Ave Sur, no. 8
On the corner of 6a Calle
Three screenings every day except Wed. Movies in English or with subtitles.

CHICHICAS-TENANGO

HOTELS

*** MAYAN INN ★
Near the market plaza
Tel. 756 1176 / 756 1212 / 756 1062 / 756 1202
Superb colonial-style rooms with fireplaces. Restaurant and good service.

HOTEL SANTO TOMAS ★
★★★

7a Ave 5–32
Tel. 756 1061/1306/1316
Delightful colonial-style hotel with an elegant patio and arcades.

HOTEL VILLA GRANDE
★★

Tel. 756 1053
This modern hotel has a swimming pool and is situated on the outskirts of the town.

PENSIÓN CHUGUILÁ
★★

5a Ave.,to the north of the Plaza Central.
Tel. 756 1134
The rooms of this hotel overlook a pleasant interior courtyard. Several of the suites have individual fireplaces. Good restaurant.

HOTEL GIRÓN
★

6a Calle
Tel. 756 1156
Built around a small interior courtyard. This is the cheapest hotel to be found in the center of town.

COBÁN

RESTAURANTS

★★ HOTEL LA POSADA
1 Calle 4-12 Zona 2
Tel. 952 1495
Regional cuisine.

★ CAFÉ CENTRO
1a Calle between 1a Ave and 2a Ave
Tel. 952 2192
Offers a varied and reasonably priced menu.

HOTELS

★★ HOTEL LA POSADA
1 Calle 4–12 Zona 2
Tel. 952 1495
Well located in the center of town. A

---

colonial-style residence with pleasant well-appointed rooms.

★ HOTEL OXIB PECK
1 Calle 12–11 Zona 1
Tel. 952 1039
Rooms have showers but no windows.

BETWEEN ANTIGUA AND SOLOLÁ

RESTAURANTS

★★ CHICHOY I
(63 miles on the Panamerican Highway)
Local cuisine.

★★ CHICHOY II
(45 miles on the Panamerican Highway)

★★ KATOK
(54 miles on the Panamerican route)
Grilled food in a typical hut.

FLORES

USEFUL INFORMATION

BANK AND BUREAU DE CHANGE
BANCO HIPOTECARIO
On the Isla Flores (near the church).
Open Mon.–Fri. 8.30am–2.30pm
It is also possible to change money at hotel receptions.

TRANSPORT

TOUR OPERATORS/ TRAVEL AGENTS
EXPLORE
Ave Centroamerica
Tel. 926 0655 / 926 0843
(Flores/Santa Elena airport office).
Guatemala City:
Ave La Reforma 12-51 Zona 10
Guatemala Ciudad 01010
Tel. 331 6243
Fax 334 1179
Other offices in Mexico, Guatemala and Belize.

EL TUCAN
Calle Centroamérica
Tel. 926 0577
Fax 926 1380
Hotel, restaurant and travel agency.
VIAJES Y REPRESENTACIONES ITZA
Near Flores in Santa Elena
Fax 926 0624
SAN JUAN TRAVEL
6a Ave "A", 2-41, Zona 1
Santa Elena
Tel. 926 0041/42, 926 0514, 926 0562
Take buses from here to Tikal, Ceibal, Uaxactún, Chetumal and Guatemala City.

CAR RENTAL
KOKA
Flores Airport
Tel. 926 1233/0526
RENTA VEHICULOS
Hotel *Tayasal*
Opposite the *Gasolinera* Chevron
Tel. 926 0333

RESTAURANTS

★★★ EL JACAL
Calle Flores
On the left on arriving in Flores
Delicious house specialties, good soups and salads. Meals are served under a straw canopy.

★★ EL TUCAN ★
Calle Centro América
Tel. 926 0577
Fax 926 1380
Closed Sun.
Excellent food served in very pleasant surroundings. Superb view over the lake, especially in the evening. Regional cuisine.

★★ LA MESA DE LOS MAYAS
Flores
(On the left coming from Santa Elena)
Tel./Fax 926 1240
Open daily.
Regional cuisine.

HOTELS

★★★ HOTEL DEL PATIO-TIKAL
Near Santa Elena airport
Tel. 926 1229/0104
A recently built colonial-style building

GUATEMALA CITY NORTH

0   100   500 yards

anillo
puente
Martin Prado

río La Barranca

ZONA 3

CEMETERIO GENERAL

6a avenida

27
30a calle
11a calle
32a calle
33a calle

7a avenida

---

which offers comfortable and reasonably priced rooms.

★★ HOTEL MAYA INTERNACIONAL
Near Santa Elena airport
Tel. 926 1276
Situated right on the shore of the lagoon, these bungalows are reached via a footbridge. Restaurant under a large straw canopy overlooking the lake.

★★ HOTEL PETÉN
Calle Centroamérica
Tel. 926 0692/0523/0593

Map of Guatemala City showing Zonas 1–6, Colonia Las Victorias, Colonia Vivibien, and key landmarks.

A friendly hotel with well-maintained, comfortable rooms. The owner has a minibus and is happy to drive guests to Tikal

★★ LA CASONA DE LA ISLA ★
Calle Centroamérica
Tel. 926 0692
Fax 926 1258
A newly built hotel with smart décor and impeccable rooms.

★★ HOTEL YUM KAX
At the end of
San Benito wharf
Tel. 926 0686
Little character but some rooms have a view of the lake.

GUATEMALA CITY

USEFUL INFORMATION

EMBASSIES, CONSULATES
AMERICAN EMBASSY
Ave la Reforma 7–01
Zona 10
Tel. 311 541
BRITISH EMBASSY
7a Ave 5–10 (8th floor)
Zona 4
Tel. 321 601 (602 and 604)
CANADIAN EMBASSY
Edificio Edyma Plaza
(8th floor)
13a Calle, 8–44
Zona 13
Tel. 448 6102

EL SALVADOR EMBASSY
18a Calle, 14–30
Zona 13
Tel. 334 3942 / 334 8196
HONDURAS EMBASSY
13a Calle, 12-33 Zona
10, Colonia Oakland
Tel. 337 4337
MEXICAN EMBASSY
Edificio Centro Ejecutivo
(7th floor)

15a Calle, 3–20
Zona 10
Tel. 448 7254 to 58
MEXICAN CONSULATE
13a Calle, 7–30 Zona 9
Tel. 331 8165 / 332 5249

BANK AND BUREAU DE CHANGE
VISA/MASTERCARD
7 Ave 6–26, Zona 9
Tel. 339 7436
Open 8am–8pm

HOSPITALS
CENTRO MÉDICO
6a Ave 3–47 Zona 10
Tel. 332 3555
HOSPITAL HERRERA LLERANDI
6a Ave 8–71, Zona 10
Tel. 336 6771 to 6775 / 332 0444 to 0448

GUATEMALA CITY SOUTH

0   100   500 yards

TOURIST OFFICE
INGUAT
7a Ave 1–17 Zona 4
Tel. 331 1333 to 1347
Fax 331 8893

MAIN POST OFFICE
OFICINA DE CORREOS
7 Ave and 12a Calle,
Zona 1
Open Mon.–Fri.,
8am–4.30pm

Stamps, poste restantes, possible to send packages weighing more than 4lb (the only post office in the country that operates this service).

CULTURE

LIBROS LUNA Y SOL
12 Calle 13 55 Zona 1
Tel. 230 2976
International bookstore.

CENTRAL MARKET
Just behind the cathedral on Ave 9, between Calles 6 and 8.

A market with plenty of character. Local crafts and souvenirs at reasonable prices.

NATIONAL PALACE
Central Park.
Open daily: 8am–4pm

IXCHEL MUSEUM OF LOCAL COSTUMES
Campus of Francisco Marroquin University,
6a Calle final, Zona 10
Tel. 331 3739 /
331 3634

NATIONAL MUSEUM OF ARCHEOLOGY AND ETHNOLOGY
Finca La Aurora,
Edificio 5, Zona 13
Tel 472 0489

Open Tue.–Fri.
9am–4pm, Sat
9am–noon and 2–4pm.
Closed Mon.

NATIONAL MUSEUM OF MODERN ART
Finca la Aurora,
Edificio 6, Zona 13
Zona 13
Open Tue.–Fri.
9am–4pm, Sat.
9am–noon and 2–4pm.
Closed Mon.

POPOL VUH MUSEUM
Ed. Galerias Reforma
Ave La Reforma 8–60
Zona 9
Tel. 334 7121
Open Mon.-Sat.
9am–5pm.

Fax 332 0372
Ticket sales:
331 8222 / 332 1886
COPA
1a Ave 10–17/Zona 10
Tel. 361 1567/1577/
1587
Fax 332 1338
LACSA
Ave Hincaple/Calle 18
Zona 13 (hangar 60)
Tel. 331 1827/1841
Fax 332 5049
TAPSA
Ave Hincaple/Calle 18
Zona 13 (hangar 14)
Tel. 331 4860/9180
Fax 334 5572
TIKAL JETS
Ave Hincaple/Calle 18
Zona 13 (hangar 8)
Tel. 332 5070 / 334 5568
Fax 334 5631
TRASLADOS
Ave Hincaple/Calle 18
Zona 13 (hangar 30)
Tel. 334 7105 / 334 7783

MOTORBIKE
RENTAL
MOTO-RENT
11 Calle Zona 9
*Hondas for rent from
around $20 for a day
(Honda XL 185).*

CAR RENTAL
AHORRENT
Bd Liberación 4–83,
Zona 9
Tel. 332 0544 / 332 7515
Fax 331 5621
Airport: 332 6491
AVIS
12a Calle 2–74 Zona 9
Tel. 331 6990 / 332 4596
Fax 332 1263
Airport: 331 0017
BUDGET
Ave la Reforma 15–0,
Zona 9
Tel. 332 2591 / 331 6546
Fax 331 2807
Airport: 331 0 273
DOLLAR
Ave la Reforma 6–14,
Zona 9
Tel. 334 8285 / 334 1538
Fax 332 6745
Airport: 331 7185
HERTZ
7 Ave 14–76 Zona 9
Tel. 332 2242 / 331 5412
Fax 331 7924
Airport: Tel. 331 1711
NATIONAL
14a Calle 1–42 Zona 10
Tel. 368 0175
Fax 337 0221
Airport: 331 8365/ 8218
TABARINI
2a Calle "A", 7-30
Zona 10
Tel. 331 6108
Fax 334 1925
Airport: 331 4755

TRANSPORT

AIRLINES
AEROVIAS
Ave Hincaple, on the
corner of Calle 18,
Zona 13
Tel. 332 5686
AVCOM
Ave Hincaple/Calle 18
Zona 13 (hangar 21)
Tel. 331 5831
Fax 332 4946
AVIATECA
Ave Hincaple, 12-22
Zona 13
Tel. 331 8222
Fax 331 7401
GROUPE
AVIATECA/LACSA/NICA/
TACA
Reservations:
Tel. 334 7222

TOUR OPERATORS/
TRAVEL AGENTS
SERVICIOS TURÍSTICOS
DEL PETÉN (STP)
2 Ave 7–78 Zona 10
Tel. 334 6236/1807/
1813
Fax 334 6237
EL TUCÁN
Tour operator, hotel and
restaurant.
6a. Ave 10–36 Zona 1
Tel. 350 1380
EXPLORE
Edificio Suites Reforma,
Bureau 1
Ave La Reforma, 12–51
Zona 10
Tel. 331 6243
Fax 334 1179
IZABAL ADVENTURE
TOURS
(ALFREDO TORRIELLO)
Edificio La Galería,
office 10,
7a Ave 14–44 Zona 9
Tel. 334 0323/0324
Fax 334 0341
*Izabal region,
Río Dulce.*
MAYA EXPEDITIONS
Edificio Tauro,
office 104
15a Calle, 1-91 Zona 10
Tel. 337 4666
Fax 594 7748
TURISMO EK CHUAH
(JEAN-LUC BRACONNIER)
3 Calle 6–24,
Zona 2
Tel. 232 0745
Fax 232 4375

RESTAURANTS

*** JEAN-FRANCOIS
Diagonal 6 (Villa de
Guadelupe), 13-63
Zona 10
Tel. 333 4785
French cuisine.

*** PUERTO BARRIOS
7a Ave 12-35 Zona 9
Tel. 334 1302
Fax 338 377
*Fashionable
restaurant with
attractive prices.*

*Décor might not be to
everyone's taste.
Specializes in fish and
seafood dishes.*

** COSTA BRAVA
15 Ave 7–79,
Zona 13
Tel. 331 1288
*International cuisine;
the Spanish dishes are
particularly good.*

** EL GRAN PAVO ★
13 Calle 4–41,
Zona 1
Tel. 251 0933
*The menu offers every
imaginable Guatemalan
specialty.*

** EL MESÓN DEL
QUIJOTE
11a Calle, 6–35 Zona 1
*Band in the evenings,
good atmosphere, late
closing. Spanish food.*

** EL PARADOR
Calzada Roosevelt,
30–92 Zona 7
*Excellent local cuisine
("platos típicos").*

** EL RODEO
7a Ave 14-84 Zona 9
Tel. 331 4028
*One of the best
steakhouses in Poptún,
very popular with the
local people.*

** LOS ANTOJITOS ★
Ave la Reforma 15-02
Zona 9
Tel. 331 3066
*Guatemalan cuisine.
Specializes in the
preparation of typical*

dishes from the country's various different regions.

* ARRIN CUAN
5a Ave 3-27 Zona 1
Tel. 238 0242, 238 0784
Guatemalan dishes.

* NAIS
Edificio Plaza, 7a Ave 6–52, Plaza 6–26, Zona 9
Tel. 331 9095
Cheese fondues, grilled steaks. Very reasonable.

* LOS CEBOLLINES
12 Calle 6–36 Zona 9
Tel. 331 7065
Another branch at 6a Ave, 9–75 Zona 1
Tel. 232 7750
Mexican food.

* ZURICH
4a Ave 12-09, Zona 10
Tel. 336 3312
Very pleasant café , ideal for afternoon teas (tea, coffee, pastries).

SPORT

WALKING AND PONY TREKKING
TURISMO EK CHUAH ★
(JEAN-LUC BRACONNIER)
3 Calle 6–24, Zona 2
Tel. 232 0745
Fax 232 4375
Walks and pony treks, with excursions to the top of volcanos, excursions in the Petén (archeology, nature), and tourist

routes around the sites of main interest (Guatemala and neighboring countries).

BUNJEE JUMPING AND RAFTING
MAYA EXPEDITIONS
(TAMMY RIDENOUR)
15 Calle 1-91, Zona 10
Tel. 337 4666
Fax 594 7748

SCUBA DIVING
PANA DIVERS
16 Calle 7–15, Zona 9
Tel. 334 3870
Fax 334 3871
On Lake Atitlán.

SCUBA DIVING AND FISHING
EXCURSIONES SPROSS
2 Ave 3–25, Zona 9
Tel./Fax 332 3594
Fishing and diving in the Cayes south of Belize (two hours from Livingston and on the islands).

CAVING
CANDELARIA
Reservations: Servicios Turísticos del Petén
2 Ave 7–78, Zona 10
Tel. 334 6235, 334 6236
Fax 334 6237
Discover the caves of Candelaria and Verapaz (Mucbilhá, Raxrujá) seven hours by road from Cobán in a four-wheel-drive vehicle.

NIGHTLIFE

CONCIERTO DE LOS 60
7 Ave and 8 Calle Zona 1
Entrance is free and drinks are affordable in this popular bar.

EL ESTABLO
Ave la Reforma 11–83 Zona 10
Bar with good music.

HOTELS

***** HOTEL CAMINO REAL
Ave la Reforma 14–1 Zona 10
Tel. 333 4663
International luxury hotel. Expensive.

***** HOTEL MARRIOTT
7a Ave 15–45 Zona 9
Tel. 331 7777
Fax 332 1877
Formerly the El Dorado.

**** HOTEL CORTIJO REFORMA
Ave la Reforma 2–18 Zona 9
Tel. 332 0712, 332 6612-16
Fax 331 8876
Rooms all have minibar, kitchenette and balcony; some have a view over the volcanos surrounding the town.

**** HOTEL GUATEMALA FIESTA
Ave La Reforma, 15–25 Zona 10
Tel. 332 2555 / 2556
Luxury hotel with heated swimming pool.

*** HOTEL CROWNE PLAZA LAS AMERICAS ★
Ave Las Americas 9–08 Zona 13
Tel. 337 0601, 333 4633
Close to the airport. High-class hotel with a swimming pool. Excellent service.

*** HOTEL DEL CENTRO
13a Calle, 4–55 Zona 1
Tel. 238 1281 / 230 6116
Fax 230 0228
Comfortable, well-equipped rooms.

*** HOTEL PAN AMERICAN ★
9a Calle, 5–63 Zona 1
Tel. 232 6807/8/9
Fax 232 6402
A local atmosphere.

*** HOTEL RITZ CONTINENTAL
9a Ave "A", 10–13 Zona 1
Tel. 238 1671–5
Fax 232 4659
Comfortable rooms and a good restaurant.

** HOTEL CENTENARIO
6a Calle 5–33 Zona 1
Tel. 238 0381
Fax 238 2039
Comfortable, clean rooms.

** HOTEL COLONIAL
7a. Ave 14–19 Zona 1
Tel. 232 6722 / 232 2955 / 238 1208
Fax 232 8671
Charming colonial hotel, very clean and quiet.

** HOTEL RESIDENCIA REFORMA "LA CASA GRANDE"
Ave La Reforma 7–67 Zona 10
Tel. 331 0907 / 331 7893
Fax 332 2736
White, square building, with a marked Spanish influence. Beautiful light rooms with shower and toilets.

** HOTEL VILLA ESPAÑOLA
2a Calle, 7–51 Zona 9
Tel. 336 5417 / 336 5611
Next to the tower of the Reformer, a discreet imitation of the Eiffel Tower. Charming, Spanish-style hotel.

** POSADA BELÉN
13 Calle "A" 10–3, Zona 1
Tel. 253 4530 / 232 9226
Superb colonial building in a quiet street in the city center. Booking essential.

* HOTEL CHALET SUIZO
14 Calle 6–82 Zona 1
Tel. 251 3786
A typical and friendly hotel. Rooms with or without bathrooms, around a small courtyard lacking in charm.

* HOTEL SPRING ★
8a Ave 12–65 Zona 1
Tel. 232 6637 / 230 2958
Large, airy rooms with windows overlooking an enormous patio.

HUEHUE-TENANGO

RESTAURANTS

** LAS VEGAS
At the intersection with the Panamerican highway.
Local and international cuisine.

* EBONY RESTAURANT ★
2 Calle/ 5 Ave (at the corner of the Plaza Central).
Open morning, lunchtime and evening.
The patron is a good source of local information and will gladly provide details of local activities, special events, timetables, and available transport. Local cuisine. Serves good breakfasts and fruit juices.

HOTELS

** HOTEL DEL PRADO
Canton San José
Zona 5
Tel. 764 2150
Situated at the entrance to the town, coming from the Panamerican highway. A fairly new hotel which provides a good standard of service.

** HOTEL ZACULEU
5a Ave 1–14 Zona 1
Tel. 764 1086
An attractive colonial building which has been recently restored. The hotel also has a very good restaurant.

** LOS CUCHUMATANES
Brasilia district
Zona 7
Tel. 764 1951 / 764 2815

LAKE IZABAL

HÔTEL

FINCA EL PARAISO
At the north shore of Lake Izabal, close to the fort San Felipe. Make reservations in Guatemala City.

LIVINGSTON

RESTAURANTS

* AFRICAN PLACE
Just before the Flamingo Hotel, twenty minutes from the wharf market place
A hotel and restaurant. Fairly comfortable rooms. The restaurant is excellent. Creole cuisine.

* EL MALECÓN
100 yards from the wharf.
A large restaurant which serves very good grilled fish. Try the "tapado" (fish and seafood cooked in coconut milk).

HOTELS

*** HOTEL TUCAN DUGU
Tel. 948 1572 / 948 1588
Livingston's chic hotel. Very comfortable rooms.

* CASA ROSADA
By the river.
Impeccably clean, fairly comfortable with communal shower.

HOTEL GARIFUNA
Dull and charmless, but excellent value for money.

PANAJACHEL

USEFUL INFORMATION

TOURIST OFFICE
OFICINA DEL INGUAT
Edificio Rincon Sai,
Ave Santander, 1-30
Zona 2
Tel. 762 1392

TRANSPORT

MOTORBIKE RENTAL
MOTO-RENT
Calle Principal
and Calle Los Arboles
Bicycle and motorbike hire by the hour, the day or the week. (Honda, Suzuki and others). A good way of exploring the neighboring towns and villages (Sololá, Chichicastenango). Note, it is not possible to do a complete tour of Lake Atitlán by motorbike.

RESTAURANTS

** AL CHISME
3a Ave 0-42
Simple food such as salads and sandwiches. Very popular with travellers.

** EL PATIO
Ave Santander 2-21
Worth for both food and atmosphere.

** RESTAURANTE LA LAGUNA
On the corner of Calle Principal and Calle Los Arboles
Regional cuisine and amazing breakfasts.

** THE LAST RESORT
Calle 14 de Febero / Ave Santander esquina, on the left approaching the beach
Excellent and moderately priced. A popular place for Americans to meet for an evening drink. Not to be missed.

HOTELS

**** HOTEL ATITLÁN ★
At the edge of Lake Atitlán, one mile from the center of town on the road to Los Encuentros.
Tel. 762 1429 / 762 1441
The best hotel in Panajachel.

Comfortable rooms, heated swimming pool and a good restaurant. Superb view of the lake and gardens.

**** HOTEL DEL LAGO
Next to Calle Rancho Grande beach
(at the end of Lake Atitlán).
Tel. 762 1555-60
Nice rooms with balconies and marble bathrooms. Swimming pool, restaurants and attractive gardens.

*** PLAYA LINDA
In the port.
Tel. 762 1159
Attractive rooms with fireplaces.

** HOTEL MONTERREY
Calle 15 de Febrero
Tel. 762 1126
One of the few hotels with a garden by the lakeside.

** HOTEL PRIMAVERA
Calle Santander
Tel. 762 1157
A small, friendly hotel with restaurant and garden.

* HOTEL GALINDO
Calle Real
Tel. 762 1168
Restaurant and hotel situated in a pleasant tropical garden.

POPTÚN

CAVES

NAJ TUNICH
Approximately 18 miles from Poptún
On a dirt track accessible only by four-wheel-drive vehicle. A guide is absolutely essential, information available in Poptún.

HOTELS

* HOTEL MARÍA ROSA
Opposite the Texaco service station at the exit

from the village toward Flores.
Reasonable rooms with shower.

★ FINCA IXOBEL ★
One mile to the south of Poptún, on the road to Río Dulce.
Several rooms with shower. Basic. Meeting point for visitors taking excursions to the surrounding caves. Four-day pony treks into the jungle organized from the finca.

★ VILLA DE LOS CASTELLANOS
6 miles from Poptún on the Flores road, by the north exit of the village Machaquila.
Tel. 927 7222

PUERTO BARRIOS

HOTELS

★★ HOTEL DEL NORTE
1a Ave 6-7,
by the sea.
Tel. 948 0087/2116
Quaint, colonial and charming hotel with a good restaurant in its large dining room.

★ HOTEL EUROPA
8a Ave between Calles 8 and 9.
Pleasant dining room.

RÍO PETEXBATÚN

HOTELS

★★ POSADA DE MATEO ★
Take a boat from Sayaxche.
Tel. 234 03 23

To organize in advance contact the Posada Caribe Agency in Sayaxché. There are several bungalows overlooking the Río Petexbatún, situated in the heart of the countryside, but nevertheless with a certain amount of luxury.

★ POSADA PETEXBATUN AND POSADA CARIBE
Take a boat from Sayaxche.
Somewhat more spartan than Posada de Mateo.

QUETZAL-TENANGO

USEFUL INFORMATION

EMBASSY, CONSULATE
CONSULAT DU MEXICO
9 Ave 6-19 Zona 1
Tel. 761 2547
Open Mon.–Fri.
9am–11am

BANK AND BUREAU DE CHANGE
BANCO DE GUATEMALA
12 Ave 5-12 Zona 1
Open:
Mon.–Thu. 8.30am–2pm
Fri. 8.30am–2.30pm
Sat. 8.30am–2pm

TELEPHONE CENTER
GUATEL
15 Ave./ 3a Calle
Open until midnight

TOURIST OFFICE
OFICINA DEL INGUAT
Casa de la Cultura
7a Calle 11–35
Zona 1
Tel. 761 4931

MAIN POST OFFICE
OFICINA DE CORREOS
15a Ave and 4 Calle,
Zona 1.

LANGUAGE COURSES

CASA XELAHU DE ESPAÑOL
9 Calle 11–26 Zona 1
Tel. 761 628
Fax 761 2628
Cost: $160 per week ($130 low-season).

CENTRO DE ESTUDIOS DE ESPAÑOL POP WUH
1 Calle 17–72
and 5 Calle 2-40,
Zona 1
Tel. 761 8286
Cost: $120 per week.

CENTRO DE LENGUAJE AMÉRICA LATINA
19 Ave 3-63 Zona 3
Tel. 761 6416
Cost: $120 per week.

ENGLISH CLUB & INTERNATIONAL LANGUAGE SCHOOL
3 Calle 15–16 Zona 1
Courses in Spanish and Mayan.

GUATEMALENSIS
19 Ave 2-41 Zona 1
Cost: $120 per week.

INEPAS
15a Ave./ 5a Calle
esquina Zona 1
Aims to finance social projects in the region.

INSTITUTO CENTRO AMÉRICA (ICA)
1 Calle 16-93 Zona 1
Tel. 761 6786
Cost: $120 per week.

MINERVA SPANISH SCHOOL
24 Ave 4-39 Zona 3
Cost: $135 per week.

SAB SPANISH CENTER
1 Calle 12-35 Zona 1
Tel. 761 2042
Full-board accommodation is available.

SPANISH SCHOOL JUAN SISAY
15 Ave 8-38 Zona 1
Cost: $120 per week.

RESTAURANTS

★★★ EL KOPETÍN
14 Ave 3–51 Zona 1
Specializes in seafood.

★★ ROYAL PARIS
2a Calle 14 "A"–32
Zona 1
Small restaurant with a pleasant atmosphere. Good value for money. Chocolate crèpes are highly recommended. French and European cuisine.

★ RESTAURANTE SHANGHAI
4 Calle 12–22 Zona 1
Tel. 761 4154
A Guatemalan version of Chinese cuisine.

★ CAFE BAVIERA ★
5a Calle 12-50
Zona 1
Open throughout the day (closes at 8pm). Coffee shop serving cakes, tea, coffee, house specials and drinks.

HOTELS

★★★ PENSION BONIFAZ
4a Calle 10-50
Zona 1
Tel. 761 2959/ 2182/ 2279
Superb ancient settings and a high standard of service.

★★★ VILLA REAL PLAZA
4a Calle 11–22 Zona 1
Tel. 761 6036/ 4045/ 6180

★ HOTEL MODELO
14a Ave "A" 2–31
Zona 1
Tel. 761 2529/ 2715
Built around a beautiful flower garden with a gallery leading to spacious, well-equipped rooms.

NIGHTLIFE

CINEMA ALPINO
Pl. Ciani, 24 Ave
and 4 Calle Zona 3

CINEMA CADORE
13 Ave and 7 Calle,
Zona 1

CINEMA ROMA
14 Ave A and Calle A
Zona 1

RÍO DULCE

HOTEL

**** CATAMARAN
ISLAND HOTEL**
Ten mins. from Río
Dulce by boat, at the
edge of Lake Izabal.
Tel. 947 8361
Make reservations from
Guatemala City on
Tel. 336 4450.
*Swimming pool, tennis
courts and restaurant.*

** HOTEL MARIMONTE
Tel. 947 8585
From Guatemala City:
Tel. 230 1421/ 6512

SANTA CATARINA PALOPÓ

HOTELS

***** HOTEL VILLA
SANTA CATARINA**
On the road from
Panajachel to Santa
Catarina.
Tel. 762 1291/ 2013
*Rooms with a view of
Lake Atitlán, some with
a view of the San Pedro
volcano. Swimming
pool and restaurant.*

SANTO TOMÁS DE CASTILLA

HOTEL

****** CAYOS
DEL DIABLO**
Aldea Las
Pavas,

four miles from Puerto
Barrios on the
Livingston road.
Tel. 948 2361/ 2363
*A luxurious and
comfortable resting
place when touring the
Caribbean coast.*

SAYAXCHÉ

TRANSPORT

**TOUR OPERATORS/
TRAVEL AGENTS**
VIAJES LA
MONTAÑA/POSADA CARIBE
Calle principal
Tel./ Fax 928 6114
*Regions: Ceibal,
Petexbatún area,
Usumacinta. This is the
best place to get
information about
traveling to Posada
Mateo which is only
accessible by boat (see
Río Petexbatún).*

HOTEL

* HOTEL GUAYACAN
Tel. 928 6111
*Basic but comfortable
rooms. Arranges trips to
the sites of Piedras
Negras, Ceibal,
Aguateca, Yaxchilán
and the Altar de
Sacrificios.*

TIKAL

HOTELS

****** HOTEL
CAMINO REAL**
Halfway between Flores
and Tikal, in the village
of El Remate.

Tel. 926 0207
Fax 926 0222
*Ideally situated at
the edge of Lake Petén
Itzá, this hotel does
not really merit its high
prices. Expensive.*

** JAGUAR INN
Situated at the
entrance to the site,
close to the
museum.
Tel. 926 0002
*Four bungalows only,
with shower and toilet.
Advance reservations
highly recommended,
either in writing or by
telephone.*

** JUNGLE LODGE
Close to the entrance
to the site.
Reserve from
Guatemala City on
Tel. 476 0294/ 8775.
*Two types of
accommodation are
offered, with different
levels of comfort: new
rooms in small
bungalows and
refurbished rooms
with showers and toilets.*

RESTAURANTS

***** RESTAURANTE
PARQUE TIKAL**
In the concrete building
of the Stele Museum .
Local dishes.

** COMEDOR TIKAL
One of the *comedores*
on the right when
entering the Tikal site.
Open all day.
*One of three or four
comedores which are
all in competition with
each other to feed the
hungry tourists after
their four-hour visit to
the ancient site. The
Comedor Pirámide is
without doubt the best
and cheapest of all of
these. Good regional
cuisine.*

UAXACTÚN

HOTEL

**** HOTEL
RESTAURANTE
CAMPAMENTO
"EL CHICLERO"**
*Basic but comfortable
rooms. Friendly
proprietor. (The price of
the room includes three
meals).*

YAXHÁ

SPORT

**RAMBLING AND PONY
TREKKING**
LODGE EL SOMBRERO
(JUAN JOSÉ DE LA HOZ
AND GABRIELA)
Melchor de Mencos
*Excursions from Yaxha,
on horseback or by jeep,
to Río Axul, including
visit to site.
Accommodation in
bungalows, or camping.*

◆

AMBERGRIS CAYE

RESTAURANTS

***** LILY'S
RESTAURANT**
At the eastern end of
Caribeña Street
(facing the sea).
Tel. 26 2059
Open daily, lunchtime
and evening.
*The best seafood
restaurant in town.*

** ELVI'S KITCHEN ★
Pescador Drive
(near Ambergris Street)
Tel. 26 2176 / 2404
Open for lunch
11.30am–2pm and
dinner 6.30–10pm.
*Popular meeting place.
Typical Belize dishes.*

** MARINO'S
Pescador Street (close
to Bucaneer Street)
Tel. 26 2174
*Good bar-restaurant
serving inexpensive
sandwiches and salads,
or langoustines and
other seafood.*

HOTELS

***** RAMON'S
VILLAGE RESORT**
Coconut Drive, San
Pedro

Tel. 26 2211/ 12/ 13,
26 2071
Fax 26 2214
Reservations: 26 2229
*Cabañas overlooking
the beach, bar
surrounded by coconut
trees, sailing boats and
watersports. Very
relaxed atmosphere.*

*** LILY'S CARIBBEAN LODGE
To the east of the
Caribeña facing the sea.
Tel. 26 2059
*Rooms with terraces
overlooking the sea.*

** EL PESCADOR
On the Punta Arena
beach, 1½ miles north of
San Pedro.
Tel. 26 2398,
26 2975/6/7/8
Fax 26 2245

** MARTHA'S HOTEL
San Pedro village.
Tel. 26 2053

* MILO'S HOTEL
San Pedro village.
Tel. 26 2033, 26 2196
*Fairly quiet and very
reasonably priced.
Often fully booked. Best
to arrive early in the day.*

SPORT

SCUBA DIVING
OUT ISLAND DIVERS
Barrier Reef Drive
PO Box 7, San Pedro
Tel. 26 2151
Fax 26 2810
UNIVERSAL TRAVEL
AND TOURS
Spindrift Hotel,
Barrier Reef Drive

BELIZE CITY

USEFUL INFORMATION

BANK AND BUREAU DE CHANGE
AMERICAN EXPRESS
TRAVEL/GLOBAL TRAVEL
41 Albert St.
Tel. 277 363/364
BARCLAY'S BANK
21 Albert St.
Tel. 277 211
Open Mon.–Fri.
8am–1pm and 3–6pm
THE BELIZE BANK
60 Market Square
(Opposite Swing
Bridge).
Tel. 277 132/069/082
Open Mon.–Thurs.
8am–1pm.
Fri. 8am–1pm, 3–6pm

TELEPHONE CENTER
BELIZEAN
TELECOMMUNICATION,
LTD (BTL.)
St. Thomas Street,
PO Box 603
Tel. 232 868, 232 096
Open Mon.–Sat.
8am–9pm,
Sun. 8am–noon

TOURIST OFFICE
THE BELIZE TOURIST
BOARD
83 North Front Street
Tel. 277 213, 273 255,
275 312
Fax 277 490

MAIN POST OFFICE
POST OFFICE
Queen Street and
North Front Street
Open Mon.–Fri.
8am–noon and 1–5pm
(Fri. 1–4.30pm)
*Stamps for sale,
possible to send
packages to a poste
restante.*

TRANSPORT

AIRLINES
AEROVIAS
55 Regent Street
Tel. 275 445/46
ISLAND AIR
Municipal Airport
Tel. 231 140/707
MAYA AIRWAYS
Municipal Airport
Tel. 235 794/95
Fax 230 585/031
SKY BIRD
Municipal Airport
Tel. 232 596
TROPIC AIR
Municipal Airport
Tel. 245 671/720
Fax 232 794

CAR RENTAL
BUDGET RENT A CAR
771 Bella Vista
Northern Highway
Tel. 232 435, 233 986
Fax 230 237
CRYSTAL AUTO RENTAL
1½ miles along Northern
Highway
Tel. 231 600
Fax 231 900
NATIONAL CAR RENTAL
12 North Front Street
Tel. 231 587 / 231 650
Fax 231 686

CENTRAL BUS STATION
BATTY BROTHERS
BUS SERVICE
15 Mosul Street
Tel 272 025, 274 037,
273 929, 277 146
Fax 278 991
*Daily departures,
connections to the west
and north of the country.*
JAME'S BUS
Pound Yard Bridge
*Very small company
(two buses).
Connections to the
south of the country.*
URBINA BUS
Cinderella Pl.
*Connections to Belize
City–Orange Walk.*
VENUS BUS LINE CO.
Magazine Road
Tel. 273 354, 277 390,
279 907
*Connections to the
north and west of the
country.*
Z-LINE BUS SERVICE
53 Main Street
Tel. 222 165
*Connections: Belize
City–Dangrige–Punta
Gorda..*

RESTAURANTS

*** THE GRILL
164 Newton Barracks
Tel. 234 201
*Considered to be one of
the best restaurants in
Belize City. International
cuisine. Variety of
dishes.*

*** NEW CHON SAAN NO. 1
55 Euphrates Ave
Tel. 272 709
*Pleasant atmosphere.
One of the best Chinese
restaurants in Belize
City. Also offers a
takeaway service.*

** MARLIN
13 Regent Street West
Facing Belize River
Tel. 276 995
Good fish and seafood

*restaurant. Varied
menu.*

* MACY'S CAFÉ
18 Bishop St.
Tel. 273 419
Open lunchtime and
evening until 10pm.
Closed Sun.
*Different menu each
day. Manageress is very
friendly. Local creole
cuisine.*

* MOM'S TRIANGLE INN
7145 Slaughter House
Road
PO Box 332
Tel. 245 073, 235 344
Open 6am–10pm
Closed Sat.
*Large cafeteria which
tends to attract a mixed
clientele. Lively, friendly
atmosphere. Music.*

* SHEN'S PEKING PANDA
Queen Street,
opposite no. 3
*Chinese restaurant
which serves delicious
food at reasonable
prices.*

HOTELS

***** RAMADA ROYAL REEF HOTEL
Newton Barracks
PO Box 1758,
Tel. 230 638, 231 591,
232 670
Fax 232 660
*Luxury hotel. Extremely
expensive.*

**** RADISSON FORT GEORGE HOTEL
2 Marine Parade
PO Box 321
Tel. 277 400
Reservations: 233 333
Fax 273 820
*Luxury hotel with
swimming pool, several
restaurants and bars.*

*** HOTEL CHATEAU CARIBBEAN
6 Marine Parade
PO Box 947
Tel. 230 658, 230 800,
272 813, 272 826
Fax 230 900
*A former hospital, this
building has been
converted into a
reasonably comfortable*

hotel with fully air-conditioned rooms and a good restaurant.

** GLENTHORNE MANOR
27 Barrack Road
PO Box 1278
Tel. 244 212
An attractive large white wooden house run by a friendly family and offering eight clean rooms with shower and toilets.

** FORT STREET GUEST HOUSE
4 Fort St.
Tel. 230 116
Fax 278 808
Breakfast included in the price of the room.

* SEA SIDE GUEST HOUSE
3 Prince St.
Tel. 278 339
Wooden house in a quiet neighborhood on the sea front. Clean and basic.

SPORT

FISHING
BLUE MARLIN LODGE
15 Mahogany Street
Dangriga
Tel. 522 243, 522 759
Fax 522 296
Fishing on the lagoon and coral reef.
MANATEE LODGE
Jamie & Amparo Claiborne
PO Box 1242
Tel./ Fax 212 040
Specializes in inland freshwater fishing.

SCUBA DIVING AND FISHING
EL PESCADOR
See this hotel in Ambergris Cave.
TURNEFFE ISLAND LODGE
PO Box 480
Tel. 230 236
Fax 223 711
Fishing and island tours of three to seven days.

EXCURSIONS, TRAVEL AGENCIES
BELIZE TRAVEL ADVENTURES
168 North Front Street
2nd floor,
PO Box 1313
Tel. 232 618
Fax 233 196
DISCOVER EXPEDITIONS BELIZE
126 Freetown Road
PO Box 1217
Tel. 230 748 / 230 749 / 231 063
Fax 230 750 / 230 263
At the Ramada Hotel:
Tel. 230 625
Airport: 252 2343

BOAT TRIPS
TIKI TOURS
23 Regent St.
Tel. 245 065
Discover the sites by boat. River route leads right up to the ruins.

NIGHTLIFE

LINDBERGH'S LANDING
162A Newton Barracks
Tel. 230 890
Outdoor bar with pleasant atmosphere (overlooking the sea).

LOUISVILLE DEMOCRATIC BAR
69 Hyde Lane
Small friendly bar in a rather dangerous area of the city. Take a taxi back to your hotel.

BELMOPÁN

HOTELS

** BELMOPÁN CONVENTION HOTEL
Bliss Parade/ Constitution Drive
Tel. 822 130, 822 327, 822 340, 823 066
Fairly expensive but comfortable.

* EL REY INN
23 Moho St.
Tel. 823 438

CAYE CAULKER

RESTAURANTS

** MARIN'S RESTAURANT
Situated to the west of the Tropical Paradise Hotel.
Closed Sun.
Tel. 2 2104
Indoor and open-air restaurant. The excellence of the food makes up for the slow service.

** THE SANDBOX ★
Front Street
Tel. 2 2200
Open: evening.
Closed Sun.
Varied international menu. Food is good and portions are generous. Indoor and outdoor restaurant with a pleasant view over the sea.

** MARTÍNEZ CARIBBEAN INN
On Front Street next to the Miramar Hotel.

HOTELS

** RAINBOW HOTEL
On the beach.
Tel. 2 2123
Basic rooms, well-kept and clean.

** TROPICAL PARADISE ★
On the beach.
Tel. 2 2124 / 2 2063
Clean, airy rooms. Restaurant and bar.

* TOM'S HOTEL
Facing the sea.
Tel. 2 2102
Very clean and reasonably priced.

SPORT

SCUBA DIVING
FRENCHIES DIVING
Tel. 2 2234
Daytime and night dives. Diving certificates awarded (PADI).

COROZAL

SPORT

WALKING AND POT-HOLING
ADVENTURE INN
Consejo Shores
Tel. 442 187

ORANGE WALK

HOTELS

** HOTEL D*VICTORIA
40 Belize-Corozal Road
Tel. 322 518, 323 050, 323 390

* JANE'S HOTEL
2 Baker's St.
Tel. 322 473

PLACENTIA

SPORT

FISHING
KINGFISHER RESTAURANT AND BAR
Tel. 623 175

SCUBA DIVING
RUM POINT INN
Tel. 623 241, 623 242
Fax 623 240

SCUBA DIVING AND FISHING
THE COVE RESORT
Point Placentia
Tel. 622 024

PUNTA GORDA

TRANSPORT

CAR RENTAL
KING ALISTAIR
Texaco Service Station
Tel. 722 126

HOTELS

* PUNTA CALIENTE
108 José María Nuñez Street
Tel. 722 561

* BELIZE TRAVEL ADVENTURES
65 Front St.
Very unlike its name, this travel agency also runs a dull hotel.

RESTAURANT

* MIRA MAR
95 Front Street
Pleasant Chinese restaurant.

SAN IGNACIO

USEFUL INFORMATION

BANK AND BUREAU DE CHANGE
THE BELIZE BANK LTD
16 Burns Ave
Tel. 92 2031
Fax 92 2263
Open: Mon.–Fri.
8am–1pm, Fri. also
3–6pm

TELEPHONE CENTER
BELIZE
TELECOMMUNICATION,
LTD (B.T.L.)
Burns Ave
Cano's Gift Shop Bldg
Tel. 92 2052
Fax 92 2057
Open: Mon.–Fri.
8am–noon and 1–4pm,
Sat. 8am–noon
Closed Sun.

HOSPITAL
At the top of Waight's
Street. (west of the town
center)
Tel. 92 2066

MAIN POST OFFICE
POST OFFICE
Government House
Buena Vista Road
(2nd floor)

RESTAURANTS

* EVA'S RESTAURANT AND BAR ★
22 Burns Avenue
Tel. 92 2267
Open morning, afternoon
and evening.
*This pleasant restaurant
is an ever-popular
meeting point for
travelers and is an
excellent information
center for the whole
area.*

* MAXIM'S CHINESE RESTAURANT
On the corner of Far
West and Bull Tree
roads

Open lunchtime
11.30am–2.30pm,
evening 5pm–midnight.
*A rather dismal location,
but the Asiatic
specialties are excellent.*

HOTELS

*** SAN IGNACIO HOTEL
18 Buena Vista Street
PO Box 33
Tel. 92 2034, 92 2125
Fax 92 2134
*Situated on a hillside
with a superb view over
the rainforest and river.
Pleasant, friendly hotel
with a restaurant, bar
and swimming pool.
Often full.*

CHAA CREEK COTTAGE
77 Burns Avenue
PO Box 53
Tel. 92 2037
Fax 92 2501
*Setting-out point for
expeditions on
horseback.*

** MAYA MOUNTAIN LODGE & TOURS
3/4 Mile Criosto Rey
Road, PO Box 46
Tel. 92 21 64
Fax 92 2029
*Bungalows in the jungle
with bed, bathroom and
toilets. Visit the ruins of
Tikal and Xunantunich,
take a trip in a kayak,
and simply explore the
breathtaking mountains
and rainforest. Meals
are included in the price
of the bungalows.*

◆

CERRO VERDE

RESTAURANT

*** MONTAÑA HOTEL RESTAURANT ★
Tel. 222 8000
Fax 222 1508

*Constructed in order to
make the most of the
breathtaking view over
the Izalco volcano.*

LAKE COATEPEQUE

HOTEL-RESTAURANT

*** HOTEL DEL LAGO
Tel. 446 9511
Fax 279 1143
*The best hotel in the
area. Swimming pool.
Pleasant restaurant with
a stunning view of the
lake. Local dishes.*

HOTEL

** HOTEL TORREMOLINOS
Tel. 446 9437
Fax 441 1859
*Swimming pool and
restaurant.*

SAN SALVADOR

USEFUL INFORMATION

EMBASSIES AND CONSULATES
AMERICAN EMBASSY
Bd Santa Elena
Antiguo Cuscatlán
Tel. 278 4444
Fax 278 6011
BELIZE EMBASSY
Condominio Médico,
Local 34 (2nd floor)
Bd Tutunichpa,
Urb. La Esperanza
Tel. 226 35 88
BRITISH EMBASSY
Paseo General Escalón,
no. 4828
Tel. 224 0473
HONDURAS EMBASSY
37a Ave Sur no. 530
Colonia Flor Blanca
Tel. 223 2222
Fax 221 2248
MEXICAN EMBASSY
Calle Circunvalación y
Pasaje no.12, Colonia
San Benito
Tel. 298 1176
Fax 298 2651
NICARAGUAN EMBASSY
71 Ave Norte and 1a
Calle Poniente no. 164
Colonia Escalón
Tel. 223 7729
Fax 223 7201

BANK AND BUREAU DE CHANGE
CITY BANK
Edificio Sisa (3rd floor)
Alameda Doctor Manuel
E. Araujo no. 3530

CREDOMATIC
55a Ave Sur, between
Alameda Roosevelt and
Ave Olimpica
Tel. 224 5100
Fax 224 4138
Open 9am–1pm
and 1.30–4pm
*Money can be changed
using Visa or
Mastercard.*

TOURIST OFFICE
INSTITUTO SALVADOREÑO
DE TURISMO (ISTUR)
Calle Rubén Darío,
no. 619
Tel. 222 8000, 222 0960
Fax 222 1208

MAIN POST OFFICE
DIRECCION DE CORREOS
Y TÉLÉGRAFOS
Centro del Gobierno
Tel. 271 4189, 271 4087
Open: Mon.–Fri.
7.30am–5pm
Sat. 7.30am–noon
Poste restante:
Mon.–Fri. 8am–noon
and 2.30–5pm
*Note! Address poste
restante mail to
"Republica de El
Salvador, Centro-
América" as there are
several "El Salvadors"
throughout the world.*

TRANSPORT

AIRLINES
COPA
Alameda . Roosevelt,
55a Ave Norte, no. 2838
Tel. 271 2333/ 3532
Fax 294 0864
TACA INTERNATIONAL
AIRLINES, AVIATECA,
LACSA-NICA
Edificio Caribe, 2nd floor
opposite Salvador del
Mundo
Tel. 298 5055/5077
Reservations: 298 5066
Fax 279 4345

CAR RENTAL
AVIS
Colonia Flor Blanca
43a Ave Sur, no. 137
Tel. 279 2344 / 224 2623
Fax 298 6272

BUDGET
Condominio Balam
Quitze, Paseo General
Escalón, office 3-A
Tel. 298 5187
DOLLAR RENT A CAR
Calle Arce no. 2226
Colonia Flor Blanca
Tel. 223 3108,
279 2069, 279 2143
Fax 279 2138
HERTZ
Calle Los Andes
Block J-16
Colonia Miramonte
Tel. 226 6579/8099
Fax 225 8412

CULTURE

**ESCUELA DE IDIOMAS
SALVADOR MIRANDA**
Correo Centro
de Govierno
PO Box 3274
Tel. 222 1352
*Language courses.
Cost: $150 for a week's
tuition.*

RESTAURANTS

*** MEDITERRANÉE
Bd El Hipódromo
no. 131
Colonia. San Benito.
Tel. 223 6137
*Seafood. Many other
similar restaurants
nearby (Marcelino's,
La Ola, Chili's,
Paradise).*

**** LA PAMPA
ARGENTINA**
Final Paseo
General Escalón
Tel. 279 11 85
*Argentinian cuisine
and grilled dishes.*

** LA ZANAHORIA
1144 Calle Arce
(between 19a and
21a Ave
Norte).

Open Mon.–Fri.
8am–6pm,
Sat. 8am–2pm.
*Large, open-air café-
restaurant. Vegetarian
cuisine.*

** SIETE MARES
Paseo General Escalón
Cond. Bálam Quitzé.
Tel. 224 3031 /
224 3763
*Good fish and seafood
restaurant. International
cuisine .*

* DON PAVO
Paseo General Escalón
and Condominio
Balám Quitzé
Rancho Alegre,
Metro Sur.
Tel. 224 3923
*Typical El Salvador
cuisine.*

*** ENTREMESES
DE FEDERICO**
1a Calle Poniente
no. 822
(between 13a
and 15a Ave Norte).
Open lunchtime only
noon–3pm.
Closed Sun.
*Housed in the
basement of the
Actoteatro building.
Large outdoor buffet.*

* KORADI
9a Ave Sur, no. 225
(close to the intersection
with 4a Calle Poniente).
Tel. 221 2545
Open Mon. to Fri.
8am–5pm.
Sat. 8am–3pm.
Closed Sun.
*Tiny but excellent
vegetarian restaurant-
pâtisserie located in the
center of town (near the
ISTU, the El Salvador
tourist office).*

HOTELS

******* HOTEL
CAMINO REAL**
Bd de los Heroes and
Ave Sisimiles
  Colonia Miramonte
    Tel. 279 3888
      Fax 223 5660

******* HOTEL
EL SALVADOR**
Calle Poniente no. 11
and Ave Norte no. 89
Escalon
Tel. 279 0766
Fax 223 2901

******* HOTEL
PRESIDENTE**
Ave La Revolución,
Colonia San Benito
Tel. 243 4444
Fax 243 4912

***** HOTEL
RAMADA INN**
Ave Sur, no. 85 and
Calle José Cañas,
Colonia Escalón
Tel. 279 1700
Fax 279 1889

* HOTEL CENTRO
10a Ave Sur, no. 410
Tel. 271 5045
*Well-kept and pleasant
hotel with comfortable
rooms at reasonable
prices.*

COMAYAGUA

TRANSPORT

AIRLINES
AVIATECA/LACSA/NICA/
TACA
Edificio Interamericana,
Bd Morazan
Tel. 31 2469/ 2472
*Other airlines at
Toncontín Airport.*

HOTEL

* HOTEL QUAN
Situated very close to
the Caridad Church.
Tel. 72 0070

RESTAURANT

* POLLOS CHALO 3
Situated between the
main square and the
market.
*The best chicken in
Comayagua.*

COPÁN

USEFUL
INFORMATION

**BANK AND BUREAU
DE CHANGE**
BANCO DEL OCCIDENTE
South corner of the
Plaza Central.
Open Mon.–Fri.
8am–noon and 2–4pm,
Sat. 8am–11am

HOSPITAL
CLINICA MÉDICA,
LUIS A. CASTRO M.D.
Next to Banco del
Occidente
Open Mon.–Sat.
8.30am–noon and
2–5pm
English spoken.

CULTURE

**IXBALANQUE
SPANISH SCHOOL**
Copán Ruinas
Tel. 98 3432
Fax 98 0004
*Weekly courses offered
with individual tuition
(five days a week, four
hours a day).
Accommodation with a
local family can be
arranged.*

**MUSEUM OF REGIONAL
ARCHAELOGY**
On the main square
(Plaza Central). The
museum exhibits ruins
from the Copán site.

HOTELS

*** HOTEL MARINA *
Close to Plaza Central.
Tel. 98 3070
Fax 57 3016
The best hotel in town.

**** HOTEL MAYA
COPÁN**
Opposite the museum.
*Well-maintained rooms
and restaurant. Local
cuisine.*

**** HACIENDA
EL JARAL**
About 7 miles on the
road from San Pedro
Sula.
Tel. 53 2070
Fax 57 5489

405

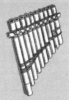

Also rents out horses, bicycles and pedalos.

* HOTEL LOS GEMELOS ★
100 yards from the Plaza Central, toward the station.
Clean and good value. Popular with visitors.

* HOTEL POPUL NAH
Plaza Central.

SPORT

WALKING, POT-HOLING AND RAFTING
GO NATIVE ADVENTURE TOURS
1½ blocks to the west of Plaza Central.
Tel. 98 3432
Fax 98 0004
XUKPI TOURS
(JORGE BARRAZA)
Copán Ruinas
Central Park
Tel. 98 3435
Open Mon.–Sat.
8am–noon and 2–5pm
Closed Sun.

RESTAURANTS

** RESTAURANT OF THE HOTEL MARINA
To the east of Plaza Central.
Tel. 98 3070
Open morning, lunchtime and evening
Large dining room overlooking the hotel's swimming pool. Local and international cuisine.

** TUNKUL BAR AND RESTAURANT
Tel. 983 410
Open all day
Excellent food, good value for money. Patronized by tourists who enjoy its friendly atmosphere (happy hour 6–8pm), and meals are served at the bar or at small tables. Music every evening. Local and international cuisine.

* LA LLAMA DEL BOSQUE
To the west of the Plaza Central (first street on the right after the museum)
Tel. 98 3431
Open morning, lunchtime and evening
Large, friendly restaurant, varied menu, local cuisine.

BAHÍA, ROATÁN ISLANDS

HOTELS

** HOTEL LOST PARADISE
West End Village
Tel. 45 1306
Fax 45 1388

** HOTEL SUNRISE
Sandy Bay
Tel. 31 0911 (Tegucigalpa)
57 8011 (San Pedro Sula)
45 1265 (from Roatán)
Comfortable rooms, bar, restaurant on the beach.

BAHÍA, UTILA ISLANDS

HOTEL

** UTILA LODGE
Utila harbor
Tel. 45 3143

BAHÍA, GUANAJA ISLANDS

HOTEL

** HOTEL ALEXANDER
South West Cay
Tel. 45 4326
Superb location. Restaurant and diving facilities.

LA CEIBA

HOTELS

** HOTEL PARTENON BEACH
On the beach.
Tel. 43 0404
Air-conditioned rooms, swimming pool and bar.

** GRAN HOTEL PARIS
Parque Central
Tel. 42 2371
Bar, swimming pool, restaurant, discotheque and tour operator.

RESTAURANTS

* CAFETERÍA EL PASTEL
Ave San Ísidro and 6a Calle
Closes 9pm.

* CRIC-CRIC BURGER
In the town center.
American-style fast-food (hamburgers, chicken) open-air restaurant.

SAN PEDRO SULA

HOTELS

** GRAN HOTEL SULA
1 Calle in front of Central Park
Tel. 52 9991-9
Fax 52 7000

* HOTEL SAN PEDRO
3a Calle and Ave 1a/2a
Tel. 53 1513

TEGUCIGALPA

USEFUL INFORMATION

TOURIST OFFICE
INSTITUTO HONDUREÑO DE TURISMO
Centro Guanacaste, Barrio Guanacaste
Tel. 22 8934
Fax 22 6621

TRANSPORT

AIRLINES
COPA
Plaza El Sol, Avenida. La Paz
Tel. 36 5760
Fax 36 7580
AVIATECA/LACSA/NICA/TACA
Edificio Interamericana, Bd Morazan
Tel 31 2469
Fax 31 2479
Airport: 33 3568/78, 33 3503

CAR RENTAL
AVIS RENT A CAR
Honduras Maya Hotel
Tel. 32 0088
Airport: 33 9548

RESTAURANTS

** RESTAURANTE DUNCAN MAYA
Ave Cristóbal Colón to the west of Plaza Central.
Basic, but good-quality food.

** RESTAURANTE EL PATIO
Calle Los Dolores 1024
Excellent meat dishes and cheese fondues. A good restaurant with a bar where one can listen to music.

* RESTAURANTE AL NATURAL
Behind the cathedral.
Specializes in fresh pasta and seafood dishes.

HOTELS

** HOTEL PLAZA SAN MARTÍN
Plaza San Martín, Colonia Palmira

** HONDURAS MAYA HOTEL
Ave Republica de Chile
Colonia Palmira
Tel. 32 3191
Also hotel at airport:
Tel. 33 5161

* VILLAS TELAMAR
Tela
Tel. 48 2196
This hotel has been built in the former storehouses of a banana company, overlooking the sea.

MUSEUMS

INSTITUTO HONDURENO DE ANTROPOLOGIA ET HISTORIA
Villa Roy,
Barrio Buenos Aires.

APPENDICES

◆ Bibliography

Essential
◆ Reading ◆

◆ Baudez (C.) and Picasso (S.), *Lost Cities of the Maya*, Thames & Hudson, London, 1992.
◆ Coe (M.D.), *The Maya*, Thames & Hudson, London, 1993.
◆ Eric (J.) and Thompson (E.), *The Rise and Fall of Maya Civilisation*, Pimlico, London, 1993.
◆ Henderson (J.), *The World of the Maya*, Cornell, Ithaca, 1981.

General
◆ Interest ◆

◆ Bernal (I.), *Ancient Mexico*, Thames & Hudson, London, 1968.
◆ Brainerd (G.W.), Morley (S.G.), and Sharer (R.J), *The Ancient Maya*, Stanford, 1983.
◆ Brunhouse (R.L.), *In Search of the Maya*, Univ. Of New Mexico Press, Albuquerque, 1973.
◆ Davies (N.), *The Aztecs*, Macmillan, London, 1973.
◆ Davies (N.), *Voyages to the New World*, W. Morrow, New York, 1979.
◆ Graham (J.A.), *Ancient Mesoamerica*, Peak Publications, Palo Alto, 1966.
◆ Riding (A.), *Distant Neighbors: A Portrait of the Mexicans*, Alfred A. Knopf, New York, 1985.
◆ Sanders (W.T.) and Price (B.J.), *Mesoamerica: The Evolution of a Civilization*, Random House, New York, 1968.
◆ Simpson (L.B.), *Many Mexicos*, Univ. of California Press, Berkeley and Los Angeles, 1964.
◆ Stuart (G.S) and Stuart (G.E.), *Lost Kingdoms of the Maya*, National Geographic Society, 1993.
◆ Townsend (R.F.), *The Aztecs*, Thames & Hudson, London, 1992.
◆ Wauchope (R.) Ed., *Handbook of Middle American Indians*, vols. 2 and 3, Univ of Texas, Austin, 1965–84.
◆ Weaver (M.P.), *The Aztecs, Maya and Their Predecessors*, Academic Press, New York, 1981.

◆ History ◆

◆ Adams (R.E.W.), *The Origins of Maya Civilization*, Albuquerque, 1977.
◆ Barrera Vasquez (A.) and Morley (S.G.), *The Maya Chronicles*, Carnegie Institution of Washington, 1949.
◆ Brainerd (G.), *The Maya Civilization*, Southwest Museum, Los Angeles, 1954.
◆ Carver (N.F.), *Silent Cities: Mexico and the Maya*, Shokokusha, Tokyo, 1966.
◆ Chamberlain (R.S.), *The Conquest and Colonization of Yucatán*, Carnegie Institution of Washington, Pub. 582, 1948.
◆ Clendinnen (I.), *Ambivalent Conquest. Maya and Spaniards in Yucatán*, Carnegie Institution of Washington, 1948.
◆ Coe (M.D.), *Breaking the Maya Code*, Thames & Hudson, London, 1992.
◆ Collis (M.), *Cortés and Montezuma*, Faber & Faber, London, 1954.
◆ Culbert (T.P.) ed., *The Classic Maya Collapse*, Univ. of New Mexico Press, Albuquerque, 1973.
◆ De Fuentes (P.), *The Conquistadores: First-Person Accounts of the Conquest of Mexico*, Orion Press, New York, 1963.
◆ Flannery (K.V.), *Maya Subsistence*, New York, 1982.
◆ Gibson (C.), *The Aztecs Under Spanish Rule*, Stanford Univ. Press, Stanford, 1964.
◆ Hammond (N.), *Ancient Maya Civilization*, Rutgers, New Brunswick, 1982.
◆ Jones (G.D.), *Anthropology and History in Yucatán*, Univ. of Texas Press, 1977.
◆ Pasztory (E.), *Middle Classic Mesoamerica*, AD 400–700, Univ. of Columbia, New York, 1978.

◆ Prescott (W.H.), *History of the Conquest of Mexico*, George Allen & Unwin, London, 1913.
◆ Ricard (R.), *The Spiritual Conquest of Mexico*, Univ. of California, Berkeley, 1966.
◆ Schele (L.) and Miller (M.), *A Forest of Kings. The Untold Story of the Ancient Maya*, W. Morrow, New York, 1990.
◆ Stuart (G.S.) and Stuart (G.E.), *The Mysterious Maya*, National Geographic Society, 1977.
◆ Thompson (J.E.S.), *Maya History and Religion*, Univ. of Oklahoma Press, Norman, 1970.
◆ Thompson (J.E.S.), *The Dresden Codex*, American Philosophical Society, 1972.
◆ Weaver (M.P.), *The Aztecs, Mayas, and their predecessors*, New York, 1981.

Religion
◆ and Society ◆

◆ Aveni (A.F.), *Skywatchers of Ancient Mexico*, Univ. of Texas, Austin, 1981.
◆ Boone (N.), *Ritual Human Sacrifice in Mesoamerica*, Washington, 1983.
◆ Bowditch (C.P.), *The Numeration, Calendar Systems and Astronomical Knowledge of the Mayas*, Cambridge Univ. Press, 1910.
◆ Bricker (V.R.), *The Indian Christ, the Indian King*, Univ. of Texas Press, 1981.
◆ Brenner (A.), *Idols Behind Altars: The Story of the Mexican Spirit*, Beacon Press, Boston, 1970.
◆ Burland (C.) and Forman (W.), *Feathered Serpent and Smoking Mirror: Gods and Fate in Ancient Mexico*, Orbis Publishing Ltd., London, 1975.
◆ Carmack (R.M.), *The Quiché Mayas of Utatlán*, Univ. of Oklahoma Press, 1981.
◆ Castaneda (C.), *Journey to Ixtlan: The Lessons of Don Juan*, Simon & Schuster, New York, 1972.

◆ Castaneda (C.), *A Separate Reality: Further Conversations with Don Juan*, Simon & Schuster, New York, 1971.
◆ Coe (M.D.), *Lords of the Underworld*, Art Museum, Princeton, 1978.
◆ Coe (M.D.), *The Maya Scribe and his World*, Grolier Club, New York, 1973.
◆ Coggins (C.) and Shane (O.C.), *Cenote of Sacrifice: Maya Treasures from the Sacred Well of Chichén Itzá*, Univ. of Texas Press, 1986.
◆ Durán, Fray (D.), *Book of the Gods and Rites and the Ancient Calendar*, TRANS. AND ED. Horcasitas (F.) and Heyden (D.), Univ. of Oklahoma Press, Norman, 1971.
◆ Flanner (K.V.) and Marcus (J.) EDS., *The Cloud People: Divergent Evolution of the Zapotec and Mixtec Civilizations*, Academic Press, New York, 1983.
◆ Helfritz (H.), *Mexican Cities of the Gods*, Praeger, New York, 1970.
◆ Léon-Portilla (M.), *Aztec Thought and Culture*, Univ. of Oklahoma Press, Norman, 1963.
◆ Miller (M.E.) and Taub (K.), *Gods and Symbols of Ancient Mexico and the Maya*, Thames & Hudson, London, 1993.
◆ Nicholson (I.), *Mexican and Central American Mythology*, Hamlyn, London, 1967.
◆ Ramos (S.), *Profile of Man and Culture in Mexico*, Univ. of Texas Press, Austin, 1962.
◆ Robicsek (F.) and Hales (D.), *The Maya Book of the Dead. The Ceramic Codex*, Univ. of Virginia Museum, 1982.
◆ Robicsek (F.), *Copán: Home of the Maya gods*, New York, 1972.
◆ Roys (R.L.), *Ritual of the Bacabs*, Univ. of Oklahoma Press, Norman, 1965.
Scholes (F.V.), *The Maya Chontal Indians of Acalan-Tixchel*, Washington, 1948.
◆ Teeple (J.E.), *Mayan Astronomy*, Carnegie Institute of

Washington, 1931.
◆ THOMPSON (J.E.S.), *Maya History and Religion,* Univ. of Oklahoma Press, Norman, 1970.
◆ TOMPKINS (P.), *Mysteries of Mexican Pyramids,* Thames & Hudson, London, 1991.

POLITICS
◆ AND ECONOMY ◆

◆ BARRY (T.), *Roots of Rebellion. Land and Hunger in Central America,* South End Press, 1987.
◆ CARMACK (R.M.), ED., *Harvest of Violence. The Maya Indians and the Guatemalan Crisis,* Univ. of Oklahoma Press, 1988.
◆ CULBERT (T.P.), *The Classic Maya Collapse,* Albuquerque, 1973.
◆ FARRISS (N.M.), *Maya Society under Colonial rule: The Collective Enterprise of Survival,* Princeton Univ. Press, 1984.
◆ FLETCHER (L.), FOLAN (W.J.) and KINTZ (E.), *Copán: A Classic Maya Metropolis,* New York, 1983.
◆ MANZ (B.), *Refugees of a Hidden War. The Aftermath of Counter-insurgency in Guatemala,* Univ. of New York Press, 1987.
◆ MARCUS (J.), *Emblem and State in the Classic Maya Lowlands,* Washington, 1976.
◆ SIMON (J.M.), *Guatemala, Eternal Spring, Eternal Tyranny,* Norton and Company, 1987.
◆ SULLIVAN (P.), *Unfinished Conversations. Mayas and Foreigners between two wars,* New York, 1989.

ART AND
◆ ARCHITECTURE ◆

◆ ANDREWS (G.F.), *Maya cities: Placemaking and Urbanization,* Univ. of Oklahoma Press, Norman, 1974.
◆ BAUDEZ (C.F.), *Maya Sculpture of Copán: The Iconography.* Univ. of Oklahoma Press, Norman, 1994.
◆ BULLARD (W.J.), *Maya Settlement Patterns in Northeastern Petén, Guatemala,* American Antiquity, Vol. 25, no. 3, 1960.
◆ COE (M.D.), *Lords of the Underworld. Masterpieces of Classic Maya Ceramics,* Princeton Univ. Press, 1978.
◆ COE (W.R.), *Tikal, a handbook of the ancient Maya ruins,* Univ. Museum, Philadelphia, 1967.
◆ CHARLOT (G.), *The Mexican Mural Renaissance 1920–1925,* Yale Univ. Press, New Haven, 1967.
◆ COVARRUBIAS (M.), *Indian Art of Mexico and Central America,* Alfred A. Knopf, New York, 1957.
◆ DOCKSTADER (F. J.), *Indian Art of Central America,* Cary, Adams and Mackay, London, 1964.
◆ GREEN ROBERTSON (M.) and RANDS (R.L.), *Maya Sculpture of the Southern Lowlands, Highlands and Pacific Piedmont,* Lederer, Street & Zens, Berkeley, 1972.
◆ GRUZINSKI (S.), *Painting the Conquest – The Mexican Indians and the European Renaissance,* Thames & Hudson, London, 1992.
◆ HANKS (W.) and RICE (D.), EDS., *Word and Image in Maya Culture,* Univ. of Utah Press, 1989.
◆ HEYDEN (D.) and GENDROP (P.), *Pre-Columbian Architecture of Mesoamerica,* Faber & Faber, London, 1980.
◆ KELEMEN (P.), *Medieval American Art: Masterpieces of the New World before Columbus,* Macmillan, New York, 1943.
◆ KUBLER (G.), *Art and Architecture of Ancient America,* Pelican Books, Harmondsworth, 1975.
◆ KUBLER (G.), *Mexican Architecture in the Sixteenth Century,* Yale Univ. Press, New Haven, 1948.
◆ LONGYEAR (J.M.), *Copán Ceramics,* Carnegie Institution of Washington, Pub. 597, 1952.

◆ LOTHROP (S.K.), *Tulum: an Archeological Study of the East Coast of Yucatán,* Carnegie Inst. of Washington Pub. 335, 1924.
◆ MILLER (A.G.), *On the Edge of the Sea: Mural painting at Tancah-Tulum,* Washington, 1982.
◆ MILLER (M.E.), *The Murals of Bonampak,* Princeton, 1986.
◆ MORLEY (S.G.), *Inscriptions at Copán,* Carnegie Institute, Washington DC, 1920.
◆ PROSKOURIAKOFF (T.), *An Album of Maya Architecture,* Carnegie Institution, Washington DC, 1946.
◆ PROSKOURIAKOFF (T.), *A Study of Classic Maya Sculpture,* Carnegie Institution, Washington DC, 1950.
◆ RAMIREZ (P.) et al., *Mexico: Art, Architecture, Archeology, Ethnography. The National Museum of Anthropology,* Harry N. Adams, New York, 1968.
◆ RIVET (P.), *Maya Cities: Ancient Cities and Temples,* Putnam, New York, 1962.
◆ ROJAS (P.), *The Art and Architecture of Mexico,* Hamlyn, Feltham, Middlesex, 1968.
◆ SABLOFF (J. A.), *The Cities of Ancient Mexico – Reconstructing a Lost World,* Thames & Hudson, London, 1990.
◆ SAYER (C.), *Arts & Crafts of Mexico,* Chronicle Books, San Francisco, 1990.
◆ SCHELE (L.) and MILLER (M.), *The Blood of Kings. Dynasty and ritual in Maya art,* George Brazillier Inc., 1986.
◆ SMITH (B.), *Mexico: a History in Art,* Phaidon Press, London, 1975.
◆ SPINDEN (H.J.), *A Study of Maya Art,* Peabody Museum Harvard, Cambridge, 1913.
◆ SUTTON (A.), *Among the Maya Ruins,* Rand-McNally, 1967.
◆ THOMPSON (J.E.), *A Preliminary Study of the Ruins of Copán,* Carnegie Institution of Washington, 1932.

◆ THOMPSON (J.E.S.), *Maya Hieroglyphics without Tears,* British Museum Publications, London, 1972.
◆ THOMPSON (J.E.S.), *Maya Hieroglyphic Writing: An Introduction,* Univ. of Oklahoma Press, Norman, 1971.
◆ TOUSSAINT (M.), *Colonial Art of Mexico,* REV. AND TRANS. Wilder Weisman (E.), Univ. of Texas Press, Austin, 1967.

◆ LITERATURE ◆

◆ ASTURIAS (M.A.), *Men of Maize,* TRANS. Partridge (F.), Gollancz. 1963 / Atheneum, New York, 1969.
◆ BARRERA VASQUEZ (A.) and MORLEY (S.G.), *The Maya Chronicles,* Carnegie Institution of Washington, 1949.
◆ BECKETT (S.) TRANS. AND ED., *Mexican Poetry,* Calder & Boyars, London, 1970.
◆ EDMONSON (M.), *Heaven Born Mérida and Its Destiny: The Book of Chilam Balam of Chumayel,* Univ. of Texas Press, Austin, 1986.
◆ TEDLOCK (D.), *Popol Vuh. The Mayan Book of the Dawn of Life,* New York, 1985.

TRAVELERS'
◆ TALES ◆

◆ GAGE (T.), *Thomas Gage's Travels in the New World,* ED. Newton (A.P), George Routledge & Sons, London, 1928.
◆ MAUDSLAY (A.C.), *A Glimpse at Guatemala,* Murray, 1899.
◆ NORMAN (B.M.), *Rambles in Yucatán,* Carey and Hart, 1849.
◆ PARKER (F.D.), *Travels in Central America 1821–1840,* Univ. of Florida Press, 1970.
◆ SEXTON (J.), *Campesino: The diary of a Guatemalan Indian,* Univ. of Arizona Press, 1985.
◆ STEPHENS (J.L.), *Incidents of Travel in Central America, Chiapas and Yucatán,* ED. Predmore (R.L.), Rutgers Univ. Press, New Brunswick, 1949.

◆ List of Illustrations

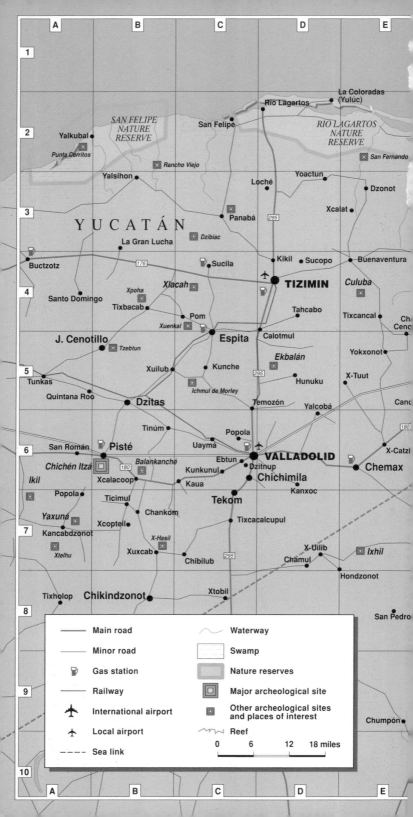